EVERYMAN, *I will go with thee,*
and be thy guide,

In thy most need to go by thy side

GEORGE GORDON
SIXTH LORD BYRON

Born 22nd January 1788. Educated at Harrow (1801–5) and at Trinity College, Cambridge (1805–8). He spent much of his time abroad between 1809 and his death at Missolonghi on 19th April 1824.

Byron's Poems

IN THREE VOLUMES : VOLUME TWO

EDITED WITH
AN INTRODUCTION BY
PROFESSOR V. DE SOLA PINTO
M.A., D.PHIL.(OXON.), F.R.S.L.

DENT: LONDON
EVERYMAN'S LIBRARY
DUTTON: NEW YORK

CONTENTS

The three volumes (Nos. 486, 487, and 488) of the Everyman's Library edition of the *Poems of Lord Byron* contain the following:

VOL. I. *Editor's Introduction, Note on the Present Edition,* Hours of Idleness (52 pieces), Occasional Pieces (58), Ode to Napoleon Buonaparte, Hebrew Melodies (23), Domestic Pieces (6), Monody on the Death of Sheridan, The Dream, Further Occasional Pieces (60), English Bards and Scotch Reviewers, Hints from Horace, The Curse of Minerva, The Waltz, The Siege of Corinth, Parisina, The Prisoner of Chillon, The Lament of Tasso, Beppo, Mazeppa, The Morgante Maggiore, The Prophecy of Dante, The Vision of Judgment, The Age of Bronze, The Island, *Select Bibliography.*

VOL. II. Childe Harold's Pilgrimage, The Giaour, The Bride of Abydos, The Corsair, Lara. *Plays*—Manfred, Marino Faliero, Cain.

VOL. III. Don Juan, *Appendix I: Byron's Preface to Cantos vi, vii, and viii, Appendix II: Byron and the Luddites, Index of First Lines.*

CHILDE HAROLD'S PILGRIMAGE

A ROMAUNT

A Romance [handwritten] *The one* [handwritten]

L'univers est une espece de livre, dont on n'a lu que la première page quand on n'a vu que son pays. J'en ai feuilleté un assez grand nombre, que j'ai trouvé également mauvaises. Cet examen ne m'a point été infructueux. Je haïssais ma patrie. Toutes les impertinences des peuples divers, parmi lesquels j'ai vécu, m'ont reconcilié avec elle. Quand je n'aurais tiré d'autre bénéfice de mes voyages que celui-là, je n'en regretterais ni les frais ni les fatigues.

LE COSMOPOLITE.[1]

[1] [By Fougeret de Monbron, Paris, 1750. Byron describes it as 'a little French volume, a great favourite of mine, which I picked up in the Archipelago'. —Letter to R. C. Dallas, 16th Sept. 1811, *Letters and Journals*, ed. R. E. Prothero, ii. 40.]

[handwritten:] The Universe is a type of book, of which only the first page has been read when only its country has been seen. I have turned over quite a large number [of pages] which I have found equally distasteful. This examination has not been unfruitful. I hated my country. All the peculiarities of its multifarious people among whom I have lived have reconciled me to her.

ORIGINAL PREFACE

Descriptive *Atmospheric*

THE following poem was written, for the most part, amidst the scenes which it attempts to describe. It was begun in Albania; and the parts relative to Spain and Portugal were composed from the author's observations in those countries. Thus much it may be necessary to state for the correctness of the descriptions. The scenes attempted to be sketched are in Spain, Portugal, Epirus, Acarnania, and Greece. There, for the present, the poem stops: its reception will determine whether the author may venture to conduct his readers to the capital of the East, through Ionia and Phrygia: these two cantos are merely experimental.

A fictitious character is introduced for the sake of giving some connection to the piece; which, however, makes no pretension to regularity. It has been suggested to me by friends, on whose opinions I set a high value, that in this fictitious character, 'Childe Harold,' I may incur the suspicion of having intended some real personage: this I beg leave, once for all, to disclaim—Harold is the child of imagination, for the purpose I have stated. In some very trivial particulars, and those merely local, there might be grounds for such a notion; but in the main points, I should hope, none whatever.

It is almost superfluous to mention that the appellation 'Childe,' as 'Childe Waters,' 'Childe Childers,' etc., is used as more consonant with the old structure of versification which I have adopted. The 'Good Night,' in the beginning of the first canto, was suggested by 'Lord Maxwell's Good Night,' in the Border Minstrelsy, edited by Mr. Scott.

With the different poems which have been published on Spanish subjects, there may be found some slight coincidence in the first part, which treats of the Peninsula, but it can only be casual; as, with the exception of a few concluding stanzas, the whole of this poem was written in the Levant.

The stanza of Spenser, according to one of our most successful poets, admits of every variety. Dr. Beattie makes the following observation: 'Not long ago I began a poem in the style and stanza of Spenser, in which I propose to give full scope to my inclination, and be either droll or pathetic, descriptive or sentimental, tender or satirical, as the humour strikes me; for, if I mistake not, the measure which I have adopted admits equally of all these kinds of composition.' [1] Strengthened in my opinion by such authority, and by the example of some in the highest order of Italian poets, I shall make no apology for attempts at similar variations in the following composition; satisfied that, if they are unsuccessful, their failure must be in the execution rather than in the design sanctioned by the practice of Ariosto, Thomson, and Beattie.

London, February 1812.

Beattie's Letters.

ADDITION TO THE PREFACE

I HAVE now waited till almost all our periodical journals have distributed their usual portion of criticism. To the justice of the generality of their criticisms I have nothing to object: it would ill become me to quarrel with their very slight degree of censure, when, perhaps, if they had been less kind they had been more candid. Returning, therefore, to all and each my best thanks for their liberality, on one point alone shall I venture an observation. Amongst the many objections justly urged to the very indifferent character of the 'vagrant Childe' (whom, notwithstanding many hints to the contrary, I still maintain to be a fictitious personage), it has been stated, that, besides the anachronism, he is very *unknightly*, as the times of the Knights were times of Love, Honour, and so forth. Now, it so happens that the good old times, when 'l'amour du bon vieux tems, l'amour antique' flourished, were the most profligate of all possible centuries. Those who have any doubts on this subject may consult Sainte-Palaye, *passim*, and more particularly vol. ii. p. 69.[1] The vows of chivalry were no better kept than any other vows whatsoever; and the songs of the Troubadours were not more decent, and certainly were much less refined, than those of Ovid. The 'Cours d'amour, parlemens d'amour, ou de courtesie et de gentilesse' had much more of love than of courtesy or gentleness. See Roland on the same subject with Sainte-Palaye. Whatever other objection may be urged to that most unamiable personage Childe Harold, he was so far perfectly knightly in his attributes—'No waiter, but a knight templar.'[2] By the by, I fear that Sir Tristrem and Sir Lancelot were no better than they should be, although very poetical personages and true knights 'sans peur,' though not 'sans reproche.' If the story of the institution of the 'Garter'

---

[1] ['Qu'on lise dans l'Auteur du roman de Gérard de Roussillon, en Provençal, les détails très-circonstanciés dans lesquels il entre sur la réception faite par le Comte Gérard à l'ambassadeur du roi Charles; on y verra des particularités singulières, qui donnent une étrange idée des mœurs et de la politesse de ces siècles aussi corrompus qu'ignorans.'—*Mémoires sur l'Ancienne Chevalerie*, par M. de la Curne de Sainte-Palaye, Paris, 1781, *loc. cit.*]

[2] 'The Rovers, or the Double Arrangement.'—[By Canning and Frere; first published in the *Anti-Jacobin*.]

be not a fable, the knights of that order have for several centuries borne the badge of a Countess of Salisbury, of indifferent memory. So much for chivalry. Burke need not have regretted that its days are over, though Marie-Antoinette was quite as chaste as most of those in whose honours lances were shivered, and knights unhorsed.

Before the days of Bayard, and down to those of Sir Joseph Banks (the most chaste and celebrated of ancient and modern times), few exceptions will be found to this statement; and I fear a little investigation will teach us not to regret these monstrous mummeries of the Middle Ages.

I now leave 'Childe Harold' to live his day, such as he is; it had been more agreeable, and certainly more easy, to have drawn an amiable character. It had been easy to varnish over his faults, to make him do more and express less, but he never was intended as an example, further than to show, that early perversion of mind and morals leads to satiety of past pleasures and disappointment in new ones, and that even the beauties of nature and the stimulus of travel (except ambition, the most powerful of all excitements) are lost on a soul so constituted, or rather misdirected. Had I proceeded with the poem, this character would have deepened as he drew to the close; for the outline which I once meant to fill up for him was; with some exceptions, the sketch of a modern Timon, perhaps a poetical Zeluco.[1]

London, 1813.

---

[1] [Moore's romance, in which were traced the fatal effects resulting from a fond mother's unconditional compliance with the humours and passions of an only child. With high advantages of person, birth, fortune, and ability, Zeluco is represented as miserable, through every scene of life, owing to the spirit of unbridled self-indulgence thus pampered in infancy.]

TO IANTHE [1]

Not in those climes where I have late been straying,
Though Beauty long hath there been matchless deem'd;
Not in those visions to the heart displaying
Forms which it sighs but to have only dream'd,
Hath aught like thee in truth or fancy seem'd:
Nor, having seen thee, shall I vainly seek
To paint those charms which varied as they beam'd—
To such as see thee not my words were weak;
To those who gaze on thee what language could they speak?

Ah! may'st thou ever be what now thou art,
Nor unbeseem the promise of thy spring,
As fair in form, as warm yet pure in heart,
Love's image upon earth without his wing,
And guileless beyond Hope's imagining!
And surely she who now so fondly rears
Thy youth, in thee, thus hourly brightening,
Beholds the rainbow of her future years,
Before whose heavenly hues all sorrow disappears.

Young Peri of the West!—'tis well for me
My years already doubly number thine;
My loveless eye unmoved may gaze on thee,
And safely view thy ripening beauties shine;
Happy, I ne'er shall see them in decline;
Happier, that while all younger hearts shall bleed,
Mine shall escape the doom thine eyes assign
To those whose admiration shall succeed,
But mix'd with pangs to Love's even loveliest hours decreed.

Oh! let that eye, which, wild as the Gazelle's,
Now brightly bold or beautifully shy,
Wins as it wanders, dazzles where it dwells,
Glance o'er this page, nor to my verse deny
That smile for which my breast might vainly sigh,

[1] [The Lady Charlotte Harley, second daughter of Edward fifth Earl of Oxford
(afterwards Lady Charlotte Bacon), in the autumn of 1812, when these lines were
addressed to her, had not completed her eleventh year. Westall's portrait of
her, painted at Lord Byron's request, is engraved in 'Finden's Illustrations.']

Could I to thee be ever more than friend:
This much, dear maid, accord; nor question why
To one so young my strain I would commend,
But bid me with my wreath one matchless lily blend.

Such is thy name with this my verse entwined;
And long as kinder eyes a look shall cast
On Harold's page, Ianthe's here enshrined
Shall thus be first beheld, forgotten last:
My days once number'd, should this homage past
Attract thy fairy fingers near the lyre
Of him who hail'd thee, loveliest as thou wast,
Such is the most my memory may desire;
Though more than Hope can claim, could Friendship less
      require?

CHILDE HAROLD'S PILGRIMAGE

CANTO THE FIRST

I

Oh, thou! in Hellas deem'd of heavenly birth,
Muse! form'd or fabled at the minstrel's will!
Since shamed full oft by later lyres on earth,
Mine dares not call thee from thy sacred hill:
Yet there I 've wander'd by thy vaunted rill;
Yes! sigh'd o'er Delphi's long deserted shrine,[1]
Where, save that feeble fountain, all is still;
Nor mote my shell awake the weary Nine
To grace so plain a tale—this lowly lay of mine.

He considers his theme unpoetic — not worthy of the muses.

II

Whilome in Albion's isle there dwelt a youth,
Who ne in virtue's ways did take delight;
But spent his days in riot most uncouth,
And vex'd with mirth the drowsy ear of Night.
Ah, me! in sooth he was a shameless wight,
Sore given to revel and ungodly glee;
Few earthly things found favour in his sight
Save concubines and carnal companie,
And flaunting wassailers of high and low degree.

III

Childe Harold was he hight:—but whence his name
And lineage long, it suits me not to say;
Suffice it, that perchance they were of fame,
And had been glorious in another day:
But one sad losel soils a name for aye,

[1] The little village of Castri stands partly on the site of Delphi. Along the path of the mountain, from Chrysso, are the remains of sepulchres hewn in and from the rock. 'One,' said the guide, 'of a king who broke his neck hunting.' His majesty had certainly chosen the fittest spot for such an achievement. A little above Castri is a cave, supposed the Pythian, of immense depth; the upper part of it is paved, and now a cowhouse. On the other side of Castri stands a Greek monastery; some way above which is the cleft in the rock, with a range of caverns difficult of ascent, and apparently leading to the interior of the mountain; probably to the Corycian Cavern mentioned by Pausanias. From this part descend the fountain and the 'Dews of Castalie.'

However mighty in the olden time;
Nor all that heralds rake from coffin'd clay,
Nor florid prose, nor honied lies of rhyme,
Can blazon evil deeds, or consecrate a crime.

IV

Childe Harold bask'd him in the noontide sun,
Disporting there like any other fly,
Nor deem'd before his little day was done
One blast might chill him into misery.
But long ere scarce a third of his pass'd by,
Worse than adversity the Childe befell;
He felt the fulness of satiety:
Then loathed he in his native land to dwell,
Which seem'd to him more lone than Eremite's sad cell.

Surfeit of corruption

V

For he through Sin's long labyrinth had run,
Nor made atonement when he did amiss,
Had sigh'd to many though he loved but one,
And that loved one, alas! could ne'er be his.
Ah, happy she! to 'scape from him whose kiss
Had been pollution unto aught so chaste;
Who soon had left her charms for vulgar bliss,
And spoil'd her goodly lands to gild his waste,
Nor calm domestic peace had ever deign'd to taste.

VI

And now Childe Harold was sore sick at heart,
And from his fellow bacchanals would flee;
'Tis said, at times the sullen tear would start,
But Pride congeal'd the drop within his ee:
Apart he stalk'd in joyless reverie,
And from his native land resolved to go,
And visit scorching climes beyond the sea;
With pleasure drugg'd, he almost long'd for woe,
And e'en for change of scene would seek the shades below.

The idea of atonement through pain

VII

The Childe departed from his father's hall:
It was a vast and venerable pile;
So old, it seemed only not to fall,
Yet strength was pillar'd in each massy aisle.
Monastic dome! condemn'd to uses vile!

Newstead?

Where Superstition once had made her den
Now Paphian girls were known to sing and smile;
And monks might deem their time was come agen,
If ancient tales say true, nor wrong these holy men.

VIII

Yet oft-times in his maddest mirthful mood
Strange pangs would flash along Childe Harold's brow
As if the memory of some deadly feud
Or disappointed passion lurk'd below:
But this none knew, nor haply cared to know;
For this was not that open, artless soul
That feels relief by bidding sorrow flow,
Nor sought he friend to counsel or condole,
Whate'er this grief mote be, which he could not control.

IX

And none did love him—though to hall and bower
He gather'd revellers from far and near,
He knew them flatt'rers of the festal hour;
The heartless parasites of present cheer.
Yea! none did love him—not his lemans dear—
But pomp and power alone are woman's care,
And where these are light Eros finds a feere;
Maidens, like moths, are ever caught by glare,
And Mammon wins his way where Seraphs might despair.

X

Childe Harold had a mother—not forgot,
Though parting from that mother he did shun;   *Augusta*
A sister whom he loved, but saw her not
Before his weary pilgrimage begun:
If friends he had, he bade adieu to none.
Yet deem not thence his breast a breast of steel:
Ye, who have known what 'tis to dote upon
A few dear objects, will in sadness feel
Such partings break the heart they fondly hope to heal.

XI

His house, his home, his heritage, his lands,
The laughing dames in whom he did delight,
Whose large blue eyes, fair locks, and snowy hands,
Might shake the saintship of an anchorite,
And long had fed his youthful appetite:

His goblets brimm'd with every coſtly wine,
And all that mote to luxury invite,
Without a sigh he left, to cross the brine,
And traverse Paynim shores, and pass Earth's central line.

XII

The sails were fill'd, and fair the light winds blew,
As glad to waft him from his native home;
And faſt the white rocks faded from his view,
And soon were loſt in circumambient foam:
And then, it may be, of his wish to roam
Repented he, but in his bosom slept
The silent thought, nor from his lips did come
One word of wail, whilſt others sate and wept,
And to the reckless gales unmanly moaning kept.

XIII

But when the sun was sinking in the sea
He seized his harp, which he at times could ſtring,
And ſtrike, albeit with untaught melody,
When deem'd he no ſtrange ear was liſtening:
And now his fingers o'er it he did fling,
And tuned his farewell in the dim twilight.
While flew the vessel on her snowy wing,
And fleeting shores receded from his sight,
Thus to the elements he pour'd his laſt 'Good Night.'

1

'ADIEU, adieu! my native shore
Fades o'er the waters blue;
The Night-winds sigh, the breakers roar,
And shrieks the wild sea-mew.
Yon Sun that sets upon the sea
We follow in his flight;
Farewell awhile to him and thee,
My native Land—Good Night!

2

'A few short hours and He will rise
To give the morrow birth;
And I shall hail the main and skies,
But not my mother earth.

Deserted is my own good hall,
Its hearth is desolate;
Wild weeds are gathering on the wall;
My dog howls at the gate.

3

'Come hither, hither, my little page!
Why doſt thou weep and wail?
Or doſt thou dread the billows' rage,
Or tremble at the gale?
But dash the tear-drop from thine eye;
Our ship is swift and ſtrong:
Our fleeteſt falcon scarce can fly
More merrily along.'

4

'Let winds be shrill, let waves roll high,
I fear not wave nor wind;
Yet marvel not, Sir Childe, that I
Am sorrowful in mind;
For I have from my father gone,
A mother whom I love,
And have no friend, save these alone,
But thee—and one above.

5

'My father bless'd me fervently,
Yet did not much complain;
But sorely will my mother sigh
Till I come back again.'
'Enough, enough, my little lad!
Such tears become thine eye;
If I thy guileless bosom had,
Mine own would not be dry.

6

'Come hither, hither, my ſtaunch yeoman,
Why doſt thou look so pale?
Or doſt thou dread a French foeman?
Or shiver at the gale?'
'Deem'ſt thou I tremble for my life?
Sir Childe, I'm not so weak;
But thinking on an absent wife
Will blanch a faithful cheek.

7

'My spouse and boys dwell near thy hall,
Along the bordering lake,
And when they on their father call,
What answer shall she make?'
'Enough, enough, my yeoman good,
Thy grief let none gainsay;
But I, who am of lighter mood,
Will laugh to flee away.

8

'For who would trust the seeming sighs
Of wife or paramour?
Fresh feres will dry the bright blue eyes
We late saw streaming o'er.
For pleasures past I do not grieve,
Nor perils gathering near;
My greatest grief is that I leave
No thing that claims a tear.

9

'And now I'm in the world alone,
Upon the wide, wide sea:
But why should I for others groan,
When none will sigh for me?
Perchance my dog will whine in vain,
Till fed by stranger hands;
But long ere I come back again
He'd tear me where he stands.

INFIDELITY

10

'With thee, my bark, I'll swiftly go
Athwart the foaming brine;
Nor care what land thou bear'st me to,
So not again to mine.
Welcome, welcome, ye dark-blue waves!
And when you fail my sight,
Welcome, ye deserts, and ye caves!
My native Land—Good Night!'

XIV

On, on the vessel flies, the land is gone,
And winds are rude in Biscay's sleepless bay.
Four days are sped, but with the fifth, anon,
New shores descried make every bosom gay;
And Cintra's mountain greets them on their way,
And Tagus dashing onward to the deep,
His fabled golden tribute bent to pay;
And soon on board the Lusian pilots leap,
And steer 'twixt fertile shores where yet few rustics reap.

XV

Oh, Christ! it is a goodly sight to see
What Heaven hath done for this delicious land!
What fruits of fragrance blush on every tree!
What goodly prospects o'er the hills expand!
But man would mar them with an impious hand:
And when the Almighty lifts his fiercest scourge
'Gainst those who most transgress his high command,
With treble vengeance will his hot shafts urge
Gaul's locust host, and earth from fellest foemen purge.

[handwritten marginalia: Accent on guilt & a purging of that guilt]

XVI

What beauties doth Lisboa first unfold!
Her image floating on that noble tide,
Which poets vainly pave with sands of gold,
But now whereon a thousand keels did ride
Of mighty strength, since Albion was allied,
And to the Lusians did her aid afford:
A nation swoln with ignorance and pride,
Who lick yet loathe the hand that waves the sword
To save them from the wrath of Gaul's unsparing lord.

[handwritten marginalia: LIBERAL SENTIMENT]

XVII

But whoso entereth within this town,
That, sheening far, celestial seems to be,
Disconsolate will wander up and down,
'Mid many things unsightly to strange ee;
For hut and palace show like filthily:
The dingy denizens are rear'd in dirt;
Ne personage of high or mean degree
Doth care for cleanness of surtout or shirt,
Though shent with Egypt's plague, unkempt, unwash'd;
    unhurt.

XVIII

Poor, paltry slaves! yet born 'midst noblest scenes—
Why, Nature, waste thy wonders on such men?
Lo! Cintra's [1] glorious Eden intervenes
In variegated maze of mount and glen.
Ah, me! what hand can pencil guide, or pen,
To follow half on which the eye dilates
Through views more dazzling unto mortal ken
Than those whereof such things the bard relates,
Who to the awe-struck world unlock'd Elysium's gates?

XIX

EXTENSIVE ALLITERATION

The horrid crags, by toppling convent crown'd,
The cork-trees hoar that clothe the shaggy steep,
The mountain-moss by scorching skies imbrown'd,
The sunken glen, whose sunless shrubs must weep,
The tender azure of the unruffled deep,
The orange tints that gild the greenest bough,
The torrents that from cliff to valley leap,
The vine on high, the willow branch below,
Mix'd in one mighty scene, with varied beauty glow.

XX

Then slowly climb the many-winding way,
And frequent turn to linger as you go,
From loftier rocks new loveliness survey,
And rest ye at 'Our Lady's house of woe;' [2]
Where frugal monks their little relics show,
And sundry legends to the stranger tell:

EXPIATION AGAIN

Here impious men have punish'd been, and lo!
Deep in yon cave Honorius long did dwell,
In hope to merit Heaven by making earth a Hell.

[1] 'To make amends for this [the filthiness of Lisbon, and its filthier inhabitants], the village of Cintra, about fifteen miles from the capital, is, perhaps in every respect, the most delightful in Europe; it contains beauties of every description, natural and artificial. Palaces and gardens rising in the midst of rocks, cataracts, and precipices; convents on stupendous heights—a distant view of the sea and the Tagus; and, besides (though that is a secondary consideration), is remarkable as the scene of Sir Hew Dalrymple's Convention. It unites in itself all the wildness of the western Highlands, with the verdure of the south of France.'—*Letter to Mrs. Byron,* 11th August 1809.

[2] The convent of 'Our Lady of Punishment,' *Nossa Señora de Pena,* on the summit of the rock. Below, at some distance, is the Cork Convent, where St. Honorius dug his den, over which is his epitaph. From the hills, the sea adds to the beauty of the view. [*Nossa Señora de Peña,* 'Our Lady of the Rock,' is the correct reading.]

XXI

And here and there, as up the crags you spring,
Mark many rude-carved crosses near the path:
Yet deem not these devotion's offering—
These are memorials frail of murderous wrath:
For wheresoe'er the shrieking victim hath
Pour'd forth his blood beneath the assassin's knife,
Some hand erects a cross of mouldering lath;
And grove and glen with thousand such are rife
Throughout this purple land, where law secures not life.[1]

XXII

On sloping mounds, or in the vale beneath,
Are domes where whilome kings did make repair;
But now the wild flowers round them only breathe;
Yet ruin'd splendour still is lingering there.
And yonder towers the Prince's palace fair:
There thou too, Vathek![2] England's wealthiest son,
Once form'd thy Paradise, as not aware
When wanton Wealth her mightiest deeds hath done,
Meek Peace voluptuous lures was ever wont to shun.

XXIII

Here didst thou dwell, here schemes of pleasure plan,
Beneath yon mountain's ever beauteous brow;
But now, as if a thing unblest by Man,
Thy fairy dwelling is as lone as thou!
Here giant weeds a passage scarce allow
To halls deserted, portals gaping wide;
Fresh lessons to the thinking bosom, how
Vain are the pleasaunces on earth supplied;
Swept into wrecks anon by Time's ungentle tide!

XXIV

Behold the hall where chiefs were late convened![3]
Oh! dome displeasing unto British eye!
With diadem hight foolscap, lo! a fiend,

[1] It is a well-known fact, that in the year 1809, the assassinations in the streets of Lisbon and its vicinity were not confined by the Portuguese to their country-men; but that Englishmen were daily butchered: and so far from redress being obtained, we were requested not to interfere if we perceived any compatriot defending himself against his allies. I was once stopped in the way to the theatre at eight o'clock in the evening, when the streets were not more empty than they generally are at that hour, opposite to an open shop, and in a carriage with a friend: had we not fortunately been armed, I have not the least doubt that we should have 'adorned a tale' instead of telling one. The crime of assassination is not confined to Portugal: in Sicily and Malta we are knocked on the head at a handsome average nightly, and not a Sicilian or Maltese is ever punished!
[2] [William Beckford.]
[3] The Convention of Cintra was signed in the palace of the Marchese Marialva.

A little fiend that scoffs incessantly,
There sits in parchment robe array'd, and by
His side is hung a seal and sable scroll,
Where blazon'd glare names known to chivalry,
And sundry signatures adorn the roll,
Whereat the Urchin points and laughs with all his soul.

XXV

Convention is the dwarfish demon styled
That foil'd the knights in Marialva's dome:
Of brains (if brains they had) he them beguiled,
And turn'd a nation's shallow joy to gloom.
Here Folly dash'd to earth the victor's plume,
And Policy regain'd what arms had lost:
For chiefs like ours in vain may laurels bloom!
Woe to the conqu'ring, not the conquer'd host,
Since baffled Triumph droops on Lusitania's coast!

[margin note:] –B. The chivalrous Mammoth must die.

XXVI

And ever since that martial synod met,
Britannia sickens, Cintra! at thy name;
And folks in office at the mention fret,
And fain would blush, if blush they could, for shame.
How will posterity the deed proclaim!
Will not our own and fellow nations sneer,
To view these champions cheated of their fame,
By foes in fight o'erthrown, yet victors here,
Where Scorn her finger points through many a coming year?

[margin note:] The Victor is oblivion o death

XXVII

So deem'd the Childe, as o'er the mountains he
Did take his way in solitary guise,
Sweet was the scene, yet soon he thought to flee,
More restless than the swallow in the skies:
Though here awhile he learn'd to moralize,
For Meditation fix'd at times on him;
And conscious Reason whisper'd to despise
His early youth, misspent in maddest whim;
But as he gazed on truth his aching eyes grew dim.

XXVIII

To horse! to horse! he quits, for ever quits
A scene of peace, though soothing to his soul:
Again he rouses from his moping fits,
But seeks not now the harlot and the bowl.
Onward he flies, nor fix'd as yet the goal

Where he shall rest him on his pilgrimage;
And o'er him many changing scenes must roll
Ere toil his thirst for travel can assuage,
Or he shall calm his breast, or learn experience sage.

[margin notes: NB]
[margin notes: Psychologically important — running from guilt]

XXIX

Yet Mafra shall one moment claim delay,[1]
Where dwelt of yore the Lusians' luckless queen;
And church and court did mingle their array,
And mass and revel were alternate seen;
Lordlings and freres—ill-sorted fry I ween!
But here the Babylonian whore hath built
A dome, where flaunts she in such glorious sheen,
That men forget the blood which she hath spilt,
And bow the knee to Pomp that loves to varnish guilt.

[margin notes: almost Calvinistic hatred of overbearing Pomp.]

XXX

O'er vales that teem with fruits, romantic hills,
(Oh, that such hills upheld a freeborn race!)
Whereon to gaze the eye with joyaunce fills,
Childe Harold wends through many a pleasant place.
Though sluggards deem it but a foolish chase,
And marvel men should quit their easy chair,
The toilsome way, and long, long league to trace,
Oh! there is sweetness in the mountain air,
And life, that bloated Ease can never hope to share.

XXXI

More bleak to view the hills at length recede,
And, less luxuriant, smoother vales extend;
Immense horizon-bounded plains succeed!
Far as the eye discerns, withouten end,
Spain's realms appear whereon her shepherds tend
Flocks, whose rich fleece right well the trader knows—
Now must the pastor's arm his lambs defend:
For Spain is compass'd by unyielding foes,
And all must shield their all, or share Subjection's woes.

XXXII

Where Lusitania and her Sister meet,
Deem ye what bounds the rival realms divide?
Or ere the jealous queens of nations greet,
Doth Tayo interpose his mighty tide?

[1] The extent of Mafra is prodigious: it contains a palace, convent, and most superb church. The six organs are the most beautiful I ever beheld, in point of decoration: we did not hear them, but were told that their tones were correspondent to their splendour. Mafra is termed the Escurial of Portugal.

Or dark Sierras rise in craggy pride?
Or fence of art, like China's vasty wall?—
Ne barrier wall, ne river deep and wide,
Ne horrid crags, nor mountains dark and tall,
Rise like the rocks that part Hispania's land from Gaul:

XXXIII

But these between a silver streamlet glides,
And scarce a name distinguisheth the brook,
Though rival kingdoms press its verdant sides.
Here leans the idle shepherd on his crook,
And vacant on the rippling waves doth look,
That peaceful still 'twixt bitterest foemen flow;
For proud each peasant as the noblest duke:
Well doth the Spanish hind the difference know
'Twixt him and Lusian slave, the lowest of the low.[1]

XXXIV

But ere the mingling bounds have far been pass'd,
Dark Guadiana rolls his power along
In sullen billows, murmuring and vast,
So noted ancient roundelays among.
Whilome upon his banks did legions throng
Of Moor and Knight, in mailed splendour drest:
Here ceased the swift their race, here sunk the strong;
The Paynim turban and the Christian crest
Mix'd on the bleeding stream, by floating hosts oppress'd.

XXXV

Oh, lovely Spain! renown'd, romantic land!
Where is that standard which Pelagio bore,
When Cava's traitor-sire first call'd the band
That dyed thy mountain streams with Gothic gore?[2]
Where are those bloody banners which of yore
Waved o'er thy sons, victorious to the gale,
And drove at last the spoilers to their shore?
Red gleam'd the cross, and waned the crescent pale,
While Afric's echoes thrill'd with Moorish matrons' wail.

[1] As I found the Portuguese, so I have characterized them. That they are since improved, at least in courage, is evident. The late exploits of Lord Wellington have effaced the follies of Cintra. He has, indeed, done wonders; he has, perhaps, changed the character of a nation, reconciled rival superstitions, and baffled an enemy who never retreated before his predecessors.—1812.

[2] Count Julian's daughter, the Helen of Spain. Pelagius preserved his independence in the fastnesses of the Asturias, and the descendants of his followers, after some centuries, completed their struggle by the conquest of Grenada.

XXXVI

Teems not each ditty with the glorious tale?
Ah! such, alas! the hero's amplest fate!
When granite moulders and when records fail,
A peasant's plaint prolongs his dubious date.
Pride! bend thine eye from heaven to thine estate.
See how the Mighty shrink into a song!
Can Volume, Pillar, Pile, preserve thee great?
Or must thou trust Tradition's simple tongue,
When Flattery sleeps with thee, and History does thee wrong?

[handwritten marginal note: The ultimate oblivion repeated]

XXXVII

Awake, ye sons of Spain! awake! advance!
Lo! Chivalry, your ancient goddess, cries;
But wields not, as of old, her thirsty lance,
Nor shakes her crimson plumage in the skies:
Now on the smoke of blazing bolts she flies,
And speaks in thunder through yon engine's roar
In every peal she calls—'Awake! arise!'
Say, is her voice more feeble than of yore,
When her war-song was heard on Andalusia's shore?

XXXVIII

Hark! heard you not those hoofs of dreadful note?
Sounds not the clang of conflict on the heath?
Saw ye not whom the reeking sabre smote;
Nor saved your brethren ere they sank beneath
Tyrants and tyrants' slaves?—the fires of death,
The bale-fires flash on high:—from rock to rock
Each volley tells that thousands cease to breathe;
Death rides upon the sulphury Siroc,
Red Battle stamps his foot, and nations feel the shock.

XXXIX

Lo! where the Giant on the mountain stands,
His blood-red tresses deep'ning in the sun,
With death-shot glowing in his fiery hands,
And eye that scorcheth all it glares upon;
Restless it rolls, now fix'd, and now anon
Flashing afar,—and at his iron feet
Destruction cowers, to mark what deeds are done;
For on this morn three potent nations meet,
To shed before his shrine the blood he deems most sweet.

[handwritten marginal note: France England Spain]

XL

By Heaven! it is a splendid sight to see
(For one who hath no friend, no brother there)
Their rival scarfs of mix'd embroidery,
Their various arms that glitter in the air!
What gallant war-hounds rouse them from their lair,
And gnash their fangs, loud yelling for the prey!
All join the chase, but few the triumph share;
The Grave shall bear the chiefest prize away,
And Havoc scarce for joy can number their array.

XLI

Three hosts combine to offer sacrifice;
Three tongues prefer strange orisons on high;
Three gaudy standards flout the pale blue skies;
The shouts are France, Spain, Albion, Victory!
The foe, the victim, and the fond ally
That fights for all, but ever fights in vain,
Are met—as if at home they could not die—
To feed the crow on Talavera's plain,
And fertilize the field that each pretends to gain.

XLII

There shall they rot—Ambition's honour'd fools!
Yes, Honour decks the turf that wraps their clay!
Vain Sophistry! in these behold the tools,
The broken tools, that tyrants cast away
By myriads, when they dare to pave their way
With human hearts—to what?—a dream alone.
Can despots compass aught that hails their sway?
Or call with truth one span of earth their own,
Save that wherein at last they crumble bone by bone?

XLIII

Oh, Albuera, glorious field of grief!
As o'er thy plain the Pilgrim prick'd his steed,
Who could foresee thee, in a space so brief,
A scene where mingling foes should boast and bleed!
Peace to the perish'd! may the warrior's meed
And tears of triumph their reward prolong!
Till others fall where other chieftains lead,
Thy name shall circle round the gaping throng,
And shine in worthless lays, the theme of transient song.

XLIV

Enough of Battle's minions! let them play
Their game of lives, and barter breath for fame:
Fame that will scarce re-animate their clay,
Though thousands fall to deck some single name.
In sooth 'twere sad to thwart their noble aim
Who strike, blest hirelings! for their country's good,
And die, that living might have proved her shame;
Perish'd perchance, in some domestic feud,
Or in a narrower sphere wild Rapine's path pursued.

XLV

Full swiftly Harold wends his lonely way
Where proud Sevilla triumphs unsubdued:
Yet is she free—the spoiler's wish'd-for prey!
Soon, soon shall Conquest's fiery foot intrude,
Blackening her lovely domes with traces rude.
Inevitable hour! 'Gainst fate to strive
Where Desolation plants her famish'd brood
Is vain, or Ilion, Tyre might yet survive,
And Virtue vanquish all, and Murder cease to thrive.

XLVI

But all unconscious of the coming doom,
The feast, the song, the revel here abounds;
Strange modes of merriment the hours consume,
Nor bleed these patriots with their country's wounds:
Nor here War's clarion, but Love's rebeck [1] sounds;
Here Folly still his votaries inthralls;
And young-eyed Lewdness walks her midnight rounds:
Girt with the silent crimes of Capitals,
Still to the last kind Vice clings to the tott'ring walls.

XLVII

Not so the rustic—with his trembling mate
He lurks, nor casts his heavy eye afar,
Lest he should view his vineyard desolate,
Blasted below the dun hot breath of war.
No more beneath soft Eve's consenting star
Fandango twirls his jocund castanet:
Ah, monarchs! could ye taste the mirth ye mar,
Not in the toils of Glory would ye fret;
The hoarse dull drum would sleep, and Man be happy yet!

[1 A kind of fiddle, with three strings, said to have been brought by the Moors into Spain.]

XLVIII

How carols now the lusty muleteer?
Of love, romance, devotion is his lay,
As whilome he was wont the leagues to cheer,
His quick bells wildly jingling on the way?
No! as he speeds, he chants 'Vivā el Rey!' [1]
And checks his song to execrate Godoy,
The royal wittol Charles, and curse the day
When first Spain's queen beheld the black-eyed boy,
And gore-faced Treason sprung from her adulterate joy.

XLIX

On yon long, level plain, at distance crown'd
With crags, whereon those Moorish turrets rest,
Wide scatter'd hoof-marks dint the wounded ground;
And, scathed by fire, the greensward's darken'd vest
Tells that the foe was Andalusia's guest:
Here was the camp, the watch-flame, and the host,
Here the bold peasant storm'd the dragon's nest;
Still does he mark it with triumphant boast,
And points to yonder cliffs, which oft were won and lost.

L

And whomsoe'er along the path you meet
Bears in his cap the badge of crimson hue,
Which tells you whom to shun and whom to greet: [2]
Woe to the man that walks in public view
Without of loyalty this token true:
Sharp is the knife, and sudden is the stroke;
And sorely would the Gallic foeman rue,
If subtle poniards, wrapt beneath the cloke,
Could blunt the sabre's edge, or clear the cannon's smoke.

LI

At every turn Morena's dusky height
Sustains aloft the battery's iron load;
And, far as mortal eye can compass sight,
The mountain-howitzer, the broken road,

---

[1] 'Vivā el Rey Fernando!' Long live King Ferdinand! is the chorus of most of
the Spanish patriotic songs. They are chiefly in dispraise of the old king Charles,
the Queen, and the Prince of Peace. I have heard many of them: some of the
airs are beautiful. Godoy, the *Principe de la Paz*, of an ancient but decayed
family, was born at Badajoz, on the frontiers of Portugal, and was originally
in the ranks of the Spanish guards; till his person attracted the queen's eyes, and
raised him to the dukedom of Alcudia, etc. etc. It is to this man that the
Spaniards universally impute the ruin of their country.
[2] The red cockade, with 'Fernando Septimo' in the centre.

The briſtling palisade, the fosse o'erflow'd,
The ſtation'd bands, the never-vacant watch,
The magazine in rocky durance stow'd,
The holſter'd ſteed beneath the shed of thatch,
The ball-piled pyramid,[1] the ever-blazing match,

LII

Portend the deeds to come:—but he whose nod
Has tumbled feebler despots from their sway,
A moment pauseth ere he lifts the rod;
A little moment deigneth to delay:
Soon will his legions sweep through these their way;
The Weſt muſt own the Scourger of the world.
Ah! Spain! how sad will be thy reckoning-day,
When soars Gaul's Vulture, with his wings unfurl'd,
And thou shalt view thy sons in crowds to Hades hurl'd.

LIII

And muſt they fall? the young, the proud, the brave,
To swell one bloated Chief's unwholesome reign?
No ſtep between submission and a grave?
The rise of rapine and the fall of Spain?
And doth the Power that man adores ordain
Their doom, nor heed the suppliant's appeal?
Is all that desperate Valour acts in vain?
And Counsel sage, and patriotic Zeal,
The Veteran's skill, Youth's fire, and Manhood's heart of ſteel?

LIV

Is it for this the Spanish maid, aroused,
Hangs on the willow her unſtrung guitar,
And, all unsex'd, the anlace hath espoused,
Sung the loud song, and dared the deed of war?
And she, whom once the semblance of a scar
Appall'd, an owlet's larum chill'd with dread,
Now views the column-scattering bay'net jar,
The falchion flash, and o'er the yet warm dead
Stalks with Minerva's ſtep where Mars might quake to tread.

[Handwritten marginal note: INTERESTING VIEW OF WOMEN IN WAR SLIGHTLY SARCASTIC AS IT WAS]

LV

Ye who shall marvel when you hear her tale,
Oh! had you known her in her softer hour,
Mark'd her black eye that mocks her coal-black veil,
Heard her light, lively tones in Lady's bower,

[1] All who have seen a battery will recollect the pyramidal form in which shot and shells are piled. The Sierra Morena was fortified in every defile through which I passed in my way to Seville.

Seen her long locks that foil the painter's power,
Her fairy form, with more than female grace,
Scarce would you deem that Saragoza's tower
Beheld her smile in Danger's Gorgon face,
Thin the closed ranks, and lead in Glory's fearful chase.

LVI

Her lover sinks—she sheds no ill-timed tear;
Her chief is slain—she fills his fatal post;
Her fellows flee—she checks their base career;
The foe retires—she heads the sallying host:
Who can appease like her a lover's ghost?
Who can avenge so well a leader's fall?
What maid retrieve when man's flush'd hope is lost?
Who hang so fiercely on the flying Gaul,
Foil'd by a woman's hand, before a batter'd wall? [1]

LVII

Yet are Spain's maids no race of Amazons,
But form'd for all the witching arts of love:
Though thus in arms they emulate her sons,
And in the horrid phalanx dare to move,
'Tis but the tender fierceness of the dove,
Pecking the hand that hovers o'er her mate:
In softness as in firmness far above
Remoter females, famed for sickening prate;
Her mind is nobler sure, her charms perchance as great.

LVIII

The seal Love's dimpling finger hath impress'd
Denotes how soft that chin which bears his touch: [2]
Her lips, whose kisses pout to leave their nest,
Bid man be valiant ere he merit such:
Her glance how wildly beautiful! how much
Hath Phoebus woo'd in vain to spoil her cheek,
Which glows yet smoother from his amorous clutch!
Who round the North for paler dames would seek?
How poor their forms appear! how languid, wan, and weak!

[1] Such were the exploits of the Maid of Saragoza, who by her valour elevated
herself to the highest rank of heroines. When the author was at Seville she
walked daily on the Prado, decorated with medals and orders, by command of
the Junta.
　　　　　　　[2] 'Sigilla in mento impressa Amoris digitulo
　　　　　　　　 Vestigio demonstrant mollitudinem.'
　　　　　　　　　　　　　　　　　　　AUL. GEL.

LIX

Match me, ye climes! which poets love to laud;
Match me, ye harams of the land! where now [1]
I strike my strain, far distant, to applaud
Beauties that ev'n a cynic must avow;
Match me those Houries, whom ye scarce allow
To taste the gale lest Love should ride the wind,
With Spain's dark-glancing daughters—deign to know,
There your wise Prophet's paradise we find,
His black-eyed maids of Heaven, angelically kind.

LX

Oh, thou Parnassus! whom I now survey, [2]
Not in the phrensy of a dreamer's eye,
Not in the fabled landscape of a lay,
But soaring snow-clad through thy native sky,
In the wild pomp of mountain majesty!
What marvel if I thus essay to sing?
The humblest of thy pilgrims passing by
Would gladly woo thine Echoes with his string,
Though from thy heights no more one Muse will wave her wing.

LXI

Oft have I dream'd of Thee! whose glorious name
Who knows not, knows not man's divinest lore:
And now I view thee, 'tis, alas! with shame
That I in feeblest accents must adore.
When I recount thy worshippers of yore
I tremble, and can only bend the knee;
Nor raise my voice, nor vainly dare to soar,
But gaze beneath thy cloudy canopy
In silent joy to think at last I look on Thee!

LXII

Happier in this than mightiest bards have been,
Whose fate to distant homes confined their lot,
Shall I unmoved behold the hallow'd scene,
Which others rave of, though they know it not?
Though here no more Apollo haunts his grot,
And thou, the Muses' seat, art now their grave,
Some gentle spirit still pervades the spot,
Sighs in the gale, keeps silence in the cave,
And glides with glassy foot o'er yon melodious wave.

[1] This stanza was written in Turkey.
[2] These stanzas were written in Castri (Delphos), at the foot of Parnassus, now called Λιακυρά (Liakura), Dec. 1809.

LXIII

Of thee hereafter.—Ev'n amidst my strain
I turn'd aside to pay my homage here;
Forgot the land, the sons, the maids of Spain;
Her fate, to every freeborn bosom dear;
And hail'd thee, not perchance without a tear.
Now to my theme—but from thy holy haunt
Let me some remnant, some memorial bear;
Yield me one leaf of Daphne's deathless plant,
Nor let thy votary's hope be deem'd an idle vaunt.

LXIV

But ne'er didst thou, fair Mount! when Greece was young,
See round thy giant base a brighter choir,
Nor e'er did Delphi, when her priestess sung
The Pythian hymn, with more than mortal fire,
Behold a train more fitting to inspire
The song of love than Andalusia's maids,
Nurst in the glowing lap of soft desire:
Ah! that to these were given such peaceful shades
As Greece can still bestow, though Glory fly her glades.

LXV

Fair is proud Seville; let her country boast
Her strength, her wealth, her site of ancient days;[1]
But Cadiz, rising on the distant coast,
Calls forth a sweeter, though ignoble praise.
Ah, Vice! how soft are thy voluptuous ways!
While boyish blood is mantling, who can 'scape
The fascination of thy magic gaze?
A Cherub-hydra round us dost thou gape,
And mould to every taste thy dear delusive shape.

LXVI

When Paphos fell by time—accursed Time!
The Queen who conquers all must yield to thee—
The Pleasures fled, but sought as warm a clime;
And Venus, constant to her native sea,
To nought else constant, hither deign'd to flee;
And fix'd her shrine within these walls of white;
Though not to one dome circumscribeth she
Her worship, but, devoted to her rite,
A thousand altars rise, for ever blazing bright.

[1] Seville was the Hispalis of the Romans.

LXVII

From morn till night, from night till startled Morn
Peeps blushing on the revel's laughing crew,
The song is heard, the rosy garland worn;
Devices quaint, and frolics ever new,
Tread on each other's kibes. A long adieu
He bids to sober joy that here sojourns;
Nought interrupts the riot, though in lieu
Of true devotion monkish incense burns,
And love and prayer unite, or rule the hour by turns.

LXVIII

The Sabbath comes, a day of blessed rest;
What hallows it upon this Christian shore?
Lo! it is sacred to a solemn feast;
Hark! heard you not the forest-monarch's roar?
Crashing the lance, he snuffs the spouting gore
Of man and steed, o'erthrown beneath his horn;
The throng'd arena shakes with shouts for more;
Yells the mad crowd o'er entrails freshly torn,
Nor shrinks the female eye, nor ev'n affects to mourn.

The seeming hypocrisy of the Sp. bullfight

LXIX

The seventh day this; the jubilee of man.
London! right well thou know'st the day of prayer:
Then thy spruce citizen, wash'd artisan,
And smug apprentice gulp their weekly air:
Thy coach of hackney, whiskey, one-horse chair,
And humblest gig through sun-dry suburbs whirl;
To Hampstead, Brentford, Harrow make repair;
Till the tired jade the wheel forgets to hurl,
Provoking envious gibe from each pedestrian churl.

LXX

Some o'er thy Thamis row the ribbon'd fair,
Others along the safer turnpike fly;
Some Richmond-hill ascend, some scud to Ware,
And many to the steep of Highgate hie.
Ask ye, Boeotian shades! the reason why? [1]
'Tis to the worship of the solemn Horn,
Grasp'd in the holy hand of Mystery,
In whose dread name both men and maids are sworn,
And consecrate the oath with draught, and dance till morn.

[1] This was written at Thebes, and consequently in the best situation for asking and answering such a question, not as the birth-place of Pindar, but as the capital of Boeotia, where the first riddle was propounded and solved.

LIGHT
HEARTED
SARCASM

LXXI

All have their fooleries—not alike are thine,
Fair Cadiz, rising o'er the dark blue sea!
Soon as the matin bell proclaimeth nine,
Thy saint adorers count the rosary:
Much is the VIRGIN teased to shrive them free
(Well do I ween the only virgin there)
From crimes as numerous as her beadsmen be;
Then to the crowded circus forth they fare:
Young, old, high, low, at once the same diversion share.

LXXII

The lists are oped, the spacious area clear'd,
Thousands on thousands piled are seated round;
Long ere the first loud trumpet's note is heard,
Ne vacant space for lated wight is found:
Here dons, grandees, but chiefly dames abound,
Skill'd in the ogle of a roguish eye,
Yet ever well inclined to heal the wound;
None through their cold disdain are doom'd to die,
As moon-struck bards complain, by Love's sad archery.

LXXIII

Hush'd is the din of tongues—on gallant steeds,
With milk-white crest, gold spur, and light-pois'd lance
Four cavaliers prepare for venturous deeds,
And lowly bending to the lists advance;
Rich are their scarfs, their chargers featly prance:
If in the dangerous game they shine to-day,
The crowd's loud shout and ladies' lovely glance,
Best prize of better acts, they bear away,
And all that kings or chiefs e'er gain their toils repay.

LXXIV

In costly sheen and gaudy cloak array'd,
But all afoot, the light-limb'd Matadore
Stands in the centre, eager to invade
The lord of lowing herds; but not before
The ground, with cautious tread, is traversed o'er,
Lest aught unseen should lurk to thwart his speed:
His arms a dart, he fights aloof, nor more
Can man achieve without the friendly steed—
Alas! too oft condemn'd for him to bear and bleed.

LXXV

Thrice sounds the clarion; lo! the signal falls,
The den expands, and Expectation mute
Gapes round the silent circle's peopled walls.
Bounds with one lashing spring the mighty brute,
And, wildly staring, spurns, with sounding foot,
The sand, nor blindly rushes on his foe:
Here, there, he points his threatening front, to suit
His first attack, wide waving to and fro
His angry tail; red rolls his eye's dilated glow.

LXXVI

Sudden he stops: his eye is fix'd: away,
Away, thou heedless boy! prepare the spear:
Now is thy time, to perish, or display
The skill that yet may check his mad career.
With well-timed croupe the nimble coursers veer;
On foams the bull, but not unscathed he goes;
Streams from his flank the crimson torrent clear:
He flies, he wheels, distracted with his throes;
Dart follows dart; lance, lance; loud bellowings speak his woes.

LXXVII

Again he comes; nor dart nor lance avail,
Nor the wild plunging of the tortured horse;
Though man and man's avenging arms assail,
Vain are his weapons, vainer is his force.
One gallant steed is stretch'd a mangled corse;
Another, hideous sight! unseam'd appears,
His gory chest unveils life's panting source;
Though death-struck, still his feeble frame he rears;
Staggering, but stemming all, his lord unharm'd he bears.

LXXVIII

Foil'd, bleeding, breathless, furious to the last,
Full in the centre stands the bull at bay,
Mid wounds, and clinging darts, and lances brast,
And foes disabled in the brutal fray:
And now the Matadores around him play,
Shake the red cloak, and poise the ready brand:
Once more through all he bursts his thundering way—
Vain rage! the mantle quits the conynge hand,
Wraps his fierce eye—'tis past—he sinks upon the sand!

LXXIX

Where his vast neck just mingles with the spine,
Sheathed in his form the deadly weapon lies.
He stops—he starts—disdaining to decline:
Slowly he falls, amidst triumphant cries,
Without a groan, without a struggle dies.
The decorated car appears on high
The corse is piled—sweet sight for vulgar eyes—
Four steeds that spurn the rein as swift as shy,
Hurl the dark bulk along, scarce seen in dashing by.

LXXX

Such the ungentle sport that oft invites
The Spanish maid, and cheers the Spanish swain.
Nurtured in blood betimes, his heart delights
In vengeance, gloating on another's pain.
What private feuds the troubled village stain!
Though now one phalanx'd host should meet the foe,
Enough, alas! in humble homes remain,
To meditate 'gainst friends the secret blow,
For some slight cause of wrath, whence life's warm stream
     must flow.

LXXXI

But Jealousy has fled: his bars, his bolts,
His wither'd centinel, Duenna sage!
And all whereat the generous soul revolts,
Which the stern dotard deem'd he could encage,
Have pass'd to darkness with the vanish'd age.
Who late so free as Spanish girls were seen,
(Ere War uprose in his volcanic rage,)
With braided tresses bounding o'er the green,
While on the gay dance shone Night's lover-loving Queen?

LXXXII

Oh! many a time, and oft, had Harold loved,
Or dream'd he loved, since Rapture is a dream;
But now his wayward bosom was unmoved,
For not yet had he drunk of Lethe's stream;
And lately had he learn'd with truth to deem
Love has no gift so grateful as his wings:
How fair, how young, how soft soe'er he seem,
Full from the fount of Joy's delicious springs
Some bitter o'er the flowers its bubbling venom flings.[1]

[1] 'Medio de fonte leporum,' etc.—Luc.

LXXXIII

Yet to the beauteous form he was not blind,
Though now it moved him as it moves the wise;
Not that Philosophy on such a mind
E'er deign'd to bend her chastely-awful eyes:
But Passion raves itself to rest, or flies;
And Vice, that digs her own voluptuous tomb,
Had buried long his hopes, no more to rise:
Pleasure's pall'd victim! life-abhorring gloom
Wrote on his faded brow curst Cain's unresting doom.

LXXXIV

Still he beheld, nor mingled with the throng;
But view'd them not with misanthropic hate:
Fain would he now have join'd the dance, the song;
But who may smile that sinks beneath his fate?
Nought that he saw his sadness could abate:
Yet once he struggled 'gainst the demon's sway,
And as in Beauty's bower he pensive sate,
Pour'd forth this unpremeditated lay,
To charms as fair as those that soothed his happier day.

TO INEZ

I

NAY, smile not at my sullen brow;
Alas! I cannot smile again:
Yet Heaven avert that ever thou
Shouldst weep, and haply weep in vain.

2

And dost thou ask, what secret woe
I bear, corroding joy and youth?
And wilt thou vainly seek to know
A pang, ev'n thou must fail to soothe?

NB. uses corroding

3

It is not love, it is not hate,
Nor low Ambition's honours lost,
That bids me loathe my present state,
And fly from all I prized the most:

4

It is that weariness which springs
From all I meet, or hear, or see:
To me no pleasure Beauty brings;
Thine eyes have scarce a charm for me.

5

It is that settled, ceaseless gloom
The fabled Hebrew wanderer bore;
That will not look beyond the tomb,
But cannot hope for rest before.

6

What Exile from himself can flee?
To zones, though more and more remote,
Still, still pursues, where'er I be,
The blight of life—the demon Thought.

7

Yet others rapt in pleasure seem,
And taste of all that I forsake;
Oh! may they still of transport dream,
And ne'er, at least like me, awake!

*The 'escape'
from himself
impossible !*

8

Through many a clime 'tis mine to go,
With many a retrospection curst;
And all my solace is to know,
Whate'er betides, I 've known the worst.

*NB. Ignorance
is bliss.*

9

What is that worst? Nay, do not ask—
In pity from the search forbear:
Smile on—nor venture to unmask
Man's heart, and view the Hell that 's there.' [1]

[1] [In place of this song, which was written at Athens, 25th January 1810, and
which contains, as Moore says, 'some of the dreariest touches of sadness that ever
Byron's pen let fall,' we find, in the first draught of the Canto, the following:

1

Oh never talk again to me
Of northern climes and British ladies;
It has not been your lot to see,
Like me, the lovely girl of Cadiz.
Although her eye be not of blue,
Nor fair her locks, like English lasses,
How far its own expressive hue
The languid azure eye surpasses!

2

Prometheus-like, from heaven she stole
The fire, that through those silken lashes
In darkest glances seems to roll,
From eyes that cannot hide their flashes:

And as along her bosom steal
In lengthen'd flow her raven tresses,
You'd swear each clustering lock could feel,
And curl'd to give her neck caresses.

3

Our English maids are long to woo,
And frigid even in possession;
And if their charms be fair to view,
Their lips are slow at Love's confession:
But born beneath a brighter sun,
For love ordain'd the Spanish maid is,
And who,—when fondly, fairly won,—
Enchants you like the Girl of Cadiz?

4

The Spanish maid is no coquette,
Nor joys to see a lover tremble,
And if she love, or if she hate,
Alike she knows not to dissemble,
Her heart can ne'er be bought or sold—
Howe'er it beats, it beats sincerely;
And, though it will not bend to gold,
'Twill love you long and love you dearly.

5

The Spanish girl that meets your love
Ne'er taunts you with a mock denial,
For every thought is bent to prove
Her passion in the hour of trial.
When thronging foemen menace Spain,
She dares the deed and shares the danger;
And should her lover press the plain,
She hurls the spear, her love's avenger.

6

And when, beneath the evening star,
She mingles in the gay Bolero,
Or sings to her attuned guitar
Of Christian knight or Moorish hero,
Or counts her beads with fairy hand
Beneath the twinkling rays of Hesper,
Or joins devotion's choral band,
To chaunt the sweet and hallow'd vesper;—

7

In each her charms the heart must move
Of all who venture to behold her;
Then let not maids less fair reprove
Because her bosom is not colder:
Through many a clime 'tis mine to roam
Where many a soft and melting maid is,
But none abroad, and few at home,
May match the dark-eyed Girl of Cadiz.]

LXXXV

Adieu, fair Cadiz! yea, a long adieu!
Who may forget how well thy walls have stood?
When all were changing thou alone wert true,
First to be free and last to be subdued:
And if amidst a scene, a shock so rude,
Some native blood was seen thy streets to dye;
A traitor only fell beneath the feud: [1]
Here all were noble, save Nobility;
None hugg'd a conqueror's chain, save fallen Chivalry!

Aristo enveighing against Aristo's

LXXXVI

Such be the sons of Spain, and strange her fate!
They fight for freedom who were never free;
A Kingless people for a nerveless state,
Her vassals combat when their chieftains flee,
True to the veriest slaves of Treachery:
Fond of a land which gave them nought but life,
Pride points the path that leads to Liberty;
Back to the struggle, baffled in the strife,
War, war is still the cry, 'War even to the knife!' [2]

LXXXVII

Ye, who would more of Spain and Spaniards know
Go, read whate'er is writ of bloodiest strife:
Whate'er keen Vengeance urged on foreign foe
Can act, is acting there against man's life:
From flashing scimitar to secret knife,
War mouldeth there each weapon to his need—
So may he guard the sister and the wife,
So may he make each curst oppressor bleed,
So may such foes deserve the most remorseless deed!

LXXXVIII

Flows there a tear of pity for the dead?
Look o'er the ravage of the reeking plain;
Look on the hands with female slaughter red;
Then to the dogs resign the unburied slain,

[1] Alluding to the conduct and death of Solano, the governor of Cadiz, in May 1809.

[2] 'War to the knife.' Palafox's answer to the French general at the siege of Saragoza. [In his proclamations, also, he stated that, should the French commit any robberies, devastations, and murders, no quarter should be given them. The dogs by whom he was beset, he said, scarcely left him time to clean his sword from their blood, but they still found their grave at Saragoza. All his addresses were in the same spirit. 'His language,' says Southey, 'had the high tone, and something of the inflation of Spanish romance, suiting the character of those to whom it was directed.' See *History of the Peninsular War*, vol. iii, p. 152.]

Then to the vulture let each corse remain;
Albeit unworthy of the prey bird's maw,
Let their bleach'd bones, and blood's unbleaching stain,
Long mark the battle-field with hideous awe:
Thus only may our sons conceive the scenes we saw!

LXXXIX

Nor yet, alas! the dreadful work is done;
Fresh legions pour adown the Pyrenees:
It deepens still, the work is scarce begun,
Nor mortal eye the distant end foresees.
Fall'n nations gaze on Spain; if freed, she frees
More than her fell Pizarros once enchain'd:
Strange retribution! now Columbia's ease
Repairs the wrongs that Quito's sons sustain'd,
While o'er the parent clime prowls Murder unrestrain'd.

XC

Not all the blood at Talavera shed,
Not all the marvels of Barossa's fight,
Not Albuera lavish of the dead,
Have won for Spain her well-asserted right.
When shall her Olive-Branch be free from blight?
When shall she breathe her from the blushing toil?
How many a doubtful day shall sink in night,
Ere the Frank robber turn him from his spoil,
And Freedom's stranger-tree grow native of the soil!

XCI

And thou, my friend![1]—since unavailing woe
Bursts from my heart, and mingles with the strain—
Had the sword laid thee with the mighty low,
Pride might forbid e'en Friendship to complain:

[1] The Honourable John Wingfield, of the Guards, who died of a fever at Coimbra. I had known him ten years, the better half of his life, and the happiest part of mine. In the short space of one month, I have lost her who gave me being, and most of those who had made that being tolerable. To me the lines of Young are no fiction:

'Insatiate archer! could not one suffice?
Thy shaft flew thrice, and thrice my peace was slain,
And thrice ere thrice yon moon had fill'd her horn.'

I should have ventured a verse to the memory of the late Charles Skinner Matthews, Fellow of Downing College, Cambridge, were he not too much above all praise of mine. His powers of mind, shown in the attainment of greater honours, against the ablest candidates, than those of any graduate on record at Cambridge, have sufficiently established his fame on the spot where it was acquired; while his softer qualities live in the recollection of friends who loved him too well to envy his superiority.

But thus unlaurel'd to descend in vain,
By all forgotten, save the lonely breast,
And mix unbleeding with the boasted slain,
While Glory crowns so many a meaner crest!
What hadst thou done to sink so peacefully to rest?

XCII

Oh, known the earliest, and esteem'd the most!
Dear to a heart where nought was left so dear!
Though to my hopeless days for ever lost,
In dreams deny me not to see thee here!
And Morn in secret shall renew the tear
Of Consciousness awaking to her woes,
And Fancy hover o'er thy bloodless bier,
Till my frail frame return to whence it rose,
And mourn'd and mourner lie united in repose.

XCIII

Here is one fytte of Harold's pilgrimage:
Ye who of him may further seek to know,
Shall find some tidings in a future page,
If he that rhymeth now may scribble moe.
Is this too much? stern Critic! say not so:
Patience! and ye shall hear what he beheld
In other lands, where he was doom'd to go:
Lands that contain the monuments of Eld,
Ere Greece and Grecian arts by barbarous hands were quell'd.

I

Come, blue-eyed maid of heaven!—but thou, alas!
Didst never yet one mortal song inspire—
Goddess of Wisdom! here thy temple was,
And is, despite of war and wasting fire,[1]
And years, that bade thy worship to expire:
But worse than steel, and flame, and ages slow,
Is the dread sceptre and dominion dire
Of men who never felt the sacred glow
That thoughts of thee and thine on polish'd breasts bestow.[2]

II

Ancient of days! august Athena! where,
Where are thy men of might? thy grand in soul?
Gone—glimmering through the dream of things that were:
First in the race that led to Glory's goal,
They won, and pass'd away—is this the whole?
A schoolboy's tale, the wonder of an hour!
The warrior's weapon and the sophist's stole
Are sought in vain, and o'er each mouldering tower,
Dim with the mist of years, gray flits the shade of power.

III

Son of the morning, rise! approach you here!
Come—but molest not yon defenceless urn:
Look on this spot—a nation's sepulchre!
Abode of gods, whose shrines no longer burn.
Even gods must yield—religions take their turn:
'Twas Jove's—'tis Mahomet's—and other creeds
Will rise with other years, till man shall learn
Vainly his incense soars, his victim bleeds;
Poor child of Doubt and Death, whose hope is built on reeds.

IV

Bound to the earth, he lifts his eye to heaven—
Is 't not enough, unhappy thing! to know
Thou art? Is this a boon so kindly given,
That being, thou would'st be again, and go,

[1] Part of the Acropolis was destroyed by the explosion of a magazine during the Venetian siege.

[2] Never did the littleness of man, and the vanity of his very best virtues, of patriotism to exalt, and of valour to defend his country, appear more conspicuous than in the record of what Athens was, and the certainty of what she now is. This theatre of contention between mighty factions, of the struggles of orators, the exaltation and deposition of tyrants, the triumph and punishment of generals, is now become a scene of petty intrigue and perpetual disturbance, between the bickering agents of certain British nobility and gentry. 'The wild foxes, the owls and serpents in the ruins of Babylon,' were surely less degrading than such inhabitants.

Thou know'st not, reck'st not to what region, so
On earth no more, but mingled with the skies?
Still wilt thou dream on future joy and woe?
Regard and weigh yon dust before it flies:
That little urn saith more than thousand homilies.

V

Or burst the vanish'd Hero's lofty mound;
Far on the solitary shore he sleeps: [1]
He fell, and falling nations mourn'd around;
But now not one of saddening thousands weeps,
Nor warlike worshipper his vigil keeps
Where demi-gods appear'd, as records tell.
Remove yon skull from out the scatter'd heaps:
Is that a temple where a God may dwell?
Why ev'n the worm at last disdains her shatter'd cell!

VI

Look on its broken arch, its ruin'd wall,
Its chambers desolate, and portals foul:
Yes, this was once Ambition's airy hall,
The dome of Thought, the palace of the Soul:
Behold through each lack-lustre, eyeless hole,
The gay recess of Wisdom and of Wit
And Passion's host, that never brook'd control:
Can all saint, sage, or sophist ever writ,
People this lonely tower, this tenement refit?

VII

Well didst thou speak, Athena's wisest son!
'All that we know is, nothing can be known.'
Why should we shrink from what we cannot shun?
Each hath his pang, but feeble sufferers groan
With brain-born dreams of evil all their own,
Pursue what Chance or Fate proclaimeth best;
Peace waits us on the shores of Acheron:
There no forced banquet claims the sated guest,
But Silence spreads the couch of ever welcome rest.

---

[1] It was not always the custom of the Greeks to burn their dead; the greater Ajax, in particular, was interred entire. Almost all the chiefs became gods after their decease; and he was indeed neglected, who had not annual games near his tomb, or festivals in honour of his memory by his countrymen, as Achilles, Brasidas, etc., and at last even Antinous, whose death was as heroic as his life was infamous.

Does Byron identify himself with the
broken countries of Spain & Greece
because they portray his own
spiritual corrosion?

VIII

Yet if, as holiest men have deem'd, there be
A land of souls beyond that sable shore,
To shame the doctrine of the Sadducee
And sophists, madly vain of dubious lore;
How sweet it were in concert to adore
With those who made our mortal labours light!
To hear each voice we fear'd to hear no more!
Behold each mighty shade reveal'd to sight,
The Bactrian, Samian sage, and all who taught the right!

IX

There, thou!—whose love and life together fled,
Have left me here to love and live in vain—
Twined with my heart, and can I deem thee dead
When busy Memory flashes on my brain?
Well—I will dream that we may meet again,
And woo the vision to my vacant breast:
If aught of young Remembrance then remain,
Be as it may Futurity's behest,
For me 'twere bliss enough to know thy spirit blest!

X

Here let me sit upon this massy stone,
The marble column's yet unshaken base;
Here, son of Saturn! was thy fav'rite throne: [1]
Mightiest of many such! Hence let me trace
The latent grandeur of thy dwelling-place.
It may not be: nor ev'n can Fancy's eye
Restore what Time hath labour'd to deface.
Yet these proud pillars claim no passing sigh;
Unmoved the Moslem sits, the light Greek carols by.

XI

But who, of all the plunderers of yon fane
On high, where Pallas linger'd, loth to flee
The latest relic of her ancient reign;
The last, the worst, dull spoiler, who was he?
Blush, Caledonia! such thy son could be!
England! I joy no child he was of thine:
Thy free-born men should spare what once was free;
Yet they could violate each saddening shrine,
And bear these altars o'er the long-reluctant brine. [2]

[1] The temple of Jupiter Olympus, of which sixteen columns, entirely of marble, yet survive: originally there were one hundred and fifty. These columns, however, are by many supposed to have belonged to the Pantheon.
[2] The ship was wrecked in the Archipelago.

XII

But moſt the modern Pict's ignoble boaſt,
To rive what Goth, and Turk, and Time hath spared:
Cold as the crags upon his native coaſt,
His mind as barren and his heart as hard,
Is he whose head conceived, whose hand prepared,
Aught to displace Athena's poor remains:
Her sons too weak the sacred shrine to guard,
Yet felt some portion of their mother's pains,[1]
And never knew, till then, the weight of Despot's chains.

XIII

What! shall it e'er be said by British tongue,
Albion was happy in Athena's tears?
Though in thy name the slaves her bosom wrung,
Tell not the deed to blushing Europe's ears;
The ocean queen, the free Britannia, bears
The laſt poor plunder from a bleeding land:
Yes, she, whose gen'rous aid her name endears,
Tore down those remnants with a harpy's hand,
Which envious Eld forbore, and tyrants left to ſtand.

XIV

Where was thine Aegis, Pallas! that appall'd
Stern Alaric and Havoc on their way?[2]
Where Peleus' son? whom Hell in vain enthrall'd,
His shade from Hades upon that dread day
Burſting to light in terrible array!
What! could not Pluto spare the chief once more,
To scare a second robber from his prey?
Idly he wander'd on the Stygian shore,
Nor now preserved the walls he loved to shield before.

XV

Cold is the heart, fair Greece, that looks on thee,
Nor feels as lovers o'er the duſt they loved;
Dull is the eye that will not weep to see
Thy walls defaced, thy mouldering shrines removed

[1] I cannot resiſt availing myself of the permission of my friend Dr. Clarke, whose name requires no comment with the public, but whose sanction will add tenfold weight to my teſtimony, to insert the following extract from a very obliging letter of his to me, as a note to the above lines: 'When the laſt of the Metopes was taken from the Parthenon, and, in moving of it, great part of the superſtructure with one of the triglyphs was thrown down by the workmen whom Lord Elgin employed, the Disdar, who beheld the mischief done to the building, took his pipe from his mouth, dropped a tear, and, in a supplicating tone of voice, said to Lusieri, Τέλος!—I was present.' The Disdar alluded to was the father of the present Disdar.

[2] According to Zosimus, Minerva and Achilles frightened Alaric from the Acropolis; but others relate that the Gothic king was nearly as mischievous as the Scottish peer.—See CHANDLER.

By British hands, which it had best behoved
To guard those relics ne'er to be restored.
Curst be the hour when from their isle they roved,
And once again thy hapless bosom gored,
And snatch'd thy shrinking Gods to northern climes abhorr'd!

XVI

But where is Harold? shall I then forget
To urge the gloomy wanderer o'er the wave?
Little reck'd he of all that men regret;
No loved-one now in feign'd lament could rave;
No friend the parting hand extended gave,
Ere the cold stranger pass'd to other climes,
Hard is his heart whom charms may not enslave;
But Harold felt not as in other times,
And left without a sigh the land of war and crimes.

XVII

He that has sail'd upon the dark blue sea
Has view'd at times, I ween, a full fair sight;
When the fresh breeze is fair as breeze may be,
The white sail set, the gallant frigate tight;
Masts, spires, and strand retiring to the right,
The glorious main expanding o'er the bow,
The convoy spread like wild swans in their flight,
The dullest sailor wearing bravely now,
So gaily curl the waves before each dashing prow.

XVIII

And oh, the little warlike world within!
The well-reeved guns, the netted canopy,[1]
The hoarse command, the busy humming din,
When, at a word, the tops are mann'd on high:
Hark, to the Boatswain's call, the cheering cry!
While through the seaman's hand the tackle glides;
Or schoolboy Midshipman that, standing by,
Strains his shrill pipe as good or ill betides,
And well the docile crew that skilful urchin guides.

XIX

White is the glassy deck, without a stain,
Where on the watch the staid Lieutenant walks:
Look on that part which sacred doth remain
For the lone chieftain, who majestic stalks,

[1] To prevent blocks or splinters from falling on deck during action.

Silent and fear'd by all—not oft he talks
With aught beneath him, if he would preserve
That strict restraint, which broken, ever balks
Conquest and Fame: but Britons rarely swerve
From law, however stern, which tends their strength to nerve.

xx

Blow! swiftly blow, thou keel-compelling gale!
Till the broad sun withdraws his lessening ray;
Then must the pennant-bearer slacken sail,
That lagging barks may make their lazy way.
Ah! grievance sore, and listless dull delay,
To waste on sluggish hulks the sweetest breeze!
What leagues are lost, before the dawn of day,
Thus loitering pensive on the willing seas,
The flapping sail haul'd down to halt for logs like these!

xxi

The moon is up; by Heaven, a lovely eve!
Long streams of light o'er dancing waves expand;
Now lads on shore may sigh, and maids believe:
Such be our fate when we return to land!
Meantime some rude Arion's restless hand
Wakes the brisk harmony that sailors love;
A circle there of merry listeners stand,
Or to some well-known measure featly move,
Thoughtless, as if on shore they still were free to rove.

xxii

Through Calpe's straits survey the steepy shore;
Europe and Afric on each other gaze!
Lands of the dark-eyed Maid and dusky Moor
Alike beheld beneath pale Hecate's blaze:
How softly on the Spanish shore she plays,
Disclosing rock, and slope, and forest brown,
Distinct, though darkening with her waning phase;
But Mauritania's giant-shadows frown,
From mountain-cliff to coast descending sombre down.

xxiii

'Tis night, when Meditation bids us feel
We once have loved, though love is at an end:
The heart, lone mourner of its baffled zeal,
Though friendless now, will dream it had a friend.

Who with the weight of years would wish to bend,
When Youth itself survives young Love and Joy?
Alas! when mingling souls forget to blend,
Death hath but little left him to destroy!
Ah! happy years! once more who would not be a boy?

search for innocence

XXIV

Thus bending o'er the vessel's laving side,
To gaze on Dian's wave-reflected sphere,
The soul forgets her schemes of Hopes and Pride,
And flies unconscious o'er each backward year.
None are so desolate but something dear,
Dearer than self, possesses or possess'd
A thought, and claims the homage of a tear;
A flashing pang! of which the weary breast
Would still, albeit in vain, the heavy heart divest.

XXV

To sit on rocks, to muse o'er flood and fell,
To slowly trace the forest's shady scene,
Where things that own not man's dominion dwell,
And mortal foot hath ne'er or rarely been;
To climb the trackless mountain all unseen,
With the wild flock that never needs a fold;
Alone o'er steeps and foaming falls to lean,
This is not solitude; 'tis but to hold
Converse with Nature's charms, and view her stores unroll'd.

XXVI

But midst the crowd, the hum, the shock of men,
To hear, to see, to feel, and to possess,
And roam along, the world's tired denizen,
With none who bless us, none whom we can bless;
Minions of splendour shrinking from distress!
None that, with kindred consciousness endued,
If we were not, would seem to smile the less
Of all that flatter'd, follow'd, sought, and sued;
This is to be alone; this, this is solitude!

XXVII

More blest the life of godly eremite,
Such as on lonely Athos may be seen,
Watching at eve upon the giant height,
Which looks o'er waves so blue, skies so serene,

That he who there at such an hour hath been
Will wistful linger on that hallow'd spot;
Then slowly tear him from the witching scene,
Sigh forth one wish that such had been his lot,
Then turn to hate a world he had almost forgot.

XXVIII

Pass we the long, unvarying course, the track
Oft trod, that never leaves a trace behind;
Pass we the calm, the gale, the change, the tack,
And each well-known caprice of wave and wind;
Pass we the joys and sorrows sailors find,
Coop'd in their winged sea-girt citadel;
The foul, the fair, the contrary, the kind,
As breezes rise and fall and billows swell,
Till on some jocund morn—lo, land! and all is well.

XXIX

But not in silence pass Calypso's isles,[1]
The sister tenants of the middle deep;
There for the weary still a haven smiles,
Though the fair goddess long hath ceased to weep,
And o'er her cliffs a fruitless watch to keep
For him who dared prefer a mortal bride:
Here, too, his boy essay'd the dreadful leap
Stern Mentor urged from high to yonder tide;
While thus of both bereft, the nymph-queen doubly sighed.

XXX

Her reign is past, her gentle glories gone:
But trust not this; too easy youth, beware!
A mortal sovereign holds her dangerous throne,
And thou may'st find a new Calypso there.
Sweet Florence![2] could another ever share
This wayward, loveless heart, it would be thine:
But check'd by every tie, I may not dare
To cast a worthless offering at thy shrine,
Nor ask so dear a breast to feel one pang for mine.

XXXI

Thus Harold deem'd, as on that lady's eye
He look'd, and met its beam without a thought,
Save Admiration glancing harmless by:
Love kept aloof, albeit not far remote,

[1] Goza is said to have been the island of Calypso.
[2] [Mrs. Spencer Smith, with whom Byron fell in love at Malta.]

Who knew his votary often lost and caught,
But knew him as his worshipper no more,
And ne'er again the boy his bosom sought:
Since now he vainly urged him to adore,
Well deem'd the little God his ancient sway was o'er.

XXXII

Fair Florence found, in sooth with some amaze,
One who, 'twas said, still sigh'd to all he saw,
Withstand, unmoved, the lustre of her gaze,
Which others hail'd with real or mimic awe,
Their hope, their doom, their punishment, their law;
All that gay Beauty from her bondsmen claims:
And such she marvell'd that a youth so raw
Nor felt, nor feign'd at least, the oft-told flames,
Which, though sometimes they frown, yet rarely anger dames.

XXXIII

Little knew she that seeming marble heart,
Now mask'd in silence or withheld by pride,
Was not unskilful in the spoiler's art,
And spread its snares licentious far and wide;
Nor from the base pursuit had turn'd aside,
As long as aught was worthy to pursue:
But Harold on such arts no more relied;
And had he doted on those eyes so blue,
Yet never would he join the lover's whining crew.

XXXIV

Not much he kens, I ween, of woman's breast,
Who thinks that wanton thing is won by sighs;
What careth she for hearts when once possess'd?
Do proper homage to thine idol's eyes;
But not too humbly, or she will despise
Thee and thy suit, though told in moving tropes:
Disguise ev'n tenderness, if thou art wise;
Brisk Confidence still best with woman copes;
Pique her and soothe in turn, soon Passion crowns thy hopes.

VERY GOOD ADVICE

XXXV

'Tis an old lesson; Time approves it true,
And those who know it best, deplore it most;
When all is won that all desire to woo,
The paltry prize is hardly worth the cost:
Youth wasted, minds degraded, honour lost,

These are thy fruits, successful Passion! these!
If, kindly cruel, early Hope is croſt,
Still to the laſt it rankles, a disease,
Not to be cured when Love itself forgets to please.

XXXVI

Away! nor let me loiter in my song,
For we have many a mountain-path to tread,
And many a varied shore to sail along,
By pensive Sadness, not by Fiction, led—
Climes, fair withal as ever mortal head
Imagined in its little schemes of thought;
Or e'er in new Utopias were ared,
To teach man what he might be, or he ought;
If that corrupted thing could ever such be taught.

XXXVII

Dear Nature is the kindeſt mother ſtill,
Though always changing, in her aspect mild;
From her bare bosom let me take my fill,
Her never-wean'd, though not her favour'd child.
Oh! she is faireſt in her features wild,
Where nothing polish'd dares pollute her path:
To me by day or night she ever smiled,
Though I have mark'd her when none other hath,
And sought her more and more, and loved her beſt in wrath.

N.B. use of pollute

XXXVIII

Land of Albania! where Iskander [1] rose,
Theme of the young, and beacon of the wise,
And he his namesake, [2] whose oft-baffled foes
Shrunk from his deeds of chivalrous emprise;
Land of Albania! let me bend mine eyes
On thee, thou rugged nurse of savage men!
The cross descends, thy minarets arise,
And the pale crescent sparkles in the glen,
Through many a cypress grove within each city's ken.

XXXIX

Childe Harold sail'd, and pass'd the barren spot
Where sad Penelope o'erlook'd the wave; [3]
And onward view'd the mount, not yet forgot,
The lover's refuge, and the Lesbian's grave.
Dark Sappho! could not verse immortal save

[1] [Alexander the Great.]   [2] [Scanderbeg.]   Ithaca.

That breast imbued with such immortal fire?
Could she not live who life eternal gave?
If life eternal may await the lyre,
That only heaven to which Earth's children may aspire.

XL

'Twas on a Grecian autumn's gentle eve
Childe Harold hail'd Leucadia's cape afar; [1]
A spot he longed to see, nor cared to leave:
Oft did he mark the scenes of vanish'd war,
Actium, Lepanto, fatal Trafalgar; [2]
Mark them unmoved, for he would not delight
(Born beneath some remote inglorious star)
In themes of bloody fray, or gallant fight,
But loathed the bravo's trade, and laughed at martial wight.

XLI

But when he saw the evening star above
Leucadia's far-projecting rock of woe,
And hail'd the last resort of fruitless love,
He felt, or deem'd he felt, no common glow:
And as the stately vessel glided slow
Beneath the shadow of that ancient mount,
He watch'd the billows' melancholy flow,
And, sunk albeit in thought as he was wont,
More placid seem'd his eye, and smooth his pallid front.

XLII

Morn dawns; and with it stern Albania's hills,
Dark Suli's rocks, and Pindus' inland peak,
Robed half in mist, bedewed with snowy rills,
Array'd in many a dun and purple streak,
Arise; and, as the clouds along them break,
Disclose the dwelling of the mountaineer:
Here roams the wolf, the eagle whets his beak,
Birds, beasts of prey, and wilder men appear,
And gathering storms around convulse the closing year.

XLIII

Now Harold felt himself at length alone,
And bade to Christian tongues a long adieu;
Now he adventured on a shore unknown,
Which all admire, but many dread to view:

[1] Leucadia, now Santa Maura. From the promontory (the Lover's Leap)
Sappho is said to have thrown herself.
[2] Actium and Trafalgar need no further mention. The battle of Lepanto,
equally bloody and considerable, but less known, was fought in the Gulf of
Patras. Here the author of *Don Quixote* lost his left hand.

His breast was arm'd 'gainst fate, his wants were few;
Peril he sought not, but ne'er shrank to meet:
The scene was savage, but the scene was new:
This made the ceaseless toil of travel sweet,
Beat back keen winter's blast, and welcomed summer's heat.

XLIV

Here the red cross, for still the cross is here,
Though sadly scoff'd at by the circumcised,
Forgets that pride to pamper'd priesthood dear;
Churchman and votary alike despised.
Foul Superstition! howsoe'er disguised,
Idol, saint, virgin, prophet, crescent, cross,
For whatsoever symbol thou art prized,
Thou sacerdotal gain, but general loss!
Who from true worship's gold can separate thy dross?

XLV

Ambracia's gulf behold, where once was lost
A world for woman, lovely, harmless thing!
In yonder rippling bay, their naval host
Did many a Roman chief and Asian king [1]
To doubtful conflict, certain slaughter bring:
Look where the second Caesar's trophies rose: [2]
Now, like the hands that reared them, withering:
Imperial anarchs, doubling human woes!
God! was thy globe ordain'd for such to win and lose?

XLVI

From the dark barriers of that rugged clime,
Ev'n to the centre of Illyria's vales,
Childe Harold pass'd o'er many a mount sublime,
Through lands scarce noticed in historic tales;
Yet in famed Attica such lovely dales
Are rarely seen; nor can fair Tempe boast
A charm they know not; loved Parnassus fails,
Though classic ground and consecrated most,
To match some spots that lurk within this lowering coast.

[1] It is said, that, on the day previous to the battle of Actium, Antony had thirteen kings at his levee.
[2] Nicopolis, whose ruins are most extensive, is at some distance from Actium) where the wall of the Hippodrome survives in a few fragments. These ruins are large masses of brickwork, the bricks of which are joined by interstices of mortar as large as the bricks themselves, and equally durable.

XLVII

He pass'd bleak Pindus, Acherusia's lake,[1]
And left the primal city of the land,
And onwards did his further journey take
To greet Albania's chief,[2] whose dread command
Is lawless law; for with a bloody hand
He sways a nation, turbulent and bold:
Yet here and there some daring mountain-band
Disdain his power, and from their rocky hold
Hurl their defiance far, nor yield, unless to gold.[3]

XLVIII

Monastic Zitza![4] from thy shady brow,
Thou small, but favour'd spot of holy ground!
Where'er we gaze, around, above, below,
What rainbow tints, what magic charms are found!
Rock, river, forest, mountain, all abound,
And bluest skies that harmonize the whole:
Beneath, the distant torrent's rushing sound
Tells where the volumed cataract doth roll
Between those hanging rocks, that shock yet please the soul.

XLIX

Amidst the grove that crowns yon tufted hill,
Which, were it not for many a mountain nigh
Rising in lofty ranks, and loftier still,
Might well itself be deem'd of dignity,
The convent's white walls glisten fair on high:
Here dwells the caloyer,[5] nor rude is he,
Nor niggard of his cheer; the passer by
Is welcome still; nor heedless will he flee
From hence, if he delight kind Nature's sheen to see.

L

Here in the sultriest season let him rest,
Fresh is the green beneath those aged trees;
Here winds of gentlest wing will fan his breast,
From heaven itself it may inhale the breeze:

[1] According to Pouqueville, the lake of Yanina: but Pouqueville is always out.
[2] The celebrated Ali Pacha. Of this extraordinary man there is an incorrect account in Pouqueville's Travels.
[3] Five thousand Suliotes, among the rocks and in the castle of Suli, withstood thirty thousand Albanians for eighteen years; the castle at last was taken by bribery. In this contest there were several acts performed not unworthy of the better days of Greece.
[4] The convent and village of Zitza are four hours' journey from Joannina, or Yanina, the capital of the Pachalic. In the valley the river Kalamas (once the Acheron) flows, and, not far from Zitza, forms a fine cataract. The situation is perhaps the finest in Greece, though the approach to Delvinachi and parts of Acarnania and Aetolia may contest the palm.
[5] The Greek monks are so called.

The plain is far beneath—oh! let him seize
Pure pleasure while he can; the scorching ray
Here pierceth not, impregnate with disease:
Then let his length the loitering pilgrim lay,
And gaze, untired, the morn, the noon, the eve away.

LI

Dusky and huge, enlarging on the sight,
Nature's volcanic amphitheatre,[1]
Chimaera's alps extend from left to right:
Beneath, a living valley seems to stir;
Flocks play, trees wave, streams flow, the mountain-fir
Nodding above; behold black Acheron![2]
Once consecrated to the sepulchre.
Pluto! if this be hell I look upon,
Close shamed Elysium's gates, my shade shall seek for none.

LII

No city's towers pollute the lovely view;
Unseen is Yanina, though not remote,
Veil'd by the screen of hills: here men are few,
Scanty the hamlet, rare the lonely cot:
But peering down each precipice, the goat
Browseth; and, pensive o'er his scatter'd flock,
The little shepherd in his white capote[3]
Doth lean his boyish form along the rock,
Or in his cave awaits the tempest's short-lived shock.

LIII

Oh! where, Dodona! is thine aged grove,
Prophetic fount, and oracle divine?
What valley echo'd the response of Jove?
What trace remaineth of the Thunderer's shrine?
All, all forgotten—and shall man repine
That his frail bonds to fleeting life are broke?
Cease, fool! the fate of gods may well be thine:
Wouldst thou survive the marble or the oak?
When nations, tongues, and worlds must sink beneath the stroke!

LIV

Epirus' bounds recede, and mountains fail;
Tired of up-gazing still, the wearied eye
Reposes gladly on as smooth a vale
As ever Spring yclad in grassy dye:

[1] The Chimariot mountains appear to have been volcanic.
[2] Now called Kalamas.   [3] Albanese cloak.

Ev'n on a plain no humble beauties lie,
Where some bold river breaks the long expanse,
And woods along the banks are waving high,
Whose shadows in the glassy waters dance,
Or with the moonbeam sleep in midnight's solemn trance.

LV

The sun had sunk behind vast Tomerit,[1]
And Laos wide and fierce came roaring by;[2]
The shades of wonted night were gathering yet,
When, down the steep banks winding warily,
Childe Harold saw, like meteors in the sky,
The glittering minarets of Tepalen,
Whose walls o'erlook the stream; and drawing nigh,
He heard the busy hum of warrior-men
Swelling the breeze that sigh'd along the lengthening glen.

LVI

He pass'd the sacred Haram's silent tower,
And underneath the wide o'er-arching gate
Survey'd the dwelling of this chief of power,
Where all around proclaim'd his high estate.
Amidst no common pomp the despot sate,
While busy preparation shook the court,
Slaves, eunuchs, soldiers, guests, and santons wait;
Within, a palace, and without, a fort:
Here men of every clime appear to make resort.

LVII

Richly caparison'd, a ready row
Of armed horse, and many a warlike store,
Circled the wide extending court below;
Above, strange groups adorn'd the corridore;
And oft-times through the area's echoing door,
Some high-capp'd Tartar spurr'd his steed away:
The Turk, the Greek, the Albanian, and the Moor,
Here mingled in their many-hued array,
While the deep war-drum's sound announced the close of day.

LVIII

The wild Albanian kirtled to his knee,
With shawl-girt head and ornamented gun,
And gold-embroider'd garments, fair to see:
The crimson-scarfed men of Macedon;

[1] Anciently Mount Tomarus.
[2] The river Laos was full at the time the author passed it; and, immediately above Tepaleen, was to the eye as wide as the Thames at Westminster; at least in the opinion of the author and his fellow-traveller. In the summer it must be much narrower. It certainly is the finest river in the Levant; neither Achelous, Alpheus, Acheron, Scamander, nor Cayster, approached it in breadth or beauty.

The Delhi with his cap of terror on,
And crooked glaive; the lively, supple Greek:
And swarthy Nubia's mutilated son;
The bearded Turk, that rarely deigns to speak,
Master of all around, too potent to be meek,

LIX

Are mix'd conspicuous: some recline in groups,
Scanning the motley scene that varies round;
There some grave Moslem to devotion stoops,
And some that smoke, and some that play, are found;
Here the Albanian proudly treads the ground;
Half whispering there the Greek is heard to prate;
Hark! from the mosque the nightly solemn sound,
The Muezzin's call doth shake the minaret,
'There is no god but God!—to prayer—lo! God is great!'

LX

Just at this season Ramazani's fast
Through the long day its penance did maintain:
But when the lingering twilight hour was past,
Revel and feast assumed the rule again:
Now all was bustle, and the menial train
Prepared and spread the plenteous board within;
The vacant gallery now seem'd made in vain,
But from the chambers came the mingling din,
As page and slave anon were passing out and in.

LXI

Here woman's voice is never heard: apart,
And scarce permitted, guarded, veil'd, to move,
She yields to one her person and her heart,
Tamed to her cage, nor feels a wish to rove:
For, not unhappy in her master's love,
And joyful in a mother's gentlest cares,
Blest cares! all other feelings far above!
Herself more sweetly rears the babe she bears,
Who never quits the breast, no meaner passion shares.

LXII

In marble-paved pavilion, where a spring
Of living water from the centre rose,
Whose bubbling did a genial freshness fling,
And soft voluptuous couches breathed repose,

ALI reclined, a man of war and woes:
Yet in his lineaments ye cannot trace,
While Gentleness her milder radiance throws
Along that aged venerable face,
The deeds that lurk beneath, and ſtain him with disgrace.

LXIII

It is not that yon hoary lengthening beard
Ill suits the passions which belong to youth;
Love conquers age—so Hafiz hath averr'd,
So sings the Teian, and he sings in sooth—
But crimes that scorn the tender voice of Ruth,
Beseeming all men ill, but moſt the man
In years, have mark'd him with a tiger's tooth;
Blood follows blood, and, through their mortal span,
In bloodier acts conclude those who with blood began.

LXIV

'Mid many things moſt new to ear and eye
The pilgrim reſted here his weary feet,
And gazed around on Moslem luxury,
Till quickly wearied with that spacious seat
Of Wealth and Wantonness, the choice retreat
Of sated Grandeur from the city's noise:
And were it humbler it in sooth were sweet;
But Peace abhorreth artificial joys,
And Pleasure, leagued with Pomp, the zeſt of both deſtroys.

use of destroys

LXV

Fierce are Albania's children, yet they lack
Not virtues, were those virtues more mature.
Where is the foe that ever saw their back?
Who can so well the toil of war endure?
Their native faſtnesses not more secure
Than they in doubtful time of troublous need:
Their wrath how deadly! but their friendship sure,
When Gratitude or Valour bids them bleed,
Unshaken rushing on where'er their chief may lead.

LXVI

Childe Harold saw them in their chieftain's tower
Thronging to war in splendour and success;
And after view'd them, when, within their power,
Himself awhile the victim of diſtress;

That saddening hour when bad men hotlier press:
But these did shelter him beneath their roof,
When less barbarians would have cheer'd him less,
And fellow-countrymen have stood aloof [1]—
In aught that tries the heart how few withstand the proof!

LXVII

It chanced that adverse winds once drove his bark
Full on the coast of Suli's shaggy shore,
When all around was desolate and dark;
To land was perilous, to sojourn more;
Yet for a while the mariners forbore,
Dubious to trust where treachery might lurk:
At length they ventured forth, though doubting sore
That those who loathe alike the Frank and Turk
Might once again renew their ancient butcher-work.

LXVIII

Vain fear! the Suliotes stretch'd the welcome hand,
Led them o'er rocks and past the dangerous swamp,
Kinder than polish'd slaves though not so bland,
And piled the hearth, and wrung their garments damp,
And fill'd the bowl, and trimm'd the cheerful lamp,
And spread their fare; though homely, all they had:
Such conduct bears Philanthropy's rare stamp—
To rest the weary and to soothe the sad,
Doth lesson happier men, and shames at least the bad.

LXIX

It came to pass, that when he did address
Himself to quit at length this mountain-land,
Combined marauders half-way barr'd egress,
And wasted far and near with glaive and brand;
And therefore did he take a trusty band
To traverse Acarnania's forest wide,
In war well season'd, and with labours tann'd,
Till he did greet white Achelous' tide,
And from his further bank Aetolia's wolds espied.

LXX

Where lone Utraikey forms its circling cove,
And weary waves retire to gleam at rest,
How brown the foliage of the green hill's grove,
Nodding at midnight o'er the calm bay's breast,

[1] Alluding to the wreckers of Cornwall.

As winds come lightly whispering from the weſt,
Kissing, not ruffling, the blue deep's serene:—
Here Harold was received a welcome gueſt;
Nor did he pass unmoved the gentle scene,
For many a joy could he from Night's soft presence glean.

LXXI

On the smooth shore the night-fires brightly blazed,
The feaſt was done, the red wine circling faſt,[1]
And he that unawares had there ygazed
With gaping wonderment had ſtared aghaſt;
For ere night's midmoſt, ſtilleſt hour was paſt,
The native revels of the troop began;
Each Palikar[2] his sabre from him caſt,
And bounding hand in hand, man link'd to man,
Yelling their uncouth dirge, long daunced the kirtled clan.

LXXII

Childe Harold at a little diſtance ſtood
And view'd, but not displeased, the revelrie,
Nor hated harmless mirth, however rude:
In sooth, it was no vulgar sight to see
Their barbarous, yet their not indecent, glee;
And, as the flames along their faces gleam'd,
Their geſtures nimble, dark eyes flashing free,
The long wild locks that to their girdles ſtream'd,
While thus in concert they this lay half sang, half scream'd:—

I

TAMBOURGI! Tambourgi![3] thy 'larum afar
Gives hope to the valiant, and promise of war;
All the sons of the mountains arise at the note,
Chimariot, Illyrian, and dark Suliote![4]

2

Oh! who is more brave than a dark Suliote,
In his snowy camese and his shaggy capote?
To the wolf and the vulture he leaves his wild flock,
And descends to the plain like the ſtream from the rock.

[1] The Albanian Mussulmans do not abſtain from wine, and, indeed, very few of the others.
[2] Palikar, shortened when addressed to a single person, from Παλικαρί, a general name for a soldier amongſt the Greeks and Albanese who speak Romaic: it means, properly, 'a lad.'
[3] Drummer.
[4] These ſtanzas are partly taken from different Albanese songs, as far as I was able to make them out by the exposition of the Albanese in Romaic and Italian.

3

Shall the sons of Chimari, who never forgive
The fault of a friend, bid an enemy live?
Let those guns so unerring such vengeance forego?
What mark is so fair as the breast of a foe?

4

Macedonia sends forth her invincible race;
For a time they abandon the cave and the chase:
But those scarfs of blood-red shall be redder, before
The sabre is sheathed and the battle is o'er.

5

Then the pirates of Parga that dwell by the waves,
And teach the pale Franks what it is to be slaves,
Shall leave on the beach the long galley and oar,
And track to his covert the captive on shore.

6

I ask not the pleasures that riches supply,
My sabre shall win what the feeble must buy;
Shall win the young bride with her long flowing hair,
And many a maid from her mother shall tear.

7

I love the fair face of the maid in her youth,
Her caresses shall lull me, her music shall soothe;
Let her bring from the chamber her many-toned lyre,
And sing us a song on the fall of her sire.

8

Remember the moment when Previsa fell,[1]
The shrieks of the conquer'd, the conquerors' yell;
The roofs that we fired, and the plunder we shared,
The wealthy we slaughter'd, the lovely we spared.

9

I talk not of mercy, I talk not of fear;
He neither must know who would serve the Vizier:
Since the days of our prophet the Crescent ne'er saw
A chief ever glorious like Ali Pashaw.

10

Dark Muchtar his son to the Danube is sped,
Let the yellow-hair'd[2] Giaours[3] view his horse-tail[4] with dread;
When his Delhis[5] come dashing in blood o'er the banks,
How few shall escape from the Muscovite ranks!

[1] It was taken by storm from the French.
[2] Yellow is the epithet given to the Russians.
[3] Infidels.   [4] The insignia of a Pacha.
[5] Horsemen, answering to our forlorn hope.

11

Seliĉtar! [1] unsheathe then our chief's scimitar:
Tambourgi! thy 'larum gives promise of war.
Ye mountains, that see us descend to the shore,
Shall view us as viĉtors, or view us no more!

LXXIII

Fair Greece! sad relic of departed worth!
Immortal, though no more; though fallen, great!
Who now shall lead thy scatter'd children forth,
And long accustom'd bondage uncreate?
Not such thy sons who whilome did await,
The hopeless warriors of a willing doom,
In bleak Thermopylae's sepulchral strait—
Oh! who that gallant spirit shall resume,
Leap from Eurotas' banks, and call thee from the tomb?

LXXIV

Spirit of freedom! when on Phyle's brow [2]
Thou sat'st with Thrasybulus and his train,
Couldst thou forebode the dismal hour which now
Dims the green beauties of thine Attic plain?
Not thirty tyrants now enforce the chain,
But every carle can lord it o'er thy land;
Nor rise thy sons, but idly rail in vain,
Trembling beneath the scourge of Turkish hand
From birth till death enslaved; in word, in deed, unmann'd.

LXXV

In all save form alone, how changed! and who
That marks the fire ĉtill sparkling in each eye,
Who but would deem their bosoms burn'd anew
With thy unquenched beam, loĉt Liberty!
And many dream withal the hour is nigh
That gives them back their fathers' heritage:
For foreign arms and aid they fondly sigh,
Nor solely dare encounter hoĉtile rage,
Or tear their name defiled from Slavery's mournful page.

LXXVI

Hereditary bondsmen! know ye not
Who would be free themselves muĉt ĉtrike the blow?
By their right arms the conqueĉt muĉt be wrought?
Will Gaul or Muscovite redress ye? no!

[1] Sword-bearer.
[2] Phyle, which commands a beautiful view of Athens, has ĉtill considerable remains: it was seized by Thrasybulus, previous to the expulsion of the Thirty.

II—C 4⁸7

True, they may lay your proud despoilers low,
But not for you will Freedom's altars flame.
Shades of the Helots! triumph o'er your foe!
Greece! change thy lords, thy state is still the same;
Thy glorious day is o'er, but not thy years of shame.

LXXVII

The city won for Allah from the Giaour,
The Giaour from Othman's race again may wrest;
And the Serai's impenetrable tower
Receive the fiery Frank, her former guest; [1]
Or Wahab's rebel brood who dared divest
The prophet's tomb of all its pious spoil, [2]
May wind their path of blood along the West;
But ne'er will freedom seek this fated soil,
But slave succeed to slave through years of endless toil.

LXXVIII

Yet mark their mirth—ere lenten days begin,
That penance which their holy rites prepare
To shrive from man his weight of mortal sin,
By daily abstinence and nightly prayer;
But ere his sackcloth garb Repentance wear,
Some days of joyaunce are decreed to all,
To take of pleasaunce each his secret share,
In motley robe to dance at masking ball,
And join the mimic train of merry Carnival.

LXXIX

And whose more rife with merriment than thine,
Oh Stamboul! once the empress of their reign?
Though turbans now pollute Sophia's shrine,
And Greece her very altars eyes in vain:
(Alas! her woes will still pervade my strain!)
Gay were her minstrels once, for free her throng,
All felt the common joy they now must feign,
Nor oft I've seen such sight, nor heard such song,
As woo'd the eye, and thrill'd the Bosphorus along.

LXXX

Loud was the lightsome tumult on the shore,
Oft Music changed, but never ceased her tone,
And timely echo'd back the measured oar,
And rippling waters made a pleasant moan:

[1] When taken by the Latins, and retained for several years.
[2] Mecca and Medina were taken some time ago by the Wahabees, a sect yearly increasing.

The Queen of tides on high consenting shone,
And when a transient breeze swept o'er the wave,
'Twas, as if darting from her heavenly throne,
A brighter glance her form reflected gave,
Till sparkling billows seem'd to light the banks they lave.

LXXXI

Glanced many a light caique along the foam,
Danced on the shore the daughters of the land,
Ne thought had man or maid of rest or home,
While many a languid eye and thrilling hand
Exchanged the look few bosoms may withstand,
Or gently prest, return'd the pressure still:
Oh Love! young Love! bound in thy rosy band,
Let sage or cynic prattle as he will,
These hours, and only these, redeem Life's years of ill!

LXXXII

But, midst the throng in merry masquerade,
Lurk there no hearts that throb with secret pain,
Even through the closest searment half betray'd?
To such the gentle murmurs of the main
Seem to re-echo all they mourn in vain;
To such the gladness of the gamesome crowd
Is source of wayward thought and stern disdain:
How do they loathe the laughter idly loud,
And long to change the robe of revel for the shroud!

LXXXIII

This must he feel, the true-born son of Greece,
If Greece one true-born patriot still can boast:
Not such as prate of war, but skulk in peace,
The bondsman's peace, who sighs for all he lost,
Yet with smooth smile his tyrant can accost,
And wield the slavish sickle, not the sword:
Ah! Greece! they love thee least who owe thee most;
Their birth, their blood, and that sublime record
Of hero sires, who shame thy now degenerate horde!

LXXXIV

When riseth Lacedemon's hardihood,
When Thebes Epaminondas rears again,
When Athens' children are with hearts endued,
When Grecian mothers shall give birth to men,
Then may'st thou be restored; but not till then.

A thousand years scarce serve to form a state;
An hour may lay it in the dust: and when
Can man its shatter'd splendour renovate,
Recall its virtues back, and vanquish Time and Fate?

LXXXV

And yet how lovely in thine age of woe,
Land of lost gods and godlike men! art thou!
Thy vales of evergreen, thy hills of snow,[1]
Proclaim thee Nature's varied favourite now;
Thy fanes, thy temples to thy surface bow,
Commingling slowly with heroic earth,
Broke by the share of every rustic plough:
So perish monuments of mortal birth,
So perish all in turn, save well-recorded Worth;

Destiny

LXXXVI

Save where some solitary column mourns
Above its prostrate brethren of the cave [2]
Save where Tritonia's airy shrine adorns
Colonna's cliff,[3] and gleams along the wave;
Save o'er some warrior's half-forgotten grave,
Where the gray stones and unmolested grass
Ages, but not oblivion, feebly brave,
While strangers only not regardless pass,
Lingering like me, perchance, to gaze, and sigh 'Alas!'

LXXXVII

Yet are thy skies as blue, thy crags as wild;
Sweet are thy groves, and verdant are thy fields,
Thine olive ripe as when Minerva smiled,
And still his honied wealth Hymettus yields;
There the blithe bee his fragrant fortress builds,
The freeborn wanderer of thy mountain-air;
Apollo still thy long, long summer gilds,
Still in his beam Mendeli's marbles glare;
Art, Glory, Freedom fail, but Nature still is fair.

Destiny

[1] On many of the mountains, particularly Liakura, the snow never is entirely melted, notwithstanding the intense heat of the summer; but I never saw it lie on the plains, even in winter.

[2] Of Mount Pentelicus, from whence the marble was dug that constructed the public edifices of Athens. The modern name is Mount Mendeli. An immense cave, formed by the quarries, still remains, and will till the end of time.

[3] In all Attica, if we except Athens itself and Marathon, there is no scene more interesting than Cape Colonna. To the antiquary and artist, sixteen columns are an inexhaustible source of observation and design; to the philosopher, the supposed scene of some of Plato's conversations will not be unwelcome; and the traveller will be struck with the beauty of the prospect over 'Isles that crown the Aegean deep': but, for an Englishman, Colonna has yet an additional interest, as the actual spot of Falconer's shipwreck.

LXXXVIII

Where'er we tread 'tis haunted, holy ground,
No earth of thine is lost in vulgar mould,
But one vast realm of wonder spreads around,
And all the Muse's tales seem truly told,
Till the sense aches with gazing to behold
The scenes our earliest dreams have dwelt upon:
Each hill and dale, each deepening glen and wold
Defies the power which crush'd thy temples gone:
Age shakes Athena's tower, but spares gray Marathon.

Early associations the reason for his love of Greece

LXXXIX

The sun, the soil, but not the slave, the same;
Unchanged in all except its foreign lord—
Preserves alike its bounds and boundless fame
The Battle-field, where Persia's victim horde
First bow'd beneath the brunt of Hellas' sword,
As on the morn to distant Glory dear,
When Marathon became a magic word; [1]
Which utter'd, to the hearer's eye appear
The camp, the host, the fight, the conqueror's career,

XC

The flying Mede, his shaftless broken bow;
The fiery Greek, his red pursuing spear;
Mountains above, Earth's, Ocean's plain below;
Death in the front, Destruction in the rear!
Such was the scene—what now remaineth here?
What sacred trophy marks the hallow'd ground,
Recording Freedom's smile and Asia's tear?
The rifled urn, the violated mound,
The dust thy courser's hoof, rude stranger! spurns around.

XCI

Yet to the remnants of thy splendour past
Shall pilgrims, pensive, but unwearied, throng;
Long shall the voyager, with th' Ionian blast,
Hail the bright clime of battle and of song;

[1] 'Siste Viator—heroa calcas!' was the epitaph on the famous Count Merci;—what then must be our feelings when standing on the tumulus of the two hundred (Greeks) who fell on Marathon? The principal barrow has recently been opened by Fauvel: few or no relics, as vases, etc., were found by the excavator. The plain of Marathon was offered to me for sale at the sum of sixteen thousand piastres, about nine hundred pounds! Alas!—'Expende—quot *libras* in duce summo—invenies!'—was the dust of Miltiades worth no more? It could scarcely have fetched less if sold by *weight*.

Long shall thine annals and immortal tongue
Fill with thy fame the youth of many a shore;
Boast of the aged! lesson of the young!
Which sages venerate and bards adore,
As Pallas and the Muse unveil their awful lore.

XCII

The parted bosom clings to wonted home,
If aught that's kindred cheer the welcome hearth;
He that is lonely, hither let him roam,
And gaze complacent on congenial earth.
Greece is no lightsome land of social mirth:
But he whom Sadness sootheth may abide,
And scarce regret the region of his birth,
When wandering slow by Delphi's sacred side,
Or gazing o'er the plains where Greek and Persian died.

XCIII

Let such approach this consecrated land,
And pass in peace along the magic waste;
But spare its relics—let no busy hand
Deface the scenes, already how defaced!
Not for such purpose were these altars placed:
Revere the remnants nations once revered:
So may our country's name be undisgraced,
So may'st thou prosper where thy youth was rear'd,
By every honest joy of love and life endear'd!

XCIV

For thee, who thus in too protracted song
Hast soothed thine idlesse with inglorious lays,
Soon shall thy voice be lost amid the throng
Of louder minstrels in these later days:
To such resign the strife for fading bays—
Ill may such contest now the spirit move
Which heeds nor keen reproach nor partial praise,
Since cold each kinder heart that might approve,
And none are left to please when none are left to love.

XCV

Thou too art gone, thou loved and lovely one!
Whom youth and youth's affections bound to me;
Who did for me what none beside have done,
Nor shrank from one albeit unworthy thee.
What is my being? thou hast ceased to be!

Nor staid to welcome here thy wanderer home,
Who mourns o'er hours which we no more shall see—
Would they had never been, or were to come!
Would he had ne'er return'd to find fresh cause to roam!

XCVI

Oh! ever loving, lovely, and beloved!
How selfish Sorrow ponders on the past,
And clings to thoughts now better far removed!
But Time shall tear thy shadow from me last,
All thou couldst have of mine, stern Death! thou hast:
The parent, friend, and now the more than friend:
Ne'er yet for one thine arrows flew so fast,
And grief with grief continuing still to blend,
Hath snatch'd the little joy that life had yet to lend.

XCVII

Then must I plunge again into the crowd,
And follow all that Peace disdains to seek?
Where Revel calls, and Laughter, vainly loud,
False to the heart, distorts the hollow cheek,
To leave the flagging spirit doubly weak;
Still o'er the features, which perforce they cheer,
To feign the pleasure or conceal the pique;
Smiles form the channel of a future tear,
Or raise the writhing lip with ill-dissembled sneer.

XCVIII

What is the worst of woes that wait on age?
What stamps the wrinkle deeper on the brow?
To view each loved one blotted from life's page,
And be alone on earth, as I am now.
Before the Chastener humbly let me bow,
O'er hearts divided and o'er hopes destroy'd:
Roll on, vain days! full reckless may ye flow,
Since Time hath reft whate'er my soul enjoy'd,
And with the ills of Eld mine earlier years alloy'd.

*Afin que cette application vous forçât de penser à autre chose; il n'y a en
vérité de remède que celui-là et le temps.*—Lettre du Roi de Prusse à
D'Alembert, 7th September 1776.

*There is a unity
of tone for each opening
of each canto*

I

Is thy face like thy mother's, my fair child!
ADA! sole daughter of my house and heart?
When last I saw thy young blue eyes they smiled,
And then we parted,—not as now we part,
But with a hope.—
                    Awaking with a start,
The waters heave around me; and on high
The winds lift up their voices: I depart,
Whither I know not; but the hour 's gone by,
When Albion's lessening shores could grieve or glad mine eye.

II

Once more upon the waters! yet once more!
And the waves bound beneath me as a steed
That knows his rider.   Welcome to their roar!
Swift be their guidance, wheresoe'er it lead!
Though the strain'd mast should quiver as a reed,
And the rent canvas fluttering strew the gale,
Still must I on; for I am as a weed,
Flung from the rock, on Ocean's foam, to sail
Where'er the surge may sweep, the tempest's breath prevail.

III

In my youth's summer I did sing of One,
The wandering outlaw of his own dark mind;
Again I seize the theme, then but begun,
And bear it with me, as the rushing wind
Bears the cloud onwards: in that Tale I find
The furrows of long thought, and dried-up tears,
Which, ebbing, leave a sterile track behind,
O'er which all heavily the journeying years
Plod the last sands of life,—where not a flower appears.

IV

NB

Since my young days of passion—joy, or pain,
Perchance my heart and harp have lost a string,
And both may jar: it may be, that in vain
I would essay as I have sung to sing.
Yet, though a dreary strain, to this I cling

66

*Childe Harold's journey is a search
for lost innocence.*

So that it wean me from the weary dream
Of selfish grief or gladness—so it fling
Forgetfulness around me—it shall seem
To me, though to none else, a not ungrateful theme.

V

He, who grown aged in this world of woe,
In deeds, not years, piercing the depths of life,
So that no wonder waits him; nor below
Can love, or sorrow, fame, ambition, strife,
Cut to his heart again with the keen knife
Of silent, sharp endurance: he can tell
Why thought seeks refuge in lone caves, yet rife
With airy images, and shapes which dwell
Still unimpair'd, though old, in the soul's haunted cell.

VI

'Tis to create, and in creating live   *Creation is a search*
A being more intense, that we endow   *for immortality*
With form our fancy, gaining as we give
The life we image, even as I do now.
What am I?   Nothing: but not so art thou,
Soul of my thought! with whom I traverse earth,
Invisible but gazing, as I glow
Mix'd with thy spirit, blended with thy birth,
And feeling still with thee in my crush'd feelings' dearth.

VII

Yet must I think less wildly:—I *have* thought
Too long and darkly, till my brain became,
In its own eddy boiling and o'erwrought,
A whirling gulf of phantasy and flame:
And thus, untaught in youth my heart to tame,
My springs of life were poison'd.   'Tis too late!
Yet am I changed; though still enough the same
In strength to bear what time can not abate,
And feed on bitter fruits without accusing Fate.

VIII

CONTINUALLY APOLOGY
FOR DIVERGENCES

Something too much of this:—but now 'tis past
And the spell closes with its silent seal.
Long absent HAROLD re-appears at last;
He of the breast which fain no more would feel,
Wrung with the wounds which kill not, but ne'er heal;

II—* c 487

Yet Time, who changes all, had alter'd him
In soul and aspect as in age: years steal
Fire from the mind as vigour from the limb;
And life's enchanted cup but sparkles near the brim.

IX

The essence of Harold's quest

His had been quaff'd too quickly, and he found
The dregs were wormwood: but he fill'd again,
And from a purer fount, on holier ground,
And deemed its spring perpetual; but in vain!
Still round him clung invisibly a chain
Which gall'd for ever, fettering though unseen,
And heavy though it clank'd not; worn with pain,
Which pined although it spoke not, and grew keen,
Entering with every step he took through many a scene.

X

Secure in guarded coldness, he had mix'd
Again in fancied safety with his kind,
And deem'd his spirit now so firmly fix'd
And sheath'd with an invulnerable mind,
That, if no joy, no sorrow lurk'd behind;
And he, as one, might 'midst the many stand
Unheeded, searching through the crowd to find
Fit speculation; such as in strange land
He found in wonder-works of God and Nature's hand.

XI

But who can view the ripen'd rose, nor seek
To wear it? who can curiously behold
The smoothness and the sheen of beauty's cheek,
Nor feel the heart can never all grow old?
Who can contemplate Fame through clouds unfold
The star which rises o'er her steep, nor climb?
Harold, once more within the vortex, roll'd
On with the giddy circle, chasing Time,
Yet with a nobler aim than in his youth's fond prime.

XII

Is there a dichotomy of sentiment here — use of "unfit" with "herd"

But soon he knew himself the most unfit
Of men to herd with Man; with whom he held
Little in common; untaught to submit
His thoughts to others, though his soul was quell'd

In youth by his own thoughts; still uncompell'd,
He would not yield dominion of his mind
To spirits against whom his own rebell'd;
Proud though in desolation; which could find
A life within itself, to breathe without mankind.

XIII

Where rose the mountains, there to him were friends;
Where roll'd the ocean, thereon was his home;
Where a blue sky, and glowing clime, extends,
He had the passion and the power to roam;
The desert, forest, cavern, breaker's foam,
Were unto him companionship; they spake
A mutual language, clearer than the tome
Of his land's tongue, which he would oft forsake
For Nature's pages glass'd by sunbeams on the lake.

XIV

Like the Chaldean, he could watch the stars,
Till he had peopled them with beings bright
As their own beams; and earth, and earth-born jars,
And human frailties, were forgotten quite:
Could he have kept his spirit to that flight
He had been happy; but this clay will sink
Its spark immortal, envying it the light
To which it mounts, as if to break the link
That keeps us from yon heaven which woos us to its brink.

XV

But in Man's dwellings he became a thing
Restless and worn, and stern and wearisome,
Droop'd as a wild-born falcon with clipt wing,
To whom the boundless air alone were home:
Then came his fit again, which to o'ercome,
As eagerly the barr'd-up bird will beat
His breast and beak against his wiry dome
Till the blood tinge his plumage, so the heat
Of his impeded soul would through his bosom eat.

XVI

Self-exiled Harold wanders forth again,
With nought of hope left, but with less of gloom;
The very knowledge that he lived in vain,
That all was over on this side the tomb,

Had made Despair a smilingness assume,
Which, though 'twere wild,—as on the plunder'd wreck,
When mariners would madly meet their doom
With draughts intemperate on the sinking deck,—
Did yet inspire a cheer, which he forbore to check.

XVII

Stop!—for thy tread is on an Empire's dust!
An Earthquake's spoil is sepulchred below!
Is the spot mark'd with no colossal bust?
Nor column trophied for triumphal show?
None; but the moral's truth tells simpler so,
As the ground was before, thus let it be;—
How that red rain hath made the harvest grow!
And is this all the world has gained by thee,
Thou first and last of fields! king-making Victory?

XVIII

And Harold stands upon this place of skulls,
The grave of France, the deadly Waterloo;
How in an hour the power which gave annuls
Its gifts, transferring fame as fleeting too!
In 'pride of place' [1] here last the eagle flew,
Then tore with bloody talon the rent plain,
Pierced by the shaft of banded nations through;
Ambition's life and labours all were vain;
He wears the shatter'd links of the world's broken chain.

XIX

Fit retribution! Gaul may champ the bit
And foam in fetters;—but is Earth more free?
Did nations combat to make *One* submit;
Or league to teach all kings true sovereignty?
What! shall reviving Thraldom again be
The patch'd-up idol of enlighten'd days?
Shall we, who struck the Lion down, shall we
Pay the Wolf homage? proffering lowly gaze
And servile knees to thrones? No; *prove* before ye praise!

XX

If not, o'er one fallen despot boast no more!
In vain fair cheeks were furrow'd with hot tears
For Europe's flowers long rooted up before
The trampler of her vineyards; in vain years

[1] 'Pride of place' is a term of falconry, and means the highest pitch of flight.
See *Macbeth*, etc.:
          'An eagle towering in his pride of place,' etc.

Of death, depopulation, bondage, fears,
Have all been borne, and broken by the accord
Of roused-up millions: all that most endears
Glory, is when the myrtle wreathes a sword
Such as Harmodius [1] drew on Athens' tyrant lord.

XXI

There was a sound of revelry by night,
And Belgium's capital had gather'd then
Her Beauty and her Chivalry, and bright
The lamps shone o'er fair women and brave men;
A thousand hearts beat happily; and when
Music arose with its voluptuous swell,
Soft eyes look'd love to eyes which spake again,
And all went merry as a marriage-bell; [2]
But hush! hark! a deep sound strikes like a rising knell!

XXII

Did ye not hear it?—No; 'twas but the wind
Or the car rattling o'er the stony street;
On with the dance! let joy be unconfined;
No sleep till morn, when Youth and Pleasure meet
To chase the glowing Hours with flying feet—
But, hark!—that heavy sound breaks in once more
As if the clouds its echo would repeat;
And nearer, clearer, deadlier than before!
Arm! Arm! it is—it is—the cannon's opening roar!

XXIII

Within a window'd niche of that high hall
Sate Brunswick's fated chieftain; he did hear
That sound the first amidst the festival,
And caught its tone with Death's prophetic ear;

[1] See the famous song on Harmodius and Aristogiton. The best English translation is in Bland's Anthology, by Mr. [later Sir Thomas] Denman:
'With myrtle my sword will I wreathe,' etc.
[2] On the night previous to the action, it is said that a ball was given at Brussels. [The popular error of the Duke of Wellington having been *surprised*, on the eve of the battle of Waterloo, at a ball given by the Duchess of Richmond at Brussels, was first corrected on authority, in the *History of Napoleon Buonaparte*, which forms a portion of the 'Family Library.' The Duke had received intelligence of Napoleon's decisive operations, and it was intended to put off the ball; but, on reflection, it seemed highly important that the people of Brussels should be kept in ignorance as to the course of events, and the Duke not only desired that the ball should proceed, but the general officers received his commands to appear at it—each taking care to quit the apartment as quietly as possible at ten o'clock, and proceed to join his respective division *en route*.]

And when they smiled because he deem'd it near,
His heart more truly knew that peal too well
Which stretch'd his father on a bloody bier,[1]
And roused the vengeance blood alone could quell:
He rush'd into the field, and, foremost fighting, fell.

XXIV

Ah! then and there was hurrying to and fro,
And gathering tears, and tremblings of distress,
And cheeks all pale, which but an hour ago
Blush'd at the praise of their own loveliness;
And there were sudden partings, such as press
The life from out young hearts, and choking sighs
Which ne'er might be repeated; who could guess
If ever more should meet those mutual eyes,
Since upon night so sweet such awful morn could rise!

XXV

And there was mounting in hot haste: the steed,
The mustering squadron, and the clattering car,
Went pouring forward with impetuous speed,
And swiftly forming in the ranks of war;
And the deep thunder peal on peal afar;
And near, the beat of the alarming drum
Roused up the soldier ere the morning star;
While throng'd the citizens with terror dumb,
Or whispering, with white lips—'The foe! they come! they
    come!'

XXVI

And wild and high the 'Cameron's gathering' rose!
The war-note of Lochiel, which Albyn's hills
Have heard, and heard, too, have her Saxon foes:—
How in the noon of night that pibroch thrills,
Savage and shrill! But with the breath which fills
Their mountain-pipe, so fill the mountaineers
With the fierce native daring which instils
The stirring memory of a thousand years,
And Evan's, Donald's [2] fame rings in each clansman's ears!

[1] [The father of the Duke of Brunswick, who fell at Quatre-bras, received his death-wound at Jena.]
[2] Sir Evan Cameron, and his descendant Donald, the 'gentle Lochiel' of the 'forty-five.'

XXVII

And Ardennes [1] waves above them her green leaves,
Dewy with nature's tear-drops, as they pass,
Grieving, if aught inanimate e'er grieves,
Over the unreturning brave,—alas!
Ere evening to be trodden like the grass
Which now beneath them, but above shall grow
In its next verdure, when this fiery mass
Of living valour, rolling on the foe
And burning with high hope shall moulder cold and low.

XXVIII

Last noon beheld them full of lusty life,
Last eve in Beauty's circle proudly gay,
The midnight brought the signal-sound of strife,
The morn the marshalling in arms,—the day
Battle's magnificently stern array!
The thunder-clouds close o'er it, which when rent
The earth is cover'd thick with other clay,
Which her own clay shall cover, heap'd and pent,
Rider and horse,—friend, foe,—in one red burial blent!

XXIX

Their praise is hymn'd by loftier harps than mine;
Yet one I would select from that proud throng,
Partly because they blend me with his line,
And partly that I did his sire some wrong,
And partly that bright names will hallow song;
And his was of the bravest, and when shower'd
The death-bolts deadliest the thinn'd files along,
Even where the thickest of war's tempest lower'd,
They reach'd no nobler breast than thine, young, gallant
    Howard!

XXX

There have been tears and breaking hearts for thee,
And mine were nothing, had I such to give;
But when I stood beneath the fresh green tree,
Which living waves where thou didst cease to live,
And saw around me the wide field revive

[1] The wood of Soignies is supposed to be a remnant of the forest of Ardennes, famous in Boiardo's *Orlando*, and immortal in Shakespeare's *As you like it*. It is also celebrated in Tacitus as being the spot of successful defence by the Germans against the Roman encroachments. I have ventured to adopt the name connected with nobler associations than those of mere slaughter.

With fruits and fertile promise, and the Spring
Come forth her work of gladness to contrive,
With all her reckless birds upon the wing,
I turn'd from all she brought to those she could not bring.[1]

XXXI

I turn'd to thee, to thousands, of whom each
And one as all a ghastly gap did make
In his own kind and kindred, whom to teach
Forgetfulness were mercy for their sake;
The Archangel's trump, not Glory's, must awake
Those whom they thirst for; though the sound of Fame
May for a moment soothe, it cannot slake
The fever of vain longing, and the name
So honour'd but assumes a stronger, bitterer claim.

XXXII

They mourn, but smile at length; and, smiling, mourn:
The tree will wither long before it fall;
The hull drives on, though mast and sail be torn;
The roof-tree sinks, but moulders on the hall
In massy hoariness; the ruin'd wall
Stands when its wind-worn battlements are gone;
The bars survive the captive they enthral;
The day drags through though storms keep out the sun;
And thus the heart will break, yet brokenly live on:

XXXIII

Even as a broken mirror, which the glass
In every fragment multiplies; and makes
A thousand images of one that was,
The same, and still the more, the more it breaks;

[1] My guide from Mont St. Jean over the field seemed intelligent and accurate. The place where Major Howard fell was not far from two tall and solitary trees (there was a third cut down, or shivered in the battle), which stand a few yards from each other at a pathway's side. Beneath these he died and was buried. The body has since been removed to England. A small hollow for the present marks where it lay, but will probably soon be effaced; the plough has been upon it, and the grain is. After pointing out the different spots where Picton and other gallant men had perished; the guide said, 'Here Major Howard lay: I was near him when wounded.' I told him my relationship, and he seemed then still more anxious to point out the particular spot and circumstances. The place is one of the most marked in the field, from the peculiarity of the two trees above mentioned. I went on horseback twice over the field, comparing it with my recollection of similar scenes. As a plain, Waterloo seems marked out for the scene of some great action, though this may be mere imagination: I have viewed with attention those of Platea, Troy, Mantinea, Leuctra, Chaeronea, and Marathon; and the field around Mont St. Jean and Hougoumont appears to want little but a better cause, and that undefinable but impressive halo which the lapse of ages throws around a celebrated spot, to vie in interest with any or all of these, except, perhaps, the last mentioned.

And thus the heart will do which not forsakes,
Living in shatter'd guise, and still, and cold,
And bloodless, with its sleepless sorrow aches,
Yet withers on till all without is old,
Showing no visible sign, for such things are untold.

XXXIV

There is a very life in our despair,
Vitality of poison,—a quick root
Which feeds these deadly branches; for it were
As nothing did we die; but Life will suit
Itself to Sorrow's most detested fruit,
Like to the apples on the Dead Sea's shore,[1]
All ashes to the taste: Did man compute
Existence by enjoyment, and count o'er
Such hours 'gainst years of life,—say, would he name three-
      score?

XXXV

The Psalmist number'd out the years of man:
They are enough; and if thy tale be *true*,
Thou, who didst grudge him even that fleeting span,
More than enough, thou fatal Waterloo!
Millions of tongues record thee, and anew
Their children's lips shall echo them, and say—
'Here, where the sword united nations drew,
Our countrymen were warring on that day!'
And this is much, and all which will not pass away.

XXXVI

There sunk the greatest, nor the worst of men,
Whose spirit antithetically mixt
One moment of the mightiest, and again
On little objects with like firmness fixt,
Extreme in all things! hadst thou been betwixt,
Thy throne had still been thine, or never been;
For daring made thy rise as fall: thou seek'st
Even now to re-assume the imperial mien,
And shake again the world, the Thunderer of the scene!

XXXVII

Conqueror and captive of the earth art thou!
She trembles at thee still, and thy wild name
Was ne'er more bruited in men's minds than now
That thou art nothing, save the jest of Fame,

[1] The (fabled) apples on the brink of the lake Asphaltes were said to be air
without, and, within, ashes.—Vide Tacitus, *Histor.*, lib. v. 7.

Who woo'd thee once, thy vassal, and became
The flatterer of thy fierceness, till thou wert
A god unto thyself; nor less the same
To the astounded kingdoms all inert,
Who deem'd thee for a time whate'er thou didst assert.

XXXVIII

Oh, more or less than man—in high or low,
Battling with nations, flying from the field;
Now making monarchs' necks thy footstool, now
More than thy meanest soldier taught to yield:
An empire thou couldst crush, command, rebuild,
But govern not thy pettiest passion, nor,
However deeply in men's spirits skill'd,
Look through thine own, nor curb the lust of war,
Nor learn that tempted Fate will leave the loftiest star.

XXXIX

Yet well thy soul hath brook'd the turning tide
With that untaught innate philosophy,
Which, be it wisdom, coldness, or deep pride,
Is gall and wormwood to an enemy.
When the whole host of hatred stood hard by,
To watch and mock thee shrinking, thou hast smiled
With a sedate and all-enduring eye;—
When Fortune fled her spoil'd and favourite child,
He stood unbow'd beneath the ills upon him piled.

XL

Sager than in thy fortunes: for in them
Ambition steel'd thee on too far to show
That just habitual scorn, which could contemn
Men and their thoughts; 'twas wise to feel, not so
To wear it ever on thy lip and brow,
And spurn the instruments thou wert to use
Till they were turn'd unto thine overthrow;
'Tis but a worthless world to win or lose;
So hath it proved to thee, and all such lot who choose.

XLI

If, like a tower upon a headlong rock,
Thou hadst been made to stand or fall alone,
Such scorn of man had help'd to brave the shock;
But men's thoughts were the steps which paved thy throne,

Their admiration thy best weapon shone;
The part of Philip's son was thine, not then
(Unless aside thy purple had been thrown)
Like stern Diogenes to mock at men;
For sceptred cynics earth were far too wide a den.[1]

XLII

But quiet to quick bosoms is a hell,
And *there* hath been thy bane; there is a fire
And motion of the soul which will not dwell
In its own narrow being, but aspire
Beyond the fitting medium of desire;
And, but once kindled, quenchless evermore,
Preys upon high adventure, nor can tire
Of aught but rest; a fever at the core,
Fatal to him who bears, to all who ever bore.

XLIII

This makes the madmen who have made men mad
By their contagion; Conquerors and Kings,
Founders of sects and systems, to whom add
Sophists, Bards, Statesmen, all unquiet things
Which stir too strongly the soul's secret springs,
And are themselves the fools to those they fool;
Envied, yet how unenviable! what stings
Are theirs!   One breast laid open were a school
Which would unteach mankind the lust to shine or rule:

XLIV

Their breath is agitation, and their life
A storm whereon they ride, to sink at last,
And yet so nursed and bigoted to strife,
That should their days, surviving perils past,
Melt to calm twilight, they feel overcast
With sorrow and supineness, and so die;
Even as a flame unfed, which runs to waste
With its own flickering, or a sword laid by,
Which eats into itself, and rusts ingloriously.

[1] The great error of Napoleon, 'if we have writ our annals true,' was a continued obtrusion on mankind of his want of all community of feeling for or with them; perhaps more offensive to human vanity than the active cruelty of more trembling and suspicious tyranny.   Such were his speeches to public assemblies as well as individuals; and the single expression which he is said to have used on returning to Paris after the Russian winter had destroyed his army, rubbing his hands over a fire, 'This is pleasanter than Moscow,' would probably alienate more favour from his cause than the destruction and reverses which led to the remark.

XLV

He who ascends to mountain-tops, shall find
The loftiest peaks most wrapt in clouds and snow.
He who surpasses or subdues mankind,
Must look down on the hate of those below.
Though high *above* the sun of glory glow,
And far *beneath* the earth and ocean spread,
Round him are icy rocks, and loudly blow
Contending tempests on his naked head,
And thus reward the toils which to those summits led.

XLVI

Away with these! true Wisdom's world will be
Within its own creation, or in thine,
Maternal Nature! for who teems like thee,
Thus on the banks of thy majestic Rhine?
There Harold gazes on a work divine,
A blending of all beauties; streams and dells,
Fruit, foliage, crag, wood, cornfield, mountain, vine,
And chiefless castles breathing stern farewells
From gray but leafy walls, where Ruin greenly dwells.

XLVII

And there they stand, as stands a lofty mind,
Worn, but unstooping to the baser crowd,
All tenantless, save to the crannying wind,
Or holding dark communion with the cloud.
There was a day when they were young and proud,
Banners on high, and battles pass'd below;
But they who fought are in a bloody shroud,
And those which waved are shredless dust ere now,
And the bleak battlements shall bear no future blow.

— B. Ultimate oblivion again

XLVIII

Beneath these battlements, within those walls,
Power dwelt amidst her passions; in proud state
Each robber chief upheld his armed halls,
Doing his evil will, nor less elate
Than mightier heroes of a longer date.
What want these outlaws[1] conquerors should have?
But History's purchased page to call them great?
A wider space, an ornamented grave?
Their hopes were not less warm, their souls were full as brave.

[1] 'What wants that knave that a king should have?' was King James's question on meeting Johnny Armstrong and his followers in full accoutrements.—See the Ballad.

XLIX

In their baronial feuds and single fields,
What deeds of prowess unrecorded died!
And Love, which lent a blazon to their shields,
With emblems well devised by amorous pride,
Through all the mail of iron hearts would glide;
But still their flame was fierceness, and drew on
Keen contest and destruction near allied,
And many a tower for some fair mischief won,
Saw the discolour'd Rhine beneath its ruin run.

L

But thou, exulting and abounding river!
Making thy waves a blessing as they flow
Through banks whose beauty would endure for ever
Could man but leave thy bright creation so,
Nor its fair promise from the surface mow
With the sharp scythe of conflict,—then to see
Thy valley of sweet waters, were to know
Earth paved like Heaven; and to seem such to me,
Even now what wants thy stream?—that it should Lethe be.

LI

A thousand battles have assail'd thy banks,
But these and half their fame have pass'd away,
And Slaughter heap'd on high his weltering ranks;
Their very graves are gone, and what are they?
Thy tide wash'd down the blood of yesterday,
And all was stainless, and on thy clear stream
Glass'd with its dancing light the sunny ray;
But o'er the blacken'd memory's blighting dream
Thy waves would vainly roll, all sweeping as they seem.

LII

Thus Harold inly said, and pass'd along,
Yet not insensibly to all which here
Awoke the jocund birds to early song
In glens which might have made even exile dear:
Though on his brow were graven lines austere,
And tranquil sternness which had ta'en the place
Of feelings fierier far but less severe,
Joy was not always absent from his face,
But o'er it in such scenes would steal with transient trace.

LIII

Nor was all love shut from him, though his days
Of passion had consumed themselves to dust.
It is in vain that we would coldly gaze
On such as smile upon us; the heart must
Leap kindly back to kindness, though disgust
Hath wean'd it from all worldlings: thus he felt,
For there was soft remembrance, and sweet trust
In one fond breast, to which his own would melt,
And in its tenderer hour on that his bosom dwelt.

LIV

And he had learn'd to love,—I know not why,
For this in such as him seems strange of mood,—
The helpless looks of blooming infancy,
Even in its earliest nurture; what subdued,
To change like this, a mind so far imbued
With scorn of man, it little boots to know;
But thus it was; and though in solitude
Small power the nipp'd affections have to grow,
In him this glow'd when all beside had ceased to glow.

LV

And there was one soft breast, as hath been said,
Which unto his was bound by stronger ties
Than the church links withal; and, though unwed,
That love was pure, and, far above disguise,
Had stood the test of mortal enmities
Still undivided, and cemented more
By peril, dreaded most in female eyes;
But this was firm, and from a foreign shore
Well to that heart might his these absent greetings pour!

I

The castled crag of Drachenfels [1]
Frowns o'er the wide and winding Rhine,
Whose breast of waters broadly swells
Between the banks which bear the vine,
And hills all rich with blossom'd trees,
And fields which promise corn and wine,

[1] The castle of Drachenfels stands on the highest summit of 'the Seven Mountains,' over the Rhine banks: it is in ruins, and connected with some singular traditions: it is the first in view on the road from Bonn, but on the opposite side of the river; on this bank, nearly facing it, are the remains of another, called the Jew's Castle, and a large cross commemorative of the murder of a chief by his brother.

And scatter'd cities crowning these,
Whose far white walls along them shine,
Have strew'd a scene, which I should see
With double joy wert *thou* with me.

Is this Augusta?

2

And peasant girls, with deep blue eyes,
And hands which offer early flowers,
Walk smiling o'er this paradise;
Above, the frequent feudal towers
Through green leaves lift their walls of gray,
And many a rock which steeply lowers,
And noble arch in proud decay,
Look o'er this vale of vintage-bowers;
But one thing want these banks of Rhine,—
Thy gentle hand to clasp in mine!

3

I send the lilies given to me;
Though long before thy hand they touch,
I know that they must wither'd be,
But yet reject them not as such;
For I have cherish'd them as dear,
Because they yet may meet thine eye,
And guide thy soul to mine even here,
When thou behold'st them drooping nigh,
And know'st them gather'd by the Rhine,
And offer'd from my heart to thine!

4

The river nobly foams and flows,
The charm of this enchanted ground,
And all its thousand turns disclose
Some fresher beauty varying round:
The haughtiest breast its wish might bound
Through life to dwell delighted here;
Nor could on earth a spot be found
To nature and to me so dear,
Could thy dear eyes in following mine
Still sweeten more these banks of Rhine!

LVI

By Coblentz, on a rise of gentle ground,
There is a small and simple pyramid,
Crowning the summit of the verdant mound;
Beneath its base are heroes' ashes hid,

Our enemy's—but let not that forbid
Honour to Marceau! o'er whose early tomb
Tears, big tears, gush'd from the rough soldier's lid,
Lamenting and yet envying such a doom,
Falling for France, whose rights he battled to resume.

LVII

Brief, brave, and glorious was his young career,—
His mourners were two hosts, his friends and foes;
And fitly may the stranger lingering here
Pray for his gallant spirit's bright repose;
For he was Freedom's champion, one of those,
The few in number, who had not o'erstept
The charter to chastise which she bestows
On such as wield her weapons; he had kept
The whiteness of his soul, and thus men o'er him wept.[1]

LVIII

Here Ehrenbreitstein,[2] with her shatter'd wall
Black with the miner's blast, upon her height
Yet shows of what she was, when shell and ball
Rebounding idly on her strength did light:
A tower of victory! from whence the flight
Of baffled foes was watch'd along the plain:
But Peace destroy'd what War could never blight
And laid those proud roofs bare to Summer's rain—
On which the iron shower for years had pour'd in vain.

LIX

Adieu to thee, fair Rhine! How long delighted
The stranger fain would linger on his way!
Thine is a scene alike where souls united
Or lonely contemplation thus might stray;

[1] The monument of the young and lamented General Marceau (killed by a rifle-ball at Alterkirchen, on the last day of the fourth year of the French republic) still remains as described. The inscriptions on his monument are rather too long, and not required: his name was enough; France adored, and her enemies admired; both wept over him. His funeral was attended by the generals and detachments from both armies.

[2] Ehrenbreitstein, i.e. 'the broad stone of honour,' one of the strongest fortresses in Europe, was dismantled and blown up by the French at the truce of Leoben. It had been, and could only be, reduced by famine or treachery. It yielded to the former, aided by surprise. After having seen the fortifications of Gibraltar and Malta, it did not much strike by comparison: but the situation is commanding. General Marceau besieged it in vain for some time, and I slept in a room where I was shown a window at which he is said to have been standing observing the progress of the siege by moonlight, when a ball struck immediately below it.

And could the ceaseless vultures cease to prey
On self-condemning bosoms, it were here,
Where Nature, nor too sombre nor too gay,
Wild but not rude, awful yet not austere,
Is to the mellow Earth as Autumn to the year.

LX

Adieu to thee again! a vain adieu!
There can be no farewell to scene like thine;
The mind is colour'd by thy every hue;
And if reluctantly the eyes resign
Their cherish'd gaze upon thee, lovely Rhine!
'Tis with the thankful glance of parting praise;
More mighty spots may rise—more glaring shine,
But none unite in one attaching maze
The brilliant, fair, and soft,—the glories of old days,

LXI

The negligently grand, the fruitful bloom
Of coming ripeness, the white city's sheen,
The rolling stream, the precipice's gloom,
The forest's growth, and Gothic walls between,
The wild rocks shaped as they had turrets been
In mockery of man's art; and these withal
A race of faces happy as the scene,
Whose fertile bounties here extend to all,
Still springing o'er thy banks, though Empires near them fall.

LXII

But these recede.   Above me are the Alps,
The palaces of Nature, whose vast walls
Have pinnacled in clouds their snowy scalps,
And throned Eternity in icy halls
Of cold sublimity, where forms and falls
The avalanche—the thunderbolt of snow!
All that expands the spirit, yet appals,
Gather around these summits, as to show
How Earth may pierce to Heaven, yet leave vain man below.

The Supremacy of nature

LXIII

But ere these matchless heights I dare to scan,
There is a spot should not be pass'd in vain,—
Morat! the proud, the patriot field! where man
May gaze on ghastly trophies of the slain,

Nor blush for those who conquer'd on that plain;
Here Burgundy bequeath'd his tombless host,
A bony heap, through ages to remain,
Themselves their monument;—the Stygian coast
Unsepulchred they roam'd, and shriek'd each wandering ghost.[1]

LXIV

While Waterloo with Cannae's carnage vies,
Morat and Marathon twin names shall stand;
They were true Glory's stainless victories,
Won by the unambitious heart and hand
Of a proud, brotherly, and civic band,
All unbought champions in no princely cause
Of vice-entail'd Corruption; they no land
Doom'd to bewail the blasphemy of laws
Making kings' rights divine, by some Draconic clause.

Draconic ?

LXV

By a lone wall a lonelier column rears
A gray and grief-worn aspect of old days;
'Tis the last remnant of the wreck of years,
And looks as with the wild bewilder'd gaze
Of one to stone converted by amaze,
Yet still with consciousness; and there it stands
Making a marvel that it not decays,
When the coeval pride of human hands,
Levell'd Aventicum,[2] hath strew'd her subject lands.

LXVI

And there—oh! sweet and sacred be the name!—
Julia—the daughter, the devoted—gave
Her youth to Heaven; her heart, beneath a claim
Nearest to Heaven's, broke o'er a father's grave.
Justice is sworn 'gainst tears, and hers would crave
The life she lived in; but the judge was just,
And then she died on him she could not save.
Their tomb was simple, and without a bust,
And held within their urn one mind, one heart, one dust.[3]

---

[1] The chapel is destroyed, and the pyramid of bones diminished to a small number by the Burgundian legion in the service of France; who anxiously effaced this record of their ancestors' less successful invasions.

[2] Aventicum, near Morat, was the Roman capital of Helvetia, where Avenches now stands.

[3] Julia Alpinula, a young Aventian priestess, died soon after a vain endeavour to save her father, condemned to death as a traitor by Aulus Caecina. Her

LXVII

But these are deeds which should not pass away,
And names that muſt not wither, though the earth
Forgets her empires with a juſt decay,
The enslavers and the enslaved, their death and birth;
The high, the mountain-majeſty of worth
Should be, and shall, survivor of its woe,
And from its immortality look forth
In the sun's face, like yonder Alpine snow,[1]
Imperishably pure beyond all things below. *concept of imperishable purity*

LXVIII

Lake Leman woos me with its cryſtal face,
The mirror where the ſtars and mountains view
The ſtillness of their aspeƈt in each trace
Its clear depth yields of their far height and hue:
There is too much of man here, to look through
With a fit mind the might which I behold;
But soon in me shall Loneliness renew
Thoughts hid, but not less cherish'd than of old,
Ere mingling with the herd had penn'd me in their fold.

LXIX

To fly from, need not be to hate, mankind:
All are not fit with them to ſtir and toil,
Nor is it discontent to keep the mind
Deep in its fountain, leſt it overboil
In the hot throng, where we become the spoil
Of our infeƈtion, till too late and long
We may deplore and ſtruggle with the coil,
In wretched interchange of wrong for wrong
Midſt a contentious world, ſtriving where none are ſtrong.

---

epitaph was discovered many years ago;—it is thus: 'Julia Alpinula: Hic jaceo. *Get translatio* Infelicis patris infelix proles. Deae Aventiae Sacerdos. Exorare patris necem non potui: Male mori in fatis ille erat. Vixi annos XXIII.' I know of no human composition so affeƈting as this, nor a hiſtory of deeper intereſt. These are the names and aƈtions which ought not to perish, and to which we turn with a true and healthy tenderness from the wretched and glittering detail of a confused mass of conqueſts and battles, with which the mind is roused for a time to a false and feverish sympathy, from whence it recurs at length with all the nausea consequent on such intoxication.

[1] This is written in the eye of Mont Blanc (3rd June, 1816), which even at this diſtance dazzles mine.—(20th July.) I this day observed for some time the diſtant refleƈtion of Mont Blanc and Mont Argentière in the calm of the lake, which I was crossing in my boat; the diſtance of these mountains from their mirror is sixty miles.

LXX

There, in a moment, we may plunge our years
In fatal penitence, and in the blight
Of our own soul turn all our blood to tears,
And colour things to come with hues of Night;
The race of life becomes a hopeless flight
To those that walk in darkness: on the sea,
The boldest steer but where their ports invite,
But there are wanderers o'er Eternity
Whose bark drives on and on, and anchor'd ne'er shall be.

LXXI

Is it not better, then, to be alone,
And love Earth only for its earthly sake?
By the blue rushing of the arrowy Rhone,[1]
Or the pure bosom of its nursing lake,
Which feeds it as a mother who doth make
A fair but froward infant her own care,
Kissing its cries away as these awake;—
Is it not better thus our lives to wear,
Than join the crushing crowd, doom'd to inflict or bear?

LXXII

I live not in myself, but I become
Portion of that around me; and to me
High mountains are a feeling, but the hum
Of human cities torture: I can see
Nothing to loathe in nature, save to be
A link reluctant in a fleshly chain,
Class'd among creatures, when the soul can flee,
And with the sky, the peak, the heaving plain
Of ocean, or the stars, mingle, and not in vain.

LXXIII

And thus I am absorb'd, and this is life:
I look upon the peopled desert past,
As on a place of agony and strife,
Where, for some sin, to sorrow I was cast,
To act and suffer, but remount at last
With a fresh pinion; which I feel to spring,
Though young, yet waxing vigorous, as the blast
Which it would cope with, on delighted wing,
Spurning the clay-cold bonds which round our being cling.

[1] The colour of the Rhone at Geneva is blue, to a depth of tint which I have never seen equalled in water, salt or fresh, except in the Mediterranean and Archipelago.

LXXIV

And when, at length, the mind shall be all free
From what it hates in this degraded form,
Reft of its carnal life, save what shall be
Existent happier in the fly and worm,—
When elements to elements conform,
And dust is as it should be, shall I not
Feel all I see, less dazzling, but more warm?
The bodiless thought? the Spirit of each spot?
Of which, even now, I share at times the immortal lot?

Search for immortality in Nature & History

LXXV

Are not the mountains, waves, and skies, a part
Of me and of my soul, as I of them?
Is not the love of these deep in my heart
With a pure passion? should I not contemn
All objects, if compared with these? and stem
A tide of suffering, rather than forego
Such feelings for the hard and worldly phlegm
Of those whose eyes are only turn'd below,
Gazing upon the ground, with thoughts which dare not glow?

NB. use of "pure passion"

LXXVI

But this is not my theme; and I return
To that which is immediate, and require
Those who find contemplation in the urn,
To look on One, whose dust was once all fire,
A native of the land where I respire
The clear air for a while—a passing guest,
Where he became a being,—whose desire
Was to be glorious; 'twas a foolish quest,
The which to gain and keep, he sacrificed all rest.

LXXVII

Here the self-torturing sophist, wild Rousseau,
The apostle of affliction, he who threw
Enchantment over passion, and from woe
Wrung overwhelming eloquence, first drew
The breath which made him wretched; yet he knew
How to make madness beautiful, and cast
O'er erring deeds and thoughts a heavenly hue
Of words, like sunbeams, dazzling as they past
The eyes, which o'er them shed tears feelingly and fast.

LXXVIII

His love was passion's essence—as a tree
On fire by lightning; with ethereal flame
Kindled he was, and blasted; for to be
Thus, and enamour'd, were in him the same.
But his was not the love of living dame,
Nor of the dead who rise upon our dreams,
But of ideal beauty, which became
In him existence, and o'erflowing teems
Along his burning page, distemper'd though it seems.

LXXIX

This breathed itself to life in Julie, *this*
Invested her with all that 's wild and sweet;
This hallow'd, too, the memorable kiss [1]
Which every morn his fever'd lip would greet,
From hers, who but with friendship his would meet;
But to that gentle touch, through brain and breast
Flash'd the thrill'd spirit's love-devouring heat;
In that absorbing sigh perchance more blest
Than vulgar minds may be with all they seek possest.

LXXX

His life was one long war with self-sought foes,
Or friends by him self-banish'd; for his mind
Had grown Suspicion's sanctuary, and chose,
For its own cruel sacrifice, the kind,
'Gainst whom he raged with fury strange and blind.
But he was phrensied,—wherefore, who may know?
Since cause might be which skill could never find;
But he was phrensied by disease or woe,
To that worst pitch of all, which wears a reasoning show.

LXXXI

For then he was inspired, and from him came,
As from the Pythian's mystic cave of yore,
Those oracles which set the world in flame,
Nor ceased to burn till kingdoms were no more:

[1] This refers to the account in his *Confessions* of his passion for the Comtesse d'Houdetot (the mistress of St. Lambert), and his long walk every morning, for the sake of the single kiss which was the common salutation of French acquaintance. Rousseau's description of his feelings on this occasion may be considered as the most passionate, yet not impure, description and expression of love that ever kindled into words; which, after all, must be felt, from their very force, to be inadequate to the delineation: a painting can give no sufficient idea of the ocean.

Did he not this for France? which lay before
Bow'd to the inborn tyranny of years?
Broken and trembling to the yoke she bore,
Till by the voice of him and his compeers
Roused up to too much wrath, which follows o'ergrown fears?

LXXXII

They made themselves a fearful monument!
The wreck of old opinions—things which grew,
Breathed from the birth of time: the veil they rent,
And what behind it lay all earth shall view.
But good with ill they also overthrew,
Leaving but ruins, wherewith to rebuild
Upon the same foundation, and renew
Dungeons and thrones, which the same hour refill'd,
As heretofore, because ambition was self-will'd.

LXXXIII

But this will not endure, nor be endured!
Mankind have felt their strength, and made it felt.
They might have used it better, but, allured
By their new vigour, sternly have they dealt
On one another; pity ceased to melt
With her once natural charities. But they,
Who in oppression's darkness caved had dwelt,
They were not eagles, nourish'd with the day;
What marvel then, at times, if they mistook their prey?

LXXXIV

What deep wounds ever closed without a scar?
The heart's bleed longest, and but heal to wear
That which disfigures it; and they who war
With their own hopes, and have been vanquish'd, bear
Silence, but not submission: in his lair
Fix'd Passion holds his breath, until the hour
Which shall atone for years; none need despair:
It came, it cometh, and will come,—the power
To punish or forgive—in *one* we shall be slower.

LXXXV

Clear, placid Leman! thy contrasted lake,
With the wild world I dwelt in, is a thing
Which warns me, with its stillness, to forsake
Earth's troubled waters for a purer spring.

This quiet sail is as a noiseless wing
To waft me from distraction; once I loved
Torn ocean's roar, but thy soft murmuring
Sounds sweet as if a Sister's voice reproved,
That I with stern delights should e'er have been so moved.

LXXXVI

It is the hush of night, and all between
Thy margin and the mountains, dusk, yet clear,
Mellow'd and mingling, yet distinctly seen,
Save darken'd Jura, whose capt heights appear
Precipitously steep; and drawing near,
There breathes a living fragrance from the shore,
Of flowers yet fresh with childhood; on the ear
Drops the light drip of the suspended oar,
Or chirps the grasshopper one good-night carol more;

LXXXVII

He is an evening reveller, who makes
His life an infancy, and sings his fill;
At intervals, some bird from out the brakes
Starts into voice a moment, then is still.
There seems a floating whisper on the hill,
But that is fancy, for the starlight dews
All silently their tears of love instil,
Weeping themselves away, till they infuse
Deep into Nature's breast the spirit of her hues.

LXXXVIII

Ye stars! which are the poetry of heaven
If in your bright leaves we would read the fate
Of men and empires,—'tis to be forgiven,
That in our aspirations to be great,
Our destinies o'erleap their mortal state,
And claim a kindred with you; for ye are
A beauty and a mystery, and create
In us such love and reverence from afar,
That fortune, fame, power, life, have named themselves a star.

LXXXIX

All heaven and earth are still—though not in sleep,
But breathless, as we grow when feeling most;
And silent, as we stand in thoughts too deep:—
All heaven and earth are still: From the high host

Of stars, to the lull'd lake and mountain-coast,
All is concenter'd in a life intense,
Where not a beam, nor air, nor leaf is lost,
But hath a part of being, and a sense
Of that which is of all Creator and defence.

XC

Then stirs the feeling infinite, so felt
In solitude, where we are *least* alone;
A truth, which through our being then doth melt
And purifies from self: it is a tone,
The soul and source of music, which makes known
Eternal harmony, and sheds a charm,
Like to the fabled Cytherea's zone,
Binding all things with beauty;—'twould disarm
The spectre Death, had he substantial power to harm.

XCI

Not vainly did the early Persian make
His altar the high places and the peak
Of earth-o'ergazing mountains,[1] and thus take
A fit and unwall'd temple, there to seek
The Spirit in whose honour shrines are weak,
Uprear'd of human hands. Come, and compare
Columns and idol-dwellings, Goth or Greek,
With Nature's realms of worship, earth and air,
Nor fix on fond abodes to circumscribe thy pray'r!

XCII

Thy sky is changed!—and such a change! Oh night,[2]
And storm, and darkness, ye are wondrous strong,
Yet lovely in your strength, as is the light
Of a dark eye in woman! Far along,
From peak to peak, the rattling crags among

[1] It is to be recollected, that the most beautiful and impressive doctrines of the divine Founder of Christianity were delivered, not in the *Temple*, but on the *Mount*.
[2] The thunderstorm to which these lines refer occurred on 13th June 1816, at midnight. I have seen, among the Acroceraunian mountains of Chimari, several more terrible, but none more beautiful.

Leaps the live thunder! Not from one lone cloud,
But every mountain now hath found a tongue,
And Jura answers, through her misty shroud,
Back to the joyous Alps, who call to her aloud!

XCIII

And this is in the night:—Most glorious night!
Thou wert not sent for slumber! let me be
A sharer in thy fierce and far delight,—
A portion of the tempest and of thee!
How the lit lake shines, a phosphoric sea,
And the big rain comes dancing to the earth!
And now again 'tis black,—and now, the glee
Of the loud hills shakes with its mountain-mirth,
As if they did rejoice o'er a young earthquake's birth.

very good

XCIV

Now, where the swift Rhone cleaves his way between
Heights which appear as lovers who have parted
In hate, whose mining depths so intervene,
That they can meet no more, though broken-hearted;
Though in their souls, which thus each other thwarted,
Love was the very root of the fond rage
Which blighted their life's bloom, and then departed:
Itself expired, but leaving them an age
Of years all winters,—war within themselves to wage.

Good insight into broken love "Of years all winters"

XCV

Now, where the quick Rhone thus hath cleft his way,
The mightiest of the storms hath ta'en his stand:
For here, not one, but many, make their play,
And fling their thunder-bolts from hand to hand,
Flashing and cast around: of all the band,
The brightest through these parted hills hath fork'd
His lightnings,—as if he did understand,
That in such gaps as desolation work'd,
There the hot shaft should blast whatever therein lurk'd.

XCVI

Sky, mountains, river, winds, lake, lightnings! ye!
With night, and clouds, and thunder, and a soul
To make these felt and feeling, well may be
Things that have made me watchful; the far roll

Of your departing voices, is the knoll
Of what in me is sleepless,—if I rest.
But where of ye, oh tempests! is the goal?
Are ye like those within the human breast?
Or do ye find, at length, like eagles, some high nest?

XCVII

Could I embody and unbosom now
That which is most within me,—could I wreak
My thoughts upon expression, and thus throw
Soul, heart, mind, passions, feelings, strong or weak,
All that I would have sought, and all I seek,
Bear, know, feel, and yet breathe—into *one* word,
And that one word were Lightning, I would speak;
But as it is, I live and die unheard,
With a most voiceless thought, sheathing it as a sword.

XCVIII

The morn is up again, the dewy morn,
With breath all incense, and with cheek all bloom,
Laughing the clouds away with playful scorn,
And living as if earth contain'd no tomb—
And glowing into day: we may resume
The march of our existence: and thus I,
Still on thy shores, fair Leman! may find room
And food for meditation, nor pass by
Much, that may give us pause, if ponder'd fittingly.

XCIX

Clarens! sweet Clarens, birthplace of deep Love,
Thine air is the young breath of passionate thought,
Thy trees take root in Love; the snows above
The very Glaciers have his colours caught,
And sunset into rose-hues sees them wrought
By rays which sleep there lovingly: the rocks,
The permanent crags, tell here of Love, who sought
In them a refuge from the worldly shocks,
Which stir and sting the soul with hope that woos, then mocks.

C

Clarens! by heavenly feet thy paths are trod,—
Undying Love's, who here ascends a throne
To which the steps are mountains; where the god
Is a pervading life and light,—so shown

Not on those summits solely, nor alone
In the still cave and forest; o'er the flower
His eye is sparkling, and his breath hath blown,
His soft and summer breath, whose tender power
Passes the strength of storms in their most desolate hour.[1]

CI

All things are here of *him*; from the black pines,
Which are his shade on high, and the loud roar
Of torrents, where he listeneth, to the vines
Which slope his green path downward to the shore,
Where the bow'd waters meet him, and adore,
Kissing his feet with murmurs; and the wood,
The covert of old trees, with trunks all hoar,
But light leaves, young as joy, stands where it stood,
Offering to him, and his, a populous solitude.

CII

A populous solitude of bees and birds,
And fairy-formed and many-colour'd things,
Who worship him with notes more sweet than words,
And innocently open their glad wings,
Fearless and full of life; the gush of springs,
And fall of lofty fountains, and the bend
Of stirring branches, and the bud which brings
The swiftest thought of beauty, here extend,
Mingling, and made by Love, unto one mighty end.

[1] See Rousseau's *Héloïse*, Lettre 17, part 4, note, and *Les Confessions*, livre iv, p. 306, Lyon, ed. 1796.—In July 1816 I made a voyage round the Lake of Geneva; and as far as my own observations have led me in a not uninterested nor inattentive survey of all the scenes most celebrated by Rousseau in his *Héloïse*, I can safely say, that in this there is no exaggeration. It would be difficult to see Clarens (with the scenes around it, Vevay, Chillon, Bôveret, St. Gingo, Meillerie, Eivan, and the entrances of the Rhone) without being forcibly struck with its peculiar adaptation to the persons and events with which it has been peopled. But this is not all: the feeling with which all around Clarens, and the opposite rocks of Meillerie, is invested, is of a still higher and more comprehensive order than the mere sympathy with individual passion; it is a sense of the existence of love in its most extended and sublime capacity, and of our own participation of its good and of its glory: it is the great principle of the universe, which is there more condensed, but not less manifested; and of which, though knowing ourselves a part, we lose our individuality, and mingle in the beauty of the whole. If Rousseau had never written, nor lived, the same associations would not less have belonged to such scenes. He has added to the interest of his works by their adoption; he has shown his sense of their beauty by the selection; but they have done that for him which no human being could do for them.

CIII

He who hath loved not, here would learn that lore,
And make his heart a spirit; he who knows
That tender myſtery, will love the more,
For this is Love's recess, where vain men's woes,
And the world's waſte, have driven him far from those,
For 'tis his nature to advance or die;
He ſtands not ſtill, but or decays, or grows
Into a boundless blessing, which may vie
With the immortal lights, in its eternity!

CIV

'Twas not for fiction chose Rousseau this spot,
Peopling it with affections; but he found
It was the scene which passion muſt allot
To the mind's purified beings; 'twas the ground
Where early Love his Psyche's zone unbound,
And hallow'd it with loveliness: 'tis lone,
And wonderful, and deep, and hath a sound,
And sense, and sight of sweetness; here the Rhone
Hath spread himself a couch, the Alps have rear'd a throne.

CV

Lausanne! and Ferney! ye have been the abodes
Of names which unto you bequeathed a name;[1]
Mortals, who sought and found, by dangerous roads
A path to perpetuity of fame:
They were gigantic minds, and their ſteep aim
Was, Titan-like, on daring doubts to pile
Thoughts which should call down thunder, and the flame
Of Heaven, again assail'd, if Heaven the while
On man and man's research could deign do more than smile.

CVI

The one was fire and fickleness, a child,
Moſt mutable in wishes, but in mind,
A wit as various,—gay, grave, sage, or wild,—
Hiſtorian, bard, philosopher, combined;
He multiplied himself among mankind,
The Proteus of their talents: But his own
Breathed moſt in ridicule,—which, as the wind,
Blew where it liſted, laying all things prone,—
Now to o'erthrow a fool, and now to shake a throne.

[1] Voltairen and Gibbo.

CVII

The other, deep and slow, exhausting thought,
And hiving wisdom with each studious year,
In meditation dwelt, with learning wrought,
And shaped his weapon with an edge severe,
Sapping a solemn creed with solemn sneer;
The lord of irony,—that master-spell,
Which stung his foes to wrath, which grew from fear,
And doom'd him to the zealot's ready Hell,
Which answers to all doubts so eloquently well.

CVIII

Yet, peace be with their ashes,—for by them,
If merited, the penalty is paid;
It is not ours to judge,—far less condemn;
The hour must come when such things shall be made
Known unto all,—or hope and dread allay'd
By slumber, on one pillow,—in the dust,
Which, thus much we are sure, must lie decay'd;
And when it shall revive, as is our trust,
'Twill be to be forgiven, or suffer what is just.

CIX

But let me quit man's works, again to read
His Maker's, spread around me, and suspend
This page, which from my reveries I feed,
Until it seems prolonging without end.
The clouds above me to the white Alps tend,
And I must pierce them, and survey whate'er
May be permitted, as my steps I bend
To their most great and growing region, where
The earth to her embrace compels the powers of air.

CX

N.B. Persistent use of dramatic (melodramatic?) openings.

Italia! too, Italia! looking on thee,
Full flashes on the soul the light of ages,
Since the fierce Carthaginian almost won thee,
To the last halo of the chiefs and sages
Who glorify thy consecrated pages;
Thou wert the throne and grave of empires; still,
The fount at which the panting mind assuages
Her thirst of knowledge, quaffing there her fill,
Flows from the eternal source of Rome's imperial hill.

CXI

Thus far have I proceeded in a theme
Renew'd with no kind auspices:—to feel
We are not what we have been, and to deem
We are not what we should be,—and to steel
The heart against itself; and to conceal,
With a proud caution, love, or hate, or aught—
Passion or feeling, purpose, grief, or zeal,—
Which is the tyrant spirit of our thought,
Is a stern task of soul:—No matter,—it is taught.

In search of mythical greatness

CXII

And for these words, thus woven into song,
It may be that they are a harmless wile,—
The colouring of the scenes which fleet along,
Which I would seize, in passing, to beguile
My breast, or that of others, for a while.
Fame is the thirst of youth,—but I am not
So young as to regard men's frown or smile,
As loss or guerdon of a glorious lot;
I stood and stand alone,—remember'd or forgot.

NB His motive for writing poem discussed

CXIII

I have not loved the world, nor the world me;
I have not flatter'd its rank breath, nor bow'd
To its idolatries a patient knee,—
Nor coin'd my cheek to smiles,—nor cried aloud
In worship of an echo; in the crowd
They could not deem me one of such; I stood
Among them, but not of them; in a shroud
Of thoughts which were not their thoughts, and still could,
Had I not filed [1] my mind, which thus itself subdued.

CXIV

I have not loved the world, nor the world me,—
But let us part fair foes; I do believe,
Though I have found them not, that there may be
Words which are things,—hopes which will not deceive,
And virtues which are merciful, or weave
Snares for the failing: I would also deem
O'er others' griefs that some sincerely grieve; [2]
That two, or one, are almost what they seem,—
That goodness is no name, and happiness no dream.

[1] 'If it be thus,
For Banquo's issue have I *filed* my mind.'
                                        MACBETH.
[2] It is said by Rochefoucault, that 'there is always something in the misfortunes of men's best friends not displeasing to them.'

CXV

My daughter! with thy name this song begun—
My daughter! with thy name thus much shall end—
I see thee not,—I hear thee not,—but none
Can be so wrapt in thee; thou art the friend
To whom the shadows of far years extend:
Albeit my brow thou never should'st behold,
My voice shall with thy future visions blend
And reach into thy heart,—when mine is cold,—
A token and a tone, even from thy father's mould.

CXVI

To aid thy mind's development,—to watch
Thy dawn of little joys,—to sit and see
Almost thy very growth,—to view thee catch
Knowledge of objects,—wonders yet to thee!
To hold thee lightly on a gentle knee,
And print on thy soft cheek a parent's kiss,—
This, it should seem, was not reserved for me;
Yet this was in my nature:—as it is,
I know not what is there, yet something like to this.

CXVII

Yet, though dull Hate as duty should be taught,
I know that thou wilt love me; though my name
Should be shut from thee, as a spell still fraught
With desolation,—and a broken claim:
Though the grave closed between us,—'twere the same,
I know that thou wilt love me; though to drain
My blood from out thy being were an aim,
And an attainment,—all would be in vain,—
Still thou would'st love me, still that more than life retain.

CXVIII

The child of love,—though born in bitterness
And nurtured in convulsion. Of thy sire
These were the elements,—and thine no less.
As yet such are around thee,—but thy fire
Shall be more temper'd, and thy hope far higher.
Sweet be thy cradled slumbers! O'er the sea,
And from the mountains where I now respire,
Fain would I waft such blessing upon thee,
As, with a sigh, I deem thou might'st have been to me!

Visto ho Toscana, Lombardia, Romagna,
Quel Monte che divide, equel che serra
Italia, e un mare e l' altro, che la bagna.
                                        ARIOSTO, Satira iii.

I

I STOOD in Venice, on the Bridge of Sighs;
A palace and a prison on each hand:
I saw from out the wave her structures rise
As from the stroke of the enchanter's wand:
A thousand years their cloudy wings expand
Around me, and a dying Glory smiles
O'er the far times, when many a subject land
Look'd to the winged Lion's marble piles,
Where Venice sate in state, throned on her hundred isles!

II

She looks a sea Cybele, fresh from ocean,[1]
Rising with her tiara of proud towers
At airy distance, with majestic motion,
A ruler of the waters and their powers:
And such she was;—her daughters had their dowers
From spoils of nations, and the exhaustless East
Pour'd in her lap all gems in sparkling showers.
In purple was she robed, and of her feast
Monarchs partook, and deem'd their dignity increased.

III

In Venice Tasso's echoes are no more,
And silent rows the songless gondolier;
Her palaces are crumbling to the shore,
And music meets not always now the ear;
Those days are gone—but Beauty still is here.
States fall, arts fade—but Nature doth not die,
Nor yet forget how Venice once was dear,
The pleasant place of all festivity,
The revel of the earth, the masque of Italy!

IV

But unto us she hath a spell beyond
Her name in story, and her long array
Of mighty shadows, whose dim forms despond
Above the dogeless city's vanish'd sway;

[1] Sabellicus, describing the appearance of Venice, has made use of the above image, which would not be poetical were it not true.—'Quo fit ut qui superne urbem contempletur, turritam telluris imaginem medio Oceano figuratam se putet inspicere.'

Ours is a trophy which will not decay
With the Rialto; Shylock and the Moor,
And Pierre, can not be swept or worn away—
The keystones of the arch! though all were o'er,
For us repeopled were the solitary shore.

V

The beings of the mind are not of clay;
Essentially immortal, they create
And multiply in us a brighter ray
And more beloved existence: that which Fate
Prohibits to dull life, in this our state
Of mortal bondage, by these spirits supplied
First exiles, then replaces what we hate;
Watering the heart whose early flowers have died,
And with a fresher growth replenishing the void.

VI

Such is the refuge of our youth and age,
The first from Hope, the last from Vacancy;
And this worn feeling peoples many a page,
And, may be, that which grows beneath mine eye:
Yet there are things whose strong reality
Outshines our fairy-land; in shape and hues
More beautiful than our fantastic sky,
And the strange constellations which the Muse
O'er her wild universe is skilful to diffuse:

VII

I saw or dream'd of such,—but let them go,—
They came like truth, and disappear'd like dreams;
And whatsoe'er they were—are now but so:
I could replace them if I would; still teems
My mind with many a form which aptly seems
Such as I sought for, and at moments found;
Let these too go—for waking Reason deems
Such overweening phantasies unsound,
And other voices speak, and other sights surround.

VIII

I've taught me other tongues—and in strange eyes
Have made me not a stranger; to the mind
Which is itself, no changes bring surprise;
Nor is it harsh to make, nor hard to find

A country with—ay, or without mankind;
Yet was I born where men are proud to be,
Not without cause; and should I leave behind
The inviolate island of the sage and free,
And seek me out a home by a remoter sea,

IX

Perhaps I loved it well; and should I lay
My ashes in a soil which is not mine,
My spirit shall resume it—if we may
Unbodied choose a sanctuary.   I twine
My hopes of being remember'd in my line
With my land's language: if too fond and far
These aspirations in their scope incline,—
If my fame should be, as my fortunes are,
Of hasty growth and blight, and dull Oblivion bar

X

My name from out the temple where the dead
Are honour'd by the nations—let it be—
And light the laurels on a loftier head!
And be the Spartan's epitaph on me—
'Sparta hath many a worthier son than he.' [1]
Meantime I seek no sympathies, nor need;
The thorns which I have reap'd are of the tree
I planted,—they have torn me,—and I bleed:
I should have known what fruit would spring from such a seed.

XI

The spouseless Adriatic mourns her lord;
And, annual marriage, now no more renew'd,
The Bucentaur lies rotting unrestored,
Neglected garment of her widowhood!
St. Mark yet sees his lion where he stood,
Stand, but in mockery of his wither'd power,
Over the proud Place where an Emperor sued,
And monarchs gazed and envied in the hour
When Venice was a queen with an unequall'd dower.

[1] The answer of the mother of Brasidas, the Lacedaemonian general, to the
strangers who praised the memory of her son.

XII

The Suabian sued, and now the Austrian reigns—
An Emperor tramples where an Emperor knelt;
Kingdoms are shrunk to provinces, and chains
Clank over sceptred cities; nations melt
From power's high pinnacle, when they have felt
The sunshine for a while, and downward go
Like lauwine loosen'd from the mountain's belt;
Oh for one hour of blind old Dandolo!
Th' octogenarian chief, Byzantium's conquering foe.

XIII

Before St. Mark still glow his steeds of brass,
Their gilded collars glittering in the sun;
But is not Doria's menace come to pass?
Are they not *bridled*?—Venice, lost and won,
Her thirteen hundred years of freedom done,
Sinks, like a sea-weed, into whence she rose!
Better be whelm'd beneath the waves, and shun,
Even in destruction's depth, her foreign foes,
From whom submission wrings an infamous repose.

XIV

In youth she was all glory,—a new Tyre,—
Her very by-word sprung from victory,
The 'Planter of the Lion,'[1] which through fire
And blood she bore o'er subject earth and sea;
Though making many slaves, herself still free,
And Europe's bulwark 'gainst the Ottomite;
Witness Troy's rival, Candia! Vouch it, ye
Immortal waves that saw Lepanto's fight!
For ye are names no time nor tyranny can blight.

XV

Statues of glass—all shiver'd—the long file
Of her dead Doges are declined to dust;
But where they dwelt, the vast and sumptuous pile
Bespeaks the pageant of their splendid trust;
Their sceptre broken, and their sword in rust,
Have yielded to the stranger: empty halls,
Thin streets, and foreign aspects, such as must
Too oft remind her who and what enthrals,
Have flung a desolate cloud o'er Venice' lovely walls.

[1] That is, the Lion of St. Mark, the standard of the republic, which is the origin
of the word Pantaloon—Piantaleone Pantaleon, Pantaloon.

XVI

When Athens' armies fell at Syracuse,
And fetter'd thousands bore the yoke of war,
Redemption rose up in the Attic Muse,[1]
Her voice their only ransom from afar:
See! as they chant the tragic hymn, the car
Of the o'ermaster'd victor stops, the reins
Fall from his hands—his idle scimitar
Starts from its belt—he rends his captive's chains,
And bids him thank the bard for freedom and his strains.

XVII

Thus, Venice, if no stronger claim were thine,
Were all thy proud historic deeds forgot,
Thy choral memory of the Bard divine,
Thy love of Tasso, should have cut the knot
Which ties thee to thy tyrants; and thy lot
Is shameful to the nations,—most of all,
Albion! to thee: the Ocean queen should not
Abandon Ocean's children; in the fall
Of Venice think of thine, despite thy watery wall.

XVIII

I loved her from my boyhood—she to me
Was as a fairy city of the heart,
Rising like water-columns from the sea,
Of joy the sojourn, and of wealth the mart;
And Otway, Radcliffe, Schiller, Shakespeare's art,[2]
Had stamp'd her image in me, and even so,
Although I found her thus, we did not part,
Perchance even dearer in her day of woe,
Than when she was a boast, a marvel, and a show.

XIX

I can repeople with the past—and of
The present there is still for eye and thought,
And meditation chasten'd down, enough;
And more, it may be, than I hoped or sought;
And of the happiest moments which were wrought
Within the web of my existence, some
From thee, fair Venice! have their colours caught:
There are some feelings Time cannot benumb,
Nor Torture shake, or mine would now be cold and dumb.

[1] The story is told in Plutarch's *Life of Nicias*.
[2] *Venice Preserved; Mysteries of Udolpho; The Ghost-Seer, or Armenian; The Merchant of Venice; Othello.*

XX

But from their nature will the tannen grow [1]
Loftiest on loftiest and least shelter'd rocks,
Rooted in barrenness, where nought below
Of soil supports them 'gainst the Alpine shocks
Of eddying storms; yet springs the trunk, and mocks
The howling tempest, till its height and frame
Are worthy of the mountains from whose blocks
Of bleak, gray granite into life it came,
And grew a giant tree;—the mind may grow the same.

XXI

Existence may be borne, and the deep root
Of life and sufferance make its firm abode
In bare and desolated bosoms: mute
The camel labours with the heaviest load,
And the wolf dies in silence,—not bestow'd
In vain should such example be; if they,
Things of ignoble or of savage mood,
Endure and shrink not, we of nobler clay
May temper it to bear,—it is but for a day.

XXII

All suffering doth destroy, or is destroy'd,
Even by the sufferer; and, in each event,
Ends:—Some, with hope replenish'd and rebuoy'd,
Return to whence they came—with like intent,
And weave their web again; some, bow'd and bent,
Wax gray and ghastly, withering ere their time,
And perish with the reed on which they leant;
Some seek devotion, toil, war, good or crime,
According as their souls were form'd to sink or climb.

XXIII

But ever and anon of griefs subdued
There comes a token like a scorpion's sting,
Scarce seen, but with fresh bitterness imbued
And slight withal may be the things which bring
Back on the heart the weight which it would fling
Aside for ever: it may be a sound—
A tone of music—summer's eve—or spring—
A flower—the wind—the ocean—which shall wound,
Striking the electric chain wherewith we are darkly bound;

[1] *Tannen* is the plural of *tanne*, a species of fir peculiar to the Alps, which only thrives in very rocky parts, where scarcely soil sufficient for its nourishment can be found. On these spots it grows to a greater height than any other mountain tree.

XXIV

And how and why we know not, nor can trace
Home to its cloud this lightning of the mind,
But feel the shock renew'd, nor can efface
The blight and blackening which it leaves behind,
Which out of things familiar, undesign'd,
When least we deem of such, calls up to view
The spectres whom no exorcism can bind,
The cold—the changed—perchance the dead—anew,
The mourn'd, the loved, the lost—too many!—yet how few!

XXV

But my soul wanders; I demand it back
To meditate amongst decay, and stand
A ruin amidst ruins; there to track
Fall'n states and buried greatness, o'er a land
Which *was* the mightiest in its old command,
And *is* the loveliest, and must ever be
The master-mould of Nature's heavenly hand,
Wherein were cast the heroic and the free,
The beautiful, the brave—the lords of earth and sea,

XXVI

The commonwealth of kings, the men of Rome!
And even since, and now, fair Italy!
Thou art the garden of the world, the home
Of all Art yields, and Nature can decree;
Even in thy desert, what is like to thee?
Thy very weeds are beautiful, thy waste
More rich than other climes' fertility;
Thy wreck a glory, and thy ruin graced
With an immaculate charm which cannot be defaced.

XXVII

The moon is up, and yet it is not night—
Sunset divides the sky with her—a sea
Of glory streams along the Alpine height
Of blue Friuli's mountains; Heaven is free
From clouds, but of all colours seems to be
Melted to one vast Iris of the West,
Where the Day joins the past Eternity;
While, on the other hand, meek Dian's crest
Floats through the azure air—an island of the blest! [1]

[1] The above description may seem fantastical or exaggerated to those who have never seen an Oriental or an Italian sky, yet it is but a literal and hardly sufficient delineation of an August evening (the eighteenth), as contemplated in one of many rides along the banks of the Brenta, near La Mira.

XXVIII

A single star is at her side, and reigns
With her o'er half the lovely heaven; but still
Yon sunny sea heaves brightly, and remains
Roll'd o'er the peak of the far Rhaetian hill,
As Day and Night contending were, until
Nature reclaim'd her order:—gently flows
The deep-dyed Brenta, where their hues instil
The odorous purple of a new-born rose,
Which streams upon her stream, and glass'd within it glows,

XXIX

Fill'd with the face of heaven, which, from afar,
Comes down upon the waters; all its hues,
From the rich sunset to the rising star,
Their magical variety diffuse:
And now they change; a paler shadow strews
Its mantle o'er the mountains; parting day
Dies like the dolphin, whom each pang imbues
With a new colour as it gasps away,
The last still loveliest, till—'tis gone—and all is gray.

XXX

There is a tomb in Arqua;—rear'd in air,
Pillar'd in their sarcophagus, repose
The bones of Laura's lover; here repair
Many familiar with his well-sung woes,
The pilgrims of his genius. He arose
To raise a language, and his land reclaim
From the dull yoke of her barbaric foes:
Watering the tree which bears his lady's name
With his melodious tears, he gave himself to fame.

XXXI

They keep his dust in Arqua, where he died;
The mountain-village where his latter days
Went down the vale of years; and 'tis their pride—
An honest pride—and let it be their praise,
To offer to the passing stranger's gaze
His mansion and his sepulchre; both plain
And venerably simple, such as raise
A feeling more accordant with his strain
Than if a pyramid form'd his monumental fane.

XXXII

And the soft quiet hamlet where he dwelt
Is one of that complexion which seems made
For those who their mortality have felt,
And sought a refuge from their hopes decay'd
In the deep umbrage of a green hill's shade,
Which shows a distant prospect far away
Of busy cities, now in vain display'd,
For they can lure no further; and the ray
Of a bright sun can make sufficient holiday,

XXXIII

Developing the mountains, leaves, and flowers,
And shining in the brawling brook, where-by,
Clear as its current, glide the sauntering hours
With a calm languor, which, though to the eye
Idlesse it seem, hath its morality.
If from society we learn to live,
'Tis solitude should teach us how to die;
It hath no flatterers; vanity can give
No hollow aid; alone—man with his God must strive:

XXXIV

Or, it may be, with demons, who impair [1]
The strength of better thoughts, and seek their prey
In melancholy bosoms, such as were
Of moody texture from their earliest day,
And loved to dwell in darkness and dismay,
Deeming themselves predestined to a doom
Which is not of the pangs that pass away;
Making the sun like blood, the earth a tomb,
The tomb a hell, and hell itself a murkier gloom.

XXXV

Ferrara! in thy wide and grass-grown streets,
Whose symmetry was not for solitude,
There seems as 'twere a curse upon the seats
Of former sovereigns, and the antique brood
Of Este, which for many an age made good
Its strength within thy walls, and was of yore
Patron or tyrant, as the changing mood
Of petty power impell'd, of those who wore
The wreath which Dante's brow alone had worn before.

[1] The struggle is to the full as likely to be with demons as with our better thoughts. Satan chose the wilderness for the temptation of our Saviour. And our unsullied John Locke preferred the presence of a child to complete solitude.

XXXVI

And Tasso is their glory and their shame.
Hark to his strain! and then survey his cell!
And see how dearly earn'd Torquato's fame,
And where Alfonso bade his poet dwell:
The miserable despot could not quell
The insulted mind he sought to quench, and blend
With the surrounding maniacs, in the hell
Where he had plunged it.　Glory without end
Scatter'd the clouds away—and on that name attend

XXXVII

The tears and praises of all time; while thine
Would rot in its oblivion—in the sink
Of worthless dust, which from thy boasted line
Is shaken into nothing; but the link
Thou formest in his fortunes bids us think
Of thy poor malice, naming thee with scorn—
Alfonso! how thy ducal pageants shrink
From thee! if in another station born,
Scarce fit to be the slave of him thou mad'st to mourn:

XXXVIII

Thou! form'd to eat, and be despised, and die,
Even as the beasts that perish, save that thou
Hadst a more splendid trough and wider sty:
He! with a glory round his furrow'd brow,
Which emanated then, and dazzles now,
In face of all his foes, the Cruscan quire,
And Boileau, whose rash envy could allow
No strain which shamed his country's creaking lyre,
That whetstone of the teeth—monotony in wire!

XXXIX

Peace to Torquato's injured shade! 'twas his
In life and death to be the mark where Wrong
Aim'd with her poison'd arrows, but to miss.
Oh, victor unsurpass'd in modern song!
Each year brings forth its millions; but how long
The tide of generations shall roll on,
And not the whole combined and countless throng
Compose a mind like thine? though all in one
Condensed their scatter'd rays, they would not form a sun.

XL

Great as thou art, yet parallel'd by those,
Thy countrymen, before thee born to shine,
The Bards of Hell and Chivalry: first rose   *Dante*
The Tuscan father's comedy divine;
Then, not unequal to the Florentine,
The southern Scott, the minstrel who call'd forth
A new creation with his magic line,
And, like the Ariosto of the North,
Sang ladye-love and war, romance and knightly worth.
Boccaccio

XLI

The lightning rent from Ariosto's bust
The iron crown of laurel's mimick'd leaves;
Nor was the ominous element unjust,
For the true laurel-wreath which Glory weaves
Is of the tree no bolt of thunder cleaves,
And the false semblance but disgraced his brow;
Yet still, if fondly Superstition grieves,
Know, that the lightning sanctifies below
Whate'er it strikes;—yon head is doubly sacred now.

XLII

Italia! oh Italia! thou who hast
The fatal gift of beauty, which became
A funeral dower of present woes and past,
On thy sweet brow is sorrow plough'd by shame,
And annals graved in characters of flame.
Oh, God! that thou wert in thy nakedness
Less lovely or more powerful, and couldst claim
Thy right, and awe the robbers back, who press
To shed thy blood, and drink the tears of thy distress;

XLIII

Then might'st thou more appal; or, less desired,
Be homely and be peaceful, undeplored
For thy destructive charms; then, still untired,
Would not be seen the armed torrents pour'd
Down the deep Alps; nor would the hostile horde
Of many-nation'd spoilers from the Po
Quaff blood and water; nor the stranger's sword
Be thy sad weapon of defence, and so,
Victor or vanquish'd, thou the slave of friend or foe.[1]

[1] The two stanzas xlii and xliii are, with the exception of a line or two, a translation of the famous sonnet of Filicaja: 'Italia, Italia, O tu cui feo la sorte!'

Childe Harolde's Pilgrimage is a search for immortality

XLIV

Wandering in youth, I traced the path of him,[1]
The Roman friend of Rome's least-mortal mind,
The friend of Tully: as my bark did skim
The bright blue waters with a fanning wind,
Came Megara before me, and behind
Aegina lay, Piraeus on the right,
And Corinth on the left; I lay reclined
Along the prow, and saw all these unite
In ruin, even as he had seen the desolate sight;

Ultimate oblivion

XLV

For Time hath not rebuilt them, but uprear'd
Barbaric dwellings on their shatter'd site,
Which only make more mourn'd and more endear'd
The few last rays of their far-scatter'd light,
And the crush'd relics of their vanish'd might.
The Roman saw these tombs in his own age,
These sepulchres of cities, which excite
Sad wonder, and his yet surviving page
The moral lesson bears, drawn from such pilgrimage.

XLVI

That page is now before me, and on mine
His country's ruin added to the mass
Of perish'd states he mourn'd in their decline,
And I in desolation: all that *was*
Of then destruction *is*; and now, alas!
Rome—Rome imperial, bows her to the storm,
In the same dust and blackness, and we pass
The skeleton of her Titanic form,[2]
Wrecks of another world, whose ashes still are warm.

[1] The celebrated letter of Servius Sulpicius to Cicero, on the death of his daughter, describes as it then was, and now is, a path which I often traced in Greece, both by sea and land, in different journeys and voyages. 'On my return from Asia, as I was sailing from Aegina towards Megara, I began to contemplate the prospect of the countries around me: Aegina was behind, Megara before me; Piraeus on the right, Corinth on the left: all which towns, once famous and flourishing, now lie overturned and buried in their ruins. Upon this sight, I could not but think presently within myself, Alas! how do we poor mortals fret and vex ourselves if any of our friends happen to die or be killed, whose life is yet so short, when the carcasses of so many noble cities lie here exposed before me in one view.'—See Middleton's *Cicero*, vol. ii, p. 371.

[2] It is Poggio, who, looking from the Capitoline hill upon ruined Rome, breaks forth into the exclamation: 'Ut nunc omni decore nudata, prostrata jacet, instar gigantei cadaveris corrupti atque undique exesi.'

XLVII

Yet, Italy! through every other land
Thy wrongs should ring, and shall, from side to side;
Mother of Arts! as once of arms; thy hand
Was then our guardian, and is still our guide;
Parent of our Religion! whom the wide
Nations have knelt to for the keys of heaven!
Europe, repentant of her parricide,
Shall yet redeem thee, and, all backward driven,
Roll the barbarian tide, and sue to be forgiven.

XLVIII

But Arno wins us to the fair white walls,
Where the Etrurian Athens claims and keeps
A softer feeling for her fairy halls.
Girt by her theatre of hills, she reaps
Her corn, and wine, and oil, and Plenty leaps
To laughing life, with her redundant horn.
Along the banks where smiling Arno sweeps
Was modern Luxury of Commerce born,
And buried Learning rose, redeem'd to a new morn.

XLIX

There, too, the Goddess loves in stone, and fills
The air around with beauty; we inhale
The ambrosial aspect, which, beheld, instils
Part of its immortality; the veil
Of heaven is half undrawn; within the pale
We stand, and in that form and face behold
What mind can make, when Nature's self would fail;
And to the fond idolaters of old
Envy the innate flash which such a soul could mould:

L

We gaze and turn away, and know not where,
Dazzled and drunk with beauty, till the heart
Reels with its fulness; there—for ever there—
Chain'd to the chariot of triumphal Art,
We stand as captives, and would not depart.
Away!—there need no words, nor terms precise,
The paltry jargon of the marble mart,
Where Pedantry gulls Folly—we have eyes?
Blood, pulse, and breast confirm the Dardan Shepherd's prize.

LI

Appear'dst thou not to Paris in this guise?
Or to more deeply blest Anchises? or,
In all thy perfect goddess-ship, when lies
Before thee thy own vanquish'd Lord of War?
And gazing in thy face as toward a star,
Laid on thy lap, his eyes to thee upturn,
Feeding on thy sweet cheek! [1] while thy lips are
With lava kisses melting while they burn,
Shower'd on his eyelids, brow, and mouth, as from an urn!

LII

Glowing, and circumfused in speechless love,
Their full divinity inadequate
That feeling to express, or to improve,
The gods become as mortals, and man's fate
Has moments like their brightest; but the weight
Of earth recoils upon us;—let it go!
We can recall such visions, and create,
From what has been, or might be, things which grow
Into thy statue's form, and look like gods below.

LIII

I leave to learned fingers, and wise hands,
The artist and his ape, to teach and tell
How well his connoisseurship understands
The graceful bend, and the voluptuous swell:
Let these describe the undescribable:
I would not their vile breath should crisp the stream
Wherein that image shall for ever dwell;
The unruffled mirror of the loveliest dream
That ever left the sky on the deep soul to beam.

LIV

In Santa Croce's holy precincts lie
Ashes which make it holier, dust which is
Even in itself an immortality,
Though there were nothing save the past, and this,
The particle of those sublimities
Which have relapsed to chaos:—here repose
Angelo's, Alfieri's bones, and his,
The starry Galileo, with his woes;
Here Machiavelli's earth return'd to whence it rose.

[1] Ὀφθαλμοὺς ἑστιᾶν.
'Atque oculos pascat uterque suos.'—OVID. *Amor.* lib. ii.

LV

These are four minds, which, like the elements,
Might furnish forth creation:—Italy!
Time, which hath wrong'd thee with ten thousand rents
Of thine imperial garment, shall deny,
And hath denied, to every other sky,
Spirits which soar from ruin:—thy decay
Is still impregnate with divinity,
Which gilds it with revivifying ray;
Such as the great of yore, Canova is to-day.

LVI

But where repose the all Etruscan three—
Dante, and Petrarch, and, scarce less than they,
The Bard of Prose, creative spirit! he
Of the Hundred Tales of love—where did they lay
Their bones, distinguish'd from our common clay
In death as life? Are they resolved to dust,
And have their country's marbles nought to say?
Could not her quarries furnish forth one bust?
Did they not to her breast their filial earth intrust?

LVII

Ungrateful Florence! Dante sleeps afar,
Like Scipio, buried by the upbraiding shore;
The factions, in their worse than civil war,
Proscribed the bard whose name for evermore
Their children's children would in vain adore
With the remorse of ages; and the crown
Which Petrarch's laureate brow supremely wore,
Upon a far and foreign soil had grown,
His life, his fame, his grave, though rifled—not thine own.

LVIII

Boccaccio to his parent earth bequeath'd
His dust,—and lies it not her Great among,
With many a sweet and solemn requiem breathed
O'er him who form'd the Tuscan's siren tongue?
That music in itself, whose sounds are song,
The poetry of speech? No;—even his tomb
Uptorn, must bear the hyaena bigot's wrong,
No more amidst the meaner dead find room,
Nor claim a passing sigh, because it told for *whom*!

LIX

And Santa Croce wants their mighty dust;
Yet for this want more noted, as of yore
The Caesar's pageant, shorn of Brutus' bust,
Did but of Rome's best Son remind her more:
Happier Ravenna! on thy hoary shore,
Fortress of falling empire! honour'd sleeps
The immortal exile;—Arqua, too, her store
Of tuneful relics proudly claims and keeps,
While Florence vainly begs her banish'd dead and weeps.

LX

What is her pyramid of precious stones?
Of porphyry, jasper, agate, and all hues
Of gem and marble, to encrust the bones
Of merchant-dukes? the momentary dews
Which, sparkling to the twilight stars, infuse
Freshness in the green turf that wraps the dead,
Whose names are mausoleums of the Muse,
Are gently prest with far more reverent tread
Than ever paced the slab which paves the princely head.

LXI

There be more things to greet the heart and eyes
In Arno's dome of Art's most princely shrine,
Where Sculpture with her rainbow sister vies;
There be more marvels yet—but not for mine;
For I have been accustom'd to entwine
My thoughts with Nature rather in the fields,
Than Art in galleries: though a work divine
Calls for my spirit's homage, yet it yields
Less than it feels, because the weapon which it wields

LXII

Is of another temper, and I roam
By Thrasimene's lake, in the defiles
Fatal to Roman rashness, more at home;
For there the Carthaginian's warlike wiles
Come back before me, as his skill beguiles
The host between the mountains and the shore,
Where Courage falls in her despairing files,
And torrents, swoll'n to rivers with their gore,
Reek through the sultry plain, with legions scatter'd o'er.

LXIII

Like to a forest fell'd by mountain winds;
And such the storm of battle on this day,
And such the frenzy, whose convulsion blinds
To all save carnage, that, beneath the fray,
An earthquake reel'd unheededly away!
None felt stern Nature rocking at his feet,
And yawning forth a grave for those who lay
Upon their bucklers for a winding sheet;
Such is the absorbing hate when warring nations meet!

LXIV

The Earth to them was as a rolling bark
Which bore them to Eternity; they saw
The Ocean round, but had no time to mark
The motions of their vessel; Nature's law,
In them suspended, reck'd not of the awe
Which reigns when mountains tremble, and the birds
Plunge in the clouds for refuge and withdraw
From their down-toppling nests; and bellowing herds
Stumble o'er heaving plains, and man's dread hath no words.

LXV

Far other scene is Thrasimene now;
Her lake a sheet of silver, and her plain
Rent by no ravage save the gentle plough;
Her aged trees rise thick as once the slain
Lay where their roots are; but a brook hath ta'en—
A little rill of scanty stream and bed—
A name of blood from that day's sanguine rain;
And Sanguinetto tells ye where the dead
Made the earth wet, and turn'd the unwilling waters red.

LXVI

But thou, Clitumnus! in thy sweetest wave
Of the most living crystal that was e'er
The haunt of river nymph, to gaze and lave
Her limbs where nothing hid them, thou dost rear
Thy grassy banks whereon the milk-white steer
Grazes; the purest god of gentle waters!
And most serene of aspect, and most clear;
Surely that stream was unprofaned by slaughters—
A mirror and a bath for Beauty's youngest daughters!

LXVII

And on thy happy shore a Temple still,
Of small and delicate proportion, keeps,
Upon a mild declivity of hill
Its memory of thee; beneath it sweeps

Thy current's calmness; oft from out it leaps
The finny darter with the glittering scales,
Who dwells and revels in thy glassy deeps;
While, chance, some scatter'd water-lily sails
Down where the shallower wave still tells its bubbling tales.

LXVIII

Pass not unblest the Genius of the place!
If through the air a zephyr more serene
Win to the brow, 'tis his; and if ye trace
Along his margin a more eloquent green,
If on the heart the freshness of the scene
Sprinkle its coolness, and from the dry dust
Of weary life a moment lave it clean
With Nature's baptism,—'tis to him ye must
Pay orisons for this suspension of disgust.

LXIX

The roar of waters!—from the headlong height
Velino cleaves the wave-worn precipice;
The fall of waters! rapid as the light
The flashing mass foams shaking the abyss;
The hell of waters! where they howl and hiss,
And boil in endless torture; while the sweat
Of their great agony, wrung out from this
Their Phlegethon, curls round the rocks of jet
That gird the gulf around, in pitiless horror set,

LXX

And mounts in spray the skies, and thence again
Returns in an unceasing shower, which round,
With its unemptied cloud of gentle rain,
Is an eternal April to the ground,
Making it all one emerald:—how profound
The gulf! and how the giant element
From rock to rock leaps with delirious bound,
Crushing the cliffs, which, downward worn and rent
With his fierce footsteps, yield in chasms a fearful vent

LXXI

To the broad column which rolls on, and shows
More like the fountain of an infant sea
Torn from the womb of mountains by the throes
Of a new world, than only thus to be

Parent of rivers, which flow gushingly,
With many windings, through the vale:—Look back!
Lo! where it comes like an eternity,
As if to sweep down all things in its track,
Charming the eye with dread,—a matchless cataract,[1]

LXXII

Horribly beautiful! but on the verge,
From side to side, beneath the glittering morn,
An Iris sits, amidst the infernal surge,[2]
Like Hope upon a death-bed, and, unworn
Its steady dyes, while all around is torn
By the distracted waters, bears serene
Its brilliant hues with all their beams unshorn:
Resembling, 'mid the torture of the scene,
Love watching Madness with unalterable mien.

LXXIII

Once more upon the woody Apennine,
The infant Alps, which—had I not before
Gazed on their mightier parents, where the pine
Sits on more shaggy summits, and where roar [3]
The thundering lauwine—might be worshipp'd more;
But I have seen the soaring Jungfrau rear
Her never-trodden snow, and seen the hoar
Glaciers of bleak Mont Blanc both far and near,
And in Chimari heard the thunder-hills of fear,

LXXIV

Th' Acroceraunian mountains of old name;
And on Parnassus seen the eagles fly
Like spirits of the spot, as 'twere for fame,

[1] I saw the 'Cascata del marmore' of Terni twice, at different periods; once from the summit of the precipice, and again from the valley below. The lower view is far to be preferred, if the traveller has time for one only; but in any point of view, either from above or below, it is worth all the cascades and torrents of Switzerland put together: the Staubach, Reichenbach, Pisse Vache, fall of Arpenaz, etc., are rills in comparative appearance. Of the fall of Schaffhausen I cannot speak, not yet having seen it.

[2] Of the time, place, and qualities of this kind of iris, the reader will see a short account, in a note to *Manfred*. The fall looks so much like 'the hell of waters,' that Addison thought the descent alluded to by the gulf in which Alecto plunged into the infernal regions. It is singular enough, that two of the finest cascades in Europe should be artificial—this of the Velino, and the one at Tivoli. The traveller is strongly recommended to trace the Velino, at least as high as the little lake, called *Pie' di Lup*. The Reatine territory was the Italian Tempe, and the ancient naturalist, amongst other beautiful varieties, remarked the daily rainbows of the lake Velinus. A scholar of great name has devoted a treatise to this district alone. See Ald. Manut., *De Reatina Urbe Agroque*.

[3] In the greater part of Switzerland, the avalanches are known by the name of lauwine.

For still they soar'd unutterably high:
I 've look'd on Ida with a Trojan's eye;
Athos, Olympus, Aetna, Atlas, made
These hills seem things of lesser dignity,
All, save the lone Soracte's heights display'd
Not *now* in snow, which asks the lyric Roman's aid

LXXV

For our remembrance, and from out the plain
Heaves like a long-swept wave about to break,
And on the curl hangs pausing: not in vain
May he, who will, his recollections rake
And quote in classic raptures, and awake
The hills with Latian echoes; I abhorr'd
Too much, to conquer for the poet's sake,
The drill'd dull lesson, forced down word by word [1]
In my repugnant youth, with pleasure to record

LXXVI

Aught that recalls the daily drug which turn'd
My sickening memory; and, though Time hath taught
My mind to meditate what then it learn'd,
Yet such the fix'd inveteracy wrought
By the impatience of my early thought,
That, with the freshness wearing out before
My mind could relish what it might have sought,
If free to choose, I cannot now restore
Its health; but what it then detested, still abhor.

LXXVII

Then farewell, Horace; whom I hated so,
Not for thy faults, but mine; it is a curse
To understand, not feel thy lyric flow.
To comprehend, but never love thy verse,
Although no deeper Moralist rehearse
Our little life, nor Bard prescribe his art,
Nor livelier Satirist the conscience pierce,
Awakening without wounding the touch'd heart,
Yet fare thee well—upon Soracte's ridge we part.

[1] These stanzas may probably remind the reader of Ensign Northerton's *
remarks: 'D—n Homo,' etc.; but the reasons for our dislike are not exactly the
same.   I wish to express, that we become tired of the task before we can comprehend the beauty; that we learn by rote before we can get by heart; that the
freshness is worn away, and the future pleasure and advantage deadened and
destroyed, by the didactic anticipation, at an age when we can neither feel nor
understand the power of compositions which it requires an acquaintance with
life, as well as Latin and Greek, to relish, or to reason upon.

* [*See* H. Fielding, *Tom Jones*, VII, 12.]

LXXVIII

Oh Rome! my country! city of the soul!
The orphans of the heart must turn to thee,
Lone mother of dead empires! and control
In their shut breasts their petty misery.
What are our woes and sufferance? Come and see
The cypress, hear the owl, and plod your way
O'er steps of broken thrones and temples, Ye!
Whose agonies are evils of a day—
A world is at our feet as fragile as our clay.

LXXIX

The Niobe of nations! there she stands,
Childless and crownless, in her voiceless woe;
An empty urn within her wither'd hands,
Whose holy dust was scatter'd long ago;
The Scipios' tomb contains no ashes now;
The very sepulchres lie tenantless
Of their heroic dwellers: dost thou flow,
Old Tiber! through a marble wilderness?
Rise, with thy yellow waves, and mantle her distress.

LXXX

The Goth, the Christian, Time, War, Flood, and Fire,
Have dealt upon the seven-hill'd city's pride;
She saw her glories star by star expire,
And up the steep barbarian monarchs ride,
Where the car climb'd the capitol; far and wide
Temple and tower went down, nor left a site:—
Chaos of ruins! who shall trace the void,
O'er the dim fragments cast a lunar light,
And say, 'here was, or is,' where all is doubly night?

LXXXI

The double night of ages, and of her,
Night's daughter, Ignorance, hath wrapt and wrap
All round us; we but feel our way to err:
The ocean hath his chart, the stars their map,
And Knowledge spreads them on her ample lap;
But Rome is as the desert, where we steer
Stumbling o'er recollections; now we clap
Our hands, and cry 'Eureka!' it is clear—
When but some false mirage of ruin rises near.

LXXXII

Alas! the lofty city! and alas!
The trebly hundred triumphs![1] and the day
When Brutus made the dagger's edge surpass
The conqueror's sword in bearing fame away!
Alas, for Tully's voice, and Virgil's lay,
And Livy's pictured page!—but these shall be
Her resurrection; all beside—decay.
Alas, for Earth, for never shall we see
That brightness in her eye she bore when Rome was free!

LXXXIII

Oh thou, whose chariot roll'd on Fortune's wheel,
Triumphant Sylla! Thou, who didst subdue
Thy country's foes ere thou wouldst pause to feel
The wrath of thy own wrongs, or reap the due
Of hoarded vengeance till thine eagles flew
O'er prostrate Asia;—thou, who with thy frown
Annihilated senates—Roman, too,
With all thy vices, for thou didst lay down
With an atoning smile a more than earthly crown—

LXXXIV

The dictatorial wreath,[2]—couldst thou divine
To what would one day dwindle that which made
Thee more than mortal? and that so supine
By aught than Romans Rome should thus be laid?
She who was named Eternal, and array'd
Her warriors but to conquer—she who veil'd
Earth with her haughty shadow, and display'd,
Until the o'er-canopied horizon fail'd,
Her rushing wings—Oh! she who was Almighty hail'd!

LXXXV

Sylla was first of victors; but our own
The sagest of usurpers, Cromwell; he
Too swept off senates while he hew'd the throne
Down to a block—immortal rebel! See
What crimes it costs to be a moment free

[1] Orosius gives 320 for the number of triumphs. He is followed by Panvinius; and Panvinius by Mr. Gibbon and the modern writers.

[2] Certainly, were it not for these two traits in the life of Sylla, alluded to in this stanza, we should regard him as a monster unredeemed by any admirable quality. The *atonement* of his voluntary resignation of empire may perhaps be accepted by us, as it seems to have satisfied the Romans, who if they had not respected must have destroyed him. There could be no mean, no division of opinion; they must have all thought, like Eucrates, that what had appeared ambition was a love of glory, and that what had been mistaken for pride was a real grandeur of soul.

And famous through all ages! but beneath
His fate the moral lurks of destiny;
His day of double victory and death
Beheld him win two realms, and, happier, yield his breath.[1]

LXXXVI

The third of the same moon whose former course
Had all but crown'd him, on the selfsame day
Deposed him gently from his throne of force,
And laid him with the earth's preceding clay.
And show'd not Fortune thus how fame and sway,
And all we deem delightful, and consume
Our souls to compass through each arduous way,
Are in her eyes less happy than the tomb?
Were they but so in man's, how different were his doom!

LXXXVII

And thou, dread statue! yet existent in
The austerest form of naked majesty,
Thou who beheldest, 'mid the assassins' din,
At thy bathed base the bloody Caesar lie,
Folding his robe in dying dignity,
An offering to thine altar from the queen
Of gods and men, great Nemesis! did he die,
And thou, too, perish, Pompey? have ye been
Victors of countless kings, or puppets of a scene?

LXXXVIII

And thou, the thunder-stricken nurse of Rome!
She-wolf! whose brazen-imaged dugs impart
The milk of conquest yet within the dome
Where, as a monument of antique art,
Thou standest:—Mother of the mighty heart,
Which the great founder suck'd from thy wild teat,
Scorch'd by the Roman Jove's ethereal dart,
And thy limbs black with lightning—dost thou yet
Guard thine immortal cubs, nor thy fond charge forget?

LXXXIX

Thou dost;—but all thy foster-babes are dead—
The men of iron; and the world hath rear'd
Cities from out their sepulchres: men bled
In imitation of the things they fear'd,
And fought and conquer'd, and the same course steer'd,

[1] On 3rd September Cromwell gained the victory of Dunbar: a year afterwards he obtained 'his crowning mercy' of Worcester; and a few years after, on the same day, which he had ever esteemed the most fortunate for him, died.

At apish distance; but as yet none have,
Nor could, the same supremacy have near'd,
Save one vain man, who is not in the grave,
But, vanquish'd by himself, to his own slaves a slave—

XC

The fool of false dominion—and a kind
Of bastard Caesar, following him of old
With steps unequal; for the Roman's mind
Was modell'd in a less terrestrial mould,
With passions fiercer, yet a judgment cold,
And an immortal instinct which redeem'd
The frailties of a heart so soft, yet bold,
Alcides with the distaff now he seem'd
At Cleopatra's feet,—and now himself he beam'd,

XCI

And came—and saw—and conquer'd! But the man
Who would have tamed his eagles down to flee,
Like a train'd falcon, in the Gallic van,
Which he, in sooth, long led to victory,
With a deaf heart which never seem'd to be
A listener to itself, was strangely framed;
With but one weakest weakness—vanity,
Coquettish in ambition—still he aim'd—
At what? can he avouch—or answer what he claim'd?

XCII

And would be all or nothing—nor could wait
For the sure grave to level him; few years
Had fixed him with the Caesars in his fate,
On whom we tread: For *this* the conqueror rears
The arch of triumph! and for this the tears
And blood of earth flow on as they have flow'd,
An universal deluge, which appears
Without an ark for wretched man's abode,
And ebbs but to reflow!—Renew thy rainbow, God!

XCIII

What from this barren being do we reap?
Our senses narrow, and our reason frail,
Life short, and truth a gem which loves the deep,
And all things weigh'd in custom's falsest scale;
Opinion an omnipotence,—whose veil

Mantles the earth with darkness, until right
And wrong are accidents, and men grow pale
Lest their own judgments should become too bright,
And their free thoughts be crimes, and earth have too much
    light.

XCIV

And thus they plod in sluggish misery,
Rotting from sire to son, and age to age,
Proud of their trampled nature, and so die,
Bequeathing their hereditary rage
To the new race of inborn slaves, who wage
War for their chains, and rather than be free,
Bleed gladiator-like, and still engage
Within the same arena where they see
Their fellows fall before, like leaves of the same tree.

XCV

I speak not of men's creeds—they rest between
Man and his Maker—but of things allow'd,
Averr'd, and known,—and daily, hourly seen—
The yoke that is upon us doubly bow'd,
And the intent of tyranny avow'd,
The edict of Earth's rulers, who are grown
The apes of him who humbled once the proud,
And shook them from their slumbers on the throne;
Too glorious, were this all his mighty arm had done.

XCVI

Can tyrants but by tyrants conquer'd be,
And Freedom find no champion and no child
Such as Columbia saw arise when she
Sprung forth a Pallas, arm'd and undefiled?
Or must such minds be nourish'd in the wild,
Deep in the unpruned forest, 'midst the roar
Of cataracts, where nursing Nature smiled
On infant Washington? Has Earth no more
Such seeds within her breast, or Europe no such shore?

XCVII

But France got drunk with blood to vomit crime,
And fatal have her Saturnalia been
To Freedom's cause, in every age and clime;
Because the deadly days which we have seen,
And vile Ambition, that built up between

Man and his hopes an adamantine wall,
And the base pageant laʃt upon the scene,
Are grown the pretext for the eternal thrall
Which nips life's tree, and dooms man's worʃt—his second fall.

XCVIII

METAPHORS
SOMEWHAT
INCONSISTANT

Yet, Freedom! yet thy banner, torn, but flying,
Streams like the thunder-ʃtorm *againʃt* the wind;
Thy trumpet voice, though broken now and dying,
The loudeʃt ʃtill the tempeʃt leaves behind;
Thy tree hath loʃt its blossoms, and the rind,
Chopp'd by the axe, looks rough and little worth,
But the sap laʃts, and ʃtill the seed we find
Sown deep, even in the bosom of the North;
So shall a better spring less bitter fruit bring forth.

XCIX

There is a ʃtern round tower of other days,[1]
Firm as a fortress, with its fence of ʃtone,
Such as an army's baffled ʃtrength delays,
Standing with half its battlements alone,
And with two thousand years of ivy grown,
The garland of eternity, where wave
The green leaves over all by time o'erthrown;—
What was this tower of ʃtrength? within its cave
What treasure lay so lock'd, so hid?—A woman's grave.

C

But who was she, the lady of the dead,
Tomb'd in a palace? Was she chaʃte and fair?
Worthy a king's—or more—a Roman's bed?
What race of chiefs and heroes did she bear?
What daughter of her beauties was the heir?
How lived—how loved—how died she? Was she not
So honour'd—and conspicuously there,
Where meaner relics muʃt not dare to rot,
Placed to commemorate a more than mortal lot?

CI

Was she as those who love their lords, or they
Who love the lords of others? such have been
Even in the olden time, Rome's annals say.
Was she a matron of Cornelia's mien,

[1] Alluding to the tomb of Cecilia Metella, called Capo di Bove.

Or the light air of Egypt's graceful queen,
Profuse of joy—or 'gainst it did she war,
Inveterate in virtue?   Did she lean
To the soft side of the heart, or wisely bar
Love from amongst her griefs?—for such the affections are.

CII

Perchance she died in youth: it may be, bow'd
With foes far heavier than the ponderous tomb
That weigh'd upon her gentle dust, a cloud
Might gather o'er her beauty, and a gloom
In her dark eye, prophetic of the doom
Heaven gives its favourites—early death; yet shed
A sunset charm around her, and illume
With hectic light, the Hesperus of the dead,
Of her consuming cheek the autumnal leaf-like red.

CIII

Perchance she died in age—surviving all,
Charms, kindred, children—with the silver gray
On her long tresses, which might yet recall,
It may be, still a something of the day
When they were braided, and her proud array
And lovely form were envied, praised, and eyed
By Rome—but whither would Conjecture stray?
Thus much alone we know—Metella died,
The wealthiest Roman's wife: Behold his love or pride!

CIV

I know not why—but standing thus by thee
It seems as if I had thine inmate known,
Thou tomb! and other days come back on me
With recollected music, though the tone
Is changed and solemn, like the cloudy groan
Of dying thunder on the distant wind;
Yet could I seat me by this ivied stone
Till I had bodied forth the heated mind,
Forms from the floating wreck which Ruin leaves behind;

CV

And from the planks, far shatter'd o'er the rocks,
Built me a little bark of hope, once more
To battle with the ocean and the shocks
Of the loud breakers, and the ceaseless roar
Which rushes on the solitary shore

Where all lies founder'd that was ever dear:
But could I gather from the wave-worn store
Enough for my rude boat, where should I steer?
There woos no home, nor hope, nor life, save what is here.

CVI

Then let the winds howl on! their harmony
Shall henceforth be my music, and the night
The sound shall temper with the owlets' cry,
As I now hear them, in the fading light
Dim o'er the bird of darkness' native site,
Answering each other on the Palatine,
With their large eyes, all glistening gray and bright,
And sailing pinions.—Upon such a shrine
What are our petty griefs?—let me not number mine.

CVII

Cypress and ivy, weed and wallflower grown
Matted and mass'd together, hillocks heap'd
On what were chambers, arch crush'd, column strown
In fragments, choked-up vaults, and frescos steep'd
In subterranean damps, where the owl peep'd,
Deeming it midnight:—Temples, baths, or halls?
Pronounce who can; for all that Learning reap'd
From her research hath been, that these are walls—
Behold the Imperial Mount! 'tis thus the mighty falls.[1]

CVIII

There is the moral of all human tales;[2]
'Tis but the same rehearsal of the past,
First Freedom, and then Glory—when that fails,
Wealth, vice, corruption,—barbarism at last.
And History, with all her volumes vast,

[1] The Palatine is one mass of ruins, particularly on the side towards the Circus Maximus. The very soil is formed of crumbled brickwork. Nothing has been told, nothing can be told, to satisfy the belief of any but a Roman antiquary.

[2] The author of the Life of Cicero, speaking of the opinion entertained of Britain by that orator and his contemporary Romans, has the following eloquent passage: 'From their railleries of this kind, on the barbarity and misery of our island, one cannot help reflecting on the surprising fate and revolutions of kingdoms; how Rome, once the mistress of the world, the seat of arts, empire, and glory, now lies sunk in sloth, ignorance, and poverty, enslaved to the most cruel as well as to the most contemptible of tyrants, superstition and religious imposture; while this remote country, anciently the jest and contempt of the polite Romans, is become the happy seat of liberty, plenty, and letters; flourishing in all the arts and refinements of civil life; yet running perhaps the same course which Rome itself had run before it, from virtuous industry to wealth; from wealth to luxury; from luxury to an impatience of discipline, and corruption of morals: till, by a total degeneracy and loss of virtue, being grown ripe for destruction, it fall a prey at last to some hardy oppressor, and, with the loss of liberty, losing everything that is valuable, sinks gradually again into its original barbarism.'

Hath, but *one* page,—'tis better written here,
Where gorgeous Tyranny hath thus amass'd
All treasures, all delights, that eye or ear,
Heart, soul could seek, tongue ask—Away with words! draw near,

CIX

Admire, exult—despise—laugh, weep,—for here
There is such matter for all feeling:—Man!
Thou pendulum betwixt a smile and tear,
Ages and realms are crowded in this span,
This mountain, whose obliterated plan
The pyramid of empires pinnacled,
Of Glory's gewgaws shining in the van
Till the sun's rays with added flame were fill'd!
Where are its golden roofs! where those who dared to build?

CX

Tully was not so eloquent as thou,
Thou nameless column with the buried base!
What are the laurels of the Caesar's brow?
Crown me with ivy from his dwelling-place.
Whose arch or pillar meets me in the face,
Titus or Trajan's?   No—'tis that of Time:
Triumph, arch, pillar, all he doth displace,
Scoffing; and apostolic statues climb
To crush the imperial urn, whose ashes slept sublime,[1]

CXI

Buried in air, the deep blue sky of Rome,
And looking to the stars: they had contain'd
A spirit which with these would find a home,
The last of those who o'er the whole earth reign'd,
The Roman globe, for after none sustain'd,
But yielded back his conquests:—he was more
Than a mere Alexander, and, unstain'd
With household blood and wine, serenely wore
His sovereign virtues—still we Trajan's name adore.[2]

[1] The column of Trajan is surmounted by St. Peter; that of Aurelius by St. Paul.

[2] Trajan was *proverbially* the best of the Roman princes; and it would be easier to find a sovereign uniting exactly the opposite characteristics, than one possessed of all the happy qualities ascribed to this emperor. 'When he mounted the throne,' says the historian Dion, 'he was strong in body, he was vigorous in mind, age had impaired none of his faculties; he was altogether free from envy and from detraction; he honoured all the good, and he advanced them; and on this account they could not be the objects of his fear, or of his hate; he never listened to informers; he gave not way to his anger; he abstained equally from unfair exactions and unjust punishments; he had rather be loved as a man than honoured as a sovereign; he was affable with his people, respectful to the senate, and universally beloved by both; he inspired none with dread but the enemies of his country.'

CXII

Where is the rock of Triumph, the high place
Where Rome embraced her heroes? where the steep
Tarpeian? fittest goal of Treason's race,
The promontory whence the Traitor's Leap
Cured all ambition.   Did the conquerors heap
Their spoils here?   Yes; and in yon field below,
A thousand years of silenced factions sleep—
The Forum, where the immortal accents glow,
And still the eloquent air breathes—burns with Cicero!

CXIII

The field of freedom, faction, fame, and blood:
Here a proud people's passions were exhaled,
From the first hour of empire in the bud
To that when further worlds to conquer fail'd;
But long before had Freedom's face been veil'd,
And Anarchy assumed her attributes;
Till every lawless soldier who assail'd
Trod on the trembling senate's slavish mutes,
Or raised the venal voice of baser prostitutes.

CXIV

Then turn we to her latest tribune's name,
From her ten thousand tyrants turn to thee,
Redeemer of dark centuries of shame—
The friend of Petrarch—hope of Italy—
Rienzi! last of Romans!   While the tree
Of freedom's wither'd trunk puts forth a leaf,
Even for thy tomb a garland let it be—
The forum's champion, and the people's chief—
Her new-born Numa thou—with reign, alas! too brief.

CXV

Egeria! sweet creation of some heart
Which found no mortal resting-place so fair
As thine ideal breast; whate'er thou art
Or wert,—a young Aurora of the air,
The nympholepsy of some fond despair;
Or, it might be, a beauty of the earth,
Who found a more than common votary there
Too much adoring; whatsoe'er thy birth,
Thou wert a beautiful thought, and softly bodied forth.

CXVI

The mosses of thy fountain still are sprinkled
With thine Elysian water-drops; the face
Of thy cave-guarded spring, with years unwrinkled,
Reflects the meek-eyed genius of the place,

Whose green, wild margin now no more erase
Art's works; nor must the delicate waters sleep,
Prison'd in marble, bubbling from the base
Of the cleft statue, with a gentle leap
The rill runs o'er, and round, fern, flowers, and ivy, creep,

CXVII

Fantastically tangled; the green hills
Are clothed with early blossoms, through the grass
The quick-eyed lizard rustles, and the bills
Of summer-birds sing welcome as ye pass;
Flowers fresh in hue, and many in their class,
Implore the pausing step, and with their dyes
Dance in the soft breeze in a fairy mass;
The sweetness of the violet's deep blue eyes,
Kiss'd by the breath of heaven, seems colour'd by its skies.

CXVIII

Here didst thou dwell, in this enchanted cover,
Egeria! thy all heavenly bosom beating
For the far footsteps of thy mortal lover;
The purple Midnight veiled that mystic meeting
With her most starry canopy, and seating
Thyself by thine adorer, what befell?
This cave was surely shaped out for the greeting
Of an enamoured Goddess, and the cell
Haunted by holy Love—the earliest oracle!

CXIX

And didst thou not, thy breast to his replying,
Blend a celestial with a human heart;
And Love, which dies as it was born, in sighing,
Share with immortal transports? could thine art
Make them indeed immortal, and impart
The purity of heaven to earthly joys,
Expel the venom and not blunt the dart—
The dull satiety which all destroys—
And root from out the soul the deadly weed which cloys?

*N.B.
Dislike of sexual
incontinence*

CXX

Alas! our young affections run to waste,
Or water but the desert; whence arise
But weeds of dark luxuriance, tares of haste,
Rank at the core, though tempting to the eyes,
Flowers whose wild odours breathe but agonies,

And trees whose gums are poison; such the plants
Which spring beneath her steps as Passion flies
O'er the world's wilderness, and vainly pants
For some celestial fruit forbidden to our wants.

CXXI

Oh Love! no habitant of earth thou art—
An unseen seraph, we believe in thee,
A faith whose martyrs are the broken heart,
But never yet hath seen, nor e'er shall see
The naked eye, thy form, as it should be;
The mind hath made thee, as it peopled heaven,
Even with its own desiring phantasy,
And to a thought such shape and image given,
As haunts the unquench'd soul—parch'd—wearied—wrung and
    riven.

CXXII

Of its own beauty is the mind diseased,
And fevers into false creation:—where,
Where are the forms the sculptor's soul hath seized?
In him alone.   Can Nature show so fair?
Where are the charms and virtues which we dare
Conceive in boyhood and pursue as men,
The unreach'd Paradise of our despair,
Which o'er-informs the pencil and the pen,
And overpowers the page where it would bloom again?

CXXIII

Who loves, raves—'tis youth's frenzy—but the cure
Is bitterer still; as charm by charm unwinds
Which robed our idols, and we see too sure
Nor worth nor beauty dwells from out the mind's
Ideal shape of such; yet still it binds
The fatal spell, and still it draws us on,
Reaping the whirlwind from the oft-sown winds;
The stubborn heart, its alchemy begun,
Seems ever near the prize—wealthiest when most undone.

CXXIV

We wither from our youth, we gasp away—
Sick—sick; unfound the boon—unslacked the thirst,
Though to the last, in verge of our decay,
Some phantom lures, such as we sought at first—
But all too late,—so are we doubly curst.
Love, fame, ambition, avarice—'tis the same,
Each idle—and all ill—and none the worst—
For all are meteors with a different name,
And Death the sable smoke where vanishes the flame.

CXXV

Few—none—find what they love or could have loved,
Though accident, blind contact, and the strong
Necessity of loving, have removed
Antipathies—but to recur, ere long,
Envenom'd with irrevocable wrong;
And Circumstance, that unspiritual god
And miscreator, makes and helps along
Our coming evils with a crutch-like rod,
Whose touch turns Hope to dust,—the dust we all have trod.

CXXVI

Our life is a false nature—'tis not in
The harmony of things,—this hard decree,
This uneradicable taint of sin,
This boundless upas, this all-blasting tree,
Whose root is earth, whose leaves and branches be
The skies which rain their plagues on men like dew—
Disease, death, bondage—all the woes we see—
And worse, the woes we see not—which throb through
The immedicable soul, with heart-aches ever new.

CXXVII

Yet let us ponder boldly—'tis a base [1]
Abandonment of reason to resign
Our right of thought—our last and only place
Of refuge; this, at least, shall still be mine:
Though from our birth the faculty divine
Is chain'd and tortured—cabin'd, cribb'd, confined,
And bred in darkness, lest the truth should shine
Too brightly on the unprepared mind,
The beam pours in, for time and skill will couch the blind.

[1] 'At all events,' says the author of the *Academical Questions*, 'I trust, whatever may be the fate of my own speculations, that philosophy will regain that estimation which it ought to possess. The free and philosophic spirit of our nation has been the theme of admiration to the world. This was the proud distinction of Englishmen, and the luminous source of all their glory. Shall we then forget the manly and dignified sentiments of our ancestors, to prate in the language of the mother or the nurse about our good old prejudices? This is not the way to defend the cause of truth. It was not thus that our fathers maintained it in the brilliant periods of our history. Prejudice may be trusted to guard the outworks for a short space of time, while reason slumbers in the citadel; but if the latter sink into a lethargy, the former will quickly erect a standard for herself. Philosophy, wisdom, and liberty support each other: he who will not reason is a bigot; he who cannot, is a fool; and he who dares not, is a slave.'

II—* E 487

CXXVIII

Arches on arches! as it were that Rome,
Collecting the chief trophies of her line,
Would build up all her triumphs in one dome,
Her Coliseum stands; the moonbeams shine
As 'twere its natural torches, for divine
Should be the light which streams here, to illume
This long-explored but still exhaustless mine
Of contemplation; and the azure gloom
Of an Italian night, where the deep skies assume

CXXIX

Hues which have words, and speak to ye of heaven,
Floats o'er this vast and wondrous monument,
And shadows forth its glory.   There is given
Unto the things of earth, which Time hath bent,
A spirit's feeling, and where he hath leant
His hand, but broke his scythe, there is a power
And magic in the ruin'd battlement,
For which the palace of the present hour
Must yield its pomp, and wait till ages are its dower.

CXXX

Oh Time! the beautifier of the dead,
Adorner of the ruin, comforter
And only healer when the heart hath bled—
Time! the corrector where our judgments err,
The test of truth, love,—sole philosopher,
For all beside are sophists, from thy thrift,
Which never loses though it doth defer—
Time, the avenger! unto thee I lift
My hands, and eyes, and heart, and crave of thee a gift:

CXXXI

Amidst this wreck, where thou hast made a shrine
And temple more divinely desolate,
Among thy mightier offerings here are mine,
Ruins of years—though few, yet full of fate:—
If thou hast ever seen me too elate,
Hear me not; but if calmly I have borne
Good, and reserved my pride against the hate
Which shall not whelm me, let me not have worn
This iron in my soul in vain—shall *they* not mourn?

CXXXII

And thou, who never yet of human wrong
Left the unbalanced scale, great Nemesis!
Here, where the ancient paid thee homage long—
Thou, who didst call the Furies from the abyss,

And round Orestes bade them howl and hiss
For that unnatural retribution—just,
Had it but been from hands less near—in this
Thy former realm, I call thee from the dust!
Dost thou not hear my heart?—Awake! thou shalt, and must.

CXXXIII

It is not that I may not have incurr'd
For my ancestral faults or mine the wound
I bleed withal, and, had it been conferr'd
With a just weapon, it had flow'd unbound;
But now my blood shall not sink in the ground;
To thee I do devote it—*thou* shalt take
The vengeance, which shall yet be sought and found,
Which if *I* have not taken for the sake——
But let that pass—I sleep, but thou shalt yet awake.

CXXXIV

And if my voice break forth, 'tis not that now
I shrink from what is suffer'd: let him speak
Who hath beheld decline upon my brow,
Or seen my mind's convulsion leave it weak;
But in this page a record will I seek.
Not in the air shall these my words disperse,
Though I be ashes; a far hour shall wreak
The deep prophetic fulness of this verse,
And pile on human heads the mountain of my curse!

CXXXV

That curse shall be Forgiveness.—Have I not—
Hear me, my mother Earth! behold it, Heaven!—
Have I not had to wrestle with my lot?
Have I not suffer'd things to be forgiven?
Have I not had my brain sear'd, my heart riven,
Hopes sapp'd, name blighted, Life's life lied away?
And only not to desperation driven,
Because not altogether of such clay
As rots into the souls of those whom I survey.

CXXXVI

From mighty wrongs to petty perfidy
Have I not seen what human things could do?
From the loud roar of foaming calumny
To the small whisper of the as paltry few,
And subtler venom of the reptile crew,

The Janus glance of whose significant eye,
Learning to lie with silence, would *seem* true,
And without utterance, save the shrug or sigh,
Deal round to happy fools its speechless obloquy.

CXXXVII

But I have lived, and have not lived in vain:
My mind may lose its force, my blood its fire,
And my frame perish even in conquering pain;
But there is that within me which shall tire
Torture and Time, and breathe when I expire;
Something unearthly, which they deem not of,
Like the remember'd tone of a mute lyre,
Shall on their soften'd spirits sink, and move
In hearts all rocky now the late remorse of love.

CXXXVIII

The seal is set.—Now welcome, thou dread power!
Nameless, yet thus omnipotent, which here
Walk'st in the shadow of the midnight hour
With a deep awe, yet all distinct from fear;
Thy haunts are ever where the dead walls rear
Their ivy mantles, and the solemn scene
Derives from thee a sense so deep and clear
That we become a part of what has been,
And grow unto the spot, all-seeing but unseen.

CXXXIX

And here the buzz of eager nations ran,
In murmur'd pity, or loud-roar'd applause,
As man was slaughter'd by his fellow man.
And wherefore slaughter'd? wherefore, but because
Such were the bloody Circus' genial laws,
And the imperial pleasure.—Wherefore not?
What matters were we fall to fill the maws
Of worms—on battle-plains or listed spot?
Both are but theatres where the chief actors rot.

CXL

I see before me the Gladiator lie:
He leans upon his hand—his manly brow
Consents to death, but conquers agony,
And his droop'd head sinks gradually low—
And through his side the last drops, ebbing slow
From the red gash, fall heavy, one by one,
Like the first of a thunder-shower; and now
The arena swims around him—he is gone,
Ere ceased the inhuman shout which hail'd the wretch who won.

CXLI

He heard it, but he heeded not—his eyes
Were with his heart, and that was far away:[1]
He reck'd not of the life he lost nor prize,
But where his rude hut by the Danube lay,
There were his young barbarians all at play,
There was their Dacian mother—he, their sire,
Butcher'd to make a Roman holiday—
All this rush'd with his blood—Shall he expire
And unavenged?—Arise! ye Goths, and glut your ire!

CXLII

But here, where Murder breathed her bloody steam;
And here, where buzzing nations choked the ways,
And roar'd or murmur'd like a mountain stream
Dashing or winding as its torrent strays;
Here, where the Roman millions' blame or praise
Was death or life, the playthings of a crowd,
My voice sounds much—and fall the stars' faint rays
On the arena void—seats crush'd—walls bow'd—
And galleries, where my steps seem echoes strangely loud.

CXLIII

A ruin—yet what ruin! from its mass
Walls, palaces, half-cities, have been rear'd;
Yet oft the enormous skeleton ye pass,
And marvel where the spoil could have appear'd.
Hath it indeed been plunder'd, or but clear'd?
Alas! developed, opens the decay,
When the colossal fabric's form is near'd:
It will not bear the brightness of the day,
Which streams too much on all years, man, have reft away.

CXLIV

But when the rising moon begins to climb
Its topmost arch, and gently pauses there;
When the stars twinkle through the loops of time,
And the low night-breeze waves along the air,
The garland forest, which the gray walls wear,

[1] Whether the wonderful statue which suggested this image be a laquearian gladiator, which, in spite of Winkelmann's criticism, has been stoutly maintained; or whether it be a Greek herald, as that great antiquary positively asserted; or whether it is to be thought a Spartan or barbarian shield-bearer, according to the opinion of his Italian editor; it must assuredly seem *a copy* of that masterpiece of Ctesilaus which represented 'a wounded man dying, who perfectly expressed what there remained of life in him.' Montfaucon and Maffei thought it the identical statue; but that statue was of bronze. The gladiator was once in the Villa Ludovizi, and was bought by Clement XII. The right arm is an entire restoration of Michael Angelo.

Like laurels on the bald first Caesar's head; [1]
When the light shines serene but doth not glare,
Then in this magic circle raise the dead:
Heroes have trod this spot—'tis on their dust ye tread.

CXLV

'While stands the Coliseum, Rome shall stand; [2]
When falls the Coliseum, Rome shall fall;
And when Rome falls—the World.'   From our own land
Thus spake the pilgrims o'er this mighty wall
In Saxon times, which we are wont to call
Ancient; and these three mortal things are still
On their foundations, and unalter'd all;
Rome and her Ruin past Redemption's skill,
The World, the same wide den—of thieves, or what ye will.

CXLVI

Simple, erect, severe, austere, sublime—
Shrine of all saints and temple of all gods,
From Jove to Jesus—spared and blest by time;
Looking tranquillity, while falls or nods
Arch, empire, each thing round thee, and man plods
His way through thorns to ashes—glorious dome!
Shalt thou not last?   Time's scythe and tyrants' rods
Shiver upon thee—sanctuary and home
Of art and piety—Pantheon!—pride of Rome!

CXLVII

Relic of nobler days, and noblest arts!
Despoil'd yet perfect, with thy circle spreads
A holiness appealing to all hearts—
To art a model; and to him who treads
Rome for the sake of ages, Glory sheds
Her light through thy sole aperture; to those
Who worship, here are altars for their beads;
And they who feel for genius may repose
Their eyes on honour'd forms, whose busts around them close. [3]

---

[1] Suetonius informs us that Julius Caesar was particularly gratified by that decree of the senate which enabled him to wear a wreath of laurel on all occasions. He was anxious, not to show that he was the conqueror of the world, but to hide that he was bald.   A stranger at Rome would hardly have guessed at the motive, nor should we without the help of the historian.

[2] This is quoted in the *Decline and Fall of the Roman Empire*, as a proof that the Coliseum was entire, when seen by the Anglo-Saxon pilgrims at the end of the seventh, or the beginning of the eighth, century.

[3] The Pantheon has been made a receptacle for the busts of modern great, or at least distinguished, men. The flood of light which once fell through the large orb above on the whole circle of divinities, now shines on a numerous assemblage of mortals, some one or two of whom have been almost deified by the veneration of their countrymen.

CXLVIII

There is a dungeon, in whose dim drear light [1]
What do I gaze on? Nothing: Look again!
Two forms are slowly shadow'd on my sight—
Two insulated phantoms of the brain:
It is not so; I see them full and plain—
An old man, and a female young and fair,
Fresh as a nursing mother, in whose vein
The blood is nectar:—but what doth she there,
With her unmantled neck, and bosom white and bare?

CXLIX

Full swells the deep pure fountain of young life,
Where *on* the heart and *from* the heart we took
Our first and sweetest nurture, when the wife,
Blest into mother, in the innocent look,
Or even the piping cry of lips that brook
No pain and small suspense, a joy perceives
Man knows not, when from out its cradled nook
She sees her little bud put forth its leaves—
What may the fruit be yet?—I know not—Cain was Eve's.

CL

But here youth offers to old age the food,
The milk of his own gift:—it is her sire
To whom she renders back the debt of blood
Born with her birth. No; he shall not expire
While in those warm and lovely veins the fire
Of health and holy feeling can provide
Great Nature's Nile, whose deep stream rises higher
Than Egypt's river:—from that gentle side
Drink, drink and live, old man! Heaven's realm holds no
        such tide.

CLI

The starry fable of the milky way
Has not thy story's purity; it is
A constellation of a sweeter ray,
And sacred Nature triumphs more in this
Reverse of her decree, than in the abyss
Where sparkle distant worlds:—Oh, holiest nurse!
No drop of that clear stream its way shall miss
To thy sire's heart, replenishing its source
With life, as our freed souls rejoin the universe.

[1] This and the next three stanzas allude to the story of the Roman daughter,
which is recalled to the traveller by the site, or pretended site, of that adventure,
now shown at the church of St. Nicholas *in Carcere*.

CLII

Turn to the Mole which Hadrian rear'd on high,[1]
Imperial mimic of old Egypt's piles,
Colossal copyist of deformity,
Whose travell'd phantasy from the far Nile's
Enormous model, doom'd the artist's toils
To build for giants, and for his vain earth,
His shrunken ashes, raise this dome: How smiles
The gazer's eye with philosophic mirth,
To view the huge design which sprung from such a birth!

CLIII

But lo! the dome—the vast and wondrous dome,[2]
To which Diana's marvel was a cell—
Christ's mighty shrine above his martyr's tomb!
I have beheld the Ephesian's miracle—
Its columns strew the wilderness, and dwell
The hyaena and the jackal in their shade;
I have beheld Sophia's bright roofs swell
Their glittering mass i' the sun, and have survey'd
Its sanctuary the while the usurping Moslem pray'd;

CLIV

But thou, of temples old, or altars new,
Standest alone—with nothing like to thee—
Worthiest of God, the holy and the true,
Since Zion's desolation, when that He
Forsook his former city, what could be,
Of earthly structures, in his honour piled,
Of a sublimer aspect?   Majesty,
Power, Glory, Strength, and Beauty, all are aisled
In this eternal ark of worship undefiled.

CLV

Enter; its grandeur overwhelms thee not;
And why? it is not lessen'd; but thy mind,
Expanded by the genius of the spot,
Has grown colossal, and can only find
A fit abode wherein appear enshrined
Thy hopes of immortality; and thou
Shalt one day, if found worthy, so defined,
See thy God face to face, as thou dost now
His Holy of Holies, nor be blasted by his brow.

[1] The castle of St. Angelo.   [2] The church of St. Peter's

CLVI

Thou movest—but increasing with the advance,
Like climbing some great Alp, which still doth rise,
Deceived by its gigantic elegance;
Vastness which grows—but grows to harmonize—
All musical in its immensities;
Rich marbles—richer painting—shrines where flame
The lamps of gold—and haughty dome which vies
In air with Earth's chief structures, though their frame
Sits on the firm-set ground—and this the clouds must claim.

CLVII

Thou seest not all; but piecemeal thou must break,
To separate contemplation, the great whole;
And as the ocean many bays will make,
That ask the eye—so here condense thy soul
To more immediate objects, and control
Thy thoughts until thy mind hath got by heart
Its eloquent proportions, and unroll
In mighty graduations, part by part,
The glory which at once upon thee did not dart,

CLVIII

Not by its fault—but thine: Our outward sense
Is but of gradual grasp—and as it is
That what we have of feeling most intense
Outstrips our faint expression; even so this
Outshining and o'erwhelming edifice
Fools our fond gaze, and greatest of the great
Defies at first our nature's littleness,
Till, growing with its growth, we thus dilate
Our spirits to the size of that they contemplate.

CLIX

Then pause, and be enlighten'd; there is more
In such a survey than the sating gaze
Of wonder pleased, or awe which would adore
The worship of the place, or the mere praise
Of art and its great masters, who could raise
What former time, nor skill, nor thought could plan;
The fountain of sublimity displays
Its depth, and thence may draw the mind of man
Its golden sands, and learn what great conceptions can.

CLX

Or, turning to the Vatican, go see
Laocoön's torture dignifying pain—
A father's love and mortal's agony
With an immortal's patience blending:—Vain
The struggle; vain, against the coiling strain
And gripe, and deepening of the dragon's grasp,
The old man's clench: the long envenom'd chain
Rivets the living links,—the enormous asp
Enforces pang on pang, and stifles gasp on gasp.

CLXI

Or view the Lord of the unerring bow,
The God of life, and poesy, and light—
The Sun in human limbs array'd, and brow
All radiant from his triumph in the fight;
The shaft hath just been shot—the arrow bright
With an immortal's vengeance; in his eye
And nostril beautiful disdain, and might
And majesty, flash their full lightnings by,
Developing in that one glance the Deity.

CLXII

But in his delicate form—a dream of Love,
Shaped by some solitary nymph, whose breast
Long'd for a deathless lover from above,
And madden'd in that vision—are exprest
All that ideal beauty ever bless'd
The mind with in its most unearthly mood,
When each conception was a heavenly guest—
A ray of immortality—and stood,
Starlike, around, until they gather'd to a god!

CLXIII

And if it be Prometheus stole from Heaven
The fire which we endure, it was repaid
By him to whom the energy was given
Which this poetic marble hath array'd
With an eternal glory—which, if made
By human hands, is not of human thought;
And Time himself hath hallow'd it, nor laid
One ringlet in the dust—nor hath it caught
A tinge of years, but breathes the flame with which 'twas
wrought.

CLXIV

But where is he, the Pilgrim of my song,
The being who upheld it through the past?
Methinks he cometh late and tarries long.
He is no more—these breathings are his last;
His wanderings done, his visions ebbing fast,
And he himself as nothing:—if he was
Aught but a phantasy, and could be class'd
With forms which live and suffer—let that pass—
His shadow fades away into Destruction's mass,

CLXV

Which gathers shadow, substance, life, and all
That we inherit in its mortal shroud,
And spreads the dim and universal pall
Through which all things grow phantoms; and the cloud
Between us sinks and all which ever glow'd,
Till Glory's self is twilight, and displays
A melancholy halo scarce allow'd
To hover on the verge of darkness; rays
Sadder than saddest night, for they distract the gaze,

CLXVI

And send us prying into the abyss,
To gather what we shall be when the frame
Shall be resolved to something less than this
Its wretched essence; and to dream of fame,
And wipe the dust from off the idle name
We never more shall hear,—but never more,
Oh, happier thought! can we be made the same:
It is enough in sooth that *once* we bore
These fardels of the heart—the heart whose sweat was gore.

CLXVII

Hark! forth from the abyss a voice proceeds,[1]
A long low distant murmur of dread sound,
Such as arises when a nation bleeds
With some deep and immedicable wound;
Through storm and darkness yawns the rending ground,
The gulf is thick with phantoms, but the chief
Seems royal still, though with her head discrown'd,
And pale, but lovely, with maternal grief
She clasps a babe, to whom her breast yields no relief.

[1] [This and the five succeeding stanzas refer to the death in childbed of
Princess Charlotte, 5th November 1817.]

CLXVIII

Scion of chiefs and monarchs, where art thou?
Fond hope of many nations, art thou dead?
Could not the grave forget thee, and lay low
Some less majestic, less beloved head?
In the sad midnight, while thy heart still bled,
The mother of a moment, o'er thy boy,
Death hush'd that pang for ever: with thee fled
The present happiness and promised joy
Which fill'd the imperial isles so full it seem'd to cloy.

CLXIX

Peasants bring forth in safety.—Can it be,
Oh thou that wert so happy, so adored!
Those who weep not for kings shall weep for thee,
And Freedom's heart, grown heavy, cease to hoard
Her many griefs for ONE; for she had pour'd
Her orisons for thee, and o'er thy head
Beheld her Iris.—Thou, too, lonely lord,
And desolate consort—vainly wert thou wed!
The husband of a year! the father of the dead!

CLXX

Of sackcloth was thy wedding garment made;
Thy bridal's fruit is ashes: in the dust
The fair-hair'd Daughter of the Isles is laid,
The love of millions! How we did intrust
Futurity to her! and, though it must
Darken above our bones, yet fondly deem'd
Our children should obey her child, and bless'd
Her and her hoped-for seed, whose promise seem'd
Like stars to shepherds' eyes:—'twas but a meteor beam'd.

CLXXI

Woe unto us, not her; for she sleeps well:
The fickle reek of popular breath, the tongue
Of hollow counsel, the false oracle,
Which from the birth of monarchy hath rung
Its knell in princely ears, till the o'erstrung
Nations have arm'd in madness, the strange fate [1]
Which tumbles mightiest sovereigns, and hath flung
Against their blind omnipotence a weight
Within the opposing scale, which crushes soon or late,—

[1] Mary died on the scaffold; Elizabeth of a broken heart; Charles V a hermit; Louis XIV a bankrupt in means and glory; Cromwell of anxiety; and, 'the greatest is behind,' Napoleon lives a prisoner. To these sovereigns a long but superfluous list might be added of names equally illustrious and unhappy.

CLXXII

These might have been her destiny; but no,
Our hearts deny it: and so young, so fair,
Good without effort, great without a foe;
But now a bride and mother—and now *there*!
How many ties did that stern moment tear!
From thy Sire's to his humblest subject's breast
Is link'd the electric chain of that despair,
Whose shock was as an earthquake's, and opprest
The land which loved thee so that none could love thee best.

CLXXIII

Lo, Nemi![1] navell'd in the woody hills
So far, that the uprooting wind which tears
The oak from his foundation, and which spills
The ocean o'er its boundary, and bears
Its foam against the skies, reluctant spares
The oval mirror of thy glassy lake;
And, calm as cherish'd hate, its surface wears
A deep cold settled aspect nought can shake,
All coil'd into itself and round, as sleeps the snake.

CLXXIV

And near Albano's scarce divided waves
Shine from a sister valley;—and afar
The Tiber winds, and the broad ocean laves
The Latian coast where sprang the Epic war,
'Arms and the Man,' whose reascending star
Rose o'er an empire:—but beneath thy right
Tully reposed from Rome;—and where yon bar
Of girdling mountains intercepts the sight
The Sabine farm was till'd, the weary bard's delight.[2]

CLXXV

But I forget.—My Pilgrim's shrine is won,
And he and I must part,—so let it be,—
His task and mine alike are nearly done;
Yet once more let us look upon the sea;
The midland ocean breaks on him and me,

[1] The village of Nemi was near the Arician retreat of Egeria, and, from the shades which embosomed the temple of Diana, has preserved to this day its distinctive appellation of *The Grove*. Nemi is but an evening's ride from the comfortable inn of Albano.

[2] The whole declivity of the Alban hill is of unrivalled beauty, and from the convent on the highest point, which has succeeded to the temple of the Latian Jupiter, the prospect embraces all the objects alluded to in this stanza; the Mediterranean; the whole scene of the latter half of the Aeneid, and the coast from beyond the mouth of the Tiber to the headland of Circaeum and the Cape of Terracina.

And from the Alban Mount we now behold
Our friend of youth, that ocean, which when we
Beheld it laſt by Calpe's rock unfold
Those waves, we follow'd on till the dark Euxine roll'd

CLXXVI

Upon the blue Symplegades: long years—
Long, though not very many, since have done
Their work on both; some suffering and some tears
Have left us nearly where we had begun:
Yet not in vain our mortal race hath run,
We have had our reward—and it is here;
That we can yet feel gladden'd by the sun,
And reap from earth, sea, joy almoſt as dear
As if there were no man to trouble what is clear.

CLXXVII

Oh! that the Desert were my dwelling-place,
With one fair Spirit for my miniſter,
That I might all forget the human race,
And, hating no one, love but only her!
Ye Elements!—in whose ennobling ſtir
I feel myself exalted—Can ye not
Accord me such a being?   Do I err
In deeming such inhabit many a spot?
Though with them to converse can rarely be our lot.

Need for a Pure "ennobling" Love.

CLXXVIII

There is a pleasure in the pathless woods,
There is a rapture on the lonely shore,
There is society, where none intrudes,
By the deep Sea, and music in its roar:
I love not Man the less, but Nature more,
From these our interviews, in which I ſteal
From all I may be, or have been before,
To mingle with the Universe, and feel
What I can ne'er express, yet cannot all conceal.

ESSENCE OF POEM

CLXXIX

Roll on, thou deep and dark blue Ocean—roll!
Ten thousand fleets sweep over thee in vain;
Man marks the earth with ruin—his control
Stops with the shore;—upon the watery plain
The wrecks are all thy deed, nor doth remain

A shadow of man's ravage, save his own,
When, for a moment, like a drop of rain,
He sinks into thy depths with bubbling groan,
Without a grave, unknell'd, uncoffin'd, and unknown.

CLXXX

His steps are not upon thy paths,—thy fields
Are not a spoil for him,—thou dost arise
And shake him from thee; the vile strength he wields
For earth's destruction thou dost all despise,
Spurning him from thy bosom to the skies,
And send'st him, shivering in thy playful spray
And howling, to his Gods, where haply lies
His petty hope in some near port or bay,
And dashest him again to earth:—there let him lay.

CLXXXI

The armaments which thunder-strike the walls
Of rock-built cities, bidding nations quake,
And monarchs tremble in their capitals,
The oak leviathans, whose huge ribs make
Their clay creator the vain title take
Of lord of thee, and arbiter of war;
These are thy toys, and, as the snowy flake,
They melt into thy yeast of waves, which mar
Alike the Armada's pride, or spoils of Trafalgar.

CLXXXII

Thy shores are empires, changed in all save thee—
Assyria, Greece, Rome, Carthage, what are they?
Thy waters wasted them while they were free,
And many a tyrant since; their shores obey
The stranger, slave, or savage; their decay
Has dried up realms to deserts:—not so thou,
Unchangeable save to thy wild waves' play—
Time writes no wrinkle on thine azure brow—
Such as creation's dawn beheld, thou rollest now.

CLXXXIII

Thou glorious mirror, where the Almighty's form
Glasses itself in tempests; in all time,
Calm or convulsed—in breeze, or gale, or storm,
Icing the pole, or in the torrid clime
Dark-heaving;—boundless, endless, and sublime—

The image of Eternity—the throne
Of the Invisible; even from out thy slime
The monsters of the deep are made; each zone
Obeys thee; thou goest forth, dread, fathomless, alone.

CLXXXIV

And I have loved thee, Ocean! and my joy
Of youthful sports was on thy breast to be
Borne, like thy bubbles, onward: from a boy
I wanton'd with thy breakers—they to me
Were a delight; and if the freshening sea
Made them a terror—'twas a pleasing fear,
For I was as it were a child of thee,
And trusted to thy billows far and near,
And laid my hand upon thy mane—as I do here.

CLXXXV

My task is done—my song hath ceased—my theme
Has died into an echo; it is fit
The spell should break of this protracted dream,
The torch shall be extinguish'd which hath lit
My midnight lamp—and what is writ, is writ,—
Would it were worthier! but I am not now
That which I have been—and my visions flit
Less palpably before me—and the glow
Which in my spirit dwelt is fluttering, faint, and low.

CLXXXVI

Farewell! a word that must be, and hath been—
A sound which makes us linger;—yet—farewell!
Ye! who have traced the Pilgrim to the scene
Which is his last, if in your memories dwell
A thought which once was his, if on ye swell
A single recollection, not in vain
He wore his sandal-shoon, and scallop-shell;
Farewell! with *him* alone may rest the pain,
If such there were—with *you*, the moral of his strain!

THE GIAOUR

A FRAGMENT OF A TURKISH TALE

One fatal remembrance—one sorrow that throws
Its bleak shade alike o'er our joys and our woes—
To which Life nothing darker nor brighter can bring,
For which joy hath no balm—and affliction no sting.

MOORE.

TO

SAMUEL ROGERS, ESQ.

AS A SLIGHT BUT MOST SINCERE TOKEN

OF ADMIRATION OF HIS GENIUS,

RESPECT FOR HIS CHARACTER,

AND GRATITUDE FOR HIS FRIENDSHIP

THIS PRODUCTION IS INSCRIBED

BY HIS OBLIGED

AND AFFECTIONATE SERVANT,

BYRON.

London, May 1813.

ADVERTISEMENT

The tale which these disjointed fragments present is founded upon circumstances now less common in the East than formerly; either because the ladies are more circumspect than in the 'olden time,' or because the Christians have better fortune, or less enterprise. The story, when entire, contained the adventures of a female slave, who was thrown, in the Mussulman manner, into the sea for infidelity, and avenged by a young Venetian, her lover, at the time the Seven Islands were possessed by the Republic of Venice, and soon after the Arnauts were beaten back from the Morea, which they had ravaged for some time subsequent to the Russian invasion. The desertion of the Mainotes, on being refused the plunder of Misitra, led to the abandonment of that enterprise, and to the desolation of the Morea, during which the cruelty exercised on all sides was unparalleled even in the annals of the faithful.

THE GIAOUR

No breath of air to break the wave
That rolls below the Athenian's grave,
That tomb [1] which, gleaming o'er the cliff
First greets the homeward-veering skiff,
High o'er the land he saved in vain:
When shall such hero live again?

*   *   *   *   *

Fair clime! where every season smiles
Benignant o'er those blessed isles,
Which, seen from far Colonna's height
Make glad the heart that hails the sight,
And lend to loneliness delight.
There mildly dimpling, Ocean's cheek
Reflects the tints of many a peak
Caught by the laughing tides that lave
These Edens of the eastern wave:
And if at times a transient breeze
Break the blue crystal of the seas,
Or sweep one blossom from the trees,
How welcome is each gentle air
That wakes and wafts the odours there!
For there—the Rose o'er crag or vale,
Sultana of the Nightingale, [2]
The maid for whom his melody,
His thousand songs are heard on high,
Blooms blushing to her lover's tale:
His queen, the garden queen, his Rose,
Unbent by winds, unchill'd by snows,
Far from the winters of the west,
By every breeze and season blest,
Returns the sweets by nature given
In softest incense back to heaven;
And grateful yields that smiling sky
Her fairest hue and fragrant sigh.
And many a summer flower is there,
And many a shade that love might share,

[1] A tomb above the rocks on the promontory, by some supposed the sepulchre of Themistocles.
[2] The attachment of the nightingale to the rose is a well-known Persian fable. If I mistake not, the 'Bulbul of a thousand tales' is one of his appellations.

151

And many a grotto, meant for rest,
That holds the pirate for a guest;
Whose bark in sheltering cove below
Lurks for the passing peaceful prow,
Till the gay mariner's guitar [1]
Is heard, and seen the evening star;
Then stealing with the muffled oar
Far shaded by the rocky shore,
Rush the night-prowlers on the prey,
And turn to groans his roundelay.
Strange—that where Nature loved to trace
As if for Gods, a dwelling place,
And every charm and grace hath mix'd
Within the paradise she fix'd,
There man, enamour'd of distress,
Should mar it into wilderness,
And trample, brute-like, o'er each flower
That tasks not one laborious hour;
Nor claims the culture of his hand
To bloom along the fairy land,
But springs as to preclude his care,
And sweetly woos him—but to spare!
Strange—that where all is peace beside,
There passion riots in her pride,
And lust and rapine wildly reign
To darken o'er the fair domain.
It is as though the fiends prevail'd
Against the seraphs they assail'd,
And, fix'd on heavenly thrones, should dwell
The free inheritors of hell;
So soft the scene, so form'd for joy,
So curst the tyrants that destroy!
He who hath bent him o'er the dead
Ere the first day of death is fled,
The first dark day of nothingness,
The last of danger and distress,
(Before Decay's effacing fingers
Have swept the lines where beauty lingers,)
And mark'd the mild angelic air,
The rapture of repose that's there,
The fix'd yet tender traits that streak
The languor of the placid cheek,
And—but for that sad shrouded eye,

[1] The guitar is the constant amusement of the Greek sailor by night; with a steady fair wind, and during a calm, it is accompanied always by the voice, and often by dancing.

That fires not, wins not, weeps not, now,
And but for that chill, changeless brow,
Where cold Obstruction's apathy [1]
Appals the gazing mourner's heart,
As if to him it could impart
The doom he dreads, yet dwells upon;
Yes, but for these and these alone,
Some moments, ay, one treacherous hour,
He still might doubt the tyrant's power;
So fair, so calm, so softly seal'd,
The first, last look by death reveal'd! [2]
Such is the aspect of this shore;
'Tis Greece, but living Greece no more!
So coldly sweet, so deadly fair,
We start, for soul is wanting there.
Hers is the loveliness in death,
That parts not quite with parting breath;
But beauty with that fearful bloom,
That hue which haunts it to the tomb,
Expression's last receding ray,
A gilded halo hovering round decay,
The farewell beam of Feeling past away!
Spark of that flame, perchance of heavenly birth,
Which gleams, but warms no more its cherish'd earth!

Clime of the unforgotten brave!
Whose land from plain to mountain-cave
Was Freedom's home or Glory's grave!
Shrine of the mighty! can it be,
That this is all remains of thee?
Approach, thou craven crouching slave:
Say, is not this Thermopylae?
These waters blue that round you lave,
Oh servile offspring of the free—
Pronounce what sea, what shore is this?
The gulf, the rock of Salamis!

[1] 'Ay, but to die and go we know not where,
    To lie in cold obstruction?'   *Measure for Measure.*

[2] I trust that few of my readers have ever had an opportunity of witnessing
what is here attempted in description, but those who have will probably retain a
painful remembrance of that singular beauty which pervades, with few exceptions, the features of the dead, a few hours, and but for a few hours, after 'the
spirit is not there.' It is to be remarked in cases of violent death by gun-shot
wounds, the expression is always that of languor, whatever the natural energy of
the sufferer's character: but in death from a stab the countenance preserves its
traits of feeling or ferocity, and the mind its bias, to the last.

These scenes, their story not unknown,
Arise, and make again your own;
Snatch from the ashes of your sires
The embers of their former fires;
And he who in the strife expires
Will add to theirs a name of fear
That Tyranny shall quake to hear,
And leave his sons a hope, a fame,
They too will rather die than shame:
For Freedom's battle once begun,
Bequeath'd by bleeding Sire to Son,
Though baffled oft is ever won.
Bear witness, Greece, thy living page,
Attest it many a deathless age!
While kings, in dusty darkness hid,
Have left a nameless pyramid,
Thy heroes, though the general doom
Hath swept the column from their tomb,
A mightier monument command,
The mountains of their native land!
There points thy Muse to stranger's eye
The graves of those that cannot die!
'Twere long to tell, and sad to trace,
Each step from splendour to disgrace;
Enough—no foreign foe could quell
Thy soul, till from itself it fell;
Yes!   Self-abasement paved the way
To villain-bonds and despot sway.

What can he tell who treads thy shore?
No legend of thine olden time,
No theme on which the muse might soar
High as thine own in days of yore,
When man was worthy of thy clime.
The hearts within thy valleys bred,
The fiery souls that might have led
Thy sons to deeds sublime,
Now crawl from cradle to the grave,
Slaves—nay the bondsmen of a slave,[1]
And callous, save to crime;
Stain'd with each evil that pollutes
Mankind, where least above the brutes;
Without even savage virtue blest,
Without one free or valiant breast,

[1] Athens is the property of the Kislar Aga (the slave of the seraglio and guardian of the women), who appoints the Waywode. A pander and eunuch —these are not polite, yet true appellations—now *governs* the *governor* of Athens!

Still to the neighbouring ports they waft
Proverbial wiles, and ancient craft;
In this the subtle Greek is found,
For this, and this alone, renown'd.
In vain might Liberty invoke
The spirit to its bondage broke,
Or raise the neck that courts the yoke:
No more her sorrows I bewail,
Yet this will be a mournful tale,
And they who listen may believe,
Who heard it first had cause to grieve.

*   *   *   *   *

Far, dark, along the blue sea glancing,
The shadows of the rocks advancing
Start on the fisher's eye like boat
Of island-pirate or Mainote;
And fearful for his light caique,
He shuns the near but doubtful creek:
Though worn and weary with his toil,
And cumber'd with his scaly spoil,
Slowly, yet strongly, plies the oar,
Till Port Leone's safer shore
Receives him by the lovely light
That best becomes an Eastern night.

*   *   *   *   *

Who thundering comes on blackest steed,
With slacken'd bit and hoof of speed?
Beneath the clattering iron's sound
The cavern'd echoes wake around
In lash for lash, and bound for bound;
The foam that streaks the courser's side
Seems gather'd from the ocean-tide:
Though weary waves are sunk to rest,
There 's none within his rider's breast;
And though to-morrow's tempest lower,
'Tis calmer than thy heart, young Giaour!
I know thee not, I loathe thy race,
But in thy lineaments I trace
What time shall strengthen, not efface:
Though young and pale, that sallow front
Is scathed by fiery passion's brunt;
Though bent on earth thine evil eye,
As meteor-like thou glidest by,
Right well I view and deem thee one
Whom Othman's sons should slay or shun.

On—on he hasten'd, and he drew
My gaze of wonder as he flew:
Though like a demon of the night
He pass'd, and vanish'd from my sight,
His aspect and his air impress'd
A troubled memory on my breast,
And long upon my startled ear
Rung his dark courser's hoofs of fear.
He spurs his steed; he nears the steep,
That, jutting, shadows o'er the deep;
He winds around; he hurries by;
The rock relieves him from mine eye;
For well I ween unwelcome he
Whose glance is fix'd on those that flee;
And not a star but shines too bright
On him who takes such timeless flight.
He wound along; but ere he pass'd
One glance he snatch'd, as if his last,
A moment check'd his wheeling steed,
A moment breathed him from his speed,
A moment on his stirrup stood—
Why looks he o'er the olive wood?
The crescent glimmers on the hill,
The Mosque's high lamps are quivering still:
Though too remote for sound to wake
In echoes of the far tophaike,[1]
The flashes of each joyous peal
Are seen to prove the Moslem's zeal,
To-night, set Rhamazani's sun;
To-night, the Bairam feast's begun;
To-night—but who and what art thou
Of foreign garb and fearful brow?
And what are these to thine or thee,
That thou should'st either pause or flee?

He stood—some dread was on his face,
Soon Hatred settled in its place:
It rose not with the reddening flush
Of transient Anger's hasty blush,
But pale as marble o'er the tomb,
Whose ghastly whiteness aids its gloom.
His brow was bent, his eye was glazed;
He raised his arm, and fiercely raised

[1] 'Tophaike,' musket.—The Bairam is announced by the cannon at sunset;
the illumination of the mosques, and the firing of all kinds of small arms, loaded
with *ball*, proclaim it during the night.

And sternly shook his hand on high,
As doubting to return or fly:
Impatient of his flight delay'd,
Here loud his raven charger neigh'd—
Down glanced that hand, and grasp'd his blade;
That sound had burst his waking dream,
As Slumber starts at owlet's scream.
The spur hath lanced his courser's sides;
Away, away, for life he rides:
Swift as the hurl'd on high jerreed [1]
Springs to the touch his startled steed;
The rock is doubled, and the shore
Shakes with the clattering tramp no more;
The crag is won, no more is seen
His Christian crest and haughty mien.
'Twas but an instant he restrain'd
That fiery barb so sternly rein'd;
'Twas but a moment that he stood,
Then sped as if by death pursued:
But in that instant o'er his soul
Winters of Memory seemed to roll,
And gather in that drop of time
A life of pain, an age of crime.
O'er him who loves, or hates, or fears
Such moment pours the grief of years:
What felt *he* then, at once opprest
By all that most distracts the breast?
That pause, which ponder'd o'er his fate,
Oh, who its dreary length shall date!
Though in Time's record nearly nought,
It was Eternity to Thought!
For infinite as boundless space
The thought that Conscience must embrace,
Which in itself can comprehend
Woe without name, or hope, or end.

The hour is past, the Giaour is gone;
And did he fly or fall alone?
Woe to that hour he came or went!
The curse for Hassan's sin was sent
To turn a palace to a tomb;

[1] 'Jerreed,' or 'Djetrid,' a blunted Turkish javelin, which is darted from horse-back with great force and precision. It is a favourite exercise of the Mussul-mans; but I know not if it can be called a *manly* one, since the most expert in the art are the Black Eunuchs of Constantinople. I think, next to these, a Mamlouk at Smyrna was the most skilful that came within my observation.

He came, he went, like the Simoom,[1]
That harbinger of fate and gloom,
Beneath whose widely-wasting breath
The very cypress droops to death—
Dark tree, still sad when others' grief is fled,
The only constant mourner o'er the dead!

The steed is vanish'd from the stall;
No serf is seen in Hassan's hall;
The lonely Spider's thin gray pall
Waves slowly widening o'er the wall;
The Bat builds in his Haram bower
And in the fortress of his power
The Owl usurps the beacon-tower;
The wild-dog howls o'er the fountain's brim,
With baffled thirst, and famine, grim;
For the stream has shrunk from its marble bed,
Where the weeds and the desolate dust are spread.
'Twas sweet of yore to see it play
And chase the sultriness of day,
As springing high the silver dew
In whirls fantastically flew,
And flung luxurious coolness round
The air, and verdure o'er the ground.
'Twas sweet, when cloudless stars were bright,
To view the wave of watery light,
And hear its melody by night.
And oft had Hassan's Childhood play'd
Around the verge of that cascade;
And oft upon his mother's breast
That sound had harmonized his rest;
And oft had Hassan's Youth along
Its bank been soothed by Beauty's song;
And softer seem'd each melting tone
Of Music mingled with its own.
But ne'er shall Hassan's Age repose
Along the brink at Twilight's close:
The stream that fill'd that font is fled—
The blood that warm'd his heart is shed!
And here no more shall human voice
Be heard to rage, regret, rejoice.
The last sad note that swell'd the gale
Was woman's wildest funeral wail:

[1] The blast of the desert, fatal to everything living, and often alluded to in eastern poetry.

That quench'd in silence, all is still,
But the lattice that flaps when the wind is shrill:
Though raves the gust, and floods the rain,
No hand shall close its clasp again.
On desert sands 'twere joy to scan
The rudest steps of fellow man,
So here the very voice of Grief
Might wake an Echo like relief—
At least 'twould say, 'All are not gone;
There lingers Life, though but in one'—
For many a gilded chamber 's there,
Which Solitude might well forbear;
Within that dome as yet Decay
Hath slowly work'd her cankering way—
But gloom is gather'd o'er the gate,
Nor there the Fakir's self will wait;
Nor there will wandering Dervise stay,
For bounty cheers not his delay;
Nor there will weary stranger halt
To bless the sacred 'bread and salt.' [1]
Alike must Wealth and Poverty
Pass heedless and unheeded by,
For Courtesy and Pity died
With Hassan on the mountain side.
His roof, that refuge unto men,
Is Desolation's hungry den.
The guest flies the hall, and the vassal from labour
Since his turban was cleft by the infidel's sabre! [2]

*   *   *   *   *

I hear the sound of coming feet,
But not a voice mine ear to greet;
More near—each turban I can scan,
And silver-sheathed ataghan; [3]
The foremost of the band is seen
An Emir by his garb of green: [4]

---

[1] To partake of food, to break bread and salt with your host, ensures the safety of the guest: even though an enemy, his person from that moment is sacred.

[2] I need hardly observe, that Charity and Hospitality are the first duties enjoined by Mahomet; and to say truth, very generally practised by his disciples. The first praise that can be bestowed on a chief, is a panegyric on his bounty; the next, on his valour.

[3] The ataghan, a long dagger worn with pistols in the belt, in a metal scabbard, generally of silver; and, among the wealthier, gilt, or of gold.

[4] Green is the privileged colour of the prophet's numerous pretended descendants; with them, as here, faith (the family inheritance) is supposed to supersede the necessity of good works: they are the worst of a very indifferent brood.

'Ho! who art thou?'—'This low salam [1]
Replies of Moslem faith I am.'—
'The burthen ye so gently bear
Seems one that claims your utmost care,
And, doubtless, holds some precious freight,
My humble bark would gladly wait.'

'Thou speakest sooth: thy skiff unmoor,
And waft us from the silent shore;
Nay, leave the sail still furl'd, and ply
The nearest oar that's scatter'd by,
And midway to those rocks where sleep
The channel'd waters dark and deep.
Rest from your task—so—bravely done,
Our course has been right swiftly run;
Yet 'tis the longest voyage, I trow,
That one of—   *   *   *
      *   *   *   *   *'

Sullen it plunged, and slowly sank,
The calm wave rippled to the bank;
I watch'd it as it sank, methought
Some motion from the current caught
Bestirr'd it more,—'twas but the beam
That checker'd o'er the living stream:
I gazed, till vanishing from view
Like lessening pebble it withdrew;
Still less and less, a speck of white
That gemm'd the tide, then mock'd the sight;
And all its hidden secrets sleep,
Known but to Genii of the deep,
Which, trembling in their coral caves,
They dare not whisper to the waves.
      *   *   *   *   *

As rising on its purple wing
The insect-queen [2] of eastern spring,
O'er emerald meadows of Kashmeer
Invites the young pursuer near,
And leads him on from flower to flower
A weary chase and wasted hour,
Then leaves him, as it soars on high,
With panting heart and tearful eye:

[1] 'Salam aleikoum! aleikoum salam!' peace be with you; be with you peace—
the salutation reserved for the faithful: to a Christian, 'Urlarula,' a good
journey; or 'saban hiresem, saban serula,' good morn, good even; and sometimes, 'may your end be happy,' are the usual salutes.
[2] The blue-winged butterfly of Kashmeer, the most rare and beautiful of the
species.

So Beauty lures the full-grown child,
With hue as bright, and wing as wild;
A chase of idle hopes and fears,
Begun in folly, closed in tears.
If won, to equal ills betray'd,
Woe waits the insect and the maid;
A life of pain, the loss of peace,
From infant's play, and man's caprice:
The lovely toy so fiercely sought
Hath lost its charm by being caught,
For every touch that woo'd its stay
Hath brush'd its brightest hues away,
Till charm, and hue, and beauty gone,
'Tis left to fly or fall alone.
With wounded wing, or bleeding breast,
Ah! where shall either victim rest?
Can this with faded pinion soar
From rose to tulip as before?
Or Beauty, blighted in an hour,
Find joy within her broken bower?
No: gayer insects fluttering by
Ne'er droop the wing o'er those that die,
And lovelier things have mercy shown
To every failing but their own,
And every woe a tear can claim
Except an erring sister's shame.

          *   *   *   *   *

The Mind, that broods o'er guilty woes,
Is like the Scorpion girt by fire,
In circle narrowing as it glows,
The flames around their captive close,
Till inly search'd by thousand throes,
And maddening in her ire,
One sad and sole relief she knows,
The sting she nourish'd for her foes,
Whose venom never yet was vain,
Gives but one pang, and cures all pain,
And darts into her desperate brain;
So do the dark in soul expire,
Or live like Scorpion girt by fire; [1]

[1] Alluding to the dubious suicide of the scorpion, so placed for experiment by gentle philosophers. Some maintain that the position of the sting, when turned towards the head, is merely a convulsive movement; but others have actually brought in the verdict *felo de se*. The scorpions are surely interested in a speedy decision of the question; as, if once fairly established as insect Catos, they will probably be allowed to live as long as they think proper, without being martyred for the sake of an hypothesis.

So writhes the mind Remorse hath riven,
Unfit for earth, undoom'd for heaven,
Darkness above, despair beneath,
Around it flame, within it death!

  *   *   *   *   *

Black Hassan from the Haram flies,
Nor bends on woman's form his eyes;
The unwonted chase each hour employs,
Yet shares he not the hunter's joys.
Not thus was Hassan wont to fly
When Leila dwelt in his Serai.
Doth Leila there no longer dwell?
That tale can only Hassan tell:
Strange rumours in our city say
Upon that eve she fled away
When Rhamazan's [1] last sun was set,
And flashing from each minaret
Millions of lamps proclaim'd the feast
Of Bairam through the boundless East.
'Twas then she went as to the bath,
Which Hassan vainly search'd in wrath;
For she was flown her master's rage
In likeness of a Georgian page,
And far beyond the Moslem's power
Had wrong'd him with the faithless Giaour.
Somewhat of this had Hassan deem'd;
But still so fond, so fair she seem'd,
Too well he trusted to the slave
Whose treachery deserved a grave:
And on that eve had gone to mosque,
And thence to feast in his kiosk.
Such is the tale his Nubians tell,
Who did not watch their charge too well;
But others say, that on that night,
By pale Phingari's [2] trembling light,
The Giaour upon his jet-black steed
Was seen, but seen alone to speed
With bloody spur along the shore,
Nor maid nor page behind him bore.

  *   *   *   *   *

Her eye's dark charm 'twere vain to tell,
But gaze on that of the Gazelle,
It will assist thy fancy well;

[1] The cannon at sunset close the Rhamazan.
[2] 'Phingari,' the moon.

As large, as languishingly dark,
But Soul beam'd forth in every spark
That darted from beneath the lid,
Bright as the jewel of Giamschid.[1]
Yea, *Soul*, and should our prophet say
That form was nought but breathing clay,
By Alla! I would answer nay;
Though on Al-Sirat's [2] arch I stood,
Which totters o'er the fiery flood,
With Paradise within my view,
And all his Houris beckoning through.
Oh! who young Leila's glance could read
And keep that portion of his creed,
Which saith that woman is but dust,
A soulless toy for tyrants's lust? [3]
On her might Muftis gaze, and own
That through her eye the Immortal shone;
On her fair cheek's unfading hue
The young pomegranate's [4] blossoms strew
Their bloom in blushes ever new;
Her hair in hyacinthine [5] flow,
When left to roll its folds below,
As midst her handmaids in the hall
She stood superior to them all,
Hath swept the marble where her feet
Gleam'd whiter than the mountain sleet
Ere from the cloud that gave it birth
It fell, and caught one stain of earth.

[1] The celebrated fabulous ruby of Sultan Giamschid, the embellisher of Istakhar; from its splendour, named Schebgerag, 'the torch of night,' also 'the cup of the sun,' etc. In the first edition, 'Giamschid' was written as a word of three syllables, so D'Herbelot has it; but I am told Richardson reduces it to a dissyllable, and writes 'Jamshid.' I have left in the text the orthography of the one with the pronunciation of the other.

[2] Al-Sirat, the bridge of breadth, narrower than the thread of a famished spider, and sharper than the edge of a sword, over which the Mussulmans must *skate* into Paradise, to which it is the only entrance; but this is not the worst, the river beneath being hell itself, into which, as may be expected, the unskilful and tender of foot contrive to tumble with a 'facilis descensus Averni,' not very pleasing in prospect to the next passenger. There is a shorter cut downwards for the Jews and Christians.

[3] A vulgar error: the Koran allots at least a third of Paradise to well-behaved women; but by far the greater number of Mussulmans interpret the text their own way, and exclude their moieties from heaven. Being enemies to Platonics, they cannot discern 'any fitness of things' in the souls of the other sex, conceiving them to be superseded by the houris.

[4] An oriental simile, which may, perhaps, though fairly stolen, be deemed 'plus Arabe qu'en Arabie.'

[5] Hyacinthine, in Arabic 'Sunbul'; as common a thought in the eastern poets as it was among the Greeks.

II—* F 487

The cygnet nobly walks the water;
So moved on earth Circassia's daughter,
The loveliest bird of Franguestan! [1]
As rears her crest the ruffled Swan,
And spurns the wave with wings of pride,
When pass the steps of stranger man
Along the banks that bound her tide;
Thus rose fair Leila's whiter neck:—
Thus arm'd with beauty would she check
Intrusion's glance, till Folly's gaze
Shrunk from the charms it meant to praise.
Thus high and graceful was her gait;
Her heart as tender to her mate;
Her mate—stern Hassan, who was he?
Alas! that name was not for thee!

    *   *   *   *   *

Stern Hassan hath a journey ta'en!
With twenty vassals in his train,
Each arm'd, as best becomes a man,
With arquebuss and ataghan;
The chief before, as deck'd for war,
Bears in his belt the scimitar
Stain'd with the best of Arnaut blood,
When in the pass the rebels stood,
And few return'd to tell the tale
Of what befell in Parne's vale.
The pistols which his girdle bore
Were those that once a pasha wore,
Which still, though gemm'd and boss'd with gold,
Even robbers tremble to behold.
'Tis said he goes to woo a bride
More true than her who left his side;
The faithless slave that broke her bower,
And, worse than faithless, for a Giaour!

    *   *   *   *   *

The sun's last rays are on the hill,
And sparkle in the fountain rill,
Whose welcome waters, cool and clear,
Draw blessings from the mountaineer:
Here may the loitering merchant Greek
Find that repose 'twere vain to seek
In cities lodged too near his lord,
And trembling for his secret hoard—
Here may he rest where none can see,
In crowds a slave, in deserts free;

[1] 'Franguestan,' Circassia.

And with forbidden wine may stain
The bowl a Moslem must not drain.

    *   *   *   *   *

The foremost Tartar 's in the gap,
Conspicuous by his yellow cap;
The rest in lengthening line the while
Wind slowly through the long defile:
Above, the mountain rears a peak,
Where vultures whet the thirsty beak,
And theirs may be a feast to-night,
Shall tempt them down ere morrow's light;
Beneath, a river's wintry stream
Has shrunk before the summer beam,
And left a channel bleak and bare,
Save shrubs that spring to perish there:
Each side the midway path there lay
Small broken crags of granite gray,
By time, or mountain lightning, riven
From summits clad in mists of heaven;
For where is he that hath beheld
The peak of Liakura unveil'd?

    *   *   *   *   *

They reach the grove of pine at last:
'Bismillah! [1] now the peril 's past;
For yonder view the opening plain,
And there we 'll prick our steeds amain:'
The Chiaus spake, and as he said,
A bullet whistled o'er his head;
The foremost Tartar bites the ground!
Scarce had they time to check the rein,
Swift from their steeds the riders bound;
But three shall never mount again:
Unseen the foes that gave the wound,
The dying asked revenge in vain.
With steel unsheath'd, and carbine bent,
Some o'er their courser's harness leant,
Half shelter'd by the steed;
Some fly behind the nearest rock,
And there await the coming shock,
Nor tamely stand to bleed
Beneath the shaft of foes unseen,
Who dare not quit their craggy screen.
Stern Hassan only from his horse
Disdains to light, and keeps his course,

---

[1] 'Bismillah,' in the name of God; the commencement of all the chapters of
the Koran but one, and of prayer and thanksgiving.

Till fiery flashes in the van
Proclaim too sure the robber-clan
Have well secured the only way
Could now avail the promised prey;
Then curl'd his very beard [1] with ire,
And glared his eye with fiercer fire:
'Though far and near the bullets hiss,
I 've 'scaped a bloodier hour than this.'
And now the foe their covert quit,
And call his vassals to submit;
But Hassan's frown and furious word
Are dreaded more than hostile sword,
Nor of his little band a man
Resign'd carbine or ataghan,
Nor raised the craven cry, Amaun! [2]
In fuller sight, more near and near,
The lately ambush'd foes appear,
And, issuing from the grove, advance
Some who on battle-charger prance.
Who leads them on with foreign brand,
Far flashing in his red right hand?
''Tis he! 'tis he! I know him now;
I know him by his pallid brow;
I know him by the evil eye [3]
That aids his envious treachery;
I know him by his jet-black barb:
Though now array'd in Arnaut garb,
Apostate from his own vile faith,
It shall not save him from the death:
'Tis he! well met in any hour,
Lost Leila's love, accursed Giaour!'

As rolls the river into ocean,
In sable torrent wildly streaming;
As the sea-tide's opposing motion,
In azure column proudly gleaming,
Beats back the current many a rood,
In curling foam and mingling flood,

[1] A phenomenon not uncommon with an angry Mussulman. In 1809, the Capitan Pacha's whiskers at a diplomatic audience were no less lively with indignation than a tiger cat's, to the horror of all the dragomans; the portentous mustachios twisted, they stood erect of their own accord, and were expected every moment to change their colour, but at last condescended to subside, which, probably, saved more heads than they contained hairs.

[2] 'Amaun,' quarter, pardon.

[3] The 'evil eye,' a common superstition in the Levant, and of which the imaginary effects are yet very singular on those who conceive themselves affected.

While eddying whirl, and breaking wave,
Roused by the blast of winter, rave;
Through sparkling spray, in thundering clash,
The lightnings of the waters flash
In awful whiteness o'er the shore,
That shines and shakes beneath the roar;
Thus—as the stream and ocean greet,
With waves that madden as they meet—
Thus join the bands, whom mutual wrong,
And fate, and fury, drive along.
The bickering sabres' shivering jar;
And pealing wide or ringing near
Its echoes on the throbbing ear,
The deathshot hissing from afar;
The shock, the shout, the groan of war,
Reverberate along that vale,
More suited to the shepherd's tale:
Though few the numbers—theirs the strife,
That neither spares nor speaks for life!
Ah! fondly youthful hearts can press,
To seize and share the dear caress:
But Love itself could never pant
For all that Beauty sighs to grant,
Which half the fervour Hate bestows
Upon the last embrace of foes,
When grappling in the fight they fold
Those arms that ne'er shall lose their hold:
Friends meet to part; Love laughs at faith;
True foes, once met, are join'd till death!

    *   *   *   *   *

With sabre shiver'd to the hilt,
Yet dripping with the blood he spilt;
Yet strain'd within the sever'd hand
Which quivers round that faithless brand;
His turban far behind him roll'd,
And cleft in twain its firmest fold;
His flowing robe by falchion torn,
And crimson as those clouds of morn
That, streak'd with dusky red, portend
The day shall have a stormy end;
A stain on every bush that bore
A fragment of his palampore,[1]
His breast with wounds unnumber'd riven,
His back to earth, his face to heaven,
Fall'n Hassan lies—his unclosed eye

[1] The flowered shawls generally worn by persons of rank.

Yet lowering on his enemy,
As if the hour that seal'd his fate
Surviving left his quenchless hate;
And o'er him bends that foe with brow
As dark as his that bled below.—

*   *   *   *   *

'Yes, Leila sleeps beneath the wave,
But his shall be a redder grave;
Her spirit pointed well the steel
Which taught that felon heart to feel.
He call'd the Prophet, but his power
Was vain against the vengeful Giaour:
He call'd on Alla—but the word
Arose unheeded or unheard.
Thou Paynim fool! could Leila's prayer
Be pass'd, and thine accorded there?
I watch'd my time, I leagued with these,
The traitor in his turn to seize;
My wrath is wreak'd, the deed is done,
And now I go—but go alone.'

*   *   *   *   *
*   *   *   *   *

The browsing camels' bells are tinkling:
His Mother look'd from her lattice high,
She saw the dews of eve besprinkling
The pasture green beneath her eye,
She saw the planets faintly twinkling:
''Tis twilight—sure his train is nigh.'
She could not rest in the garden-bower,
But gazed through the grate of his steepest tower:
'Why comes he not? his steeds are fleet,
Nor shrink they from the summer heat;
Why sends not the Bridegroom his promised gift:
Is his heart more cold, or his barb less swift?
Oh, false reproach! yon Tartar now
Has gain'd our nearest mountain's brow,
And warily the steep descends,
And now within the valley bends;
And he bears the gift at his saddle bow—
How could I deem his courser slow?
Right well my largess shall repay
His welcome speed, and weary way.'

The Tartar lighted at the gate,
But scarce upheld his fainting weight:
His swarthy visage spake distress,

But this might be from weariness;
His garb with sanguine spots was dyed,
But these might be from his courser's side;
He drew the token from his vest—
Angel of Death! 'tis Hassan's cloven crest!
His calpac [1] rent—his caftan red—
'Lady, a fearful bride thy Son hath wed:
Me, not from mercy, did they spare,
But this empurpled pledge to bear.
Peace to the brave! whose blood is spilt;
Woe to the Giaour! for his the guilt.'

    *   *   *   *   *

A turban [2] carved in coarsest stone,
A pillar with rank weeds o'ergrown,
Whereon can now be scarcely read
The Koran verse that mourns the dead,
Point out the spot where Hassan fell
A victim in that lonely dell.
There sleeps as true an Osmanlie
As e'er at Mecca bent the knee;
As ever scorn'd forbidden wine,
Or pray'd with face towards the shrine,
In orisons resumed anew
At solemn sound of 'Alla Hu!' [3]
Yet died he by a stranger's hand,
And stranger in his native land;
Yet died he as in arms he stood,
And unavenged, at least in blood.
But him the maids of Paradise
Impatient to their halls invite,
And the dark Heaven of Houris' eyes
On him shall glance for ever bright;
They come—their kerchiefs green they wave, [4]
And welcome with a kiss the brave!

---

[1] The calpac is the solid cap or centre part of the head-dress; the shawl is wound round it and forms the turban.

[2] The turban, pillar, and inscriptive verse, decorate the tombs of the Osmanlies, whether in the cemetery or the wilderness. In the mountains you frequently pass similar mementoes: and on inquiry you are informed that they record some victim of rebellion, plunder, or revenge.

[3] 'Alla Hu!' the concluding words of the muezzin's call to prayer from the highest gallery on the exterior of the minaret. On a still evening, when the muezzin has a fine voice, which is frequently the case, the effect is solemn and beautiful beyond all the bells in Christendom.

[4] The following is part of a battle song of the Turks: 'I see—I see a dark-eyed girl of Paradise, and she waves a handkerchief, a kerchief of green; and cries aloud, "Come, kiss me, for I love thee,"' etc.

Who falls in battle 'gainst a Giaour
Is worthiest an immortal bower.

*   *   *   *   *

But thou, false Infidel! shalt writhe
Beneath avenging Monkir's [1] scythe;
And from its torment 'scape alone
To wander round lost Eblis' throne;
And fire unquench'd, unquenchable,
Around, within, thy heart shall dwell!
Nor ear can hear nor tongue can tell
The tortures of that inward hell!
But first, on earth as vampire [2] sent,
Thy corse shall from its tomb be rent:
Then ghastly haunt thy native place,
And suck the blood of all thy race;
There from thy daughter, sister, wife,
At midnight drain the stream of life;
Yet loathe the banquet which perforce
Must feed thy livid living corse:
Thy victims ere they yet expire
Shall know the demon for their sire,
As cursing thee, thou cursing them,
The flowers are wither'd on the stem.
But one that for thy crime must fall,
The youngest, most beloved of all,
Shall bless thee with a *father's* name—
That word shall wrap thy heart in flame!
Yet must thou end thy task, and mark
Her cheek's last tinge, her eye's last spark,
And the last glassy glance must view
Which freezes o'er its lifeless blue;
Then with unhallow'd hand shall tear
The tresses of her yellow hair,

[1] Monkir and Nekir are the inquisitors of the dead, before whom the corpse undergoes a slight novitiate and preparatory training for damnation. If the answers are none of the clearest, he is hauled up with a scythe and thumped down with a red-hot mace till properly seasoned, with a variety of subsidiary probations. The office of these angels is no sinecure; there are but two, and the number of orthodox deceased being in a small proportion to the remainder, their hands are always full. See *Relig. Ceremon.* and Sale's *Koran.*

[2] The vampire superstition is still general in the Levant. Honest Tournefort tells a long story, which Mr. Southey, in the notes on *Thalaba*, quotes, about these 'Vroucolochas,' as he calls them. The Romaic term is 'Vardoulacha.' I recollect a whole family being terrified by the scream of a child, which they imagined must proceed from such a visitation. The Greeks never mention the word without horror. I find that 'Broucolokas' is an old legitimate Hellenic appellation—at least is so applied to Arsenius, who, according to the Greeks, was after his death animated by the Devil.—The moderns, however, use the word I mention.

Of which in life a lock when shorn
Affection's fondest pledge was worn,
But now is borne away by thee,
Memorial of thine agony!
Wet with thine own best blood shall drip [1]
Thy gnashing tooth and haggard lip;
Then stalking to thy sullen grave,
Go—and with Gouls and Afrits rave;
Till these in horror shrink away
From spectre more accursed than they!

* * * * *

'How name ye yon lone Caloyer?
His features I have scanned before
In mine own land: 'tis many a year,
Since, dashing by the lonely shore,
I saw him urge as fleet a steed
As ever served a horseman's need.
But once I saw that face, yet then
It was so mark'd with inward pain,
I could not pass it by again;
It breathes the same dark spirit now,
As death were stamp'd upon his brow.

''Tis twice three years at summer tide
Since first among our freres he came;
And here it soothes him to abide
For some dark deed he will not name.
But never at our vesper prayer,
Nor e'er before confession chair
Kneels he, nor recks he when arise
Incense or anthem to the skies,
But broods within his cell alone,
His faith and race alike unknown.
The sea from Paynim land he crost,
And here ascended from the coast;
Yet seems he not of Othman race,
But only Christian in his face:
I'd judge him some stray renegade,
Repentant of the change he made,
Save that he shuns our holy shrine,
Nor tastes the sacred bread and wine.
Great largess to these walls he brought,
And thus our abbot's favour bought;

[1] The freshness of the face, and the wetness of the lip with blood, are the never-failing signs of a vampire. The stories told in Hungary and Greece of these foul feeders are singular, and some of them most *incredibly* attested.

But were I prior, not a day
Should brook such stranger's further stay,
Or pent within our penance cell
Should doom him there for aye to dwell.
Much in his visions mutters he
Of maiden whelm'd beneath the sea;
Of sabres clashing, foemen flying,
Wrongs avenged, and Moslem dying.
On cliff he hath been known to stand,
And rave as to some bloody hand
Fresh sever'd from its parent limb,
Invisible to all but him,
Which beckons onward to his grave,
And lures to leap into the wave.'

   *   *   *   *   *
   *   *   *   *   *

Dark and unearthly is the scowl
That glares beneath his dusky cowl:
The flash of that dilating eye
Reveals too much of times gone by;
Though varying, indistinct its hue
Oft will his glance the gazer rue,
For in it lurks that nameless spell,
Which speaks, itself unspeakable,
A spirit yet unquell'd and high,
That claims and keeps ascendency;
And like the bird whose pinions quake,
But cannot fly the gazing snake,
Will others quail beneath his look,
Nor 'scape the glance they scarce can brook.
From him the half-affrighted Friar
When met alone would fain retire,
As if that eye and bitter smile
Transferr'd to others fear and guile:
Not oft to smile descendeth he,
And when he doth 'tis sad to see
That he but mocks at Misery.
How that pale lip will curl and quiver!
Then fix once more as if for ever;
As if his sorrow or disdain
Forbade him e'er to smile again.
Well were it so—such ghastly mirth
From joyaunce ne'er derived its birth.
But sadder still it were to trace
What once were feelings in that face:

Time hath not yet the features fix'd,
But brighter traits with evil mix'd;
And there are hues not always faded,
Which speak a mind not all degraded
Even by the crimes through which it waded:
The common crowd but see the gloom
Of wayward deeds, and fitting doom;
The close observer can espy
A noble soul, and lineage high:
Alas! though both bestow'd in vain,
Which Grief could change, and Guilt could stain,
It was no vulgar tenement
To which such lofty gifts were lent,
And still with little less than dread
On such the sight is riveted.
The roofless cot, decay'd and rent,
Will scarce delay the passer by;
The tower by war or tempest bent,
While yet may frown one battlement,
Demands and daunts the stranger's eye;
Each ivied arch, and pillar lone,
Pleads haughtily for glories gone!

'His floating robe around him folding,
Slow sweeps he through the column'd aisle;
With dread beheld, with gloom beholding
The rites that sanctify the pile.
But when the anthem shakes the choir,
And kneel the monks, his steps retire;
By yonder lone and wavering torch
His aspect glares within the porch;
There will he pause till all is done—
And hear the prayer, but utter none.
See—by the half-illumined wall
His hood fly back, his dark hair fall,
That pale brow wildly wreathing round,
As if the Gorgon there had bound
The sablest of the serpent-braid
That o'er her fearful forehead stray'd:
For he declines the convent oath,
And leaves those locks unhallow'd growth,
But wears our garb in all beside;
And, not from piety but pride,
Gives wealth to walls that never heard
Of his one holy vow nor word.

Lo!—mark ye, as the harmony
Peals louder praises to the sky,
That livid cheek, that stony air
Of mix'd defiance and despair!
Saint Francis, keep him from the shrine!
Else may we dread the wrath divine
Made manifest by awful sign.
If ever evil angel bore
The form of mortal, such he wore:
By all my hope of sins forgiven,
Such looks are not of earth nor heaven!'

To love the softest hearts are prone,
But such can ne'er be all his own;
Too timid in his woes to share,
Too meek to meet, or brave despair;
And sterner hearts alone may feel
The wound that time can never heal.
The rugged metal of the mine
Must burn before its surface shine,
But plunged within the furnace-flame,
It bends and melts—though still the same;
Then temper'd to thy want, or will,
'Twill serve thee to defend or kill;
A breast-plate for thine hour of need,
Or blade to bid thy foeman bleed;
But if a dagger's form it bear,
Let those who shape its edge, beware!
Thus passion's fire, and woman's art,
Can turn and tame the sterner heart;
From these its form and tone are ta'en,
And what they make it, must remain,
But break—before it bend again.

        *   *   *   *   *
        *   *   *   *   *

If solitude succeed to grief,
Release from pain is slight relief;
The vacant bosom's wilderness
Might thank the pang that made it less.
We loathe what none are left to share:
Even bliss—'twere woe alone to bear;
The heart once left thus desolate
Must fly at last for ease—to hate.
It is as if the dead could feel
The icy worm around them steal,

And shudder, as the reptiles creep
To revel o'er their rotting sleep,
Without the power to scare away
The cold consumers of their clay!
It is as if the desert-bird,[1]
Whose beak unlocks her bosom's stream
To still her famish'd nestlings' scream,
Nor mourns a life to them transferr'd,
Should rend her rash devoted breast,
And find them flown her empty nest.
The keenest pangs the wretched find
Are rapture to the dreary void,
The leafless desert of the mind,
The waste of feelings unemploy'd.
Who would be doom'd to gaze upon
A sky without a cloud or sun?
Less hideous far the tempest's roar
Than ne'er to brave the billows more—
Thrown, when the war of winds is o'er,
A lonely wreck on fortune's shore,
'Mid sullen calm, and silent bay,
Unseen to drop by dull decay;—
Better to sink beneath the shock
Than moulder piecemeal on the rock!

*   *   *   *   *

'Father! thy days have pass'd in peace,
'Mid counted beads, and countless prayer;
To bid the sins of others cease,
Thyself without a crime or care,
Save transient ills that all must bear,
Has been thy lot from youth to age;
And thou wilt bless thee from the rage
Of passions fierce and uncontroll'd,
Such as thy penitents unfold,
Whose secret sins and sorrows rest
Within thy pure and pitying breast.
My days, though few, have pass'd below
In much of joy, but more of woe;
Yet still in hours of love or strife,
I've 'scaped the weariness of life:
Now leagued with friends, now girt by foes,
I loathed the languor of repose.
Now nothing left to love or hate,
No more with hope or pride elate,

[1] The pelican is, I believe, the bird so libelled, by the imputation of feeding her chickens with her blood.

I 'd rather be the thing that crawls
Most noxious o'er a dungeon's walls,
Than pass my dull, unvarying days,
Condemn'd to meditate and gaze.
Yet, lurks a wish within my breast
For rest—but not to feel 'tis rest.
Soon shall my fate that wish fulfil;
And I shall sleep without the dream
Of what I was, and would be still,
Dark as to thee my deeds may seem:
My memory now is but the tomb
Of joys long dead; my hope, their doom:
Though better to have died with those
Than bear a life of lingering woes.
My spirit shrunk not to sustain
The searching throes of ceaseless pain;
Nor sought the self-accorded grave
Of ancient fool and modern knave:
Yet death I have not fear'd to meet;
And in the field it had been sweet,
Had danger woo'd me on to move
The slave of glory, not of love.
I 've braved it—not for honour's boast;
I smile at laurels won or lost;
To such let others carve their way,
For high renown, or hireling pay:
But place again before my eyes
Aught that I deem a worthy prize,
The maid I love, the man I hate;
And I will hunt the steps of fate,
To save or slay, as these require,
Through rending steel, and rolling fire:
Nor needst thou doubt this speech from one
Who would but do—what he *hath* done.
Death is but what the haughty brave,
The weak must bear, the wretch must crave;
Then let Life go to him who gave:
I have not quail'd to danger's brow
When high and happy—need I *now*?
　　*　　　　*　　　　*　　　　*
'I loved her, Friar! nay, adored—
But these are words that all can use—
I proved it more in deed than word;
There 's blood upon that dinted sword,
A stain its steel can never lose:
'Twas shed for her, who died for me,

It warmed the heart of one abhorr'd:
Nay, start not—no—nor bend thy knee,
Nor midst my sins such act record;
Thou wilt absolve me from the deed,
For he was hostile to thy creed!
The very name of Nazarene
Was wormwood to his Paynim spleen.
Ungrateful fool! since but for brands
Well wielded in some hardy hands,
And wounds by Galileans given,
The surest pass to Turkish heaven,
For him his Houris still might wait
Impatient at the Prophet's gate.
I loved her—love will find its way
Through paths where wolves would fear to prey;
And if it dares enough, 'twere hard
If passion met not some reward—
No matter how, or where, or why,
I did not vainly seek, nor sigh:
Yet sometimes, with remorse, in vain
I wish she had not loved again.
She died—I dare not tell thee how;
But look—'tis written on my brow!
There read of Cain the curse and crime,
In characters unworn by time:
Still, ere thou dost condemn me, pause;
Not mine the act, though I the cause.
Yet did he but what I had done
Had she been false to more than one.
Faithless to him, he gave the blow;
But true to me, I laid him low:
Howe'er deserved her doom might be,
Her treachery was truth to me:
To me she gave her heart, that all
Which tyranny can ne'er enthrall;
And I, alas! too late to save!
Yet all I then could give, I gave,
'Twas some relief, our foe a grave.
His death sits lightly; but her fate
Has made me—what thou well may'st hate.
His doom was seal'd—he knew it well,
Warn'd by the voice of stern Taheer,
Deep in whose darkly boding ear [1]

[1] This superstition of a second hearing (for I never met with downright second sight in the East) fell once under my own observation. On my third journey to Cape Colonna, early in 1811, as we passed through the defile that

The deathshot peal'd of murder near,
As filed the troop to where they fell!
He died too in the battle broil,
A time that heeds nor pain nor toil;
One cry to Mahomet for aid,
One prayer to Alla all he made:
He knew and cross'd me in the fray—
I gazed upon him where he lay,
And watch'd his spirit ebb away:
Though pierced like pard by hunters' steel,
He felt not half that now I feel.
I search'd, but vainly search'd, to find
The workings of a wounded mind;
Each feature of that sullen corse
Betray'd his rage, but no remorse.
Oh, what had Vengeance given to trace
Despair upon his dying face!

leads from the hamlet between Keratia and Colonna, I observed Dervish Tahiri riding rather out of the path, and leaning his head upon his hand, as if in pain. I rode up and inquired. 'We are in peril,' he answered. 'What peril? we are not now in Albania, nor in the passes to Ephesus, Messalunghi, or Lepanto; there are plenty of us, well armed, and the Choriates have not courage to be thieves.'—'True, Affendi, but nevertheless the shot is ringing in my ears.'— 'The shot! not a tophaike has been fired this morning.'—'I hear it, notwithstanding—Bom—Bom—as plainly as I hear your voice.'—'Psha!'—'As you please, Affendi; it if is written, so will it be.'—I left this quick-eared predestinarian, and rode up to Basili, his Christian compatriot, whose ears, though not at all prophetic, by no means relished the intelligence. We all arrived at Colonna, remained some hours, and returned leisurely, saying a variety of brilliant things, in more languages than spoiled the building of Babel, upon the mistaken seer. Romaic, Arnaout, Turkish, Italian, and English were all exercised, in various conceits, upon the unfortunate Mussulman. While we were contemplating the beautiful prospect, Dervish was occupied about the columns. I thought he was deranged into an antiquarian, and asked him if he had become a 'Palaocastro' man? 'No,' said he, 'but these pillars will be useful in making a stand,' and added other remarks, which at least evinced his own belief in his troublesome faculty of *forebearing*. On our return to Athens we heard from Leoné (a prisoner set ashore some days after) of the intended attack of the Mainotes. I was at some pains to question the man, and he described the dresses, arms, and marks of the horses of our party so accurately, that, with other circumstances, we could not doubt of *his* having been in 'villanous company,' and ourselves in a bad neighbourhood. Dervish became a soothsayer for life, and I dare say is now hearing more musketry than ever will be fired, to the great refreshment of the Arnaouts of Berat, and his native mountains. I shall mention one trait more of this singular race. In March 1811 a remarkably stout and active Arnaout came (I believe the fiftieth on the same errand) to offer himself as an attendant, which was declined: 'Well, Affendi,' quoth he, 'may you live!—you would have found me useful. I shall leave the town for the hills to-morrow, in the winter I return, perhaps you will then receive me.'—Dervish, who was present, remarked as a thing of course, and of no consequence, 'in the mean time he will join the Klephtes' (robbers), which was true to the letter. If not cut off, they come down in the winter, and pass it unmolested in some town, where they are often as well known as their exploits.

The late repentance of that hour,
When Penitence hath lost her power
To tear one terror from the grave,
And will not soothe, and cannot save.

   *   *   *   *   *

'The cold in clime are cold in blood,
Their love can scarce deserve the name:
But mine was like the lava flood
That boils in Aetna's breast of flame.
I cannot prate in puling strain
Of ladye-love, and beauty's chain:
If changing cheek, and scorching vein,
Lips taught to writhe, but not complain,
If bursting heart, and madd'ning brain,
And daring deed, and vengeful steel,
And all that I have felt, and feel,
Betoken love—that love was mine,
And shown by many a bitter sign.
'Tis true, I could not whine nor sigh,
I knew but to obtain or die.
I die—but first I have possess'd,
And come what may, I *have been* blest.
Shall I the doom I sought upbraid?
No—reft of all, yet undismay'd
But for the thought of Leila slain,
Give me the pleasure with the pain,
So would I live and love again.
I grieve, but not, my holy guide!
For him who dies, but her who died:
She sleeps beneath the wandering wave—
Ah! had she but an earthly grave,
This breaking heart and throbbing head
Should seek and share her narrow bed.
She was a form of life and light,
That, seen, became a part of sight;
And rose, where'er I turn'd mine eye,
The Morning-star of Memory!

'Yes, Love indeed is light from heaven;
A spark of that immortal fire
With angels shared, by Alla given,
To lift from earth our low desire.
Devotion wafts the mind above,
But Heaven itself descends in love;
A feeling from the Godhead caught,
To wean from self each sordid thought;

A Ray of him who form'd the whole;
A Glory circling round the soul!
I grant *my* love imperfect, all
That mortals by the name miscall;
Then deem it evil, what thou wilt;
But say, oh say, *hers* was not guilt!
She was my life's unerring light:
That quench'd, what beam shall break my night?
Oh! would it shone to lead me still,
Although to death or deadliest ill!
Why marvel ye, if they who lose
This present joy, this future hope,
No more with sorrow meekly cope;
In phrensy then their fate accuse:
In madness do those fearful deeds
That seem to add but guilt to woe?
Alas! the breast that inly bleeds
Hath nought to dread from outward blow:
Who falls from all he knows of bliss,
Cares little into what abyss.
Fierce as the gloomy vulture's now
To thee, old man, my deeds appear:
I read abhorrence on thy brow,
And this too was I born to bear!
'Tis true, that, like that bird of prey,
With havoc have I mark'd my way:
But this was taught me by the dove,
To die—and know no second love.
This lesson yet hath man to learn,
Taught by the thing he dares to spurn:
The bird that sings within the brake,
The swan that swims upon the lake,
One mate, and one alone, will take.
And let the fool still prone to range,
And sneer on all who cannot change,
Partake his jest with boasting boys;
I envy not his varied joys,
But deem such feeble, heartless man,
Less than yon solitary swan;
Far, far beneath the shallow maid
He left believing and betray'd.
Such shame at least was never mine—
Leila! each thought was only thine!
My good, my guilt, my weal, my woe,
My hope on high—my all below.
Earth holds no other like to thee,

Or, if it doth, in vain for me:
For worlds I dare not view the dame
Resembling thee, yet not the same.
The very crimes that mar my youth,
This bed of death—attest my truth!
'Tis all too late—thou wert, thou art
The cherish'd madness of my heart!

'And she was lost—and yet I breathed,
But not the breath of human life:
A serpent round my heart was wreathed,
And stung my every thought to strife.
Alike all time, abhorr'd all place,
Shuddering I shrunk from Nature's face,
Where every hue that charm'd before
The blackness of my bosom wore.
The rest thou dost already know,
And all my sins, and half my woe.
But talk no more of penitence;
Thou see'st I soon shall part from hence:
And if thy holy tale were true,
The deed that's done canst *thou* undo?
Think me not thankless—but this grief
Looks not to priesthood for relief.[1]
My soul's estate in secret guess:
But wouldst thou pity more, say less.
When thou canst bid my Leila live,
Then will I sue thee to forgive;
Then plead my cause in that high place
Where purchased masses proffer grace.
Go, when the hunter's hand hath wrung
From forest-cave her shrieking young,
And calm the lonely lioness:
But soothe not—mock not *my* distress!

'In earlier days, and calmer hours,
When heart with heart delights to blend,
Where bloom my native valley's bowers
I had—Ah! have I now?—a friend!
To him this pledge I charge thee send,
Memorial of a youthful vow;
I would remind him of my end:

[1] The monk's sermon is omitted. It seems to have had so little effect upon the patient, that it could have no hopes from the reader. It may be sufficient to say, that it was of a customary length (as may be perceived from the interruptions and uneasiness of the patient), and was delivered in the usual tone of all orthodox preachers.

Though souls absorb'd like mine allow
Brief thought to distant friendship's claim,
Yet dear to him my blighted name.
'Tis strange—he prophesied my doom,
And I have smiled—I then could smile—
When Prudence would his voice assume,
And warn—I reck'd not what—the while:
But now remembrance whispers o'er
Those accents scarcely mark'd before.
Say—that his bodings came to pass,
And he will start to hear their truth,
And wish his words had not been sooth:
Tell him, unheeding as I was,
Through many a busy bitter scene
Of all our golden youth had been,
In pain, my faltering tongue had tried
To bless his memory ere I died;
But Heaven in wrath would turn away,
If Guilt should for the guiltless pray.
I do not ask him not to blame,
Too gentle he to wound my name;
And what have I to do with fame?
I do not ask him not to mourn,
Such cold request might sound like scorn;
And what than friendship's manly tear
May better grace a brother's bier?
But bear this ring, his own of old,
And tell him—what thou dost behold!
The wither'd frame, the ruin'd mind,
The wrack by passion left behind,
A shrivelled scroll, a scatter'd leaf,
Sear'd by the autumn blast of grief!

           *   *   *   *   *

'Tell me no more of fancy's gleam,
No, father, no, 'twas not a dream;
Alas! the dreamer first must sleep,
I only watch'd, and wish'd to weep;
But could not, for my burning brow
Throbb'd to the very brain as now:
I wish'd but for a single tear,
As something welcome, new, and dear:
I wish'd it then, I wish it still;
Despair is stronger than my will.
Waste not thine orison, despair
Is mightier than thy pious prayer:

I would not, if I might, be blest;
I want no paradise, but rest.
'Twas then, I tell thee, father! then
I saw her; yes, she lived again;
And shining in her white symar,[1]
As through yon pale gray cloud the star
Which now I gaze on, as on her,
Who look'd and looks far lovelier;
Dimly I view its trembling spark;
To-morrow's night shall be more dark;
And I, before its rays appear,
That lifeless thing the living fear.
I wander, father! for my soul
Is fleeting towards the final goal.
I saw her, friar! and I rose
Forgetful of our former woes;
And rushing from my couch, I dart,
And clasp her to my desperate heart;
I clasp—what is it that I clasp?
No breathing form within my grasp,
No heart that beats reply to mine,
Yet, Leila! yet the form is thine!
And art thou, dearest, changed so much,
As meet my eye, yet mock my touch?
Ah! were thy beauties e'er so cold,
I care not; so my arms enfold
The all they ever wish'd to hold.
Alas! around a shadow prest
They shrink upon my lonely breast;
Yet still 'tis there! In silence stands,
And beckons with beseeching hands!
With braided hair, and bright-black eye—
I knew 'twas false—she could not die!
But he is dead! within the dell
I saw him buried where he fell;
He comes not, for he cannot break
From earth; why then art thou awake?
They told me wild waves roll'd above
The face I view, the form I love;
They told me—'twas a hideous tale!
I'd tell it, but my tongue would fail:
If true, and from thine ocean-cave
Thou com'st to claim a calmer grave,
Oh! pass thy dewy fingers o'er
This brow that then will burn no more;

[1] 'Symar,' a shroud.

Or place them on my hopeless heart:
But, shape or shade! whate'er thou art,
In mercy ne'er again depart!
Or farther with thee bear my soul
Than winds can waft or waters roll!

    *   *   *   *   *

'Such is my name, and such my tale.
Confessor! to thy secret ear
I breathe the sorrows I bewail,
And thank thee for the generous tear
This glazing eye could never shed.
Then lay me with the humblest dead,
And, save the cross above my head,
Be neither name nor emblem spread,
By prying stranger to be read,
Or stay the passing pilgrim's tread.'

He pass'd—nor of his name and race
Hath left a token or a trace,
Save what the father must not say
Who shrived him on his dying day:
This broken tale was all we knew
Of her he loved, or him he slew.[1]

---

[1] The circumstance to which the above story relates was not very uncommon in Turkey. A few years ago the wife of Muchtar Pacha complained to his father of his son's supposed infidelity; he asked with whom, and she had the barbarity to give in a list of the twelve handsomest women in Yanina. They were seized, fastened up in sacks, and drowned in the lake the same night! One of the guards who was present informed me that not one of the victims uttered a cry, or showed a symptom of terror at so sudden a 'wrench from all we know, from all we love.' The fate of Phrosine, the fairest of this sacrifice, is the subject of many a Romaic and Arnaout ditty. The story in the text is one told of a young Venetian many years ago, and now nearly forgotten. I heard it by accident recited by one of the coffee-house story-tellers who abound in the Levant, and sing or recite their narratives. The additions and interpolations by the translator will be easily distinguished from the rest, by the want of Eastern imagery; and I regret that my memory has retained so few fragments of the original. For the contents of some of the notes I am indebted partly to D'Herbelot, and partly to that most Eastern, and, as Mr. Weber justly entitles it, 'sublime tale,' the *Caliph Vathek.* I do not know from what source the author of that singular volume may have drawn his materials; some of his incidents are to be found in the *Bibliothèque Orientale*; but for correctness of costume, beauty of description, and power of imagination, it far surpasses all European imitations; and bears such marks of originality, that those who have visited the East will find some difficulty in believing it to be more than a translation.

THE BRIDE OF ABYDOS

A TURKISH TALE

Had we never loved so kindly,
Had we never loved so blindly,
Never met or never parted,
We had ne'er been broken-hearted.

BURNS.

THE BRIDE OF ABYDOS

I

KNOW ye the land where the cypress and myrtle
Are emblems of deeds that are done in their clime,
Where the rage of the vulture, the love of the turtle,
Now melt into sorrow, now madden to crime?
Know ye the land of the cedar and vine,
Where the flowers ever blossom, the beams ever shine;
Where the light wings of Zephyr, oppress'd with perfume,
Wax faint o'er the gardens of Gúl [1] in her bloom;
Where the citron and olive are fairest of fruit,
And the voice of the nightingale never is mute.
Where the tints of the earth, and the hues of the sky,
In colour though varied, in beauty may vie,
And the purple of Ocean is deepest in dye;
Where the virgins are soft as the roses they twine,
And all, save the spirit of man, is divine?
'Tis the clime of the East; 'tis the land of the Sun—
Can he smile on such deeds as his children have done? [2]
Oh! wild as the accents of lovers' farewell
Are the hearts which they bear, and the tales which they tell.

II

Begirt with many a gallant slave,
Apparell'd as becomes the brave,
Awaiting each his lord's behest
To guide his steps, or guard his rest,
Old Giaffir sate in his Divan:
Deep thought was in his aged eye;
And though the face of Mussulman
Not oft betrays to standers by
The mind within, well skill'd to hide
All but unconquerable pride,
His pensive cheek and pondering brow
Did more than he was wont avow.

III

'Let the chamber be clear'd.'—The train disappear'd—
'Now call me the chief of the Haram guard.'
With Giaffir is none but his only son,
And the Nubian awaiting the sire's award.

---

[1] 'Gúl,' the rose.
[2] 'Souls made of fire, and children of the Sun,
  With whom revenge is virtue.'
                                        YOUNG's *Revenge*.

'Haroun—when all the crowd that wait
Are pass'd beyond the outer gate,
(Woe to the head whose eye beheld
My child Zuleika's face unveil'd!)
Hence, lead my daughter from her tower;
Her fate is fix'd this very hour:
Yet not to her repeat my thought;
By me alone be duty taught!'

'Pacha! to hear is to obey.'
No more must slave to despot say—
Then to the tower had ta'en his way,
But here young Selim silence brake,
First lowly rendering reverence meet;
And downcast look'd, and gently spake,
Still standing at the Pacha's feet:
For son of Moslem must expire,
Ere dare to sit before his sire!

'Father! for fear that thou shouldst chide
My sister, or her sable guide,
Know—for the fault, if fault there be,
Was mine, then fall thy frowns on me—
So lovelily the morning shone,
That—let the old and weary sleep—
I could not; and to view alone
The fairest scenes of land and deep,
With none to listen and reply
To thoughts with which my heart beat high
Were irksome—for whate'er my mood,
In sooth I love not solitude;
I on Zuleika's slumber broke,
And, as thou knowest that for me
Soon turns the Haram's grating key,
Before the guardian slaves awoke
We to the cypress groves had flown,
And made earth, main, and heaven our own!
There linger'd we, beguiled too long
With Mejnoun's tale, or Sadi's song; [1]
Till I, who heard the deep tambour [2]
Beat thy Divan's approaching hour,
To thee, and to my duty true,
Warn'd by the sound, to greet thee flew:

[1] Mejnoun and Leila, the Romeo and Juliet of the East. Sadi, the moral
poet of Persia.
[2] 'Tambour,' Turkish drum, which sounds at sunrise, noon, and twilight.

But there Zuleika wanders yet—
Nay, Father, rage not—nor forget
That none can pierce that secret bower
But those who watch the women's tower.'

IV

'Son of a slave'—the Pacha said—
'From unbelieving mother bred,
Vain were a father's hope to see
Aught that beseems a man in thee.
Thou, when thine arm should bend the bow,
And hurl the dart, and curb the steed,
Thou, Greek in soul if not in creed,
Must pore where babbling waters flow,
And watch unfolding roses blow.
Would that yon orb, whose matin glow
Thy listless eyes so much admire,
Would lend thee something of his fire!
Thou, who wouldst see this battlement
By Christian cannon piecemeal rent;
Nay, tamely view old Stambol's wall
Before the dogs of Moscow fall,
Nor strike one stroke for life and death
Against the curs of Nazareth!
Go—let thy less than woman's hand
Assume the distaff—not the brand.
But, Haroun!—to my daughter speed:
And hark—of thine own head take heed—
If thus Zuleika oft takes wing—
Thou see'st yon bow—it hath a string!'

V

No sound from Selim's lip was heard,
At least that met old Giaffir's ear,
But every frown and every word
Pierced keener than a Christian's sword,
'Son of a slave!—reproach'd with fear!
Those gibes had cost another dear.
Son of a slave!—and *who* my sire?'
Thus held his thoughts their dark career;
And glances ev'n of more than ire
Flash forth, then faintly disappear.
Old Giaffir gazed upon his son

And started; for within his eye
He read how much his wrath had done;
He saw rebellion there begun:
'Come hither, boy—what, no reply?
I mark thee—and I know thee too:
But there be deeds thou dar'st not do:
But if thy beard had manlier length,
And if thy hand had skill and strength,
I 'd joy to see thee break a lance,
Albeit against my own perchance.'

As sneeringly these accents fell,
On Selim's eye he fiercely gazed:
That eye return'd him glance for glance,
And proudly to his sire's was raised,
Till Giaffir's quail'd and shrunk askance—
And why—he felt, but durst not tell.
'Much I misdoubt this wayward boy
Will one day work me more annoy:
I never loved him from his birth,
And—but his arm is little worth,
And scarcely in the chase could cope
With timid fawn or antelope,
Far less would venture into strife
Where man contends for fame and life—
I would not trust that look or tone:
No—nor the blood so near my own.
That blood—he hath not heard—no more—
I 'll watch him closer than before.
He is an Arab [1] to my sight,
Or Christian crouching in the fight—
But hark!—I hear Zuleika's voice;
Like Houris' hymn it meets mine ear:
She is the offspring of my choice;
Oh! more than ev'n her mother dear,
With all to hope, and nought to fear—
My Peri! ever welcome here!
Sweet as the desert fountain's wave
To lips just cool'd in time to save—
Such to my longing sight art thou;
Nor can they waft to Mecca's shrine
More thanks for life, than I for thine.
Who blest thy birth, and bless thee now.'

[1] The Turks abhor the Arabs (who return the compliment a hundredfold) even
more than they hate the Christians.

VI

Fair, as the first that fell of womankind,
When on that dread yet lovely serpent smiling,
Whose image then was stamp'd upon her mind—
But once beguil'd—and ever more beguiling;
Dazzling, as that, oh! too transcendent vision
To Sorrow's phantom-peopled slumbers given,
When heart meets heart again in dreams Elysian,
And paints the lost on Earth revived in Heaven;
Soft, as the memory of buried love;
Pure, as the prayer which Childhood wafts above
Was she—the daughter of that rude old Chief,
Who met the maid with tears—but not of grief.

Who hath not proved how feebly words essay
To fix one spark of Beauty's heavenly ray?
Who doth not feel, until his failing sight
Faints into dimness with its own delight,
His changing cheek, his sinking heart confess
The might—the majesty of Loveliness?
Such was Zuleika—such around her shone
The nameless charms unmark'd by her alone;
The light of love, the purity of grace,
The mind, the Music [1] breathing from her face,
The heart whose softness harmonized the whole—
And, oh! that eye was in itself a Soul!

Her graceful arms in meekness bending
Across her gently-budding breast;
At one kind word those arms extending
To clasp the neck of him who blest
His child caressing and carest,

[1] This expression has met with objections. I will not refer to 'Him who hath not Music in his soul,' but merely request the reader to recollect, for ten seconds, the features of the woman whom he believes to be the most beautiful; and, if he then does not comprehend fully what is feebly expressed in the above line, I shall be sorry for us both. For an eloquent passage in the latest work of the first female writer of this, perhaps of any, age, on the analogy (and the immediate comparison excited by that analogy) between 'painting and music,' see *De l'Allemagne*, iii. 10 [by Mme de Staël]. And is not this connection still stronger with the original than the copy? With the colouring of Nature than of Art? After all, this is rather to be felt than described; still, I think there are some who will understand it, at least they would have done had they beheld the countenance whose speaking harmony suggested the idea; for this passage is not drawn from imagination but memory, that mirror which Affliction dashes to the earth, and looking down upon the fragments, only beholds the reflection multiplied!

Zuleika came—and Giaffir felt
His purpose half within him melt:
Not that against her fancied weal
His heart though stern could ever feel;
Affection chain'd her to that heart:
Ambition tore the links apart.

VII

'Zuleika! child of gentleness!
How dear this very day must tell,
When I forget my own distress,
In losing what I love so well,
To bid thee with another dwell:
Another! and a braver man
Was never seen in battle's van.
We Moslem reck not much of blood;
But yet the line of Carasman [1]
Unchanged, unchangeable hath stood
First of the bold Timariot bands
That won and well can keep their lands.
Enough that he who comes to woo
Is kinsman of the Bey Oglou:
His years need scarce a thought employ;
I would not have thee wed a boy.
And thou shalt have a noble dower:
And his and my united power
Will laugh to scorn the death-firman,
Which others tremble but to scan,
And teach the messenger [2] what fate
The bearer of such boon may wait.
And now thou know'st thy father's will;
All that thy sex hath need to know:
'Twas mine to teach obedience still—
The way to love, thy lord may show.'

---

[1] Carasman Oglou, or Kara Osman Oglou, is the principal landholder in Turkey; he governs Magnesia: those who, by a kind of feudal tenure, possess land on condition of service, are called Timariots: they serve as Spahis, according to the extent of territory, and bring a certain number into the field, generally cavalry.

[2] When a Pacha is sufficiently strong to resist, the single messenger, who is always the first bearer of the order for his death, is strangled instead, and sometimes five or six, one after the other on the same errand, by command of the refractory patient; if, on the contrary, he is weak or loyal, he bows, kisses the Sultan's respectable signature, and is bowstrung with great complacency. In 1810, several of these presents were exhibited in the niche of the Seraglio gate; among others, the head of the Pacha of Bagdat, a brave young man, cut off by treachery, after a desperate resistance.

VIII

In silence bow'd the virgin's head;
And if her eye was fill'd with tears
That stifled feeling dare not shed,
And changed her cheek from pale to red,
And red to pale, as through her ears
Those winged words like arrows sped,
What could such be but maiden fears?
So bright the tear in Beauty's eye,
Love half regrets to kiss it dry;
So sweet the blush of Bashfulness,
Even Pity scarce can wish it less!

Whate'er it was the sire forgot;
Or if remember'd, mark'd it not;
Thrice clapp'd his hands, and call'd his steed,[1]
Resign'd his gem-adorn'd chibouque,[2]
And mounting featly for the mead,
With Maugrabee[3] and Mamaluke,
His way amid his Delis took,[4]
To witness many an active deed
With sabre keen, or blunt jerreed.
The Kislar only and his Moors
Watch well the Haram's massy doors.

IX

His head was leant upon his hand,
His eye looked o'er the dark blue water
That swiftly glides and gently swells
Between the winding Dardanelles;
But yet he saw nor sea nor strand,
Nor even his Pacha's turban'd band
Mix in the game of mimic slaughter,
Careering cleave the folded felt[5]

[1] Clapping of the hands calls the servants. The Turks hate a superfluous expenditure of voice, and they have no bells.

[2] 'Chibouque,' the Turkish pipe, of which the amber mouthpiece, and sometimes the ball which contains the leaf, is adorned with precious stones, if in possession of the wealthier orders.

[3] 'Maugrabee,' Moorish mercenaries.

[4] 'Delis,' bravoes who form the forlorn hope of the cavalry, and always begin the action.

[5] A twisted fold of *felt* is used for scimitar practice by the Turks, and few but Mussulman arms can cut through it at a single stroke: sometimes a tough turban is used for the same purpose. The jerreed is a game of blunt javelins, animated and graceful.

With sabre stroke right sharply dealt;
Nor mark'd the javelin-darting crowd,
Nor heard their Ollahs [1] wild and loud—
He thought but of old Giaffir's daughter!

x

No word from Selim's bosom broke;
One sigh Zuleika's thought bespoke:
Still gazed he through the lattice grate,
Pale, mute, and mournfully sedate.
To him Zuleika's eye was turn'd;
But little from his aspect learn'd:
Equal her grief, yet not the same;
Her heart confess'd a gentler flame:
But yet that heart alarm'd or weak,
She knew not why, forbade to speak.
Yet speak she must—but when essay?
'How strange he thus should turn away!
Not thus we e'er before have met;
Not thus shall be our parting yet.'
Thrice paced she slowly through the room,
And watch'd his eye—it still was fixed:
She snatch'd the urn wherein was mix'd
The Persian Atar-gul's [2] perfume,
And sprinkled all its odours o'er
The pictured roof [3] and marble floor:
The drops, that through his glittering vest
The playful girl's appeal address'd,
Unheeded o'er his bosom flew,
As if that breast were marble too.
'What, sullen yet? it must not be—
Oh! gentle Selim, this from thee!'
She saw in curious order set
The fairest flowers of eastern land—
'He lov'd them once; may touch them yet,
If offer'd by Zuleika's hand.'
The childish thought was hardly breathed
Before the Rose was pluck'd and wreathed;

[1] 'Ollahs,' Alla il Allah, the 'Leilies,' as the Spanish poets call them, the sound is Ollah; a cry of which the Turks, for a silent people, are somewhat profuse. particularly during the jerreed, or in the chase, but mostly in battle. Their animation in the field, and gravity in the chamber, with their pipes and comboloios, form an amusing contrast.

[2] 'Atar-gul,' attar of roses. The Persian is the finest.

[3] The ceilings and wainscots, or rather walls, of the Mussulman apartments are generally painted, in great houses, with one eternal and highly coloured view of Constantinople, wherein the principal feature is a noble contempt of perspective; below, arms, scimitars, etc., are in general fancifully and not inelegantly disposed.

The next fond moment saw her seat
Her fairy form at Selim's feet:
'This rose to calm my brother's cares
A message from the Bulbul [1] bears;
It says to-night he will prolong
For Selim's ear his sweetest song;
And though his note is somewhat sad,
He'll try for once a strain more glad,
With some faint hope his alter'd lay
May sing these gloomy thoughts away.

XI

'What! not receive my foolish flower?
Nay then I am indeed unblest:
On me can thus thy forehead lower?
And know'st thou not who loves thee best?
Oh, Selim dear! oh, more than dearest!
Say, is it me thou hat'st or fearest?
Come, lay thy head upon my breast,
And I will kiss thee into rest,
Since words of mine, and songs must fail,
Ev'n from my fabled nightingale.
I knew our sire at times was stern,
But this from thee had yet to learn:
Too well I know he loves thee not;
But is Zuleika's love forgot?
Ah! deem I right? the Pacha's plan—
This kinsman Bey of Carasman
Perhaps may prove some foe of thine.
If so, I swear by Mecca's shrine,
If shrines that ne'er approach allow
To woman's step admit her vow,
Without thy free consent, command,
The Sultan should not have my hand!
Think'st thou that I could bear to part
With thee, and learn to halve my heart?
Ah! were I sever'd from thy side,
Where were thy friend—and who my guide?
Years have not seen, Time shall not see,
The hour that tears my soul from thee:

[1] It has been much doubted whether the notes of this 'Lover of the rose' are sad or merry; and Mr. Fox's remarks on the subject have provoked some learned controversy as to the opinions of the ancients on the subject. I dare not venture a conjecture on the point, though a little inclined to the 'errare mallem,' etc., if Mr. Fox was mistaken.

Ev'n Azrael,[1] from his deadly quiver
When flies that shaft, and fly it must,
That parts all else, shall doom for ever
Our hearts to undivided dust!'

XII

He lived—he breathed—he moved—he felt;
He raised the maid from where she knelt;
His trance was gone—his keen eye shone
With thoughts that long in darkness dwelt;
With thoughts that burn—in rays that melt.
As the stream late conceal'd
By the fringe of its willows,
When it rushes reveal'd
In the light of its billows;
As the bolt burst on high
From the black cloud that bound it,
Flash'd the soul of that eye
Through the long lashes round it.
A war-horse at the trumpet's sound,
A lion roused by heedless hound,
A tyrant waked to sudden strife
By graze of ill-directed knife,
Starts not to more convulsive life
Than he, who heard that vow, display'd,
And all, before repress'd, betray'd:
'Now thou art mine, for ever mine,
With life to keep, and scarce with life resign;
Now thou art mine, that sacred oath,
Though sworn by one, hath bound us both.
Yes, fondly, wisely hast thou done;
That vow hath saved more heads than one;
But blench not thou—thy simplest tress
Claims more from me than tenderness;
I would not wrong the slenderest hair
That clusters round thy forehead fair,
For all the treasures buried far
Within the caves of Istakar.[2]
This morning clouds upon me lower'd,
Reproaches on my head were shower'd,
And Giaffir almost call'd me coward!
Now I have motive to be brave;
The son of his neglected slave,
Nay, start not, 'twas the term he gave,

[1] 'Azrael,' the angel of death.
[2] The treasures of the pre-Adamite Sultans.—See D'Herbelot, article *Istakar*.

May show, though little apt to vaunt,
A heart his words nor deeds can daunt.
His son, indeed!—yet, thanks to thee,
Perchance I am, at least shall be;
But let our plighted secret vow
Be only known to us as now.
I know the wretch who dares demand
From Giaffir thy reluctant hand;
More ill-got wealth, a meaner soul
Holds not a Musselim's [1] control:
Was he not bred in Egripo? [2]
A viler race let Israel show;
But let that pass—to none be told
Our oath; the rest shall time unfold.
To me and mine leave Osman Bey;
I've partisans for peril's day:
Think not I am what I appear;
I've arms, and friends, and vengeance near.'

XIII

'Think not thou art what thou appearest!
My Selim, thou art sadly changed:
This morn I saw thee gentlest, dearest;
But now thou 'rt from thyself estranged.
My love thou surely knew'st before,
It ne'er was less, nor can be more.
To see thee, hear thee, near thee stay,
And hate the night I know not why,
Save that we meet not but by day;
With thee to live, with thee to die,
I dare not to my hope deny:
Thy cheek, thine eyes, thy lips to kiss,
Like this—and this—no more than this:
For, Alla! sure thy lips are flame:
What fever in thy veins is flushing?
My own have nearly caught the same,
At least I feel my cheek too blushing.
To soothe thy sickness, watch thy health,
Partake, but never waste thy wealth,
Or stand with smiles unmurmuring by,

---

[1] 'Musselim,' a governor, the next in rank after a Pacha; a Waywode is the third; and then come the Agas.
[2] 'Egripo,' the Negropont. According to the proverb, the Turks of Egripo, the Jews of Salonica, and the Greeks of Athens, are the worst of their respective races.

And lighten half thy poverty;
Do all but close thy dying eye,
For that I could not live to try:
To these alone my thoughts aspire:
More can I do? or thou require?
But, Selim, thou must answer why
We need so much of mystery?
The cause I cannot dream nor tell,
But be it, since thou say'st 'tis well;
Yet what thou mean'st by "arms" and "friends,"
Beyond my weaker sense extends.
I meant that Giaffir should have heard
The very vow I plighted thee;
His wrath would not revoke my word:
But surely he would leave me free.
Can this fond wish seem strange in me,
To be what I have ever been?
What other hath Zuleika seen
From simple childhood's earliest hour?
What other can she seek to see
Than thee, companion of her bower,
The partner of her infancy?
These cherish'd thoughts with life begun,
Say, why must I no more avow?
What change is wrought to make me shun
The truth; my pride, and thine till now?
To meet the gaze of stranger's eyes,
Our law, our creed, our God denies;
Nor shall one wandering thought of mine
At such, our Prophet's will, repine:
No! happier made by that decree,
He left me all in leaving thee.
Deep were my anguish, thus compell'd
To wed with one I ne'er beheld:
This wherefore should I not reveal?
Why wilt thou urge me to conceal?
I know the Pacha's haughty mood
To thee hath never boded good;
And he so often storms at nought,
Allah! forbid that e'er he ought!
And why I know not, but within
My heart concealment weighs like sin.
If then such secrecy be crime,
And such it feels while lurking here;
Oh, Selim! tell me yet in time,
Nor leave me thus to thoughts of fear.

Ah! yonder see the Tchocadar,[1]
My father leaves the mimic war;
I tremble now to meet his eye—
Say, Selim, canst thou tell me why?'

XIV

'Zuleika—to thy tower's retreat
Betake thee—Giaffir I can greet:
And now with him I fain must prate
Of firmans, impost, levies, state.
There's fearful news from Danube's banks,
Our Vizier nobly thins his ranks,
For which the Giaour may give him thanks!
Our Sultan hath a shorter way
Such costly triumph to repay.
But, mark me, when the twilight drum
Hath warn'd the troops to food and sleep,
Unto thy cell will Selim come:
Then softly from the Haram creep
Where we may wander by the deep:
Our garden-battlements are steep;
Nor these will rash intruder climb
To list our words, or stint our time;
And if he doth, I want not steel
Which some have felt, and more may feel.
Then shalt thou learn of Selim more
Than thou hast heard or thought before:
Trust me, Zuleika—fear not me!
Thou know'st I hold a Haram key.'

'Fear thee, my Selim! ne'er till now
Did word like this—'
                              'Delay not thou;
I keep the key—and Haroun's guard
Have *some*, and hope of *more* reward.
To-night, Zuleika, thou shalt hear
My tale, my purpose, and my fear:
I am not, love! what I appear.'

[1] 'Tchocadar'—one of the attendants who precedes a man of authority.

I

THE winds are high on Helle's wave,
As on that night of stormy water
When Love, who sent, forgot to save
The young, the beautiful, the brave,
The lonely hope of Sestos' daughter.
Oh! when alone along the sky
Her turret-torch was blazing high,
Though rising gale, and breaking foam,
And shrieking sea-birds warn'd him home;
And clouds aloft and tides below,
With signs and sounds, forbade to go,
He could not see, he would not hear,
Or sound or sign foreboding fear;
His eye but saw the light of love,
The only star it hail'd above;
His ear but rang with Hero's song,
'Ye waves, divide not lovers long!'—
That tale is old, but love anew
May nerve young hearts to prove as true.

II

The winds are high, and Helle's tide
Rolls darkly heaving to the main;
And Night's descending shadows hide
That field with blood bedew'd in vain,
The desert of old Priam's pride;
The tombs, sole relics of his reign,
All—save immortal dreams that could beguile
The blind old man of Scio's rocky isle!

III

Oh! yet—for there my steps have been;
These feet have press'd the sacred shore,
These limbs that buoyant wave hath borne—
Minstrel! with thee to muse, to mourn,
To trace again those fields of yore,
Believing every hillock green
Contains no fabled hero's ashes,
And that around the undoubted scene
Thine own 'broad Hellespont'[1] still dashes,

[1] The wrangling about this epithet, 'the broad Hellespont' or the 'boundless Hellespont,' whether it means one or the other, or what it means at all, has been beyond all possibility of detail. I have even heard it disputed on the spot; and not foreseeing a speedy conclusion to the controversy, amused myself with

Be long my lot! and cold were he
Who there could gaze denying thee!

IV

The night hath closed on Helle's stream,
Nor yet hath risen on Ida's hill
That moon, which shone on his high theme:
No warrior chides her peaceful beam,
But conscious shepherds bless it still.
Their flocks are grazing on the mound
Of him who felt the Dardan's arrow:
That mighty heap of gather'd ground
Which Ammon's son ran proudly round,[1]
By nations raised, by monarchs crown'd,
Is now a lone and nameless barrow!
Within—thy dwelling-place how narrow!
Without—can only strangers breathe
The name of him that *was* beneath:
Dust long outlasts the storied stone;
But Thou—thy very dust is gone!

V

Late, late to-night will Dian cheer
The swain, and chase the boatman's fear:
Till then—no beacon on the cliff
May shape the course of struggling skiff;
The scatter'd lights that skirt the bay,
All, one by one, have died away;
The only lamp of this lone hour
Is glimmering in Zuleika's tower.
Yes! there is light in that lone chamber,
And o'er her silken Ottoman
Are thrown the fragrant beads of amber,
O'er which her fairy fingers ran:[2]
Near these, with emerald rays beset,
(How could she thus that gem forget?)

swimming across it in the meantime; and probably may again, before the point
is settled. Indeed, the question as to the truth of 'the tale of Troy divine'
still continues, much of it resting upon the talismanic word 'ἄπειρος': probably
Homer had the same notion of distance that a coquette has of time; and when
he talks of boundless, means half a mile; as the latter, by a like figure, when she
says *eternal* attachment, simply specifies three weeks.

[1] Before his Persian invasion, and crowned the altar with laurel, etc. He was
afterwards imitated by Caracalla in his race. It is believed that the last also
poisoned a friend, named Festus, for the sake of new Patroclan games. I have
seen the sheep feeding on the tombs of Aesietes and Antilochus: the first is in the
centre of the plain.

[2] When rubbed, the amber is susceptible of a perfume, which is slight but *not*
disagreeable.

Her mother's sainted amulet,[1]
Whereon engraved the Koorsee text,
Could smooth this life, and win the next;
And by her comboloio [2] lies
A Koran of illumined dyes;
And many a bright emblazon'd rhyme
By Persian scribes redeem'd from time;
And o'er those scrolls, not oft so mute,
Reclines her now neglected lute;
And round her lamp of fretted gold
Bloom flowers in urns of China's mould;
The richest work of Iran's loom,
And Sheeraz' tribute of perfume;
All that can eye or sense delight
Are gather'd in that gorgeous room;
But yet it hath an air of gloom.
She, of this Peri cell the sprite,
What doth she hence, and on so rude a night?

VI

Wrapt in the darkest sable vest,
Which none save noblest Moslem wear,
To guard from winds of heaven the breast
As heaven itself to Selim dear,
With cautious steps the thicket threading,
And starting oft, as through the glade
The gust its hollow moanings made,
Till on the smoother pathway treading,
More free her timid bosom beat,
The maid pursued her silent guide;
And though her terror urged retreat,
How could she quit her Selim's side?
How teach her tender lips to chide?

VII

They reach'd at length a grotto, hewn
By nature, but enlarged by art,
Where oft her lute she wont to tune,
And oft her Koran conn'd apart;

---

[1] The belief in amulets engraved on gems, or enclosed in gold boxes, containing scraps from the Koran, worn round the neck, wrist, or arm, is still universal in the East. The Koorsee (throne) verse in the second cap. of the Koran describes the attributes of the Most High, and is engraved in this manner, and worn by the pious, as the most esteemed and sublime of all sentences.

[2] 'Comboloio,' a Turkish rosary. The MSS., particularly those of the Persians, are richly adorned and illuminated. The Greek females are kept in utter ignorance; but many of the Turkish girls are highly accomplished, though not actually qualified for a Christian coterie. Perhaps some of our own 'blues' might not be the worse for bleaching.

And oft in youthful reverie
She dream'd what Paradise might be:
Where woman's parted soul shall go
Her Prophet had disdain'd to show;
But Selim's mansion was secure,
Nor deem'd she, could he long endure
His bower in other worlds of bliss,
Without *her*, most beloved in this!
Oh! who so dear with him could dwell?
What Houri soothe him half so well?

VIII

Since last she visited the spot
Some change seem'd wrought within the grot;
It might be only that the night
Disguised things seen by better light:
That brazen lamp but dimly threw
A ray of no celestial hue;
But in a nook within the cell
Her eye on stranger objects fell.
There arms were piled, not such as wield
The turban'd Delis in the field;
But brands of foreign blade and hilt,
And one was red—perchance with guilt!
Ah! how without can blood be spilt?
A cup too on the board was set
That did not seem to hold sherbet.
What may this mean? she turn'd to see
Her Selim—'Oh! can this be he?'

IX

His robe of pride was thrown aside,
His brow no high-crown'd turban bore,
But in its stead a shawl of red,
Wreathed lightly round, his temples wore:
That dagger, on whose hilt the gem
Were worthy of a diadem,
No longer glitter'd at his waist,
Where pistols unadorn'd were braced;
And from his belt a sabre swung,
And from his shoulder loosely hung
The cloak of white, the thin capote
That decks the wandering Candiote;
Beneath—his golden plated vest
Clung like a cuirass to his breast;
The greaves below his knee that wound
With silvery scales were sheathed and bound.

But were it not that high command
Spake in his eye, and tone, and hand,
All that a careless eye could see
In him was some young Galiongée.[1]

x

'I said I was not what I seem'd;
And now thou see'st my words were true:
I have a tale thou hast not dream'd,
If sooth—its truth must others rue.
My story now 'twere vain to hide,
I must not see thee Osman's bride:
But had not thine own lips declared
How much of that young heart I shared,
I could not, must not, yet have shown
The darker secret of my own.
In this I speak not now of love;
That, let time, truth, and peril prove:
But first—Oh! never wed another—
Zuleika! I am not thy brother!'

xi

'Oh! not my brother!—yet unsay—
God! am I left alone on earth
To mourn—I dare not curse—the day
That saw my solitary birth?
Oh! thou wilt love me now no more!
My sinking heart foreboded ill;
But know *me* all I was before,
Thy sister—friend—Zuleika still.
Thou led'st me here perchance to kill;
If thou hast cause for vengeance, see!
My breast is offer'd—take thy fill!
Far better with the dead to be
Than live thus nothing now to thee:
Perhaps far worse, for now I know
Why Giaffir always seem'd thy foe;
And I, alas! am Giaffir's child,
For whom thou wert contemn'd, reviled.
If not thy sister—would'st thou save
My life, oh! bid me be thy slave!'

---

[1] 'Galiongée,' or 'Galiongi,' a sailor, that is, a Turkish sailor; the Greeks navigate, the Turks work the guns. Their dress is picturesque; and I have seen the Capitan Pacha more than once wearing it as a kind of *incog.* Their legs, however, are generally naked. The buskins described in the text as sheathed behind with silver are those of an Arnaut robber, who was my host (he had quitted the profession) at his Pyrgo, near Gastouni in the Morea; they were plated in scales one over the other, like the back of an armadillo.

XII

'My slave, Zuleika!—nay, I'm thine:
But, gentle love, this transport calm,
Thy lot shall yet be link'd with mine;
I swear it by our Prophet's shrine,
And be that thought thy sorrow's balm.
So may the Koran [1] verse display'd
Upon its steel direct my blade,
In danger's hour to guard us both,
As I preserve that awful oath!
The name in which thy heart hath prided
Must change; but, my Zuleika, know,
That tie is widen'd, not divided,
Although thy Sire's my deadliest foe.
My father was to Giaffir all
That Selim late was deem'd to thee;
That brother wrought a brother's fall,
But spared, at least, my infancy;
And lull'd me with a vain deceit
That yet a like return may meet.
He rear'd me, not with tender help,
But like the nephew of a Cain; [2]
He watch'd me like a lion's whelp,
That gnaws and yet may break his chain.
My father's blood in every vein
Is boiling; but for thy dear sake
No present vengeance will I take;
Though here I must no more remain.
But first, beloved Zuleika! hear
How Giaffir wrought this deed of fear.

[1] The characters on all Turkish scimitars contain sometimes the name of the place of their manufacture, but more generally a text from the Koran, in letters of gold. Amongst those in my possession is one with a blade of singular construction; it is very broad, and the edge notched into serpentine curves like the ripple of water, or the wavering of flame. I asked the Arminian who sold it, what possible use such a figure could add: he said, in Italian, that he did not know; but the Mussulmans had an idea that those of this form gave a severer wound; and liked it because it was *piu feroce*. I did not much admire the reason, but bought it for its peculiarity.

[2] It is to be observed, that every allusion to any thing or personage in the Old Testament, such as the Ark, or Cain, is equally the privilege of Mussulman and Jew: indeed, the former profess to be much better acquainted with the lives, true and fabulous, of the patriarchs, than is warranted by our own sacred writ; and not content with Adam, they have a biography of pre-Adamites. Solomon is the monarch of all necromancy, and Moses a prophet inferior only to Christ and Mahomet. Zuleika is the Persian name of Potiphar's wife; and her amour with Joseph constitutes one of the finest poems in their language. It is, therefore, no violation of costume to put the names of Cain, or Noah, into the mouth of a Moslem.

XIII

'How first their strife to rancour grew,
If love or envy made them foes,
It matters little if I knew;
In fiery spirits, slights, though few
And thoughtless, will disturb repose
In war Abdallah's arm was strong,
Remember'd yet in Bosniac song,
And Paswan's [1] rebel hordes attest
How little love they bore such guest:
His death is all I need relate,
The stern effect of Giaffir's hate;
And how my birth disclosed to me,
Whate'er beside it makes, hath made me free.

XIV

'When Paswan, after years of strife,
At last for power, but first for life,
In Widin's walls too proudly sate,
Our Pachas rallied round the state;
Nor last nor least in high command,
Each brother led a separate band;
They gave their horsetails [2] to the wind,
And mustering in Sophia's plain
Their tents were pitch'd, their post assign'd;
To one, alas! assign'd in vain!
What need of words? the deadly bowl,
By Giaffir's order drugg'd and given,
With venom subtle as his soul,
Dismiss'd Abdallah's hence to heaven.
Reclined and feverish in the bath,
He, when the hunter's sport was up,
But little deem'd a brother's wrath
To quench his thirst had such a cup:
The bowl a bribed attendant bore;
He drank one draught [3] nor needed more!
If thou my tale, Zuleika, doubt,
Call Haroun—he can tell it out.

[1] Paswan Oglou, the rebel of Widin; who, for the last years of his life, set the whole power of the Porte at defiance.

[2] 'Horsetail,' the standard of a Pacha.

[3] Giaffir, Pacha of Argyro Castro, or Scutari, I am not sure which, was actually taken off by the Albanian Ali, in the manner described in the text. Ali Pacha, while I was in the country, married the daughter of his victim, some years after the event had taken place at a bath in Sophia, or Adrianople. The poison was mixed in the cup of coffee, which is presented before the sherbet by the bath-keeper, after dressing.

XV

'The deed once done, and Paswan's feud
In part suppress'd, though ne'er subdued,
Abdallah's Pachalick was gain'd:—
Thou know'st not what in our Divan
Can wealth procure for worse than man—
Abdallah's honours were obtain'd
By him a brother's murder stain'd;
'Tis true, the purchase nearly drain'd
His ill got treasure, soon replaced.
Wouldst question whence?   Survey the waste,
And ask the squalid peasant how
His gains repay his broiling brow!—
Why me the stern usurper spared,
Why thus with me his palace shared,
I know not.   Shame, regret, remorse,
And little fear from infant's force;
Besides, adoption as a son
By him whom Heaven accorded none,
Or some unknown cabal, caprice,
Preserved me thus;—but not in peace:
He cannot curb his haughty mood,
Nor I forgive a father's blood.

XVI

'Within thy father's house are foes;
Not all who break his bread are true:
To these should I my birth disclose,
His days, his very hours were few:
They only want a heart to lead,
A hand to point them to the deed.
But Haroun only knows or knew
This tale, whose close is almost nigh:
He in Abdallah's palace grew,
And held that post in his Serai
Which holds he here—he saw him die:
But what could single slavery do?
Avenge his lord? alas! too late;
Or save his son from such a fate?
He chose the last, and when elate
With foes subdued, or friends betray'd,
Proud Giaffir in high triumph sate,
He led me helpless to his gate,
And not in vain it seems essay'd
To save the life for which he pray'd.
The knowledge of my birth secured

From all and each, but most from me;
Thus Giaffir's safety was ensured.
Removed he too from Roumelie
To this our Asiatic side,
Far from our seats by Danube's tide,
With none but Haroun, who retains
Such knowledge—and that Nubian feels
A tyrant's secrets are but chains,
From which the captive gladly steals,
And this and more to me reveals:
Such still to guilt just Alla sends—
Slaves, tools, accomplices—no friends!

XVII

'All this, Zuleika, harshly sounds;
But harsher still my tale must be:
Howe'er my tongue thy softness wounds,
Yet I must prove all truth to thee.
I saw thee start this garb to see,
Yet is it one I oft have worn,
And long must wear: this Galiongée,
To whom thy plighted vow is sworn,
Is leader of those pirate hordes,
Whose laws and lives are on their swords;
To hear whose desolating tale
Would make thy waning cheek more pale;
Those arms thou see'st my band have brought.
The hands that wield are not remote;
This cup too for the rugged knaves
Is fill'd—once quaff'd, they ne'er repine:
Our prophet might forgive the slaves;
They 're only infidels in wine.

XVIII

'What could I be?   Proscribed at home,
And taunted to a wish to roam;
And listless left—for Giaffir's fear
Denied the courser and the spear—
Though oft—Oh, Mahomet! how oft!—
In full Divan the despot scoff'd,
As if my weak unwilling hand
Refused the bridle or the brand:
He ever went to war alone,
And pent me here untried—unknown;
To Haroun's care with women left,
By hope unblest, of fame bereft,

While thou—whose softness long endear'd,
Though it unmann'd me, still had cheer'd—
To Brusa's walls for safety sent,
Awaited'st there the field's event.
Haroun, who saw my spirit pining
Beneath inaction's sluggish yoke,
His captive, though with dread resigning,
My thraldom for a season broke,
On promise to return before
The day when Giaffir's charge was o'er.
'Tis vain—my tongue can not impart
My almost drunkenness of heart,
When first this liberated eye
Survey'd Earth, Ocean, Sun, and Sky,
As if my spirit pierced them through,
And all their inmost wonders knew!
One word alone can paint to thee
That more than feeling—I was Free!
E'en for thy presence ceased to pine;
The World—nay, Heaven itself was mine!

XIX

'The shallop of a trusty Moor
Convey'd me from this idle shore;
I long'd to see the isles that gem
Old Ocean's purple diadem:
I sought by turns, and saw them all; [1]
But when and where I join'd the crew,
With whom I'm pledged to rise or fall,
When all that we design to do
Is done, 't will then be time more meet
To tell thee, when the tale 's complete.

XX

''T is true, they are a lawless brood,
But rough in form, nor mild in mood;
And every creed, and every race,
With them hath found—may find a place:
But open speech, and ready hand,
Obedience to their chief's command;
A soul for every enterprise,
That never sees with Terror's eyes;
Friendship for each, and faith to all,
And vengeance vow'd for those who fall,

---

[1] The Turkish notions of almost all islands are confined to the Archipelago, the sea alluded to.

Have made them fitting instruments
For more than ev'n my own intents.
And some—and I have studied all
Distinguish'd from the vulgar rank,
But chiefly to my council call
The wisdom of the cautious Frank—
And some to higher thoughts aspire,
The last of Lambro's [1] patriots there
Anticipated freedom share;
And oft around the cavern fire
On visionary schemes debate,
To snatch the Rayahs [2] from their fate.
So let them ease their hearts with prate
Of equal rights, which man ne'er knew;
I have a love for freedom too.
Ay! let me like the Ocean-Patriarch [3] roam,
Or only know on land the Tartar's home! [4]
My tent on shore, my galley on the sea,
Are more than cities and Serais to me:
Borne by my steed, or wafted by my sail,
Across the desert, or before the gale,
Bound where thou wilt, my barb! or glide, my prow!
But be the star that guides the wanderer, Thou!
Thou, my Zuleika, share and bless my bark;
The Dove of peace and promise to mine ark!
Or, since that hope denied in worlds of strife,
Be thou the rainbow to the storms of life!
The evening beam that smiles the clouds away,
And tints to-morrow with prophetic ray!
Blest—as the Muezzin's strain from Mecca's wall
To pilgrims pure and prostrate at his call;
Soft—as the melody of youthful days,
That steals the trembling tear of speechless praise;
Dear—as his native song to Exile's ears,
Shall sound each tone thy long-loved voice endears.

[1] Lambro Canzani, a Greek, famous for his efforts, in 1789–90, for the independence of his country. Abandoned by the Russians, he became a pirate, and the Archipelago was the scene of his enterprises. He is said to be still alive at Petersburg. He and Riga are the two most celebrated of the Greek revolutionists.

[2] 'Rayahs,' all who pay the capitation tax, called the 'Haratch.'

[3] The first of voyages is one of the few with which the Mussulmans profess much acquaintance.

[4] The wandering life of the Arabs, Tartars, and Turkomans, will be found well detailed in any book of Eastern travels. That it possesses a charm peculiar to itself cannot be denied. A young French renegado confessed to Chateaubriand, that he never found himself alone, galloping in the desert, without a sensation approaching to rapture which was indescribable.

For thee in those bright isles is built a bower
Blooming as Aden [1] in its earliest hour.
A thousand swords, with Selim's heart and hand,
Wait—wave—defend—destroy—at thy command!
Girt by my band, Zuleika at my side,
The spoil of nations shall bedeck my bride.
The Haram's languid years of listless ease
Are well resign'd for cares—for joys like these:
Not blind to fate, I see, where'er I rove,
Unnumbered perils,—but one only love!
Yet well my toils shall that fond breast repay,
Though fortune frown, or falser friends betray.
How dear the dream in darkest hours of ill,
Should all be changed, to find thee faithful still!
Be but thy soul, like Selim's, firmly shown;
To thee be Selim's tender as thine own;
To soothe each sorrow, share in each delight,
Blend every thought, do all—but disunite!
Once free, 'tis mine our horde again to guide;
Friends to each other, foes to aught beside:
Yet there we follow but the bent assign'd
By fatal Nature to man's warring kind:
Mark! where his carnage and his conquests cease!
He makes a solitude, and calls it—peace!
I like the rest must use my skill or strength,
But ask no land beyond my sabre's length:
Power sways but by division—her resource
The blest alternative of fraud or force!
Ours be the last; in time deceit may come
When cities cage us in a social home:
There ev'n thy soul might err—how oft the heart
Corruption shakes which peril could not part!
And woman, more than man, when death or woe,
Or even Disgrace, would lay her lover low,
Sunk in the lap of Luxury will shame—
Away suspicion! *not* Zuleika's name!
But life is hazard at the best; and here
No more remains to win, and much to fear:
Yes, fear!—the doubt, the dread of losing thee,
By Osman's power, and Giaffir's stern decree.
That dread shall vanish with the favouring gale,
Which love to-night hath promised to my sail:
No danger daunts the pair his smile hath blest,
Their steps still roving, but their hearts at rest.
With thee all toils are sweet, each clime hath charms;

[1] 'Jannat al Aden,' the perpetual abode, the Mussulman paradise.

Earth—sea alike—our world within our arms!
Ay—let the loud winds whistle o'er the deck,
So that those arms cling closer round my neck:
The deepest murmur of this lip shall be
No sigh for safety, but a prayer for thee!
The war of elements no fears impart
To Love, whose deadliest bane is human Art:
There lie the only rocks our course can check;
Here moments menace—*there* are years of wreck!
But hence ye thoughts that rise in Horror's shape!
This hour bestows, or ever bars escape.
Few words remain of mine my tale to close:
Of thine but *one* to waft us from our foes;
Yes—foes—to me will Giaffir's hate decline?
And is not Osman, who would part us, thine?

XXI

'His head and faith from doubt and death
Return'd in time my guard to save;
Few heard, none told, that o'er the wave
From isle to isle I roved the while:
And since, though parted from my band,
Too seldom now I leave the land,
No deed they 've done, nor deed shall do,
Ere I have heard and doom'd it too:
I form the plan, decree the spoil,
'Tis fit I oftener share the toil.
But now too long I 've held thine ear;
Time presses, floats my bark, and here
We leave behind but hate and fear.
To-morrow Osman with his train
Arrives—to-night must break thy chain:
And wouldst thou save that haughty Bey,—
Perchance *his* life who gave thee thine,—
With me, this hour away—away!
But yet, though thou art plighted mine,
Wouldst thou recall thy willing vow,
Appall'd by truths imparted now
Here rest I—not to see thee wed:
But be that peril on *my* head!'

XXII

Zuleika, mute and motionless,
Stood like that statue of distress,
When, her last hope for ever gone,
The mother harden'd into stone;

All in the maid that eye could see
Was but a younger Niobé.
But ere her lip, or even her eye,
Essay'd to speak or look reply,
Beneath the garden's wicket porch
Far flash'd on high a blazing torch!
Another—and another—and another—
'Oh! fly—no more—yet now my more than brother!'
Far, wide, through every thicket spread,
The fearful lights are gleaming red;
Nor these alone—for each right hand
Is ready with a sheathless brand.
They part, pursue, return, and wheel
With searching flambeau, shining steel;
And last of all, his sabre waving,
Stern Giaffir in his fury raving:
And now almost they touch the cave—
Oh! must that grot be Selim's grave?

XXIII

Dauntless he stood—''Tis come—soon past—
One kiss, Zuleika—'tis my last:
But yet my band not far from shore
May hear this signal, see the flash;
Yet now too few—the attempt were rash:
No matter—yet one effort more.'
Forth to the cavern mouth he stept;
His pistol's echo rang on high,
Zuleika started not, nor wept,
Despair benumb'd her breast and eye!—
'They hear me not, or if they ply
Their oars, 'tis but to see me die;
That sound hath drawn my foes more nigh.
Then forth my father's scimitar,
Thou ne'er hast seen less equal war!
Farewell, Zuleika!—Sweet! retire:
Yet stay within—here linger safe,
At thee his rage will only chafe.
Stir not—lest even to thee perchance
Some erring blade or ball should glance.
Fear'st thou for him?—may I expire
If in this strife I seek thy sire!
No—though by him that poison pour'd;
No—though again he call me coward!
But tamely shall I meet their steel?
No—as each crest save *his* may feel!'

XXIV

One bound he made, and gain'd the sand:
Already at his feet hath sunk
The foremost of the prying band,
A gasping head, a quivering trunk:
Another falls—but round him close
A swarming circle of his foes;
From right to left his path he cleft,
And almost met the meeting wave:
His boat appears—not five oars' length—
His comrades strain with desperate strength—
Oh! are they yet in time to save?
His feet the foremost breakers lave;
His band are plunging in the bay,
Their sabres glitter through the spray;
Wet—wild—unwearied to the strand
They struggle—now they touch the land!
They come—'tis but to add to slaughter—
His heart's best blood is on the water.

XXV

Escaped from shot, unharm'd by steel,
Or scarcely grazed its force to feel,
Had Selim won, betray'd, beset,
To where the strand and billows met;
There as his last step left the land,
And the last death-blow dealt his hand—
Ah! wherefore did he turn to look
For her his eye but sought in vain?
That pause, that fatal gaze he took,
Hath doom'd his death, or fix'd his chain.
Sad proof, in peril and in pain,
How late will Lover's hope remain!
His back was to the dashing spray;
Behind, but close, his comrades lay,
When, at the instant, hiss'd the ball—
'So may the foes of Giaffir fall!'
Whose voice is heard? whose carbine rang?
Whose bullet through the night-air sang,
Too nearly, deadly aim'd to err?
'Tis thine—Abdallah's Murderer!
The father slowly rued thy hate,
The son hath found a quicker fate:

Fast from his breast the blood is bubbling,
The whiteness of the sea-foam troubling—
If aught his lips essay'd to groan,
The rushing billows choked the tone!

XXVI

Morn slowly rolls the clouds away;
Few trophies of the fight are there:
The shouts that shook the midnight-bay
Are silent; but some signs of fray
That strand of strife may bear,
And fragments of each shiver'd brand;
Steps stamp'd; and dash'd into the sand
The print of many a struggling hand
May there be mark'd; nor far remote
A broken torch, an oarless boat;
And tangled on the weeds that heap
The beach where shelving to the deep
There lies a white capote!
'Tis rent in twain—one dark-red stain
The wave yet ripples o'er in vain:
But where is he who wore?
Ye! who would o'er his relics weep,
Go, seek them where the surges sweep
Their burthen round Sigaeum's steep
And cast on Lemnos' shore:
The sea-birds shriek above the prey,
O'er which their hungry beaks delay,
As shaken on his restless pillow,
His head heaves with the heaving billow;
That hand, whose motion is not life,
Yet feebly seems to menace strife,
Flung by the tossing tide on high,
Then levell'd with the wave—
What recks it, though that corse shall lie
Within a living grave?
The bird that tears that prostrate form
Hath only robb'd the meaner worm;
The only heart, the only eye
Had bled or wept to see him die,
Had seen those scatter'd limbs composed,
And mourn'd above his turban-stone,[1]
That heart hath burst—that eye was closed—
Yea—closed before his own!

[1] A turban is carved in stone above the graves of *men* only.

XXVII

By Helle's stream there is a voice of wail!
And woman's eye is wet—man's cheek is pale:
Zuleika! last of Giaffir's race,
Thy destined lord is come too late:
He sees not—ne'er shall see thy face!
Can he not hear
The loud Wul-wulleh [1] warn his distant ear?
Thy handmaids weeping at the gate,
The Koran-chanters of the hymn of fate,
The silent slaves with folded arms that wait,
Sighs in the hall, and shrieks upon the gale,
Tell him thy tale!
Thou didst not view thy Selim fall!
That fearful moment when he left the cave
Thy heart grew chill:
He was thy hope—thy joy—thy love—thine all—
And that last thought on him thou couldst not save
Sufficed to kill:
Burst forth in one wild cry—and all was still.
Peace to thy broken heart, and virgin grave!
Ah! happy! but of life to lose the worst!
That grief—though deep—though fatal—was thy first!
Thrice happy! ne'er to feel nor fear the force
Of absence, shame, pride, hate, revenge, remorse!
And, oh! that pang where more than Madness lies!
The worm that will not sleep—and never dies;
Thought of the gloomy day and ghastly night,
That dreads the darkness, and yet loathes the light,
That winds around and tears the quivering heart!
Ah! wherefore not consume it—and depart!
Woe to thee, rash and unrelenting chief!
Vainly thou heap'st the dust upon thy head,
Vainly the sackcloth o'er thy limbs dost spread:
By that same hand Abdallah—Selim bled.
Now let it tear thy beard in idle grief:
Thy pride of heart, thy bride for Osman's bed,
She, whom thy sultan had but seen to wed,
Thy Daughter 's dead!
Hope of thine age, thy twilight's lonely beam,

---

[1] The death-song of the Turkish women. The 'silent slaves' are the men,
whose notions of decorum forbid complaint in *public*.

The Star hath set that shone on Helle's stream.
What quench'd its ray?—the blood that thou hast shed!
Hark! to the hurried question of Despair:
'Where is my child?'—an Echo answers—'Where?'[1]

XXVIII

Within the place of thousand tombs
That shine beneath, while dark above
The sad but living cypress glooms,
And withers not, though branch and leaf
Are stamp'd with an eternal grief,
Like early unrequited Love,
One spot exists, which ever blooms,
Ev'n in that deadly grove—
A single rose is shedding there
Its lonely lustre, meek and pale:
It looks as planted by Despair—
So white—so faint—the slightest gale
Might whirl the leaves on high;
And yet, though storms and blight assail,
And hands more rude than wintry sky
May wring it from the stem—in vain—
To-morrow sees it bloom again!
The stalk some spirit gently rears,
And waters with celestial tears;
For well may maids of Helle deem
That this can be no earthly flower,
Which mocks the tempest's withering hour,
And buds unshelter'd by a bower;
Nor droops, though spring refuse her shower,
Nor woos the summer beam:
To it the livelong night there sings
A bird unseen—but not remote:
Invisible his airy wings,
But soft as harp that Houri strings
His long entrancing note!
It were the Bulbul; but his throat,
Though mournful, pours not such a strain;
For they who listen cannot leave
The spot, but linger there and grieve,
As if they loved in vain!
And yet so sweet the tears they shed,
'Tis sorrow so unmix'd with dread,
They scarce can bear the morn to break

[1] 'I came to the place of my birth, and cried: "The friends of my youth, where
are they?" and an Echo answered: "Where are they?"'—*From an Arabic MS.*

That melancholy spell,
And longer yet would weep and wake,
He sings so wild and well!
But when the day-blush bursts from high
Expires that magic melody.
And some have been who could believe,
(So fondly youthful dream deceive,
Yet harsh be they that blame,)
That note so piercing and profound
Will shape and syllable [1] its sound
Into Zuleika's name.
'Tis from her cypress summit heard,
That melts in air the liquid word:
'Tis from her lowly virgin earth
That white rose takes its tender birth.
There late was laid a marble stone;
Eve saw it placed—the Morrow gone!
It was no mortal arm that bore
That deep-fix'd pillar to the shore;
For there, as Helle's legends tell,
Next morn 'twas found where Selim fell;
Lash'd by the tumbling tide, whose wave
Denied his bones a holier grave:
And there by night, reclined, 'tis said,
Is seen a ghastly turban'd head:
And hence extended by the billow,
'Tis named the ' Pirate-phantom's pillow!'
Where first it lay that mourning flower
Hath flourished; flourisheth this hour,
Alone and dewy, coldly pure and pale;
As weeping Beauty's cheek at Sorrow's tale!

[1] 'And airy tongues that *syllable* men's names.'
                                        MILTON.

For a belief that the souls of the dead inhabit the form of birds, we need not travel to the East. Lord Lyttelton's ghost story, the belief of the Duchess of Kendal, that George I flew into her window in the shape of a raven (see Orford's *Reminiscences*), and many other instances, bring this superstition nearer home. The most singular was the whim of a Worcester lady, who, believing her daughter to exist in the shape of a singing bird, literally furnished her pew in the cathedral with cages full of the kind; and as she was rich, and a benefactress in beautifying the church, no objection was made to her harmless folly. For this anecdote, see Orford's *Letters*.

THE CORSAIR

A TALE

. . I suoi pensieri in lui dormir non ponno.
TASSO, Gerusalemme Liberata, canto **x.**

TO THOMAS MOORE, ESQ.

My dear Moore,

I dedicate to you the last production with which I shall trespass on public patience, and your indulgence, for some years; and I own that I feel anxious to avail myself of this latest and only opportunity of adorning my pages with a name, consecrated by unshaken public principle, and the most undoubted and various talents. While Ireland ranks you among the firmest of her patriots; while you stand alone the first of her bards in her estimation, and Britain repeats and ratifies the decree, permit one, whose only regret, since our first acquaintance, has been the years he had lost before it commenced, to add the humble but sincere suffrage of friendship, to the voice of more than one nation. It will at least prove to you, that I have neither forgotten the gratification derived from your society, nor abandoned the prospect of its renewal, whenever your leisure or inclination allows you to atone to your friends for too long an absence. It is said among those friends, I trust truly, that you are engaged in the composition of a poem whose scene will be laid in the East; none can do those scenes so much justice. The wrongs of your own country, the magnificent and fiery spirit of her sons, the beauty and feeling of her daughters, may there be found; and Collins, when he denominated his Oriental his Irish Eclogues, was not aware how true, at least, was a part of his parallel. Your imagination will create a warmer sun, and less clouded sky; but wildness, tenderness, and originality, are part of your national claim of oriental descent, to which you have already thus far proved your title more clearly than the most zealous of your country's antiquarians.

May I add a few words on a subject on which all men are supposed to be fluent, and none agreeable,—Self? I have written much, and published more than enough to demand a longer silence than I now meditate; but, for some years to come, it is my intention to tempt no further the award of 'Gods, men, nor columns.' In the present composition I have attempted not the most difficult, but, perhaps, the best adapted measure to our language, the good old and now neglected heroic couplet. The stanza of Spenser is perhaps too slow and dignified for narrative; though, I confess, it is the measure most after my own heart: Scott alone, of the present generation, has hitherto completely triumphed over the fatal facility of the octo-syllabic verse; and this is not the least victory of his fertile and mighty genius: in blank verse, Milton, Thomson, and our dramatists, are the beacons that shine along the deep, but warn us from the rough and barren rock on which they are kindled. The heroic couplet is not the most popular measure certainly; but as I did not deviate into the other from a wish to flatter what is called public opinion, I shall quit it without further apology, and take my chance once more with that versification, in which I have hitherto published nothing but compositions whose former circulation is part of my present, and will be of my future regret.

With regard to my story, and stories in general, I should have been glad to have rendered my personages more perfect and amiable, if possible, inasmuch as I have been sometimes criticized, and considered no less responsible for their deeds and qualities than if all had been personal. Be it so—if I have deviated into the gloomy vanity of 'drawing from self,' the pictures are probably like, since they are unfavourable; and if not, those who know me are undeceived, and those who do not, I have little interest in undeceiving. I have no particular desire that any but my acquaintance should think the author better than the beings of his imagining; but I cannot help a little surprise, and perhaps amusement, at some odd critical exceptions in the present instance, when I see several bards (far more deserving, I allow) in very reputable plight, and quite exempted from all participation in the faults of those heroes, who, nevertheless, might be found with little more morality than *The Giaour*, and perhaps—but no—I must admit Childe Harold to be a very repulsive personage; and as to his identity, those who like it must give him whatever 'alias' they please.

If, however, it were worth while to remove the impression, it might be of some service to me, that the man who is alike the delight of his readers and his friends, the poet of all circles, and the idol of his own, permits me here and elsewhere to subscribe myself,

> Most truly,
> And affectionately,
> His obedient servant,
> BYRON.

2nd January 1814.

THE CORSAIR[1]

. . . nessun maggior dolore,
Che ricordarsi del tempo felice
Nella miseria . . .
DANTE.

I

'O'ER the glad waters of the dark blue sea,
Our thoughts as boundless, and our souls as free,
Far as the breeze can bear, the billows foam,
Survey our empire, and behold our home!
These are our realms, no limits to their sway—
Our flag the sceptre all who meet obey.
Ours the wild life in tumult still to range
From toil to rest, and joy in every change.
Oh, who can tell? not thou, luxurious slave!
Whose soul would sicken o'er the heaving wave;
Not thou, vain lord of wantonness and ease!
Whom slumber soothes not—pleasure cannot please—
Oh, who can tell, save he whose heart hath tried,
And danced in triumph o'er the waters wide,
The exulting sense—the pulse's maddening play,
That thrills the wanderer of that trackless way?
That for itself can woo the approaching fight,
And turn what some deem danger to delight;
That seeks what cravens shun with more than zeal,
And where the feebler faint—can only feel—
Feel—to the rising bosom's inmost core,
Its hope awaken and its spirit soar?
No dread of death—if with us die our foes—
Save that it seems even duller than repose:
Come when it will—we snatch the life of life—
When lost—what recks it—by disease or strife?
Let him who crawls enamour'd of decay
Cling to his couch, and sicken years away;
Heave his thick breath, and shake his palsied head;
Ours—the fresh turf, and not the feverish bed.
While gasp by gasp he falters forth his soul,
Ours with one pang—one bound—escapes control.
His corse may boast its urn and narrow cave,
And they who loath'd his life may gild his grave:

The time in this poem may seem too short for the occurrences, but the whole of the Aegean isles are within a few hours' sail of the continent, and the reader must be kind enough to take the *wind* as I have often found it.

Ours are the tears, though few, sincerely shed,
When Ocean shrouds and sepulchres our dead.
For us, even banquets fond regret supply
In the red cup that crowns our memory;
And the brief epitaph in danger's day,
When those who win at length divide the prey,
And cry, Remembrance saddening o'er each brow,
How had the brave who fell exulted *now*!'

II

Such were the notes that from the Pirate's isle
Around the kindling watch-fire rang the while:
Such were the sounds that thrill'd the rocks along,
And unto ears as rugged seem'd a song!
In scatter'd groups upon the golden sand,
They game—carouse—converse—or whet the brand;
Select the arms—to each his blade assign,
And careless eye the blood that dims its shine;
Repair the boat, replace the helm or oar,
While others straggling muse along the shore;
For the wild bird the busy springes set,
Or spread beneath the sun the dripping net;
Gaze where some distant sail a speck supplies,
With all the thirsting eye of Enterprise;
Tell o'er the tales of many a night of toil,
And marvel where they next shall seize a spoil:
No matter where—their chief's allotment this;
Theirs, to believe no prey nor plan amiss.
But who that CHIEF? his name on every shore
Is famed and fear'd—they ask and know no more.
With these he mingles not but to command;
Few are his words, but keen his eyes and hand.
Ne'er seasons he with mirth their jovial mess,
But they forgive his silence for success.
Ne'er for his lips the purpling cup they fill,
That goblet passes him untasted still—
And for his fare—the rudest of his crew
Would that, in turn, have pass'd untasted too;
Earth's coarsest bread, the garden's homeliest roots,
And scarce the summer luxury of fruits,
His short repast in humbleness supply
With all a hermit's board would scarce deny.
But while he shuns the grosser joys of sense,
His mind seems nourished by that abstinence.
'Steer to that shore!'—they sail. 'Do this!'—'tis done:
'Now form and follow me!'—the spoil is won.

Thus prompt his accents and his actions still,
And all obey and few inquire his will;
To such, brief answer and contemptuous eye
Convey reproof, nor further deign reply.

III

'A sail!—a sail!' a promised prize to Hope!
Her nation—flag—how speaks the telescope?
No prize, alas!—but yet a welcome sail:
The blood-red signal glitters in the gale.
Yes—she is ours—a home-returning bark—
Blow fair, thou breeze!—she anchors ere the dark.
Already doubled is the cape—our bay
Receives that prow which proudly spurns the spray.
How gloriously her gallant course she goes!
Her white wings flying—never from her foes—
She walks the waters like a thing of life,
And seems to dare the elements to strife.
Who would not brave the battle-fire—the wreck—
To move the monarch of her peopled deck?

IV

Hoarse o'er her side the rustling cable rings;
The sails are furl'd; and anchoring round she swings:
And gathering loiterers on the land discern
Her boat descending from the latticed stern.
'Tis mann'd—the oars keep concert to the strand,
Till grates her keel upon the shallow sand.
Hail to the welcome shout!—the friendly speech!
When hand grasps hand uniting on the beach;
The smile, the question, and the quick reply,
And the heart's promise of festivity!

V

The tidings spread, and gathering grows the crowd.
The hum of voices, and the laughter loud,
And woman's gentler anxious tone is heard—
Friends'—husbands'—lovers' names in each dear word:
'Oh! are they safe? we ask not of success—
But shall we see them? will their accents bless?
From where the battle roars—the billows chafe—
They doubtless boldly did—but who are safe?
Here let them haste to gladden and surprise,
And kiss the doubt from these delighted eyes!'

VI

'Where is our chief? for him we bear report—
And doubt that joy—which hails our coming—short;
Yet thus sincere—'tis cheering, though so brief;
But, Juan! instant guide us to our chief:
Our greeting paid, we'll feast on our return,
And all shall hear what each may wish to learn.
Ascending slowly by the rock-hewn way,
To where his watch-tower beetles o'er the bay,
By bushy brake, and wild flowers blossoming,
And freshness breathing from each silver spring,
Whose scatter'd streams from granite basins burst,
Leap into life, and sparkling woo your thirst;
From crag to cliff they mount—Near yonder cave,
What lonely straggler looks along the wave?
In pensive posture leaning on the brand,
Not oft a resting-staff to that red hand?
''Tis he—'tis Conrad—here, as wont, alone;
On—Juan!—on—and make our purpose known.
The bark he views—and tell him we would greet
His ear with tidings he must quickly meet:
We dare not yet approach—thou know'st his mood,
When strange or uninvited steps intrude.'

VII

Him Juan sought, and told of their intent;—
He spake not—but a sign expressed assent.
These Juan calls—they come—to their salute
He bends him slightly, but his lips are mute.
'These letters, Chief, are from the Greek—the spy,
Who still proclaims our spoil or peril nigh:
Whate'er his tidings, we can well report,
Much that'—'Peace, peace!'—he cuts their prating short.
Wondering they turn, abash'd, while each to each
Conjecture whispers in his muttering speech:
They watch his glance with many a stealing look,
To gather how that eye the tidings took;
But, this as if he guess'd, with head aside,
Perchance from some emotion, doubt, or pride,
He read the scroll—'My tablets, Juan, hark—
Where is Gonsalvo?'
                              'In the anchor'd bark.'
'There let him stay—to him this order bear—
Back to your duty—for my course prepare:
Myself this enterprise to-night will share.'
'To-night, Lord Conrad?'

'Ay! at set of sun:
The breeze will freshen when the day is done.
My corslet, cloak—one hour and we are gone.
Sling on thy bugle—see that free from rust
My carbine-lock springs worthy of my trust;
Be the edge sharpen'd of my boarding-brand,
And give its guard more room to fit my hand.
This let the armourer with speed dispose;
Last time, it more fatigued my arm than foes:
Mark that the signal-gun be duly fired,
To tell us when the hour of stay 's expired.'

VIII

They make obeisance, and retire in haste,
Too soon to seek again the watery waste:
Yet they repine not—so that Conrad guides;
And who dare question aught that he decides?
That man of loneliness and mystery,
Scarce seen to smile, and seldom heard to sigh;
Whose name appals the fiercest of his crew,
And tints each swarthy cheek with sallower hue;
Still sways their souls with that commanding art
That dazzles, leads, yet chills the vulgar heart.
What is that spell, that thus his lawless train
Confess and envy, yet oppose in vain?
What should it be, that thus their faith can bind?
The power of Thought—the magic of the Mind!
Link'd with success, assumed and kept with skill,
That moulds another's weakness to its will;
Wields with their hands, but, still to these unknown,
Makes even their mightiest deeds appear his own.
Such hath it been—shall be—beneath the sun
The many still must labour for the one!
'Tis Nature's doom—but let the wretch who toils,
Accuse not, hate not *him* who wears the spoils.
Oh! if he knew the weight of splendid chains,
How light the balance of his humbler pains!

IX

Unlike the heroes of each ancient race,
Demons in act, but Gods at least in face,
In Conrad's form seems little to admire,
Though his dark eyebrow shades a glance of fire:
Robust but not Herculean—to the sight
No giant frame sets forth his common height;
Yet, in the whole, who paused to look again,
Saw more than marks the crowd of vulgar men;

They gaze and marvel how—and still confess
That thus it is, but why they cannot guess.
Sun-burnt his cheek, his forehead high and pale
The sable curls in wild profusion veil;
And oft perforce his rising lip reveals
The haughtier thought it curbs, but scarce conceals.
Though smooth his voice, and calm his general mien,
Still seems there something he would not have seen:
His features' deepening lines and varying hue
At times attracted, yet perplex'd the view,
As if within that murkiness of mind
Work'd feelings fearful, and yet undefined;
Such might it be—that none could truly tell—
Too close inquiry his stern glance would quell.
There breathe but few whose aspect might defy
The full encounter of his searching eye:
He had the skill, when Cunning's gaze would seek
To probe his heart and watch his changing cheek,
At once the observer's purpose to espy,
And on himself roll back his scrutiny,
Lest he to Conrad rather should betray
Some secret thought, than drag that chief's to-day.
There was a laughing Devil in his sneer,
That raised emotions both of rage and fear;
And where his frown of hatred darkly fell
Hope withering fled—and Mercy sigh'd farewell! [1]

                              x

Slight are the outward signs of evil thought,
Within—within—'twas there the spirit wrought!
Love shows all changes—Hate, Ambition, Guile,
Betray no further than the bitter smile;

[1] That Conrad is a character not altogether out of nature, I shall attempt to prove by some historical coincidences which I have met with since writing *The Corsair.*

'Eccelin prisonnier,' dit Rolandini, 's'enfermoit dans un silence menaçant, il fixoit sur la terre son visage féroce, et ne donnoit point d'essor à sa profonde indignation. De toutes partes cependant les soldats et les peuples accouroient; ils vouloient voir cet homme, jadis si puissant, et la joie universelle éclatoit de toutes partes. . . . Eccelin étoit d'une petite taille; mais tout l'aspect de sa personne, tous ses mouvemens, indiquoient un soldat.—Son langage étoit amer, son déportement superbe—et par son seul regard, il faisoit trembler les plus hardis.'—*Sismondi*, tome iii, p. 219.

Again, 'Gizericus (Genseric, king of the Vandals, the conqueror of both Carthage and Rome), staturâ mediocris, et equi casu claudicans, animo profundus, sermone rarus, luxuriae contemptor, irâ turbidus, habendi cupidus, ad solicitandas gentes providentissimus,' etc.—*Jornandes de Rebus Geticis*, c. 33.

I beg leave to quote these gloomy realities to keep in countenance my Giaour and Corsair.

The lip's least curl, the lightest paleness thrown
Along the govern'd aspect, speak alone
Of deeper passions; and to judge their mien,
He, who would see, must be himself unseen.
Then—with the hurried tread, the upward eye,
The clenched hand, the pause of agony,
That listens, starting, lest the step too near
Approach intrusive on that mood of fear:
Then—with each feature working from the heart,
With feelings loosed to strengthen—not depart:
That rise—convulse—contend—that freeze or glow,
Flush in the cheek, or damp upon the brow;
Then—Stranger! if thou canst, and tremblest not,
Behold his soul—the rest that soothes his lot!
Mark how that lone and blighted bosom sears
The scathing thought of execrated years!
Behold—but who hath seen, or e'er shall see,
Man as himself—the secret spirit free?

XI

Yet was not Conrad thus by Nature sent
To lead the guilty—guilt's worst instrument—
His soul was changed, before his deeds had driven
Him forth to war with man and forfeit heaven.
Warp'd by the world in Disappointment's school,
In words too wise, in conduct *there* a fool;
Too firm to yield, and far too proud to stoop,
Doom'd by his very virtues for a dupe,
He cursed those virtues as the cause of ill,
And not the traitors who betray'd him still;
Nor deem'd that gifts bestow'd on better men
Had left him joy, and means to give again.
Fear'd, shunn'd, belied—ere youth had lost her force,
He hated man too much to feel remorse,
And thought the voice of wrath a sacred call,
To pay the injuries of some on all.
He knew himself a villain—but he deem'd
The rest no better than the thing he seem'd;
And scorn'd the best as hypocrites who hid
Those deeds the bolder spirit plainly did.
He knew himself detested, but he knew
The hearts that loath'd him, crouch'd and dreaded too.
Lone, wild, and strange, he stood alike exempt
From all affection and from all contempt:
His name could sadden, and his acts surprise;
But they that fear'd him dared not to despise:

Man spurns the worm, but pauses ere he wake
The slumbering venom of the folded snake;
The first may turn—but not avenge the blow;
The last expires—but leaves no living foe;
Fast to the doom'd offender's form it clings,
And he may crush—not conquer—still it stings!

XII

None are all evil—quickening round his heart,
One softer feeling would not yet depart;
Oft could he sneer at others as beguiled
By passions worthy of a fool or child;
Yet 'gainst that passion vainly still he strove,
And even in him it asks the name of Love!
Yes, it was love—unchangeable—unchanged,
Felt but for one from whom he never ranged;
Though fairest captives daily met his eye,
He shunn'd, nor sought, but coldly passed them by;
Though many a beauty droop'd in prison'd bower,
None ever sooth'd his most unguarded hour.
Yes—it was Love—if thoughts of tenderness,
Tried in temptation, strengthen'd by distress,
Unmoved by absence, firm in every clime,
And yet—oh more than all!—untired by time;
Which nor defeated hope, nor baffled wile,
Could render sullen were she near to smile,
Nor rage could fire, nor sickness fret to vent
On her one murmur of his discontent;
Which still would meet with joy, with calmness part,
Lest that his look of grief should reach her heart;
Which nought removed, nor menaced to remove—
If there be love in mortals—this was love!
He was a villain—ay—reproaches shower
On him—but not the passion, nor its power,
Which only proved, all other virtues gone,
Not guilt itself could quench this loveliest one!

XIII

He paused a moment—till his hastening men
Pass'd the first winding downward to the glen.
'Strange tidings!—many a peril have I pass'd,
Nor know I why this next appears the last!
Yet so my heart forebodes, but must not fear,
Nor shall my followers find me falter here.
'Tis rash to meet, but surer death to wait
Till here they hunt us to undoubted fate;

And, if my plan but hold, and Fortune smile,
We 'll furnish mourners for our funeral pile.
Ay—let them slumber—peaceful be their dreams!
Morn ne'er awoke them with such brilliant beams
As kindle high to-night (but blow, thou breeze!)
To warm these slow avengers of the seas.
Now to Medora—Oh! my sinking heart,
Long may her own be lighter than thou art!
Yet was I brave—mean boast where all are brave!
Ev'n insects sting for aught they seek to save.
This common courage which with brutes we share,
That owes its deadliest efforts to despair,
Small merit claims—but 'twas my nobler hope
To teach my few with numbers still to cope;
Long have I led them—not to vainly bleed;
No medium now—we perish or succeed!
So let it be—it irks not me to die;
But thus to urge them whence they cannot fly.
My lot hath long had little of my care,
But chafes my pride thus baffled in the snare:
Is this my skill? my craft? to set at last
Hope, power, and life upon a single cast?
Oh, Fate!—accuse thy folly, not thy fate—
She may redeem thee still—nor yet too late.'

XIV

Thus with himself communion held he, till
He reach'd the summit of his tower-crown'd hill:
There at the portal paused—for wild and soft
He heard those accents never heard too oft;
Through the high lattice far yet sweet they rung,
And these the notes the bird of beauty sung:

1

'Deep in my soul that tender secret dwells,
    Lonely and lost to light for evermore,
Save when to thine my heart responsive swells,
    Then trembles into silence as before.

2

'There, in its centre, a sepulchral lamp
    Burns the slow flame, eternal—but unseen;
Which not the darkness of despair can damp,
    Though vain its ray as it had never been.

3

'Remember me—Oh! pass not thou my grave
Without one thought whose relics there recline:
The only pang my bosom dare not brave
Must be to find forgetfulness in thine.

4

'My fondest, faintest, latest accents hear—
Grief for the dead not Virtue can reprove;
Then give me all I ever ask'd—a tear,
The first—last—sole reward of so much love!'

He pass'd the portal—cross'd the corridor,
And reach'd the chamber as the strain gave o'er:
'My own Medora! sure thy song is sad—'

'In Conrad's absence wouldst thou have it glad?
Without thine ear to listen to my lay,
Still must my song my thoughts, my soul betray:
Still must each accent to my bosom suit,
My heart unhush'd—although my lips were mute!
Oh! many a night on this lone couch reclined,
My dreaming fear with storms hath wing'd the wind,
And deem'd the breath that faintly fann'd thy sail
The murmuring prelude of the ruder gale;
Though soft, it seem'd the low prophetic dirge,
That mourn'd thee floating on the savage surge:
Still would I rise to rouse the beacon fire,
Lest spies less true should let the blaze expire;
And many a restless hour outwatch'd each star,
And morning came—and still thou wert afar.
Oh! how the chill blast on my bosom blew,
And day broke dreary on my troubled view,
And still I gazed and gazed—and not a prow
Was granted to my tears—my truth—my vow!
At length—'twas noon—I hail'd and blest the mast
That met my sight—it near'd—Alas! it pass'd!
Another came—Oh God! 'twas thine at last!
Would that those days were over! wilt thou ne'er,
My Conrad! learn the joys of peace to share?
Sure thou hast more than wealth, and many a home
As bright as this invites us not to roam:
Thou know'st it is not peril that I fear,
I only tremble when thou art not here;
Then not for mine, but that far dearer life,

Which flies from love and languishes for strife—
How strange that heart, to me so tender still,
Should war with nature and its better will!'

'Yea, strange indeed—that heart hath long been changed;
Worm-like 'twas trampled—adder-like avenged,
Without one hope on earth beyond thy love,
And scarce a glimpse of mercy from above.
Yet the same feeling which thou dost condemn,
My very love to thee is hate to them,
So closely mingling here, that disentwined,
I cease to love thee when I love mankind:
Yet dread not this—the proof of all the past
Assures the future that my love will last;
But—Oh, Medora! nerve thy gentler heart,
This hour again—but not for long—we part.'

'This hour we part!—my heart foreboded this:
Thus ever fade my fairy dreams of bliss.
This hour—it cannot be—this hour away!
Yon bark hath hardly anchor'd in the bay;
Her consort still is absent, and her crew
Have need of rest before they toil anew:
My love! thou mock'st my weakness; and wouldst steel
My breast before the time when it must feel;
But trifle now no more with my distress,
Such mirth hath less of play than bitterness.
Be silent, Conrad!—dearest! come and share
The feast these hands delighted to prepare;
Light toil! to cull and dress thy frugal fare!
See, I have pluck'd the fruit that promised best,
And where not sure, perplex'd, but pleased, I guess'd
At such as seem'd the fairest; thrice the hill
My steps have wound to try the coolest rill;
Yes! thy sherbet to-night will sweetly flow,
See how it sparkles in its vase of snow!
The grapes' gay juice thy bosom never cheers;
Thou more than Moslem when the cup appears:
Think not I mean to chide—for I rejoice
What others deem a penance is thy choice.
But come, the board is spread; our silver lamp
Is trimm'd, and heeds not the sirocco's damp:
Then shall my handmaids while the time along,
And join with me the dance, or wake the song;
Or my guitar, which still thou lov'st to hear,
Shall soothe or lull—or, should it vex thine ear,

We 'll turn the tale, by Ariosto told,
Of fair Olympia loved and left of old.[1]
Why—thou wert worse than he who broke his vow
To that lost damsel, shouldst thou leave me now;
Or even that traitor chief—I 've seen thee smile,
When the clear sky show'd Ariadne's Isle,
Which I have pointed from these cliffs the while:
And thus half sportive, half in fear, I said,
Lest time should raise that doubt to more than dread,
Thus Conrad, too, will quit me for the main:
And he deceived me—for—he came again!'

'Again, again—and oft again—my love!
If there be life below, and hope above,
He will return—but now, the moments bring
The time of parting with redoubled wing:
The why—the where—what boots it now to tell?
Since all must end in that wild word—farewell!
Yet would I fain—did time allow—disclose—
Fear not—these are no formidable foes;
And here shall watch a more than wonted guard,
For sudden siege and long defence prepared:
Nor be thou lonely—though thy lord 's away,
Our matrons and thy handmaids with thee stay;
And this thy comfort—that, when next we meet,
Security shall make repose more sweet.
List!—'tis the bugle—Juan shrilly blew—
One kiss—one more—another—Oh! Adieu!'

She rose—she sprung—she clung to his embrace,
Till his heart heaved beneath her hidden face.
He dared not raise to his that deep-blue eye,
Which downcast droop'd in tearless agony.
Her long fair hair lay floating o'er his arms,
In all the wildness of dishevell'd charms;
Scarce beat that bosom where his image dwelt
So full—*that* feeling seem'd almost unfelt!
Hark—peals the thunder of the signal-gun!
It told 'twas sunset—and he cursed that sun.
Again—again—that form he madly press'd,
Which mutely clasp'd, imploringly caress'd!
And tottering to the couch his bride he bore,
One moment gazed—as if to gaze no more;
Felt—that for him earth held but her alone,
Kiss'd her cold forehead—turn'd—is Conrad gone?

[1] *Orlando Furioso*, canto x.

XV

'And is he gone?'—on sudden solitude
How oft that fearful question will intrude!
''Twas but an instant past—and here he stood!
And now'—without the portal's porch she rush'd,
And then at length her tears in freedom gush'd;
Big, bright, and fast, unknown to her they fell;
But still her lips refused to send—'Farewell!'
For in that word—that fatal word—howe'er
We promise, hope, believe, there breathes despair.
O'er every feature of that still, pale face,
Had sorrow fix'd what time can ne'er erase:
The tender blue of that large loving eye
Grew frozen with its gaze on vacancy,
Till—Oh, how far!—it caught a glimpse of him,
And then it flow'd—and phrensied seem'd to swim
Through those long, dark, and glistening lashes dew'd
With drops of sadness oft to be renew'd.
'He 's gone!'—against her heart that hand is driven,
Convulsed and quick—then gently raised to heaven;
She look'd and saw the heaving of the main;
The white sail set—she dared not look again;
But turn'd with sickening soul within the gate—
'It is no dream—and I am desolate!'

XVI

From crag to crag descending—swiftly sped
Stern Conrad down, nor once he turn'd his head;
But shrunk whene'er the windings of his way
Forced on his eye what he would not survey,
His lone, but lovely dwelling on the steep,
That hail'd him first when homeward from the deep:
And she—the dim and melancholy star,
Whose ray of beauty reach'd him from afar,
On her he must not gaze, he must not think,
There he might rest—but on Destruction's brink:
Yet once almost he stopp'd—and nearly gave
His fate to chance, his projects to the wave:
But no—it must not be—a worthy chief
May melt, but not betray to woman's grief.
He sees his bark, he notes how fair the wind,
And sternly gathers all his might of mind.
Again he hurries on—and as he hears
The clang of tumult vibrate on his ears,
The busy sounds, the bustle of the shore,
The shout, the signal, and the dashing oar;

As marks his eye the seaboy on the mast,
The anchors rise, the sails unfurling fast,
The waving kerchiefs of the crowd that urge
That mute adieu to those who stem the surge;
And more than all, his blood-red flag aloft,
He marvell'd how his heart could seem so soft.
Fire in his glance, and wildness in his breast,
He feels of all his former self possest;
He bounds—he flies—until his footsteps reach
The verge where ends the cliff, begins the beach,
There checks his speed; but pauses less to breathe
The breezy freshness of the deep beneath,
Than there his wonted statelier step renew;
Nor rush, disturb'd by haste, to vulgar view:
For well had Conrad learn'd to curb the crowd,
By arts that veil, and oft preserve the proud;
His was the lofty port, the distant mien,
That seems to shun the sight—and awes if seen:
The solemn aspect, and the highborn eye,
That checks low mirth, but lacks not courtesy;
All these he wielded to command assent:
But where he wished to win, so well unbent,
That kindness cancell'd fear in those who heard,
And others' gifts show'd mean beside his word,
When echo'd to the heart as from his own,
His deep yet tender melody of tone:
But such was foreign to his wonted mood,
He cared not what he soften'd, but subdued;
The evil passions of his youth had made
Him value less who loved—than what obey'd.

XVII

Around him mustering ranged his ready guard.
Before him Juan stands—'Are all prepared?'
'They are—nay more—embark'd: the latest boat
Waits but my chief——'
                              'My sword, and my capote.'
Soon firmly girded on, and lightly slung,
His belt and cloak were o'er his shoulder flung:
'Call Pedro here!' He comes—and Conrad bends,
With all the courtesy he deign'd his friends;
'Receive these tablets, and peruse with care,
Words of high trust and truth are graven there;
Double the guard, and when Anselmo's bark
Arrives, let him alike these orders mark:

In three days (serve the breeze) the sun shall shine
On our return—till then all peace be thine!'
This said, his brother Pirate's hand he wrung,
Then to his boat with haughty gesture sprung.
Flash'd the dipt oars, and sparkling with the stroke,
Around the waves' phosphoric brightness broke; [1]
They gain the vessel—on the deck he stands,—
Shrieks the shrill whistle—ply the busy hands—
He marks how well the ship her helm obeys,
How gallant all her crew—and deigns to praise.
His eyes of pride to young Gonsalvo turn—
Why doth he start, and inly seem to mourn?
Alas! those eyes beheld his rocky tower,
And live a moment o'er the parting hour;
She—his Medora—did she mark the prow?
Ah! never loved he half so much as now!
But much must yet be done ere dawn of day—
Again he mans himself and turns away;
Down to the cabin with Gonsalvo bends,
And there unfolds his plan—his means—and ends;
Before them burns the lamp, and spreads the chart
And all that speaks and aids the naval art;
They to the midnight watch protract debate;
To anxious eyes what hour is ever late?
Meantime, the steady breeze serenely blew,
And fast and falcon-like the vessel flew;
Pass'd the high headlands of each clustering isle
To gain their port—long—long ere morning smile:
And soon the night-glass through the narrow bay
Discovers where the Pacha's galleys lay.
Count they each sail—and mark how there supine
The lights in vain o'er heedless Moslem shine.
Secure, unnoted, Conrad's prow pass'd by,
And anchor'd where his ambush meant to lie;
Screen'd from espial by the jutting cape,
That rears on high its rude fantastic shape,
Then rose his band to duty—not from sleep—
Equipp'd for deeds alike on land or deep;
While lean'd their leader o'er the fretting flood,
And calmly talk'd—and yet he talk'd of blood!

By night, particularly in a warm latitude, every stroke of the oar, every
motion of the boat or ship, is followed by a slight flash like sheet lightning from
the water.

Conosceste i dubiosi desiri?
DANTE.

I

In Coron's bay floats many a galley light,
Through Coron's lattices the lamps are bright,
For Seyd, the Pacha, makes a feast to-night:
A feast for promised triumph yet to come,
When he shall drag the fetter'd Rovers home;
This hath he sworn by Alla and his sword,
And faithful to his firman and his word,
His summon'd prows collect along the coast,
And great the gathering crews, and loud the boast,
Already shared the captives and the prize,
Though far the distant foe they thus despise;
'Tis but to sail—no doubt to-morrow's Sun
Will see the Pirates bound—their haven won!
Meantime the watch may slumber, if they will,
Nor only wake to war, but dreaming kill.
Though all, who can, disperse on shore and seek
To flesh their glowing valour on the Greek;
How well such deed becomes the turban'd brave—
To bare the sabre's edge before a slave!
Infest his dwelling—but forbear to slay,
Their arms are strong yet merciful to-day,
And do not deign to smite because they may!
Unless some gay caprice suggests the blow,
To keep in practice for the coming foe.
Revel and rout the evening hours beguile,
And they who wish to wear a head must smile;
For Moslem mouths produce their choicest cheer,
And hoard their curses, till the coast is clear.

II

High in his hall reclines the turban'd Seyd;
Around—the bearded chiefs he came to lead.
Removed the banquet, and the last pilaff—
Forbidden draughts, 'tis said, he dared to quaff,
Though to the rest the sober berry's juice [1]
The slaves bear round for rigid Moslems use;
The long chibouque's [2] dissolving cloud supply,
While dance the Almas [3] to wild minstrelsy.

[1] Coffee. [2] 'Chibouque,' pipe. [3] Dancing girls.

The rising morn will view the chiefs embark;
But waves are somewhat treacherous in the dark:
And revellers may more securely sleep
On silken couch than o'er the rugged deep;
Feast there who can—nor combat till they must,
And less to conquest than to Korans trust;
And yet the numbers crowded in his host
Might warrant more than even the Pacha's boast.

III

With cautious reverence from the outer gate
Slow stalks the slave, whose office there to wait,
Bows his bent head—his hand salutes the floor,
Ere yet his tongue the trusted tidings bore:
'A captive Dervise, from the pirate's nest
Escaped, is here—himself would tell the rest.' [1]
He took the sign from Seyd's assenting eye,
And led the holy man in silence nigh.
His arms were folded on his dark-green vest,
His step was feeble, and his look deprest;
Yet worn he seem'd of hardship more than years,
And pale his cheek with penance, not from fears.
Vow'd to his God—his sable locks he wore,
And these his lofty cap rose proudly o'er:
Around his form his loose long robe was thrown,
And wrapt a breast bestow'd on heaven alone;
Submissive, yet with self-possession mann'd,
He calmly met the curious eyes that scann'd;
And question of his coming fain would seek,
Before the Pacha's will allow'd to speak.

IV

'Whence com'st thou, Dervise?'
                                        'From the outlaw's den,
A fugitive—'
                    'Thy capture where and when?'
'From Scalanovo's port to Scio's isle,
The Saick was bound; but Alla did not smile

[1] It has been observed, that Conrad's entering disguised as a spy is out of
nature. Perhaps so. I find something not unlike it in history.—'Anxious to
explore with his own eyes the state of the Vandals, Majorian ventured, after
disguising the colour of his hair, to visit Carthage in the character of his own
ambassador; and Genseric was afterwards mortified by the discovery that he had
entertained and dismissed the Emperor of the Romans. Such an anecdote may
be rejected as an improbable fiction; but it is a fiction which would not have been
imagined unless in the life of a hero.'—See Gibbon's *Decline and Fall*, vol. vi.
p. 180.

Upon our course—the Moslem merchant's gains
The Rovers won: our limbs have worn their chains.
I had no death to fear, nor wealth to boast,
Beyond the wandering freedom which I lost;
At length a fisher's humble boat by night
Afforded hope, and offer'd chance of flight;
I seized the hour, and find my safety here—
With thee—most mighty Pacha! who can fear?'

'How speed the outlaws? stand they well prepared,
Their plunder'd wealth, and robber's rock, to guard?
Dream they of this our preparation, doom'd
To view with fire their scorpion nest consumed?'

'Pacha! the fetter'd captive's mourning eye,
That weeps for flight, but ill can play the spy;
I only heard the reckless waters roar,
Those waves that would not bear me from the shore;
I only mark'd the glorious sun and sky,
Too bright—too blue—for my captivity;
And felt—that all which Freedom's bosom cheers,
Must break my chain before it dried my tears.
This may'st thou judge, at least, from my escape,
They little deem of aught in peril's shape;
Else vainly had I pray'd or sought the chance
That leads me here—if eyed with vigilance;
The careless guard that did not see me fly,
May watch as idly when thy power is nigh:
Pacha!—my limbs are faint—and nature craves
Food for my hunger, rest from tossing waves:
Permit my absence—peace be with thee!   Peace
With all around!—now grant repose—release.'

'Stay, Dervise!   I have more to question—stay,
I do command thee—sit—dost hear?—obey!
More I must ask, and food the slaves shall bring;
Thou shalt not pine where all are banqueting:
The supper done—prepare thee to reply,
Clearly and full—I love not mystery.'
'Twere vain to guess what shook the pious man,
Who look'd not lovingly on that Divan;
Nor show'd high relish for the banquet prest,
And less respect for every fellow guest.
'Twas but a moment's peevish hectic past
Along his cheek, and tranquillized as fast:

He sate him down in silence, and his look
Resumed the calmness which before forsook:
The feast was usher'd in—but sumptuous fare
He shunn'd as if some poison mingled there.
For one so long condemn'd to toil and fast,
Methinks he strangely spares the rich repast.
'What ails thee, Dervise? eat—dost thou suppose
This feast a Christian's? or my friends thy foes?
Why dost thou shun the salt? that sacred pledge,
Which, once partaken, blunts the sabre's edge,
Makes even contending tribes in peace unite,
And hated hosts seem brethren to the sight!'

'Salt seasons dainties—and my food is still
The humblest root, my drink the simplest rill;
And my stern vow and order's [1] laws oppose
To break or mingle bread with friends or foes;
It may seem strange—if there be aught to dread,
That peril rests upon my single head;
But for thy sway—nay more—thy Sultan's throne,
I taste nor bread nor banquet—save alone;
Infringed our order's rule, the Prophet's rage
To Mecca's dome might bar my pilgrimage.'
'Well—as thou wilt—ascetic as thou art—
One question answer; then in peace depart.
How many?—Ha! it cannot sure be day?
What star—what sun is bursting on the bay?
It shines a lake of fire!—away—away!
Ho! treachery! my guards! my scimitar!
The galleys feed the flames—and I afar!
Accursed Dervise!—these thy tidings—thou
Some villain spy—seize—cleave him—slay him now!'

Up rose the Dervise with that burst of light,
Nor less his change of form appall'd the sight:
Up rose that Dervise—not in saintly garb,
But like a warrior bounding on his barb,
Dash'd his high cap, and tore his robe away—
Shone his mail'd breast, and flash'd his sabre's ray!
His close but glittering casque, and sable plume,
More glittering eye, and black brow's sabler gloom,
Glared on the Moslems' eyes some Afrit sprite,
Whose demon death-blow left no hope for fight.
The wild confusion, and the swarthy glow
Of flames on high, and torches from below;

[1] The Dervises are in colleges, and of different orders, as the monks.

The shriek of terror, and the mingling yell—
For swords began to clash, and shouts to swell—
Flung o'er that spot of earth the air of hell!
Distracted, to and fro, the flying slaves
Behold but bloody shore and fiery waves;
Nought heeded they the Pacha's angry cry,
They seize that Dervise!—seize on Zatanai![1]
He saw their terror—check'd the first despair
That urged him but to stand and perish there,
Since far too early and too well obey'd,
The flame was kindled ere the signal made;
He saw their terror—from his baldric drew
His bugle—brief the blast—but shrilly blew;
'Tis answer'd—'Well ye speed, my gallant crew!
Why did I doubt their quickness of career?
And deem design had left me single here?'
Sweeps his long arm—that sabre's whirling sway
Sheds fast atonement for its first delay;
Completes his fury, what their fear begun,
And makes the many basely quail to one.
The cloven turbans o'er the chamber spread,
And scarce an arm dare rise to guard its head:
Even Seyd, convulsed, o'erwhelm'd, with rage, surprise,
Retreats before him, though he still defies.
No craven he—and yet he dreads the blow,
So much Confusion magnifies his foe!
His blazing galleys still distract his sight,
He tore his beard, and foaming fled the fight;[2]
For now the pirates pass'd the Haram gate,
And burst within—and it were death to wait;
Where wild Amazement shrieking—kneeling—throws
The sword aside—in vain—the blood o'erflows!
The Corsairs pouring, haste to where within
Invited Conrad's bugle, and the din
Of groaning victims, and wild cries for life,
Proclaim'd how well he did the work of strife.
They shout to find him grim and lonely there,
A glutted tiger mangling in his lair!
But short their greeting—shorter his reply—
''Tis well—but Seyd escapes, and he must die—
Much hath been done, but more remains to do—
Their galleys blaze—why not their city too?'

'Zatanai,' Satan.

[2] A common and not very novel effect of Mussulman anger. See Prince
Eugene's *Memoirs*, p. 24. 'The Seraskier received a wound in the thigh; he
plucked up his beard by the roots, because he was obliged to quit the field.'

V

Quick at the word they seized him each a torch,
And fire the dome from minaret to porch.
A stern delight was fix'd in Conrad's eye,
But sudden sunk—for on his ear the cry
Of women struck, and like a deadly knell
Knock'd at that heart unmoved by battle's yell.
'Oh! burst the Haram—wrong not on your lives
One female form—remember—*we* have wives.
On them such outrage Vengeance will repay;
Man is our foe, and such 'tis ours to slay:
But still we spared—must spare the weaker prey.
Oh! I forgot—but Heaven will not forgive
If at my word the helpless cease to live:
Follow who will—I go—we yet have time
Our souls to lighten of at least a crime.'
He climbs the crackling stair—he bursts the door,
Nor feels his feet glow scorching with the floor;
His breath choked gasping with the volumed smoke,
But still from room to room his way he broke.
They search—they find—they save: with lusty arms
Each bears a prize of unregarded charms;
Calm their loud fears; sustain their sinking frames
With all the care defenceless beauty claims:
So well could Conrad tame their fiercest mood,
And check the very hands with gore imbrued.
But who is she? whom Conrad's arms convey
From reeking pile and combat's wreck away—
Who but the love of him he dooms to bleed?
The Haram queen—but still the slave of Seyd!

VI

Brief time had Conrad now to greet Gulnare,[1]
Few words to reassure the trembling fair;
For in that pause compassion snatch'd from war,
The foe before retiring, fast and far,
With wonder saw their footsteps unpursued,
First slowlier fled—then rallied—then withstood.
This Seyd perceives, then first perceives how few,
Compared with his, the Corsair's roving crew,
And blushes o'er his error, as he eyes
The ruin wrought by panic and surprise.
Alla il Alla! Vengeance swells the cry—
Shame mounts to rage that must atone or die!

[1] Gulnare, a female name; it means, literally, the flower of the pomegranate.

And flame for flame and blood for blood must tell,
The tide of triumph ebbs that flow'd too well—
When wrath returns to renovated strife,
And those who fought for conquest strike for life.
Conrad beheld the danger—he beheld
His followers faint by freshening foes repell'd:
'One effort—one—to break the circling host!'
They form—unite—charge—waver—all is lost!
Within a narrower ring compress'd, beset,
Hopeless, not heartless, strive and struggle yet—
Ah! now they fight in firmest file no more,
Hemm'd in—cut off—cleft down—and trampled o'er;
But each strikes singly, silently, and home,
And sinks outwearied rather than o'ercome,
His last faint quittance rendering with his breath,
Till the blade glimmers in the grasp of death!

VII

But first, ere came the rallying host to blows,
And rank to rank, and hand to hand oppose,
Gulnare and all her Haram handmaids freed,
Safe in the dome of one who held their creed,
By Conrad's mandate safely were bestow'd,
And dried those tears for life and fame that flow'd:
And when that dark-eyed lady, young Gulnare,
Recall'd those thoughts late wandering in despair,
Much did she marvel o'er the courtesy
That smooth'd his accents; soften'd in his eye:
'Twas strange—*that* robber thus with gore bedew'd,
Seem'd gentler then than Seyd in fondest mood.
The Pacha woo'd as if he deem'd the slave
Must seem delighted with the heart he gave;
The Corsair vow'd protection, soothed affright,
As if his homage were a woman's right.
'The wish is wrong—nay, worse for female—vain:
Yet much I long to view that chief again;
If but to thank for, what my fear forgot,
The life my loving lord remember'd not!'

VIII

And him she saw, where thickest carnage spread,
But gather'd breathing from the happier dead;
Far from his band, and battling with a host
That deem right dearly won the field he lost,
Fell'd—bleeding—baffled of the death he sought,
And snatch'd to expiate all ills he wrought;

Preserved to linger and to live in vain,
While Vengeance ponder'd o'er new plans of pain,
And stanch'd the blood she saves to shed again—
But drop for drop, for Seyd's unglutted eye
Would doom him ever dying—ne'er to die!
Can this be he? triumphant late she saw,
When his red hand's wild gesture waved, a law!
'Tis he indeed—disarm'd but undeprest,
His sole regret the life he still possest;
His wounds too slight, though taken with that will,
Which would have kiss'd the hand that then could kill.
Oh were there none, of all the many given,
To send his soul—he scarcely ask'd to heaven?
Must he alone of all retain his breath,
Who more than all had striven and struck for death?
He deeply felt—what mortal hearts must feel,
When thus reversed on faithless fortune's wheel,
For crimes committed, and the victor's threat
Of lingering tortures to repay the debt—
He deeply, darkly felt; but evil pride
That led to perpetrate, now serves to hide
Still in his stern and self-collected mien
A conqueror's more than captive's air is seen,
Though faint with wasting toil and stiffening wound,
But few that saw—so calmly gazed around:
Though the far shouting of the distant crowd,
Their tremors o'er, rose insolently loud,
The better warriors who beheld him near,
Insulted not the foe who taught them fear;
And the grim guards that to his durance led
In silence eyed him with a secret dread.

IX

The Leech was sent—but not in mercy—there,
To note how much the life yet left could bear;
He found enough to load with heaviest chain,
And promise feeling for the wrench of pain:
To-morrow—yea—to-morrow's evening sun
Will sinking see impalement's pangs begun,
And rising with the wonted blush of morn
Behold how well or ill those pangs are borne.
Of torments this the longest and the worst,
Which adds all other agony to thirst,
That day by day death still forbears to slake,
While famish'd vultures flit around the stake.

'Oh! water—water!'—smiling Hate denies
The victim's prayer—for if he drinks—he dies.
This was his doom;—the Leech, the guard, were gone,
And left proud Conrad fetter'd and alone.

X

'Twere vain to paint to what his feelings grew—
It even were doubtful if their victim knew.
There is a war, a chaos of the mind,
When all its elements convulsed—combined—
Lie dark and jarring with perturbed force,
And gnashing with impenitent Remorse;
That juggling fiend—who never spake before—
But cries 'I warn'd thee!' when the deed is o'er.
Vain voice! the spirit burning but unbent,
May writhe—rebel—the weak alone repent!
Even in that lonely hour when most it feels,
And, to itself, all—all that self reveals,
No single passion, and no ruling thought
That leaves the rest at once unseen, unsought;
But the wild prospect when the soul reviews—
All rushing through their thousand avenues,
Ambition's dreams expiring, love's regret,
Endangered glory, life itself beset;
The joy untasted, the contempt or hate
'Gainst those who fain would triumph in our fate;
The hopeless past, the hasting future driven
Too quickly on to guess if hell or heaven;
Deeds, thoughts, and words, perhaps remember'd not
So keenly till that hour, but ne'er forgot;
Things light or lovely in their acted time,
But now to stern reflection each a crime;
The withering sense of evil unreveal'd,
Not cankering less because the more conceal'd—
All, in a word, from which all eyes must start,
That opening sepulchre—the naked heart
Bares with its buried woes, till Pride awake,
To snatch the mirror from the soul—and break.
Ay—Pride can veil, and Courage brave it all,
All—all—before—beyond—the deadliest fall.
Each has some fear, and he who least betrays,
The only hypocrite deserving praise:
Not the loud recreant wretch who boasts and flies;
But he who looks on death—and silent dies.
So steel'd by pondering o'er his far career,
He half-way meets him should he menace near!

XI

In the high chamber of his highest tower
Sate Conrad, fetter'd in the Pacha's power.
His palace perish'd in the flame—this fort
Contain'd at once his captive and his court.
Not much could Conrad of his sentence blame,
His foe, if vanquish'd, had but shared the same:—
Alone he sate—in solitude had scann'd
His guilty bosom, but that breast he mann'd:
One thought alone he could not—dared not meet—
'Oh, how these tidings will Medora greet?'
Then—only then—his clanking hands he raised,
And strain'd with rage the chain on which he gazed:
But soon he found, or feign'd, or dream'd relief,
And smiled in self-derision of his grief,
'And now come torture when it will—or may,
More need of rest to nerve me for the day!'
This said, with languor to his mat he crept,
And, whatsoe'er his visions, quickly slept.
'Twas hardly midnight when that fray begun,
For Conrad's plans matured, at once were done;
And Havoc loathes so much the waste of time,
She scarce had left an uncommitted crime.
One hour beheld him since the tide he stemm'd—
Disguised, discover'd, conquering, ta'en, condemn'd,
A chief on land—an outlaw on the deep—
Destroying, saving, prison'd, and asleep!

XII

He slept in calmest seeming, for his breath
Was hush'd so deep—Ah! happy if in death!
He slept—Who o'er his placid slumber bends?
His foes are gone, and here he hath no friends;
Is it some seraph sent to grant him grace?
No, 'tis an earthly form with heavenly face!
Its white arm raised a lamp—yet gently hid,
Lest the ray flash abruptly on the lid
Of that closed eye, which opens but to pain,
And once unclosed—but once may close again.
That form, with eye so dark, and cheek so fair,
And auburn waves of gemm'd and braided hair;
With shape of fairy lightness—naked foot,
That shines like snow, and falls on earth as mute—
Through guards and dunnest night how came it there?
Ah! rather ask what will not woman dare?
Whom youth and pity lead like thee, Gulnare!

She could not sleep—and while the Pacha's rest
In muttering dreams yet saw his pirate-guest,
She left his side—his signet-ring she bore,
Which oft in sport adorn'd her hand before—
And with it, scarcely question'd, won her way
Through drowsy guards that must that sign obey.
Worn out with toil, and tired with changing blows,
Their eyes had envied Conrad his repose;
And chill and nodding at the turret door,
They stretch their listless limbs, and watch no more:
Just raised their heads to hail the signet-ring,
Nor ask or what or who the sign may bring.

XIII

She gazed in wonder, 'Can he calmly sleep,
While other eyes his fall or ravage weep?
And mine in restlessness are wandering here—
What sudden spell hath made this man so dear?
True—'tis to him my life, and more, I owe,
And me and mine he spared from worse than woe:
'Tis late to think—but soft—his slumber breaks—
How heavily he sighs!—he starts—awakes!'

He raised his head—and dazzled with the light,
His eye seem'd dubious if it saw aright:
He moved his hand—the grating of his chain
Too harshly told him that he lived again.
'What is that form? if not a shape of air,
Methinks, my jailor's face shows wondrous fair!'

'Pirate! thou know'st me not—but I am one,
Grateful for deeds thou hast too rarely done;
Look on me—and remember her, thy hand
Snatch'd from the flames, and thy more fearful band.
I come through darkness,—and I scarce know why—
Yet not to hurt—I would not see thee die.'

'If so, kind lady! thine the only eye
That would not here in that gay hope delight:
Theirs is the chance—and let them use their right.
But still I thank their courtesy or thine,
That would confess me at so fair a shrine!'
Strange though it seem—yet with extremest grief
Is link'd a mirth—it doth not bring relief—
That playfulness of Sorrow ne'er beguiles,
And smiles in bitterness—but still it smiles;

And sometimes with the wisest and the best,
Till even the scaffold [1] echoes with their jest!
Yet not the joy to which it seems akin—
It may deceive all hearts, save that within.
Whate'er it was that flash'd on Conrad, now
A laughing wildness half unbent his brow;
And these his accents had a sound of mirth,
As if the last he could enjoy on earth;
Yet 'gainst his nature—for through that short life,
Few thoughts had he to spare from gloom and strife.

XIV

'Corsair! thy doom is named—but I have power
To soothe the Pacha in his weaker hour.
Thee would I spare—nay more—would save thee now,
But this—time—hope—nor even thy strength allow;
But all I can, I will: at least delay
The sentence that remits thee scarce a day.
More now were ruin—even thyself were loth
The vain attempt should bring but doom to both.'

'Yes! loth indeed:—my soul is nerved to all,
Or fall'n too low to fear a further fall:
Tempt not thyself with peril; me with hope
Of flight from foes with whom I could not cope:
Unfit to vanquish—shall I meanly fly,
The one of all my band that would not die?
Yet there is one—to whom my memory clings,
Till to these eyes her own wild softness springs.
My sole resources in the path I trod
Were these—my bark, my sword, my love, my God!
The last I left in youth—he leaves me now—
And Man but works his will to lay me low.
I have no thought to mock his throne with prayer
Wrung from the coward crouching of despair;
It is enough—I breathe, and I can bear.
My sword is shaken from the worthless hand
That might have better kept so true a brand;
My bark is sunk or captive—but my love—
For her in sooth my voice would mount above:

---

[1] In Sir Thomas More, for instance, on the scaffold, and Anne Boleyn, in the Tower, when grasping her neck, she remarked, that it 'was too slender to trouble the headsman much.' During one part of the French Revolution, it became a fashion to leave some *mot* as a legacy; and the quantity of facetious last words spoken during that period would form a melancholy jest-book of a considerable size.

Oh! she is all that still to earth can bind—
And this will break a heart so more than kind,
And blight a form—till thine appear'd, Gulnare!
Mine eye ne'er ask'd if others were as fair.'

'Thou lov'st another then?—but what to me
Is this—'tis nothing—nothing e'er can be:
But yet—thou lov'st—and—Oh! I envy those
Whose hearts on hearts as faithful can repose,
Who never feel the void—the wandering thought
That sighs o'er visions—such as mine hath wrought.'
'Lady—methought thy love was his, for whom
This arm redeem'd thee from a fiery tomb.'
'My love stern Seyd's! Oh—No—No—not my love—
Yet much this heart, that strives no more, once strove
To meet his passion—but it would not be.
I felt—I feel—love dwells with—with the free.
I am a slave, a favour'd slave at best,
To share his splendour, and seem very blest!
Oft must my soul the question undergo,
Of—"Dost thou love?" and burn to answer, "No!"
Oh! hard it is that fondness to sustain,
And struggle not to feel averse in vain;
But harder still the heart's recoil to bear,
And hide from one—perhaps another there.
He takes the hand I give not—nor withhold—
Its pulse nor check'd—nor quicken'd—calmly cold:
And when resign'd, it drops a lifeless weight
From one I never loved enough to hate.
No warmth these lips return by his imprest,
And chill'd remembrance shudders o'er the rest.
Yes—had I ever proved that passion's zeal,
The change to hatred were at least to feel:
But still he goes unmourn'd, returns unsought,
And oft when present—absent from my thought.
Or when reflection comes—and come it must—
I fear that henceforth 'twill but bring disgust;
I am his slave—but, in despite of pride,
'Twas worse than bondage to become his bride.
Oh! that this dotage of his breast would cease!
Or seek another and give mine release,
But yesterday—I could have said, to peace!
Yes, if unwonted fondness now I feign,
Remember, captive! 'tis to break thy chain;
Repay the life that to thy hand I owe;

To give thee back to all endear'd below,
Who share such love as I can never know.
Farewell—morn breaks—and I must now away:
'Twill cost me dear—but dread no death to-day!'

XV

She press'd his fetter'd fingers to her heart,
And bow'd her head, and turn'd her to depart,
And noiseless as a lovely dream is gone.
And was she here? and is he now alone?
What gem hath dropp'd and sparkles o'er his chain?
The tear most sacred, shed for others' pain,
That starts at once—bright—pure—from Pity's mine
Already polish'd by the hand divine!
Oh! too convincing—dangerously dear—
In woman's eye the unanswerable tear!
That weapon of her weakness she can wield,
To save, subdue—at once her spear and shield:
Avoid it—Virtue ebbs and Wisdom errs,
Too fondly gazing on that grief of hers!
What lost a world, and bade a hero fly?
The timid tear in Cleopatra's eye.
Yet be the soft triumvir's fault forgiven,
By this—how many lose not earth—but heaven!
Consign their souls to man's eternal foe,
And seal their own to spare some wanton's woe.

XVI

'Tis morn—and o'er his alter'd features play
The beams—without the hope of yesterday.
What shall he be ere night? perchance a thing
O'er which the raven flaps her funeral wing:
By his closed eye unheeded and unfelt,
While sets that sun, and dews of evening melt,
Chill, wet, and misty round each stiffen'd limb,
Refreshing earth—reviving all but him!

CANTO THE THIRD

Come vedi—ancor non m'abbandona.

DANTE.

I

Slow sinks, more lovely ere his race be run,[1]
Along Morea's hills the setting sun;
Not, as in Northern climes, obscurely bright,
But one unclouded blaze of living light!
O'er the hush'd deep the yellow beam he throws,
Gilds the green wave, that trembles as it glows.
On old Aegina's rock, and Idra's isle,
The god of gladness sheds his parting smile;
O'er his own regions lingering, loves to shine,
Though there his altars are no more divine.
Descending fast the mountain shadows kiss
Thy glorious gulf, unconquer'd Salamis!
Their azure arches through the long expanse
More deeply purpled meet his mellowing glance,
And tenderest tints, along their summits driven,
Mark his gay course, and own the hues of heaven;
Till, darkly shaded from the land and deep,
Behind his Delphian cliff he sinks to sleep.

On such an eve, his palest beam he cast,
When—Athens! here thy Wisest look'd his last.
How watch'd thy better sons his farewell ray,
That closed their murder'd sage's [2] latest day!
Not yet—not yet—Sol pauses on the hill—
The precious hour of parting lingers still;
But sad his light to agonizing eyes,
And dark the mountain's once delightful dyes:
Gloom o'er the lovely land he seem'd to pour,
The land, where Phoebus never frown'd before;
But ere he sank below Cithaeron's head,
The cup of woe was quaff'd—the spirit fled;
The soul of him who scorn'd to fear or fly—
Who lived and died, as none can live or die!

But lo! from high Hymettus to the plain,
The queen of night asserts her silent reign.[3]

[1] The opening lines, as far as section ii, have perhaps, little business here, and were annexed to an unpublished (though printed) poem [*The Curse of Minerva*]; but they were written on the spot, in the spring of 1811, and—I scarce know why—the reader must excuse their appearance here—if he can.

[2] Socrates drank the hemlock a short time before sunset (the hour of execution), notwithstanding the entreaties of his disciples to wait till the sun went down.

[3] The twilight in Greece is much shorter than in our own country; the days in winter are longer, but in summer of shorter duration.

252

No murky vapour, herald of the ſtorm,
Hides her fair face, nor girds her glowing form;
With cornice glimmering as the moon-beams play,
There the white column greets her grateful ray,
And, bright around with quivering beams beset,
Her emblem sparkles o'er the minaret:
The groves of olive scatter'd dark and wide
Where meek Cephisus pours his scanty tide,
The cypress saddening by the sacred mosque,
The gleaming turret of the gay kiosk,[1]
And, dun and sombre 'mid the holy calm,
Near Theseus' fane yon solitary palm,
All tinged with varied hues arreſt the eye—
And dull were his that pass'd them heedless by.
Again the Aegean, heard no more afar,
Lulls his chafed breaſt from elemental war;
Again his waves in milder tints unfold
Their long array of sapphire and of gold,
Mix'd with the shades of many a diſtant isle,
That frown—where gentler ocean seems to smile.

II

Not now my theme—why turn my thoughts to thee?
Oh! who can look along thy native sea,
Nor dwell upon thy name whate'er the tale,
So much its magic muſt o'er all prevail?
Who that beheld that Sun upon thee set,
Fair Athens! could thine evening face forget?
Not he—whose heart nor time nor diſtance frees,
Spell-bound within the cluſtering Cyclades!
Nor seems this homage foreign to his ſtrain,
His Corsair's isle was once thine own domain—
Would that with freedom it were thine again!

III

The Sun hath sunk—and, darker than the night,
Sinks with its beam upon the beacon height
Medora's heart—the third day's come and gone—
With it he comes not—sends not—faithless one!
The wind was fair though light; and ſtorms were none.
Laſt eve Anselmo's bark return'd, and yet
His only tidings that they had not met!

The kiosk is a Turkish summer-house: the palm is without the present walls of Athens, not far from the temple of Theseus, between which and the tree the wall intervenes.—Cephisus' ſtream is indeed scanty, and Ilissus has no ſtream at all.

Though wild, as now, far different were the tale
Had Conrad waited for that single sail.

The night-breeze freshens—she that day had pass'd
In watching all that Hope proclaim'd a mast;
Sadly she sate on high—Impatience bore
At last her footsteps to the midnight shore,
And there she wander'd, heedless of the spray
That dash'd her garments oft, and warn'd away:
She saw not, felt not this—nor dared depart,
Nor deem'd it cold—her chill was at her heart;
Till grew such certainty from that suspense—
His very sight had shock'd from life or sense!

It came at last—a sad and shatter'd boat,
Whose inmates first beheld whom first they sought;
Some bleeding—all most wretched—these the few—
Scarce knew they how escaped—*this* all they knew.
In silence, darkling, each appear'd to wait
His fellow's mournful guess at Conrad's fate:
Something they would have said; but seem'd to fear
To trust their accents to Medora's ear.
She saw at once, yet sunk not—trembled not—
Beneath that grief, that loneliness of lot,
Within that meek fair form, were feelings high,
That deem'd not till they found their energy.
While yet was Hope they soften'd, flutter'd, wept—
All lost—that softness died not—but it slept;
And o'er its slumber rose that Strength which said,
'With nothing left to love—there's nought to dread.'
'Tis more than nature's; like the burning might
Delirium gathers from the fever's height.

'Silent you stand—nor would I hear you tell
What—speak not—breathe not—for I know it well—
Yet would I ask—almost my lip denies
The—quick your answer—tell me where he lies.'

'Lady! we know not—scarce with life we fled;
But here is one denies that he is dead:
He saw him bound; and bleeding—but alive.'

She heard no further—'twas in vain to strive—
So throbb'd each vein—each thought—till then withstood;
Her own dark soul—these words at once subdued:
She totters—falls—and senseless had the wave
Perchance but snatch'd her from another grave;

But that with hands though rude, yet weeping eyes,
They yield such aid as Pity's haste supplies:
Dash o'er her deathlike cheek the ocean dew,
Raise, fan, sustain—till life returns anew;
Awake her handmaids, with the matrons leave
That fainting form o'er which they gaze and grieve;
Then seek Anselmo's cavern, to report
The tale too tedious—when the triumph short.

IV

In that wild council words wax'd warm and strange
With thoughts of ransom, rescue, and revenge;
All, save repose or flight: still lingering there
Breathed Conrad's spirit, and forbade despair;
Whate'er his fate—the breasts he form'd and led
Will save him living, or appease him dead.
Woe to his foes! there yet survive a few,
Whose deeds are daring, as their hearts are true.

V

Within the Haram's secret chamber sate
Stern Seyd, still pondering o'er his Captive's fate;
His thoughts on love and hate alternate dwell,
Now with Gulnare, and now in Conrad's cell;
Here at his feet the lovely slave reclined
Surveys his brow—would soothe his gloom of mind:
While many an anxious glance her large dark eye
Sends in its idle search for sympathy,
His only bends in seeming o'er his beads,[1]
But inly views his victim as he bleeds.

'Pacha! the day is thine; and on thy crest
Sits Triumph—Conrad taken—fall'n the rest!
His doom is fix'd—he dies: and well his fate
Was earn'd—yet much too worthless for thy hate:
Methinks, a short release, for ransom told
With all his treasure, not unwisely sold;
Report speaks largely of his pirate-hoard—
Would that of this my Pacha were the lord!
While baffled, weaken'd by this fatal fray—
Watch'd—follow'd—he were then an easier prey;
But once cut off—the remnant of his band
Embark their wealth, and seek a safer strand.'

'Gulnare!—if for each drop of blood a gem
Were offer'd rich as Stamboul's diadem;

[1] The comboloio, or Mahometan rosary; the beads are in number ninety-nine.

If for each hair of his a massy mine
Or virgin ore should supplicating shine;
If all our Arab tales divulge or dream
Of wealth were here—that gold should not redeem!
It had not now redeem'd a single hour;
But that I know him fetter'd, in my power;
And, thirsting for revenge, I ponder still
On pangs that longest rack, and latest kill.'

'Nay, Seyd!—I seek not to restrain thy rage,
Too justly moved for mercy to assuage;
My thoughts were only to secure for thee
His riches—thus released, he were not free:
Disabled, shorn of half his might and band,
His capture could but wait thy first command.'

'His capture *could*!—and shall I then resign
One day to him—the wretch already mine?
Release my foe!—at whose remonstrance?—thine!
Fair suitor!—to thy virtuous gratitude,
That thus repays this Giaour's relenting mood,
Which thee and thine alone of all could spare,
No doubt—regardless if the prize were fair,
My thanks and praise alike are due—now hear!
I have a counsel for thy gentler ear:
I do mistrust thee, woman! and each word
Of thine stamps truth on all Suspicion heard.
Borne in his arms through fire from yon Serai—
Say, wert thou lingering there with him to fly?
Thou need'st not answer—thy confession speaks,
Already reddening on thy guilty cheeks;
Then, lovely dame, bethink thee! and beware:
'Tis not *his* life alone may claim such care!
Another word and—nay—I need no more.
Accursed was the moment when he bore
Thee from the flames, which better far—but no—
I then had mourn'd thee with a lover's woe—
Now 'tis thy lord that warns—deceitful thing!
Know'st thou that I can clip thy wanton wing?
In words alone I am not wont to chafe:
Look to thyself—nor deem thy falsehood safe!'

He rose—and slowly, sternly thence withdrew,
Rage in his eye and threats in his adieu:
Ah! little reck'd that chief of womanhood—
Which frowns ne'er quell'd, nor menaces subdued;

And little deem'd he what thy heart, Gulnare!
When soft could feel, and when incensed could dare.
His doubts appear'd to wrong—nor yet she knew
How deep the root from whence compassion grew—
She was a slave—from such may captives claim
A fellow-feeling, differing but in name;
Still half unconscious—heedless of his wrath,
Again she ventured on the dangerous path,
Again his rage repell'd—until arose
That strife of thought, the source of woman's woes!

                              VI

Meanwhile long, anxious, weary, still the same
Roll'd day and night: his soul could terror tame—
This fearful interval of doubt and dread,
When every hour might doom him worse than dead,
When every step that echo'd by the gate
Might entering lead where axe and stake await;
When every voice that grated on his ear
Might be the last that he could ever hear;
Could terror tame—that spirit stern and high
Had proved unwilling as unfit to die;
'Twas worn—perhaps decay'd—yet silent bore
That conflict, deadlier far than all before:
The heat of fight, the hurry of the gale,
Leave scarce one thought inert enough to quail;
But bound and fix'd in fetter'd solitude,
To pine, the prey of every changing mood;
To gaze on thine own heart; and meditate
Irrevocable faults, and coming fate—
Too late the last to shun—the first to mend—
To count the hours that struggle to thine end,
With not a friend to animate, and tell
To other ears that death became thee well:
Around thee foes to forge the ready lie,
And blot life's latest scene with calumny;
Before thee tortures, which the soul can dare,
Yet doubts how well the shrinking flesh may bear;
But deeply feels a single cry would shame,
To valour's praise thy last and dearest claim;
The life thou leav'st below, denied above
By kind monopolists of heavenly love;
And more than doubtful paradise—thy heaven
Of earthly hope—thy loved one from thee riven.

Such were the thoughts that outlaw must sustain,
And govern pangs surpassing mortal pain:
And those sustain'd he—boots it well or ill?
Since not to sink beneath, is something still!

VII

The first day pass'd—he saw not her—Gulnare—
The second—third—and still she came not there;
But what her words avouch'd, her charms had done,
Or else he had not seen another sun.
The fourth day roll'd along, and with the night
Came storm and darkness in their mingling might:
Oh! how he listen'd to the rushing deep,
That ne'er till now so broke upon his sleep:
And his wild spirit wilder wishes sent,
Roused by the roar of his own element!
Oft had he ridden on that winged wave,
And loved its roughness for the speed it gave;
And now its dashing echo'd on his ear,
A long known voice—alas! too vainly near!
Loud sung the wind above; and, doubly loud,
Shook o'er his turret cell the thunder-cloud;
And flash'd the lightning by the latticed bar,
To him more genial than the midnight star:
Close to the glimmering grate he dragg'd his chain,
And hoped *that* peril might not prove in vain.
He raised his iron hand to Heaven, and pray'd
One pitying flash to mar the form it made:
His steel and impious prayer attract alike—
The storm roll'd onward and disdain'd to strike;
Its peal wax'd fainter—ceased—he felt alone,
As if some faithless friend had spurn'd his groan!

VIII

The midnight pass'd—and to the massy door
A light step came—it paused—it moved once more;
Slow turns the grating bolt and sullen key:
'Tis as his heart foreboded—that fair she!
Whate'er her sins, to him a guardian saint,
And beauteous still as hermit's hope can paint;
Yet changed since last within that cell she came,
More pale her cheek, more tremulous her frame:
On him she cast her dark and hurried eye,
Which spoke before her accents—'Thou must die!
Yes, thou must die—there is but one resource,
The last—the worst—if torture were not worse.'

'Lady! I look to none—my lips proclaim
What last proclaim'd they—Conrad still the same:
Why shouldst thou seek an outlaw's life to spare,
And change the sentence I deserve to bear?
Well have I earn'd—nor here alone—the meed
Of Seyd's revenge, by many a lawless deed.'

'Why should I seek? because—Oh! didst thou not
Redeem my life from worse than slavery's lot?
Why should I seek?—hath misery made thee blind
To the fond workings of a woman's mind!
And must I say? albeit my heart rebel
With all that woman feels, but should not tell—
Because—despite thy crimes—that heart is moved:
It fear'd thee, thank'd thee, pitied, madden'd, loved.
Reply not, tell not now thy tale again,
Thou lov'st another—and I love in vain;
Though fond as mine her bosom, form more fair,
I rush through peril which she would not dare.
If that thy heart to hers were truly dear,
Were I thine own—thou wert not lonely here:
An outlaw's spouse—and leave her lord to roam!
What hath such gentle dame to do with home?
But speak not now—o'er thine and o'er my head
Hangs the keen sabre by a single thread;
If thou hast courage still, and wouldst be free,
Receive this poniard—rise and follow me!'

'Ay—in my chains! my steps will gently tread,
With these adornments, o'er each slumbering head!
Thou hast forgot—is this a garb for flight?
Or is that instrument more fit for fight?'

'Misdoubting Corsair! I have gain'd the guard,
Ripe for revolt, and greedy for reward.
A single word of mine removes that chain:
Without some aid how here could I remain?
Well, since we met, hath sped my busy time,
If in aught evil, for thy sake the crime:
The crime—'tis none to punish those of Seyd.
That hated tyrant, Conrad—he must bleed!
I see thee shudder—but my soul is changed—
Wrong'd, spurn'd, reviled—and it shall be avenged—
Accused of what till now my heart disdain'd—
Too faithful, though to bitter bondage chain'd.
Yes, smile!—but he had little cause to sneer,
I was not treacherous then—nor thou too dear:
II—*I 487

But he has said it—and the jealous well—
Those tyrants, teasing, tempting to rebel—
Deserve the fate their fretting lips foretell.
I never loved—he bought me—somewhat high—
Since with me came a heart he could not buy.
I was a slave unmurmuring: he hath said,
But for his rescue I with thee had fled.
'Twas false thou know'st—but let such augurs rue,
Their words are omens insult renders true.
Nor was thy respite granted to my prayer;
This fleeting grace was only to prepare
New torments for thy life, and my despair.
Mine too he threatens; but his dotage still
Would fain reserve me for his lordly will:
When wearier of these fleeting charms and me,
There yawns the sack—and yonder rolls the sea!
What, am I then a toy for dotard's play,
To wear but till the gilding frets away?
I saw thee—loved thee—owe thee all—would save,
If but to show how grateful is a slave.
But had he not thus menaced fame and life,
(And well he keeps his oaths pronounced in strife,)
I still had saved thee—but the Pacha spared.
Now I am all thine own—for all prepared:
Thou lov'st me not—nor know'st—or but the worst.
Alas! *this* love—*that* hatred—are the first—
Oh! couldst thou prove my truth, thou wouldst not start,
Nor fear the fire that lights an Eastern heart;
'Tis now the beacon of thy safety—now
It points within the port a Mainote prow:
But in one chamber, where our path must lead,
There sleeps—he must not wake—the oppressor Seyd!'

'Gulnare—Gulnare—I never felt till now
My abject fortune, wither'd fame so low:
Seyd is mine enemy: had swept my band
From earth with ruthless but with open hand,
And therefore came I, in my bark of war,
To smite the smiter with the scimitar;
Such is my weapon—not the secret knife—
Who spares a woman's seeks not slumber's life.
Thine saved I gladly, Lady, not for this—
Let me not deem that mercy shown amiss.
Now fare thee well—more peace be with thy breast!
Night wears apace—my last of earthly rest!'

'Rest! rest! by sunrise must thy sinews shake,
And thy limbs writhe around the ready stake.
I heard the order—saw—I will not see—
If thou wilt perish, I will fall with thee.
My life, my love, my hatred—all below
Are on this cast—Corsair! 'tis but a blow!
Without it flight were idle—how evade
His sure pursuit? my wrongs too unrepaid,
My youth disgraced—the long long wasted years,
One blow shall cancel with our future fears;
But since the dagger suits thee less than brand,
I'll try the firmness of a female hand.
The guards are gain'd—one moment all were o'er—
Corsair! we meet in safety or no more;
If errs my feeble hand, the morning cloud
Will hover o'er thy scaffold, and my shroud.'

IX

She turn'd, and vanish'd ere he could reply,
But his glance followed far with eager eye;
And gathering, as he could, the links that bound
His form, to curl their length, and curb their sound,
Since bar and bolt no more his steps preclude,
He, fast as fetter'd limbs allow, pursued.
'Twas dark and winding, and he knew not where
That passage led; nor lamp nor guard were there:
He sees a dusky glimmering—shall he seek
Or shun that ray so indistinct and weak?
Chance guides his steps—a freshness seems to bear
Full on his brow, as if from morning air—
He reach'd an open gallery—on his eye
Gleam'd the last star of night, the clearing sky:
Yet scarcely heeded these—another light
From a lone chamber struck upon his sight.
Towards it he moved; a scarcely closing door
Reveal'd the ray within, but nothing more.
With hasty step a figure outward past,
Then paused, and turn'd—and paused—'tis she at last!
No poniard in that hand—nor sign of ill—
'Thanks to that softening heart—she could not kill!'
Again he look'd, the wildness of her eye
Starts from the day abrupt and fearfully.
She stopp'd—threw back her dark far-floating hair,
That nearly veil'd her face and bosom fair:
As if she late had bent her leaning head
Above some object of her doubt or dread.

They meet—upon her brow—unknown, forgot—
Her hurrying hand had left—'twas but a spot—
Its hue was all he saw, and scarce withstood—
Oh! slight but certain pledge of crime—'tis blood!

X

He had seen battle—he had brooded lone
O'er promised pangs to sentenced guilt foreshown;
He had been tempted, chasten'd, and the chain
Yet on his arms might ever there remain:
But ne'er from strife, captivity, remorse—
From all his feelings in their inmost force—
So thrill'd, so shuddered every creeping vein,
As now they froze before that purple stain.
That spot of blood, that light but guilty streak,
Had banish'd all the beauty from her cheek!
Blood he had view'd—could view unmoved—but then
It flow'd in combat, or was shed by men!

XI

''Tis done—he nearly waked—but it is done.
Corsair! he perish'd—thou art dearly won.
All words would now be vain—away—away!
Our bark is tossing—'tis already day.
The few gain'd over, now are wholly mine,
And these thy yet surviving band shall join:
Anon my voice shall vindicate my hand,
When once our sail forsakes this hated strand.'

XII

She clapp'd her hands—and through the gallery pour,
Equipp'd for flight, her vassals—Greek and Moor;
Silent but quick they stoop, his chains unbind;
Once more his limbs are free as mountain wind!
But on his heavy heart such sadness sate,
As if they there transferr'd that iron weight.
No words are utter'd—at her sign, a door
Reveals the secret passage to the shore;
The city lies behind—they speed, they reach
The glad waves dancing on the yellow beach;
And Conrad following, at her beck, obey'd,
Nor cared he now if rescued or betray'd;
Resistance were as useless as if Seyd
Yet lived to view the doom his ire decreed.

XIII

Embark'd, the sail unfurl'd, the light breeze blew—
How much had Conrad's memory to review!
Sunk he in contemplation, till the cape
Where last he anchor'd rear'd its giant shape.
Ah!—since that fatal night, though brief the time,
Had swept an age of terror, grief, and crime.
As its far shadow frown'd above the mast,
He veil'd his face, and sorrow'd as he pass'd;
He thought of all—Gonsalvo and his band,
His fleeting triumph and his failing hand;
He thought on her afar, his lonely bride:
He turn'd and saw—Gulnare, the homicide!

XIV

She watch'd his features till she could not bear
Their freezing aspect and averted air,
And that strange fierceness foreign to her eye,
Fell quench'd in tears, too late to shed or dry.
She knelt beside him and his hand she press'd,
'Thou may'st forgive though Allah's self detest;
But for that deed of darkness what wert thou?
Reproach me—but not yet—Oh! spare me *now*!
I am not what I seem—this fearful night
My brain bewilder'd—do not madden quite!
If I had never loved, though less my guilt,
Thou hadst not lived to—hate me—if thou wilt.'

XV

She wrongs his thoughts, they more himself upbraid
Than her, though undesign'd, the wretch he made;
But speechless all, deep, dark, and unexprest,
They bleed within that silent cell—his breast.
Still onward, fair the breeze, nor rough the surge,
The blue waves sport around the stern they urge;
Far on the horizon's verge appears a speck,
A spot—a mast—a sail—an armed deck!
Their little bark her men of watch descry,
And ampler canvas woos the wind from high;
She bears her down majestically near,
Speed on her prow, and terror in her tier;
A flash is seen—the ball beyond her bow
Booms harmless, hissing to the deep below.
Up rose keen Conrad from his silent trance,
A long, long absent gladness in his glance;

''Tis mine—my blood-red flag! again—again—
I am not all deserted on the main!'
They own the signal, answer to the hail,
Hoist out the boat at once, and slacken sail.
''Tis Conrad! Conrad!' shouting from the deck,
Command nor duty could their transport check!
With light alacrity and gaze of pride,
They view him mount once more his vessel's side;
A smile relaxing in each rugged face,
Their arms can scarce forbear a rough embrace.
He, half forgetting danger and defeat,
Returns their greeting as a chief may greet,
Wrings with a cordial grasp Anselmo's hand,
And feels he yet can conquer and command!

XVI

These greetings o'er, the feelings that o'erflow,
Yet grieve to win him back without a blow;
They sail'd prepared for vengeance—had they known
A woman's hand secured that deed her own,
She were their queen—less scrupulous are they
Than haughty Conrad how they win their way.
With many an asking smile, and wondering stare,
They whisper round, and gaze upon Gulnare;
And her, at once above—beneath her sex,
Whom blood appall'd not, their regards perplex.
To Conrad turns her faint imploring eye,
She drops her veil, and stands in silence by;
Her arms are meekly folded on that breast,
Which—Conrad safe—to fate resign'd the rest.
Though worse than frenzy could that bosom fill,
Extreme in love or hate, in good or ill,
The worst of crimes had left her woman still!

XVII

This Conrad mark'd, and felt—ah! could he less?—
Hate of that deed, but grief for her distress;
What she has done no tears can wash away,
And Heaven must punish on its angry day:
But—it was done: he knew, whate'er her guilt,
For him that poniard smote, that blood was spilt;
And he was free!—and she for him had given
Her all on earth, and more than all in heaven!
And now he turn'd him to that dark'd-eyed slave
Whose brow was bow'd beneath the glance he gave,

Who now seem'd changed and humbled, faint and meek,
But varying oft the colour of her cheek
To deeper shades of paleness—all its red
That fearful spot which stain'd it from the dead!
He took that hand—it trembled—now too late—
So soft in love, so wildly nerved in hate;
He clasp'd that hand—it trembled—and his own
Had lost its firmness, and his voice its tone.
'Gulnare!'—but she replied not—'dear Gulnare!'
She raised her eye—her only answer there—
At once she sought and sunk in his embrace:
If he had driven her from that resting-place,
His had been more or less than mortal heart,
But—good or ill—it bade her not depart.
Perchance, but for the bodings of his breast,
His latest virtue then had join'd the rest.
Yet even Medora might forgive the kiss
That ask'd from form so fair no more than this,
The first, the last that Frailty stole from Faith—
To lips where Love had lavish'd all his breath,
To lips—whose broken sighs such fragrance fling
As he had fann'd them freshly with his wing!

XVIII

They gain by twilight's hour their lonely isle.
To them the very rocks appear to smile;
The haven hums with many a cheering sound,
The beacons blaze their wonted stations round,
The boats are darting o'er the curly bay,
And sportive dolphins bend them through the spray;
Even the hoarse sea-bird's shrill, discordant shriek,
Greets like the welcome of his tuneless beak!
Beneath each lamp that through its lattice gleams,
Their fancy paints the friends that trim the beams.
Oh! what can sanctify the joys of home,
Like Hope's gay glance from Ocean's troubled foam!

XIX

The lights are high on beacon and from bower,
And 'midst them Conrad seeks Medora's tower;
He looks in vain—'tis strange—and all remark,
Amid so many, hers alone is dark.
'Tis strange—of yore its welcome never fail'd,
Nor now, perchance, extinguish'd, only veil'd.
With the first boat descends he for the shore,
And looks impatient on the lingering oar.

Oh! for a wing beyond the falcon's flight,
To bear him like an arrow to that height!
With the first pause the resting rowers gave,
He waits not—looks not—leaps into the wave,
Strives through the surge, bestrides the beach, and high
Ascends the path familiar to his eye.

He reach'd his turret door—he paused—no sound
Broke from within; and all was night around.
He knock'd, and loudly—footstep nor reply
Announced that any heard or deem'd him nigh;
He knock'd, but faintly—for his trembling hand
Refused to aid his heavy heart's demand.
The portal opens—'tis a well-known face,
But not the form he panted to embrace.
Its lips are silent—twice his own essay'd,
And fail'd to frame the question they delay'd;
He snatch'd the lamp—its light will answer all—
It quits his grasp, expiring in the fall.
He would not wait for that reviving ray—
As soon could he have linger'd there for day;
But, glimmering through the dusky corridor,
Another chequers o'er the shadow'd floor;
His steps the chamber gain—his eyes behold
All that his heart believed not—yet foretold!

XX

He turn'd not—spoke not—sunk not—fix'd his look,
And set the anxious frame that lately shook:
He gazed—how long we gaze despite of pain,
And know, but dare not own, we gaze in vain!
In life itself she was so still and fair,
That death with gentler aspect wither'd there;
And the cold flowers [1] her colder hand contain'd,
In that last grasp as tenderly were strain'd
As if she scarcely felt, but feign'd a sleep,
And made it almost mockery yet to weep:
The long dark lashes fringed her lids of snow,
And veil'd—thought shrinks from all that lurk'd below—
Oh! o'er the eye Death most exerts his might,
And hurls the spirit from her throne of light!
Sinks those blue orbs in that long last eclipse,
But spares, as yet, the charm around her lips—

[1] In the Levant it is the custom to strew flowers on the bodies of the dead, and in the hands of young persons to place a nosegay.

Yet, yet they seem as they forbore to smile,
And wish'd repose—but only for a while;
But the white shroud, and each extended tress,
Long, fair—but spread in utter lifelessness,
Which, late the sport of every summer wind,
Escaped the baffled wreath that strove to bind;
These—and the pale pure cheek, became the bier—
But she is nothing—wherefore is he here?

XXI

He ask'd no question—all were answer'd now
By the first glance on that still, marble brow.
It was enough—she died—what reck'd it how?
The love of youth, the hope of better years,
The source of softest wishes, tenderest fears,
The only living thing he could not hate,
Was reft at once—and he deserved his fate,
But did not feel it less;—the good explore,
For peace, those realms where guilt can never soar:
The proud, the wayward—who have fix'd below
Their joy, and find this earth enough for woe,
Lose in that one their all—perchance a mite—
But who in patience parts with all delight?
Full many a stoic eye and aspect stern
Mask hearts where grief hath little left to learn:
And many a withering thought lies hid, not lost,
In smiles that least befit who wear them most.

XXII

By those, that deepest feel, is ill exprest
The indistinctness of the suffering breast;
Where thousand thoughts begin to end in one,
Which seeks from all the refuge found in none;
No words suffice the secret soul to show,
For Truth denies all eloquence to Woe.
On Conrad's stricken soul exhaustion prest,
And stupor almost lull'd it into rest;
So feeble now—his mother's softness crept
To those wild eyes, which like an infant's wept:
It was the very weakness of his brain,
Which thus confess'd without relieving pain.
None saw his trickling tears—perchance, if seen,
That useless flood of grief had never been:
Now long they flow'd—he dried them to depart,
In helpless—hopeless—brokenness of heart:
The sun goes forth—but Conrad's day is dim;
And the night cometh—ne'er to pass from him.

There is no darkness like the cloud of mind,
On Grief's vain eye—the blindest of the blind!
Which may not—dare not see—but turns aside
To blackest shade—nor will endure a guide!

XXIII

His heart was form'd for softness—warp'd to wrong;
Betray'd too early, and beguiled too long;
Each feeling pure—as falls the dropping dew
Within the grot; like that had harden'd too;
Less clear, perchance, its earthly trials pass'd,
But sunk, and chill'd, and petrified at last.
Yet tempests wear, and lightning cleaves the rock,
If such his heart, so shatter'd it the shock.
There grew one flower beneath its rugged brow,
Though dark the shade—it shelter'd—saved till now.
The thunder came—that bolt hath blasted both,
The Granite's firmness, and the Lily's growth:
The gentle plant hath left no leaf to tell
Its tale, but shrunk and wither'd where it fell;
And of its cold protector, blacken round
But shiver'd fragments on the barren ground!

XXIV

'Tis morn—to venture on his lonely hour
Few dare; though now Anselmo sought his tower.
He was not there—nor seen along the shore;
Ere night, alarm'd, their isle is traversed o'er:
Another morn—another bids them seek,
And shout his name till echo waxeth weak;
Mount, grotto, cavern, valley search'd in vain,
They find on shore a sea-boat's broken chain:
Their hope revives—they follow o'er the main.
'Tis idle all—moons roll on moons away,
And Conrad comes not—came not since that day:
Nor trace, nor tidings of his doom declare
Where lives his grief, or perish'd his despair!
Long mourn'd his band whom none could mourn beside;
And fair the monument they gave his bride:
For him they raise not the recording stone—·
His death yet dubious, deeds too widely known;
He left a Corsair's name to other times,
Link'd with one virtue, and a thousand crimes.

LARA

A TALE

LARA

I

THE Serfs [1] are glad through Lara's wide domain,
And Slavery half forgets her feudal chain;
He, their unhoped, but unforgotten lord,
The long self-exiled chieftain, is restored:
There be bright faces in the busy hall,
Bowls on the board, and banners on the wall;
Far checkering o'er the pictured window, plays
The unwonted faggots' hospitable blaze;
And gay retainers gather round the hearth,
With tongues all loudness, and with eyes all mirth.

II

The chief of Lara is return'd again:
And why had Lara cross'd the bounding main?
Left by his sire, too young such loss to know,
Lord of himself,—that heritage of woe,
That fearful empire which the human breast
But holds to rob the heart within of rest!—
With none to check, and few to point in time
The thousand paths that slope the way to crime;
Then, when he most required commandment, then
Had Lara's daring boyhood govern'd men.
It skills not, boots not step by step to trace
His youth through all the mazes of its race;
Short was the course his restlessness had run,
But long enough to leave him half undone.

III

And Lara left in youth his fatherland;
But from the hour he waved his parting hand
Each trace wax'd fainter of his course, till all
Had nearly ceased his memory to recall.

[1] The reader is apprised, that the name of Lara being Spanish, and no circumstance of local and natural description fixing the scene or hero of the poem to any country or age, the word 'Serf,' which could not be correctly applied to the lower classes in Spain, who were never vassals of the soil, has nevertheless been employed to designate the followers of our fictitious chieftain.—[Lara is really meant for a chief of the Morea.]

His sire was dust, his vassals could declare,
'Twas all they knew, that Lara was not there;
Nor sent, nor came he, till conjecture grew
Cold in the many, anxious in the few.
His hall scarce echoes with his wonted name,
His portrait darkens in its fading frame,
Another chief consoled his destined bride,
The young forgot him, and the old had died;
'Yet doth he live!' exclaims the impatient heir,
And sighs for sables which he must not wear.
A hundred scutcheons deck with gloomy grace
The Laras' last and longest dwelling-place;
But one is absent from the mouldering file,
That now were welcome in that Gothic pile.

IV

He comes at last in sudden loneliness,
And whence they know not, why they need not guess;
They more might marvel, when the greeting 's o'er,
Not that he came, but came not long before:
No train is his beyond a single page,
Of foreign aspect, and of tender age.
Years had roll'd on, and fast they speed away
To those that wander as to those that stay;
But lack of tidings from another clime
Had lent a flagging wing to weary Time.
They see, they recognise, yet almost deem
The present dubious, or the past a dream.

He lives, nor yet is past his manhood's prime,
Though sear'd by toil, and something touch'd by time;
His faults, whate'er they were, if scarce forgot,
Might be untaught him by his varied lot;
Nor good nor ill of late were known, his name
Might yet uphold his patrimonial fame:
His soul in youth was haughty, but his sins
No more than pleasure from the stripling wins;
And such, if not yet harden'd in their course,
Might be redeem'd, nor ask a long remorse.

V

And they indeed were changed—'tis quickly seen,
Whate'er he be, 'twas not what he had been:
That brow in furrow'd lines had fix'd at last,
And spake of passions, but of passion past:

The pride, but not the fire, of early days,
Coldness of mien, and carelessness of praise;
A high demeanour, and a glance that took
Their thoughts from others by a single look;
And that sarcastic levity of tongue,
The stinging of a heart the world hath stung,
That darts in seeming playfulness around,
And makes those feel that will not own the wound;
All these seem'd his, and something more beneath
Than glance could well reveal, or accent breathe.
Ambition, glory, love, the common aim,
That some can conquer, and that all would claim,
Within his breast appear'd no more to strive,
Yet seem'd as lately they had been alive;
And some deep feeling it were vain to trace
At moments lighten'd o'er his livid face.

VI

Not much he loved long question of the past,
Nor told of wondrous wilds, and deserts vast,
In those far lands where he had wander'd lone,
And—as himself would have it seem—unknown:
Yet these in vain his eye could scarcely scan,
Nor glean experience from his fellow man;
But what he had beheld he shunn'd to show,
As hardly worth a stranger's care to know;
If still more prying such inquiry grew,
His brow fell darker, and his words more few.

VII

Not unrejoiced to see him once again,
Warm was his welcome to the haunts of men;
Born of high lineage, link'd in high command,
He mingled with the magnates of his land;
Join'd the carousals of the great and gay,
And saw them smile or sigh their hours away;
But still he only saw, and did not share,
The common pleasure or the general care;
He did not follow what they all pursued
With hope still baffled still to be renew'd;
Nor shadowy honour, nor substantial gain,
Nor beauty's preference, and the rival's pain:
Around him some mysterious circle thrown
Repell'd approach, and show'd him still alone;
Upon his eye sat something of reproof,
That kept at least frivolity aloof;

And things more timid that beheld him near,
In silence gazed, or whisper'd mutual fear;
And they the wiser, friendlier few confess'd
They deem'd him better than his air express'd.

VIII

'Twas strange—in youth all action and all life,
Burning for pleasure, not averse from strife;
Woman, the field, the ocean, all that gave
Promise of gladness, peril of a grave,
In turn he tried—he ransack'd all below,
And found his recompense in joy or woe,
No tame, trite medium; for his feelings sought
In that intenseness an escape from thought:
The tempest of his heart in scorn had gazed
On that the feebler elements hath raised;
The rapture of his heart had look'd on high,
And ask'd if greater dwelt beyond the sky:
Chain'd to excess, the slave of each extreme,
How woke he from the wildness of that dream?
Alas! he told not—but he did awake
To curse the wither'd heart that would not break.

IX

Books, for his volume heretofore was Man,
With eye more curious he appeared to scan,
And oft, in sudden mood, for many a day,
From all communion he would start away:
And then, his rarely call'd attendants said,
Through night's long hours would sound his hurried tread
O'er the dark gallery, where his fathers frown'd
In rude but antique portraiture around:
They heard, but whisper'd—'*that* must not be known—
The sound of words less earthly than his own.
Yes, they who chose might smile, but some had seen
They scarce knew what, but more than should have been.
Why gazed he so upon the ghastly head
Which hands profane had gather'd from the dead,
That still beside his open'd volume lay,
As if to startle all save him away?
Why slept he not when others were at rest?
Why heard no music, and received no guest?
All was not well, they deem'd—but where the wrong?
Some knew perchance—but 'twere a tale too long;

And such besides were too discreetly wise,
To more than hint their knowledge in surmise;
But if they would—they could'—around the board,
Thus Lara's vassals prattled of their lord.

x

It was the night—and Lara's glassy stream
The stars are studding, each with imaged beam;
So calm, the waters scarcely seem to stray,
And yet they glide like happiness away;
Reflecting far and fairy-like from high
The immortal lights that live along the sky:
Its banks are fringed with many a goodly tree,
And flowers the fairest that may feast the bee;
Such in her chaplet infant Dian wove,
And Innocence would offer to her love.
These deck the shore; the waves their channel make
In windings bright and mazy like the snake.
All was so still, so soft in earth and air,
You scarce would start to meet a spirit there;
Secure that nought of evil could delight
To walk in such a scene, on such a night!
It was a moment only for the good:
So Lara deem'd, nor longer there he stood,
But turn'd in silence to his castle-gate;
Such scene his soul no more could contemplate:
Such scene reminded him of other days,
Of skies more cloudless, moon of purer blaze,
Of nights more soft and frequent, hearts that now—
No—no—the storm may beat upon his brow,
Unfelt, unsparing—but a night like this,
A night of beauty, mock'd such breast as his.

XI

He turn'd within his solitary hall,
And his high shadow shot along the wall:
There were the painted forms of other times,
'Twas all they left of virtues or of crimes,
Save vague tradition; and the gloomy vaults
That hid their dust, their foibles, and their faults;
And half a column of the pompous page,
That speeds the specious tale from age to age;
Where history's pen its praise or blame supplies,
And lies like truth, and still most truly lies.
He wandering mused, and as the moonbeam shone
Through the dim lattice o'er the floor of stone,

And the high fretted roof, and saints, that there
O'er Gothic windows knelt in pictured prayer,
Reflected in fantastic figures grew,
Like life, but not like mortal life, to view;
His bristling locks of sable, brow of gloom,
And the wide waving of his shaken plume,
Glanced like a spectre's attributes, and gave
His aspect all that terror gives the grave.

XII

'Twas midnight—all was slumber; the lone light
Dimm'd in the lamp, as loth to break the night.
Hark! there be murmurs heard in Lara's hall—
A sound—a voice—a shriek—a fearful call!
A long, loud shriek—and silence—did they hear
That frantic echo burst the sleeping ear?
They heard and rose, and, tremulously brave,
Rush where the sound invoked their aid to save;
They come with half-lit tapers in their hands,
And snatch'd in startled haste unbelted brands.

XIII

Cold as the marble where his length was laid,
Pale as the beam that o'er his features play'd,
Was Lara stretch'd; his half-drawn sabre near,
Dropp'd it should seem in more than nature's fear;
Yet he was firm, or had been firm till now,
And still defiance knit his gather'd brow;
Though mix'd with terror, senseless as he lay,
There lived upon his lip the wish to slay;
Some half-form'd threat in utterance there had died,
Some imprecation of despairing pride;
His eye was almost seal'd, but not forsook
Even in its trance the gladiator's look,
That oft awake his aspect could disclose,
And now was fix'd in horrible repose.
They raise him—bear him;—hush! he breathes, he speaks,
The swarthy blush recolours in his cheeks,
His lip resumes its red, his eye, though dim,
Rolls wide and wild, each slowly quivering limb
Recalls its function, but his words are strung
In terms that seem not of his native tongue;
Distinct but strange, enough they understand
To deem them accents of another land;
And such they were, and meant to meet an ear
That hears him not—alas! that cannot hear!

XIV

His page approach'd, and he alone appear'd
To know the import of the words they heard;
And, by the changes of his cheek and brow,
They were not such as Lara should avow,
Nor he interpret,—yet with less surprise
Than those around their chieftain's state he eyes,
But Lara's prostrate form he bent beside,
And in that tongue which seem'd his own replied,
And Lara heeds those tones that gently seem
To soothe away the horrors of his dream—
If dream it were, that thus could overthrow
A breast that needed not ideal woe.

XV

Whate'er his frenzy dream'd or eye beheld,
If yet remember'd ne'er to be reveal'd,
Rests at his heart: the custom'd morning came,
And breathed new vigour in his shaken frame;
And solace sought he none from priest nor leech,
And soon the same in movement and in speech
As heretofore he fill'd the passing hours,
Nor less he smiles, nor more his forehead lowers,
Than these were wont; and if the coming night
Appear'd less welcome now to Lara's sight,
He to his marvelling vassals show'd it not,
Whose shuddering proved *their* fear was less forgot.
In trembling pairs (alone they dared not) crawl
The astonish'd slaves, and shun the fated hall;
The waving banner, and the clapping door,
The rustling tapestry, and the echoing floor;
The long dim shadows of surrounding trees,
The flapping bat, the night song of the breeze;
Aught they behold or hear their thought appals,
As evening saddens o'er the dark grey walls.

XVI

Vain thought! that hour of ne'er unravell'd gloom
Came not again, or Lara could assume
A seeming of forgetfulness, that made
His vassals more amazed nor less afraid.
Had memory vanish'd then with sense restored?
Since word, nor look, nor gesture of their lord
Betray'd a feeling that recall'd to these
That fever'd moment of his mind's disease.

Was it a dream? was his the voice that spoke
Those strange wild accents; his the cry that broke
Their slumber? his the oppress'd, o'erlabour'd heart
That ceased to beat, the look that made them start?
Could he who thus had suffer'd so forget,
When such as saw that suffering shudder yet?
Or did that silence prove his memory fix'd
Too deep for words, indelible, unmix'd
In that corroding secrecy which gnaws
The heart to show the effect, but not the cause?
Not so in him; his breast had buried both,
Nor common gazers could discern the growth
Of thoughts that mortal lips must leave half told;
They choke the feeble words that would unfold.

XVII

In him inexplicably mix'd appear'd
Much to be loved and hated, sought and fear'd;
Opinion varying o'er his hidden lot,
In praise or railing ne'er his name forgot:
His silence form'd a theme for others' prate—
They guess'd, they gazed, they fain would know his fate.
What had he been? what was he, thus unknown,
Who walk'd their world, his lineage only known?
A hater of his kind? yet some would say,
With them he could seem gay amidst the gay;
But own'd that smile, if oft observed and near,
Waned in its mirth, and wither'd to a sneer;
That smile might reach his lips, but pass'd not by,
None e'er could trace its laughter to his eye:
Yet there was softness too in his regard,
At times, a heart as not by nature hard,
But once perceived, his spirit seem'd to chide
Such weakness, as unworthy of its pride,
And steel'd itself, as scorning to redeem
One doubt from others' half withheld esteem;
In self-inflicted penance of a breast
Which tenderness might once have wrung from rest;
In vigilance of grief that would compel
The soul to hate for having loved too well.

XVIII

There was in him a vital scorn of all:
As if the worst had fall'n which could befall,
He stood a stranger in this breathing world,
An erring spirit from another hurl'd;

A thing of dark imaginings, that shaped
By choice the perils he by chance escaped;
But 'scaped in vain, for in their memory yet
His mind would half exult and half regret:
With more capacity for love than earth
Bestows on most of mortal mould and birth,
His early dreams of good outstripp'd the truth,
And troubled manhood follow'd baffled youth;
With thought of years in phantom chase misspent,
And wasted powers for better purpose lent;
And fiery passions that had pour'd their wrath
In hurried desolation o'er his path,
And left the better feelings all at strife
In wild reflection o'er his stormy life;
But haughty still, and loth himself to blame,
He call'd on Nature's self to share the shame,
And charged all faults upon the fleshly form
She gave to clog the soul, and feast the worm;
Till he at last confounded good and ill,
And half mistook for fate the acts of will:
Too high for common selfishness, he could
At times resign his own for others' good,
But not in pity, not because he ought,
But in some strange perversity of thought,
That sway'd him onward with a secret pride
To do what few or none would do beside;
And this same impulse would, in tempting time,
Mislead his spirit equally to crime;
So much he soar'd beyond, or sunk beneath,
The men with whom he felt condemn'd to breathe,
And long'd by good or ill to separate
Himself from all who shared his mortal state;
His mind abhorring this had fix'd her throne
Far from the world, in regions of her own:
Thus coldly passing all that pass'd below,
His blood in temperate seeming now would flow:
Ah! happier if it ne'er with guilt had glow'd,
But ever in that icy smoothness flow'd!
'Tis true, with other men their path he walk'd,
And like the rest in seeming did and talk'd,
Nor outraged Reason's rules by flaw nor start,
His madness was not of the head, but heart;
And rarely wander'd in his speech, or drew
His thoughts so forth as to offend the view.

XIX

With all that chilling mystery of mien,
And seeming gladness to remain unseen,
He had (if 'twere not nature's boon) an art
Of fixing memory on another's heart:
It was not love perchance, nor hate, nor aught
That words can image to express the thought;
But they who saw him did not see in vain,
And once beheld, would ask of him again:
And those to whom he spake remember'd well,
And on the words, however light, would dwell:
None knew nor how, nor why, but he entwined
Himself perforce around the hearer's mind;
There he was stamp'd, in liking, or in hate,
If greeted once; however brief the date
That friendship, pity, or aversion knew,
Still there within the inmost thought he grew.
You could not penetrate his soul, but found,
Despite your wonder, to your own he wound;
His presence haunted still; and from the breast
He forced an all unwilling interest:
Vain was the struggle in that mental net,
His spirit seem'd to dare you to forget!

XX

There is a festival, where knights and dames,
And aught that wealth or lofty lineage claims,
Appear—a high-born and a welcome guest
To Otho's hall came Lara with the rest.
The long carousal shakes the illumined hall,
Well speeds alike the banquet and the ball;
And the gay dance of bounding Beauty's train
Links grace and harmony in happiest chain:
Blest are the early hearts and gentle hands
That mingle there in well according bands;
It is a sight the careful brow might smooth,
And make Age smile, and dream itself to youth,
And Youth forget such hour was past on earth,
So springs the exulting bosom to that mirth!

XXI

And Lara gazed on these, sedately glad,
His brow belied him if his soul was sad;
And his glance follow'd fast each fluttering fair,
Whose steps of lightness woke no echo there:

He lean'd against the lofty pillar nigh,
With folded arms and long attentive eye,
Nor mark'd a glance so sternly fix'd on his—
Ill brook'd high Lara scrutiny like this:
At length he caught it, 'tis a face unknown,
But seems as searching his, and his alone;
Prying and dark, a stranger's by his mien,
Who still till now had gazed on him unseen:
At length encountering meets the mutual gaze
Of keen inquiry, and of mute amaze;
On Lara's glance emotion gathering grew,
As if distrusting that the stranger threw;
Along the stranger's aspect, fix'd and stern,
Flash'd more than thence the vulgar eye could learn.

XXII

''Tis he!' the stranger cried, and those that heard
Re-echoed fast and far the whisper'd word.
''Tis he!'—''Tis who?' they question far and near,
Till louder accents rung on Lara's ear;
So widely spread, few bosoms well could brook
The general marvel, or that single look:
But Lara stirr'd not, changed not, the surprise
That sprung at first to his arrested eyes
Seem'd now subsided, neither sunk nor raised
Glanced his eye round, though still the stranger gazed;
And drawing nigh, exclaim'd, with haughty sneer,
''Tis he!—how came he thence?—what doth he here?'

XXIII

It were too much for Lara to pass by
Such questions, so repeated fierce and high;
With look collected, but with accent cold,
More mildly firm than petulantly bold,
He turn'd, and met the inquisitorial tone—
'My name is Lara!—when thine own is known,
Doubt not my fitting answer to requite
The unlook'd-for courtesy of such a knight.
'Tis Lara!—further wouldst thou mark or ask?
I shun no question, and I wear no mask.'

'Thou shunn'st no question!   Ponder—is there none
Thy heart must answer, though thine ear would shun?
And deem'st thou me unknown too?   Gaze again!
At least thy memory was not given in vain.

Oh! never canst thou cancel half her debt,
Eternity forbids thee to forget.'
With slow and searching glance upon his face
Grew Lara's eyes, but nothing there could trace
They knew, or chose to know—with dubious look
He deign'd no answer, but his head he shook,
And half contemptuous turn'd to pass away;
But the stern stranger motion'd him to stay.
'A word!—I charge thee stay, and answer here
To one, who, wert thou noble, were thy peer,
But as thou wast and art—nay, frown not, lord,
If false, 'tis easy to disprove the word—
But as thou wast and art, on thee looks down,
Distrusts thy smiles, but shakes not at thy frown.
Art thou not he? whose deeds——'
                                    'Whate'er I be,
Words wild as these, accusers like to thee
I list no further; those with whom they weigh
May hear the rest, nor venture to gainsay
The wondrous tale no doubt thy tongue can tell,
Which thus begins so courteously and well.
Let Otho cherish here his polish'd guest,
To him my thanks and thoughts shall be express'd.'
And here their wondering host hath interposed—
'Whate'er there be between you undisclosed,
This is no time nor fitting place to mar
The mirthful meeting with a wordy war.
If thou, Sir Ezzelin, hast aught to show
Which it befits Count Lara's ear to know,
To-morrow, here, or elsewhere, as may best
Beseem your mutual judgment, speak the rest;
I pledge myself for thee, as not unknown,
Though, like Count Lara, now return'd alone
From other lands, almost a stranger grown;
And if from Lara's blood and gentle birth
I augur right of courage and of worth,
He will not that untainted line belie,
Nor aught that knighthood may accord, deny.'
'To-morrow be it,' Ezzelin replied,
'And here our several worth and truth be tried;
I gage my life, my falchion to attest
My words, so may I mingle with the blest!'
What answers Lara? to its centre shrunk
His soul, in deep abstraction sudden sunk;
The words of many, and the eyes of all
That there were gather'd, seem'd on him to fall;

But his were silent, his appear'd to stray
In far forgetfulness away—away—
Alas! that heedlessness of all around
Bespoke remembrance only too profound.

XXIV

'To-morrow!—ay, to-morrow!' further word
Than those repeated none from Lara heard;
Upon his brow no outward passion spoke;
From his large eye no flashing anger broke;
Yet there was something fix'd in that low tone,
Which show'd resolve, determined, though unknown.
He seized his cloak—his head he slightly bow'd,
And passing Ezzelin, he left the crowd;
And, as he pass'd him, smiling met the frown
With which that chieftain's brow would bear him down:
It was nor smile of mirth, nor struggling pride
That curbs to scorn the wrath it cannot hide;
But that of one in his own heart secure
Of all that he would do, or could endure.
Could this mean peace? the calmness of the good?
Or guilt grown old in desperate hardihood?
Alas! too like in confidence are each,
For man to trust to mortal look or speech;
From deeds, and deeds alone, may he discern
Truths which it wrings the unpractised heart to learn.

XXV

And Lara call'd his page, and went his way—
Well could that stripling word or sign obey:
His only follower from those climes afar,
Where the soul glows beneath a brighter star;
For Lara left the shore from whence he sprung,
In duty patient, and sedate though young;
Silent as him he served, his faith appears
Above his station, and beyond his years.
Though not unknown the tongue of Lara's land,
In such from him he rarely heard command;
But fleet his step, and clear his tones would come,
When Lara's lip breathed forth the words of home:
Those accents, as his native mountains dear,
Awake their absent echoes in his ear,
Friends', kindred's, parents' wonted voice recall,
Now lost, abjured, for one—his friend, his all:
For him earth now disclosed no other guide;
What marvel then he rarely left his side?

XXVI

Light was his form, and darkly delicate
That brow whereon his native sun had sate,
But had not marr'd, though in his beams he grew,
The cheek where oft the unbidden blush shone through;
Yet not such blush as mounts when health would show
All the heart's hue in that delighted glow;
But 'twas a hectic tint of secret care
That for a burning moment fever'd there;
And the wild sparkle of his eye seem'd caught
From high, and lighten'd with electric thought,
Though its black orb those long low lashes' fringe
Had temper'd with a melancholy tinge;
Yet less of sorrow than of pride was there,
Or, if 'twere grief, a grief that none should share:
And pleased not him the sports that please his age,
The tricks of youth, the frolics of the page;
For hours on Lara he would fix his glance,
As all-forgotten in that watchful trance;
And from his chief withdrawn, he wander'd lone,
Brief were his answers, and his questions none;
His walk the wood, his sport some foreign book;
His resting-place the bank that curbs the brook:
He seem'd, like him he served, to live apart
From all that lures the eye, and fills the heart;
To know no brotherhood, and take from earth
No gift beyond that bitter boon—our birth.

XXVII

If aught he loved, 'twas Lara; but was shown
His faith in reverence and in deeds alone;
In mute attention; and his care, which guess'd
Each wish, fulfill'd it ere the tongue express'd.
Still there was haughtiness in all he did,
A spirit deep that brook'd not to be chid;
His zeal, though more than that of servile hands,
In act alone obeys, his air commands;
As if 'twas Lara's less than *his* desire
That thus he served, but surely not for hire.
Slight were the tasks enjoin'd him by his lord,
To hold the stirrup, or to bear the sword;
To tune his lute, or, if he will'd it more,
On tomes of other times and tongues to pore;
But ne'er to mingle with the menial train,
To whom he show'd nor deference nor disdain,

But that well-worn reserve which proved he knew
No sympathy with that familiar crew:
His soul, whate'er his station or his stem,
Could bow to Lara, not descend to them.
Of higher birth he seem'd, and better days,
Nor mark of vulgar toil that hand betrays,
So femininely white it might bespeak
Another sex, when match'd with that smooth cheek,
But for his garb, and something in his gaze,
More wild and high than woman's eye betrays;
A latent fierceness that far more became
His fiery climate than his tender frame:
True, in his words it broke not from his breast,
But from his aspect might be more than guess'd.
Kaled his name, though rumour said he bore
Another ere he left his mountain-shore;
For sometimes he would hear, however nigh,
That name repeated loud without reply,
As unfamiliar, or, if roused again,
Start to the sound, as but remember'd then;
Unless 'twas Lara's wonted voice that spake,
For then, ear, eyes, and heart would all awake.

XXVIII

He had look'd down upon the festive hall,
And mark'd that sudden strife so mark'd of all;
And when the crowd around and near him told
Their wonder at the calmness of the bold,
Their marvel how the high-born Lara bore
Such insult from a stranger, doubly sore,
The colour of young Kaled went and came,
The lip of ashes, and the cheek of flame;
And o'er his brow the dampening heart-drops threw
The sickening iciness of that cold dew,
That rises as the busy bosom sinks
With heavy thoughts from which reflection shrinks.
Yes—there be things which we must dream and dare,
And execute ere thought be half aware:
Whate'er might Kaled's be, it was enow
To seal his lip, but agonize his brow.
He gazed on Ezzelin till Lara cast
That sidelong smile upon the knight he past;
When Kaled saw that smile his visage fell
As if on something recognised right well,
His memory read in such a meaning more
Than Lara's aspect unto others wore:

Forward he sprung—a moment, both were gone,
And all within that hall seem'd left alone;
Each had so fix'd his eye on Lara's mien,
All had so mix'd their feelings with that scene,
That when his long dark shadow through the porch
No more relieves the glare of yon high torch,
Each pulse beats quicker, and all bosoms seem
To bound as doubting from too black a dream,
Such as we know is false, yet dread in sooth,
Because the worst is ever nearest truth.
And they are gone—but Ezzelin is there,
With thoughtful visage and imperious air;
But long remain'd not; ere an hour expired
He waved his hand to Otho, and retired.

XXIX

The crowds are gone, the revellers at rest;
The courteous host, and all-approving guest,
Again to that accustom'd couch must creep
Where joy subsides, and sorrow sighs to sleep,
And man, o'erlabour'd with his being's strife,
Shrinks to that sweet forgetfulness of life:
There lie love's feverish hope, and cunning's guile,
Hate's working brain, and lull'd ambition's wile;
O'er each vain eye oblivion's pinions wave,
And quench'd existence crouches in a grave.
What better name may slumber's bed become?
Night's sepulchre, the universal home,
Where weakness, strength, vice, virtue, sunk supine,
Alike in naked helplessness recline;
Glad for a while to heave unconscious breath,
Yet wake to wrestle with the dread of death,
And shun, though day but dawn on ills increased,
That sleep, the loveliest, since it dreams the least.

I

NIGHT wanes—the vapours round the mountains curl'd
Melt into morn, and Light awakes the world.
Man has another day to swell the past,
And lead him near to little, but his last;
But mighty Nature bounds as from her birth,
The sun is in the heavens, and life on earth;
Flowers in the valley, splendour in the beam,
Health on the gale, and freshness in the stream.
Immortal man! behold her glories shine,
And cry, exulting inly, 'They are thine!'
Gaze on, while yet thy gladden'd eye may see;
A morrow comes when they are not for thee:
And grieve what may above thy senseless bier,
Nor earth nor sky will yield a single tear;
Nor cloud shall gather more, nor leaf shall fall,
Nor gale breathe forth one sigh for thee, for all;
But creeping things shall revel in their spoil,
And fit thy clay to fertilise the soil.

II

'Tis morn—'tis noon—assembled in the hall,
The gather'd chieftains come to Otho's call:
'Tis now the promised hour, that must proclaim
The life or death of Lara's future fame;
When Ezzelin his charge may here unfold,
And whatsoe'er the tale, it must be told.
His faith was pledged, and Lara's promise given,
To meet it in the eye of man and heaven.
Why comes he not? Such truths to be divulged,
Methinks the accuser's rest is long indulged.

III

The hour is past, and Lara too is there,
With self-confiding, coldly patient air;
Why comes not Ezzelin? The hour is past,
And murmurs rise, and Otho's brow's o'ercast.
'I know my friend! his faith I cannot fear,
If yet he be on earth, expect him here;
The roof that held him in the valley stands
Between my own and noble Lara's lands;
My hall from such a guest had honour gain'd,
Nor had Sir Ezzelin his host disdain'd,
But that some previous proof forbade his stay,
And urged him to prepare against to-day;
The word I pledged for his I pledge again,
Or will myself redeem his knighthood's stain.'

He ceased—and Lara answer'd, 'I am here
To lend at thy demand a listening ear
To tales of evil from a stranger's tongue,
Whose words already might my heart have wrung,
But that I deem'd him scarcely less than mad,
Or, at the worst, a foe ignobly bad.
I know him not—but me it seems he knew
In lands where—but I must not trifle too:
Produce this babbler—or redeem the pledge;
Here in thy hold, and with thy falchion's edge.'

Proud Otho on the instant, reddening, threw
His glove on earth, and forth his sabre flew.
'The last alternative befits me best,
And thus I answer for mine absent guest.'

With cheek unchanging from its sallow gloom,
However near his own or other's tomb;
With hand, whose almost careless coolness spoke
Its grasp well-used to deal the sabre-stroke;
With eye, though calm, determined not to spare,
Did Lara too his willing weapon bare.
In vain the circling chieftains round them closed,
For Otho's frenzy would not be opposed;
And from his lip those words of insult fell—
His sword is good who can maintain them well.

IV

Short was the conflict; furious, blindly rash,
Vain Otho gave his bosom to the gash:
He bled, and fell; but not with deadly wound,
Stretch'd by a dextrous sleight along the ground
'Demand thy life!' He answer'd not: and then
From that red floor he ne'er had risen again,
For Lara's brow upon the moment grew
Almost to blackness in its demon hue;
And fiercer shook his angry falchion now
Than when his foe's was levell'd at his brow;
Then all was stern collectedness and art,
Now rose the unleaven'd hatred of his heart;
So little sparing to the foe he fell'd,
That when the approaching crowd his arm withheld,
He almost turn'd the thirsty point on those
Who thus for mercy dared to interpose;
But to a moment's thought that purpose bent;
Yet look'd he on him still with eye intent,

As if he loathed the ineffectual strife
That left a foe, howe'er o'erthrown, with life;
As if to search how far the wound he gave
Had sent his victim onward to his grave.

V

They raised the bleeding Otho, and the Leech
Forbade all present question, sign, and speech;
The others met within a neighbouring hall,
And he, incensed and heedless of them all,
The cause and conqueror in this sudden fray,
In haughty silence slowly strode away;
He back'd his steed, his homeward path he took,
Nor cast on Otho's towers a single look.

VI

But where was he? that meteor of a night,
Who menaced but to disappear with light.
Where was this Ezzelin? who came and went
To leave no other trace of his intent.
He left the dome of Otho long ere morn,
In darkness, yet so well the path was worn
He could not miss it: near his dwelling lay;
But there he was not, and with coming day
Came fast inquiry, which unfolded nought
Except the absence of the chief it sought.
A chamber tenantless, a steed at rest,
His host alarm'd, his murmuring squires distress'd:
Their search extends along, around the path,
In dread to meet the marks of prowlers' wrath:
But none are there, and not a brake hath borne
Nor gout of blood, nor shred of mantle torn;
Nor fall nor struggle hath defaced the grass,
Which still retains a mark where murder was;
Nor dabbling fingers left to tell the tale,
The bitter print of each convulsive nail,
When agonised hands that ceased to guard,
Wound in that pang the smoothness of the sward.
Some such had been, if here a life was reft,
But these were not; and doubting hope is left;
And strange suspicion, whispering Lara's name,
Now daily mutters o'er his blacken'd fame;
Then sudden silent when his form appear'd,
Awaits the absence of the thing it fear'd;
Again its wonted wondering to renew,
And dye conjecture with a darker hue.

VII

Days roll along, and Otho's wounds are heal'd,
But not his pride; and hate no more conceal'd:
He was a man of power, and Lara's foe,
The friend of all who sought to work him woe,
And from his country's justice now demands
Account of Ezzelin at Lara's hands.
Who else than Lara could have cause to fear
His presence? who had made him disappear,
If not the man on whom his menaced charge
Had sate too deeply were he left at large?
The general rumour ignorantly loud,
The mystery dearest to the curious crowd;
The seeming friendlessness of him who strove
To win no confidence, and wake no love;
The sweeping fierceness which his soul betray'd,
The skill with which he wielded his keen blade;
Where had his arm unwarlike caught that art?
Where had that fierceness grown upon his heart?
For it was not the blind capricious rage
A word can kindle and a word assuage;
But the deep working of a soul unmix'd
With aught of pity where its wrath had fix'd;
Such as long power and overgorged success
Concentrates into all that's merciless:
These, link'd with that desire which ever sways
Mankind, the rather to condemn than praise,
'Gainst Lara gathering raised at length a storm,
Such as himself might fear, and foes would form,
And he must answer for the absent head
Of one that haunts him still, alive or dead.

VIII

Within that land was many a malcontent,
Who cursed the tyranny to which he bent;
That soil full many a wringing despot saw,
Who work'd his wantonness in form of law;
Long war without and frequent broil within
Had made a path for blood and giant sin,
That waited but a signal to begin
New havoc, such as civil discord blends,
Which knows no neuter, owns but foes or friends;
Fix'd in his feudal fortress each was lord,
In word and deed obey'd, in soul abhorr'd.

Thus Lara had inherited his lands,
And with them pining hearts and sluggish hands;
But that long absence from his native clime
Had left him stainless of oppression's crime,
And now, diverted by his milder sway,
All dread by slow degrees had worn away.
The menials felt their usual awe alone,
But more for him than them that fear was grown;
They deem'd him now unhappy, though at first
Their evil judgment augur'd of the worst,
And each long restless night, and silent mood,
Was traced to sickness, fed by solitude:
And though his lonely habits threw of late
Gloom o'er his chamber, cheerful was his gate;
For thence the wretched ne'er unsoothed withdrew,
For them, at least, his soul compassion knew.
Cold to the great, contemptuous to the high,
The humble pass'd not his unheeding eye;
Much he would speak not, but beneath his roof
They found asylum oft, and ne'er reproof.
And they who watch'd might mark that, day by day,
Some new retainers gather'd to his sway;
But most of late, since Ezzelin was lost,
He play'd the courteous lord and bounteous host:
Perchance his strife with Otho made him dread
Some snare prepared for his obnoxious head;
Whate'er his view, his favour more obtains
With these, the people, than his fellow thanes.
If this were policy, so far 'twas sound,
The million judged but of him as they found;
From him by sterner chiefs to exile driven
They but required a shelter, and 'twas given.
By him no peasant mourn'd his rifled cot,
And scarce the Serf could murmur o'er his lot;
With him old avarice found its hoard secure,
With him contempt forbore to mock the poor;
Youth present cheer and promised recompense
Detain'd, till all too late to part from thence:
To hate he offer'd, with the coming change.
The deep reversion of delay'd revenge;
To love, long baffled by the unequal match,
The well-won charms success was sure to snatch.
All now was ripe, he waits but to proclaim
That slavery nothing which was still a name.
The moment came, the hour when Otho thought
Secure at last the vengeance which he sought:

His summons found the destined criminal
Begirt by thousands in his swarming hall,
Fresh from their feudal fetters newly riven,
Defying earth, and confident of heaven.
That morning he had freed the soil-bound slaves
Who dig no land for tyrants but their graves!
Such is their cry—some watchword for the fight
Must vindicate the wrong, and warp the right;
Religion—freedom—vengeance—what you will,
A word's enough to raise mankind to kill;
Some factious phrase by cunning caught and spread,
That guilt may reign, and wolves and worms be fed!

IX

Throughout that clime the feudal chiefs had gain'd
Such sway, their infant monarch hardly reign'd;
Now was the hour for faction's rebel growth,
The Serfs contemn'd the one, and hated both:
They waited but a leader, and they found
One to their cause inseparably bound;
By circumstance compell'd to plunge again,
In self-defence, amidst the strife of men.
Cut off by some mysterious fate from those
Whom birth and nature meant not for his foes,
Had Lara from that night, to him accurst,
Prepared to meet, but not alone, the worst:
Some reason urged, whate'er it was, to shun
Inquiry into deeds at distance done;
By mingling with his own the cause of all,
E'en if he fail'd he still delay'd his fall.
The sullen calm that long his bosom kept,
The storm that once had spent itself and slept,
Roused by events that seem'd foredoom'd to urge
His gloomy fortunes to their utmost verge,
Burst forth, and made him all he once had been,
And is again; he only changed the scene.
Light care had he for life, and less for fame,
But not less fitted for the desperate game;
He deem'd himself mark'd out for others' hate,
And mock'd at ruin so they shared his fate.
What cared he for the freedom of the crowd?
He raised the humble but to bend the proud.
He had hoped quiet in his sullen lair,
But man and destiny beset him there:
Inured to hunters, he was found at bay;
And they must kill, they cannot snare the prey.

Stern, unambitious, silent, he had been
Henceforth a calm spectator of life's scene;
But dragg'd again upon the arena, stood
A leader not unequal to the feud;
In voice—mien—gesture—savage nature spoke,
And from his eye the gladiator broke.

x

What boots the oft-repeated tale of strife,
The feast of vultures, and the waste of life?
The varying fortune of each separate field,
The fierce that vanquish, and the faint that yield?
The smoking ruin, and the crumbled wall?
In this the struggle was the same with all;
Save that distemper'd passions lent their force
In bitterness that banish'd all remorse.
None sued, for Mercy knew her cry was vain,
The captive died upon the battle-slain:
In either cause, one rage alone possess'd
The empire of the alternate victor's breast;
And they that smote for freedom or for sway,
Deem'd few were slain, while more remain'd to slay.
It was too late to check the wasting brand,
And Desolation reap'd the famish'd land;
The torch was lighted, and the flame was spread,
And Carnage smiled upon her daily dead.

xi

Fresh with the nerve the newborn impulse strung,
The first success to Lara's numbers clung:
But that vain victory hath ruin'd all;
They form no longer to their leader's call:
In blind confusion on the foe they press,
And think to snatch is to secure success.
The lust of booty, and the thirst of hate,
Lure on the broken brigands to their fate:
In vain he doth whate'er a chief may do,
To check the headlong fury of that crew;
In vain their stubborn ardour he would tame,
The hand that kindles cannot quench the flame;
The wary foe alone hath turn'd their mood,
And shown their rashness to that erring brood:
The feign'd retreat, the nightly ambuscade,
The daily harass, and the fight delay'd,
The long privation of the hoped supply,
The tentless rest beneath the humid sky,

The stubborn wall that mocks the leaguer's art,
And palls the patience of his baffled heart,
Of these they had not deem'd: the battle-day
They could encounter as a veteran may;
But more preferr'd the fury of the strife,
And present death, to hourly suffering life:
And famine wrings, and fever sweeps away
His numbers melting fast from their array;
Intemperate triumph fades to discontent,
And Lara's soul alone seems still unbent:
But few remain to aid his voice and hand,
And thousands dwindled to a scanty band:
Desperate, though few, the last and best remain'd
To mourn the discipline they late disdain'd.
One hope survives, the frontier is not far,
And thence they may escape from native war;
And bear within them to the neighbouring state
An exile's sorrows, or an outlaw's hate:
Hard is the task their fatherland to quit,
But harder still to perish or submit.

XII

It is resolved—they march—consenting Night
Guides with her star their dim and torchless flight;
Already they perceive its tranquil beam
Sleep on the surface of the barrier stream;
Already they descry—Is yon the bank?
Away! 'tis lined with many a hostile rank.
Return or fly!—What glitters in the rear?
'Tis Otho's banner—the pursuer's spear!
Are those the shepherds' fires upon the height?
Alas! they blaze too widely for the flight:
Cut off from hope, and compass'd in the toil,
Less blood perchance hath bought a richer spoil!

XIII

A moment's pause—'tis but to breathe their band,
Or shall they onward press, or here withstand?
It matters little—if they charge the foes
Who by their border-stream their march oppose,
Some few, perchance, may break and pass the line,
However link'd to baffle such design.
'The charge be ours! to wait for their assault
Were fate well worthy of a coward's halt.'

Forth flies each sabre, rein'd is every steed,
And the next word shall scarce outstrip the deed:
In the next tone of Lara's gathering breath
How many shall but hear the voice of death!

XIV

His blade is bared,—in him there is an air
As deep, but far too tranquil for despair;
A something of indifference more than then
Becomes the bravest, if they feel for men.
He turn'd his eye on Kaled, ever near,
And still too faithful to betray one fear;
Perchance 'twas but the moon's dim twilight threw
Along his aspect an unwonted hue
Of mournful paleness, whose deep tint express'd
The truth, and not the terror of his breast.
This Lara mark'd, and laid his hand on his:
It trembled not in such an hour as this;
His lip was silent, scarcely beat his heart,
His eye alone proclaim'd, 'We will not part!
Thy band may perish, or thy friends may flee,
Farewell to life, but not adieu to thee!'

The word hath pass'd his lips, and onward driven,
Pours the link'd band through ranks asunder riven;
Well has each steed obey'd the armed heel,
And flash the scimitars, and rings the steel;
Outnumber'd, not outbraved, they still oppose
Despair to daring, and a front to foes;
And blood is mingled with the dashing stream,
Which runs all redly till the morning beam.

XV

Commanding, aiding, animating all,
Where foe appear'd to press, or friend to fall,
Cheers Lara's voice, and waves or strikes his steel,
Inspiring hope himself had ceased to feel.
None fled, for well they knew that flight were vain;
But those that waver turn to smite again,
While yet they find the firmest of the foe
Recoil before their leader's look and blow:
Now girt with numbers, now almost alone,
He foils their ranks, or re-unites his own;
Himself he spared not—once they seem'd to fly—
Now was the time, he waved his hand on high,

And shook—Why sudden droops that plumed crest?
The shaft is sped—the arrow's in his breast!
That fatal gesture left the unguarded side,
And Death has stricken down yon arm of pride.
The word of triumph fainted from his tongue;
That hand, so raised, how droopingly it hung!
But yet the sword instinctively retains,
Though from its fellow shrink the falling reins;
These Kaled snatches: dizzy with the blow,
And senseless bending o'er his saddle-bow,
Perceives not Lara that his anxious page
Beguiles his charger from the combat's rage:
Meantime his followers charge, and charge again;
Too mix'd the slayers now to heed the slain!

XVI

Day glimmers on the dying and the dead,
The cloven cuirass, and the helmless head;
The war-horse masterless is on the earth,
And that last gasp hath burst his bloody girth;
And near, yet quivering with what life remain'd,
The heel that urged him and the hand that rein'd;
And some too near that rolling torrent lie,
Whose waters mock the lip of those that die;
That panting thirst which scorches in the breath
Of those that die the soldier's fiery death,
In vain impels the burning mouth to crave
One drop—the last—to cool it for the grave;
With feeble and convulsive effort swept,
Their limbs along the crimson'd turf have crept;
The faint remains of life such struggles waste,
But yet they reach the stream, and bend to taste:
They feel its freshness, and almost partake—
Why pause?   No further thirst have they to slake—
It is unquench'd, and yet they feel it not;
It was an agony—but now forgot!

XVII

Beneath a lime, remoter from the scene,
Where but for him that strife had never been,
A breathing but devoted warrior lay:
'Twas Lara bleeding fast from life away.
His follower once, and now his only guide,
Kneels Kaled watchful o'er his welling side,
And with his scarf would stanch the tides that rush,
With each convulsion, in a blacker gush;

And then, as his faint breathing waxes low,
In feebler, not less fatal tricklings flow:
He scarce can speak, but motions him 'tis vain,
And merely adds another throb to pain.
He clasps the hand that pang which would assuage,
And sadly smiles his thanks to that dark page,
Who nothing fears, nor feels, nor heeds, nor sees,
Save that damp brow which rests upon his knees;
Save that pale aspect, where the eye, though dim,
Held all the light that shone on earth for him.

XVIII

The foe arrives, who long had search'd the field,
Their triumph nought till Lara too should yield;
They would remove him, but they see 'twere vain,
And he regards them with a calm disdain,
That rose to reconcile him with his fate,
And that escape to death from living hate:
And Otho comes, and leaping from his steed,
Looks on the bleeding foe that made him bleed,
And questions of his state; he answers not,
Scarce glances on him as on one forgot,
And turns to Kaled:—each remaining word
They understood not, if distinctly heard;
His dying tones are in that other tongue,
To which some strange remembrance wildly clung.
They spake of other scenes, but what—is known
To Kaled, whom their meaning reach'd alone;
And he replied, though faintly to their sound,
While gazed the rest in dumb amazement round:
They seem'd even then—that twain—unto the last
To half forget the present in the past;
To share between themselves some separate fate,
Whose darkness none beside should penetrate.

XIX

Their words though faint were many—from the tone
Their import those who heard could judge alone;
From this, you might have deem'd young Kaled's death
More near than Lara's by his voice and breath,
So sad, so deep, and hesitating broke
The accents his scarce-moving pale lips spoke;
But Lara's voice, though low, at first was clear
And calm, till murmuring death gasp'd hoarsely near:
But from his visage little could we guess,
So unrepentant, dark, and passionless,

Save that when struggling nearer to his last,
Upon the page his eye was kindly cast;
And once, as Kaled's answering accents ceased,
Rose Lara's hand, and pointed to the East:
Whether (as then the breaking sun from high
Roll'd back the clouds) the morrow caught his eye,
Or that 'twas chance, or some remember'd scene,
That raised his arm to point where such had been,
Scarce Kaled seem'd to know, but turn'd away
As if his heart abhorr'd that coming day,
And shrunk his glance before that morning light,
To look on Lara's brow—where all grew night.
Yet sense seem'd left, though better were its loss;
For when one near display'd the absolving cross,
And proffer'd to his touch the holy bead,
Of which his parting soul might own the need,
He look'd upon it with an eye profane,
And smiled—Heaven pardon! if 'twere with disdain:
And Kaled, though he spoke not, nor withdrew
From Lara's face his fix'd despairing view,
With brow repulsive, and with gesture swift,
Flung back the hand which held the sacred gift,
As if such but disturb'd the expiring man,
Nor seem'd to know his life but *then* began,
That life of Immortality, secure
To none, save them whose faith in Christ is sure.

XX

But gasping heaved the breath that Lara drew,
And dull the film along his dim eye grew;
His limbs stretch'd fluttering, and his head droop'd o'er
The weak yet still untiring knee that bore;
He press'd the hand he held upon his heart—
It beats no more, but Kaled will not part
With the cold grasp, but feels, and feels in vain,
For that faint throb which answers not again.
'It beats!'—Away, thou dreamer! he is gone—
It once was Lara which thou look'st upon.

XXI

He gazed, as if not yet had pass'd away
The haughty spirit of that humble clay;
And those around have roused him from his trance,
But cannot tear from thence his fixed glance;
And when, in raising him from where he bore
Within his arms the form that felt no more,

He saw the head his breast would still sustain,
Roll down like earth to earth upon the plain;
He did not dash himself thereby, nor tear
The glossy tendrils of his raven hair,
But strove to stand and gaze, but reel'd and fell,
Scarce breathing more than that he loved so well.
Than that *he* loved! Oh! never yet beneath
The breast of man such trusty love may breathe!
That trying moment hath at once reveal'd
The secret long and yet but half conceal'd;
In baring to revive that lifeless breast,
Its grief seem'd ended, but the sex confess'd;
And life return'd, and Kaled felt no shame—
What now to her was Womanhood or Fame?

XXII

And Lara sleeps not where his fathers sleep,
But where he died his grave was dug as deep;
Nor is his mortal slumber less profound,
Though priest nor bless'd nor marble deck'd the mound;
And he was mourn'd by one whose quiet grief,
Less loud, outlasts a people's for their chief.
Vain was all question ask'd her of the past,
And vain e'en menace—silent to the last;
She told nor whence, nor why she left behind
Her all for one who seem'd but little kind.
Why did she love him? Curious fool!—be still—
Is human love the growth of human will?
To her he might be gentleness; the stern
Have deeper thoughts than your dull eyes discern,
And when they love, your smilers guess not how
Beats the strong heart, though less the lips avow.
They were not common links, that form'd the chain
That bound to Lara Kaled's heart and brain;
But that wild tale she brook'd not to unfold,
And seal'd is now each lip that could have told.

XXIII

They laid him in the earth, and on his breast,
Besides the wound that sent his soul to rest,
They found the scatter'd dints of many a scar,
Which were not planted there in recent war;
Where'er had pass'd his summer years of life,
It seems they vanish'd in a land of strife;

But all unknown his glory or his guilt,
These only told that somewhere blood was spilt,
And Ezzelin, who might have spoke the past,
Return'd no more—that night appear'd his last.

XXIV

Upon that night (a peasant's is the tale)
A Serf that cross'd the intervening vale,
When Cynthia's light almost gave way to morn,
And nearly veil'd in mist her waning horn;
A Serf, that rose betimes to thread the wood,
And hew the bough that bought his children's food,
Pass'd by the river that divides the plain
Of Otho's lands and Lara's broad domain:
He heard a tramp—a horse and horseman broke
From out the wood—before him was a cloak
Wrapt round some burthen at his saddle-bow,
Bent was his head, and hidden was his brow.
Roused by the sudden sight at such a time,
And some foreboding that it might be crime,
Himself unheeded watch'd the stranger's course,
Who reach'd the river, bounded from his horse,
And lifting thence the burthen which he bore,
Heaved up the bank, and dash'd it from the shore,
Then paused, and look'd, and turn'd, and seem'd to watch,
And still another hurried glance would snatch,
And follow with his step the stream that flow'd,
As if even yet too much its surface show'd:
At once he started, stoop'd, around him strown
The winter floods had scatter'd heaps of stone;
Of these the heaviest thence he gather'd there,
And slung them with a more than common care.
Meantime the Serf had crept to where unseen
Himself might safely mark what this might mean;
He caught a glimpse, as of a floating breast,
And something glitter'd starlike on the vest;
But ere he well could mark the buoyant trunk,
A massy fragment smote it, and it sunk:
It rose again, but indistinct to view,
And left the waters of a purple hue,
Then deeply disappear'd: the horseman gazed
Till ebb'd the latest eddy it had raised;
Then turning, vaulted on his pawing steed,
And instant spurr'd him into panting speed.
His face was mask'd—the features of the dead,
If dead it were, escaped the observer's dread;

But if in sooth a star its bosom bore,
Such is the badge that knighthood ever wore,
And such 'tis known Sir Ezzelin had worn
Upon the night that led to such a morn.
If thus he perish'd, Heaven receive his soul!
His undiscover'd limbs to ocean roll;
And charity upon the hope would dwell
It was not Lara's hand by which he fell.

XXV

And Kaled—Lara—Ezzelin, are gone,
Alike without their monumental stone!
The first, all efforts vainly strove to wean
From lingering where her chieftain's blood had been;
Grief had so tamed a spirit once too proud,
Her tears were few, her wailing never loud;
But furious would you tear her from the spot
Where yet she scarce believed that he was not,
Her eye shot forth with all the living fire
That haunts the tigress in her whelpless ire;
But left to waste her weary moments there,
She talk'd all idly unto shapes of air,
Such as the busy brain of Sorrow paints,
And woos to listen to her fond complaints:
And she would sit beneath the very tree
Where lay his drooping head upon her knee;
And in that posture where she saw him fall,
His words, his looks, his dying grasp recall;
And she had shorn, but saved her raven hair,
And oft would snatch it from her bosom there,
And fold, and press it gently to the ground,
As if she stanch'd anew some phantom's wound.
Herself would question, and for him reply;
Then rising, start, and beckon him to fly
From some imagined spectre in pursuit;
Then seat her down upon some linden's root,
And hide her visage with her meagre hand,
Or trace strange characters along the sand—
This could not last—she lies by him she loved;
Her tale untold—her truth too dearly proved.

MANFRED

A DRAMATIC POEM

There are more things in heaven and earth, Horatio,
Than are dreamt of in your philosophy.

EXTRACTS from Lord Byron's letters to Mr. Murray respecting the composition of *Manfred*:

Venice, 15th February 1817.—'I forgot to mention to you, that a kind of Poem in dialogue (in blank verse) or Drama, from which "the Incantation" is an extract, begun last summer in Switzerland, is finished: it is in three acts, but of a very wild, metaphysical, and inexplicable kind. Almost all the persons—but two or three—are Spirits of the earth and air, or the waters; the scene is in the Alps; the hero a kind of magician, who is tormented by a species of remorse, the cause of which is left half unexplained. He wanders about invoking these Spirits, which appear to him, and are of no use; he at last goes to the very abode of the Evil Principle, *in propria persona*, to evocate a ghost, which appears, and gives him an ambiguous and disagreeable answer; and, in the third act, he is found by his attendants dying in a tower where he had studied his art. You may perceive, by this outline, that I have no great opinion of this piece of fantasy; but I have at least rendered it *quite impossible* for the stage, for which my intercourse with Drury Lane has given me the greatest contempt. I have not even copied it off, and feel too lazy at present to attempt the whole; but when I have, I will send it you, and you may either throw it into the fire or not.'

3rd March.—'I sent you the other day, in two covers, the first act of *Manfred*, a drama as mad as Nat. Lee's Bedlam tragedy, which was in twenty-five acts and some odd scenes: mine is but in three acts.'

9th March.—'In remitting the third act of the sort of dramatic poem of which you will by this time have received the two first, I have little to observe, except that you must not publish it (if it ever is published) without giving me previous notice. I have really and truly no notion whether it is good or bad; and as this was not the case with the principal of my former publications, I am, therefore, inclined to rank it very humbly. You will submit it to Mr. Gifford, and to whomsoever you please besides. The thing, you will see at a glimpse, could never be attempted or thought of for the stage; I much doubt if for publication even. It is too much in my old style; but I composed it actually with a *horror* of the stage, and with a view to render the thought of it impracticable, knowing the zeal of my friends that I should try that for which I have an invincible repugnance, viz. a representation. I certainly am a devil of a mannerist, and must leave off; but what could I do? Without exertion of some kind, I should have sunk under my imagination and reality.'

25th March.—'With regard to the *Witch Drama*, I repeat, that I have not an idea if it is good or bad. If bad, it must, on no account, be risked in publication; if good, it is at your service. I value it at three hundred guineas, or less, if you like it. Perhaps, if published, the best way will be to add it to your winter volume, and not publish separately. The price will show you I don't pique myself upon it; so speak out. You may put it into the fire, if you like, and Gifford don't like.'

9th April.—'As for *Manfred*, the two first acts are the best; the third so so; but I was blown with the first and second heats. You may call it "a Poem," for it is no Drama, and I do not choose to have it called by so d—d a name,—"a Poem in dialogue," or—Pantomime, if you will; anything but a green-room synonyme; and this is your motto:

> "There are more things in heaven and earth, Horatio,
>   Than are dreamt of in your philosophy."'

The third act was rewritten before publication. We give here the most important paragraphs of the ablest critique that immediately followed the appearance of the poem:

'In Manfred, we recognize at once the gloom and potency of that soul which burned and blasted and fed upon itself, in Harold, and Conrad, and Lara—and which comes again in this piece, more in sorrow than in anger—more proud, perhaps, and more awful than ever—but with the fiercer traits of its misanthropy subdued, as it were, and quenched in the gloom of a deeper despondency. Manfred does not, like Conrad and Lara, wreak the anguish of his burning heart in the dangers and daring of desperate and predatory war—nor seek to drown bitter thoughts in the tumult of perpetual contention; nor yet, like Harold, does he sweep over the peopled scenes of the earth with high disdain and aversion, and make his survey of the business, and pleasures, and studies of man an occasion for taunts and sarcasms, and the food of an unmeasurable spleen. He is fixed by the genius of the poet in the majestic solitudes of the central Alps—where, from his youth up, he has lived in proud but calm seclusion from the ways of men, conversing only with the magnificent forms and aspects of nature by which he is surrounded, and with the Spirits of the Elements over whom he has acquired dominion, by the secret and unhallowed studies of sorcery and magic. He is averse, indeed, from mankind, and scorns the low and frivolous nature to which he belongs; but he cherishes no animosity or hostility to that feeble race. Their concerns excite no interest—their pursuits no sympathy—their joys no envy. It is irksome and vexatious for him to be crossed by them in his melancholy musings,—but he treats them with gentleness and pity; and, except when stung to impatience by too importunate an intrusion, is kind and considerate to the comforts of all around him.—This piece is properly entitled a dramatic poem—for it is merely poetical, and is not at all a drama or play in the modern acceptation of the term. It has no action, no plot, and no characters; Manfred merely muses and suffers from the beginning to the end. His distresses are the same at the opening of the scene and at its closing, and the temper in which they are borne is the same. A hunter and a priest, and some domestics, are indeed introduced, but they have no connection with the passions or sufferings on which the interest depends; and Manfred is substantially alone throughout the whole piece.   He holds no communion but with the memory of the Being he had loved; and the immortal Spirits whom he evokes to reproach with his misery, and their inability to relieve it. These unearthly beings approach nearer to the character of persons of the drama—but still they are but choral accompaniments to the performance; and Manfred is, in reality, the only actor and sufferer on the scene.   To delineate his character indeed—to render conceivable his feelings—is plainly the whole scope and design of the poem; and the conception and execution are, in this respect, equally admirable.   It is a grand and terrific vision of a being invested with superhuman attributes, in order that he may be capable of more than human sufferings, and be sustained under them by more than human force and pride.   To object to the improbabliity of the fiction, is to mistake the end and aim of the author.   Probabilities, we apprehend, did not enter at all into his consideration; his object was, to produce effect—to exalt and dilate the character through whom he was to interest or appal us—and to raise our conception of it, by all the helps that could be derived from the majesty of nature, or the dread of superstition.   It is enough, therefore, if the situation in which he has placed him is *conceivable*, and if the supposition of its reality enhances our emotions and kindles our imagination;—for it is Manfred only that we are required to fear, to pity, or admire.   If we can once conceive of him as a real existence, and enter into the depth and the height of his pride and his sorrows, we may deal as we please with the means that have been used to furnish us with this impression, or to enable us to attain to this conception.   We may regard them but as types, or metaphors, or allegories; but HE is the thing to be expressed, and the feeling and the intellect of which all these are but shadows.'—JEFFREY.

DRAMATIS PERSONAE

MANFRED.

CHAMOIS HUNTER.

ABBOT OF ST. MAURICE.

MANUEL.

HERMAN.

WITCH OF THE ALPS.

ARIMANES.

NEMESIS.

THE DESTINIES.

SPIRITS, ETC.

The Scene of the Drama is amongst the Higher Alps—partly in the Castle of Manfred, and partly in the Mountains.

MANFRED

ACT I

SCENE I

Manfred alone.—Scene, a Gothic Gallery.—Time, Midnight

Man. The lamp must be replenish'd, but even then
  It will not burn so long as I must watch:
  My slumbers—if I slumber—are not sleep,
  But a continuance of enduring thought,
  Which then I can resist not: in my heart
  There is a vigil, and these eyes but close
  To look within; and yet I live, and bear
  The aspect and the form of breathing men.
  But grief should be the instructor of the wise;
  Sorrow is knowledge: they who know the most
  Must mourn the deepest o'er the fatal truth,
  The Tree of Knowledge is not that of Life.
  Philosophy and science, and the springs
  Of wonder, and the wisdom of the world,
  I have essay'd, and in my mind there is
  A power to make these subject to itself—
  But they avail not: I have done men good,
  And I have met with good even among men—
  But this avail'd not: I have had my foes,
  And none have baffled, many fallen before me—
  But this avail'd not:—Good, or evil, life,
  Powers, passions, all I see in other beings,
  Have been to me as rain unto the sands,
  Since that all-nameless hour. I have no dread,
  And feel the curse to have no natural fear,
  Nor fluttering throb, that beats with hopes or wishes,
  Or lurking love of something on the earth.—
  Now to my task.—
          Mysterious Agency!
  Ye spirits of the unabounded Universe!
  Whom I have sought in darkness and in light—
  Ye, who do compass earth about, and dwell
  In subtler essence—ye, to whom the tops
  Of mountains inaccessible are haunts,
  And earth's and ocean's caves familiar things—

I call upon ye by the written charm
Which gives me power upon you——Rise! appear!   [*A pause.*
They come not yet.—Now by the voice of him
Who is the first among you—by this sign,
Which makes you tremble—by the claims of him
Who is undying,——Rise! appear!—Appear!   [*A pause.*
If it be so.—Spirits of earth and air,
Ye shall not thus elude me: by a power,
Deeper than all yet urged, a tyrant-spell,
Which had its birthplace in a star condemn'd,
The burning wreck of a demolish'd world,
A wandering hell in the eternal space;
By the strong curse which is upon my soul,
The thought which is within me and around me,
I do compel ye to my will.—Appear!

[*A star is seen at the darker end of the gallery: it is stationary;
and a voice is heard singing.*

FIRST SPIRIT

Mortal! to thy bidding bow'd,
From my mansion in the cloud,
Which the breath of twilight builds,
And the summer's sunset gilds
With the azure and vermilion,
Which is mix'd for my pavilion;
Though thy quest may be forbidden,
On a star-beam I have ridden;
To thine adjuration bow'd,
Mortal—be thy wish avow'd!

Voice of the SECOND SPIRIT

Mont Blanc is the monarch of mountains;
They crown'd him long ago
On a throne of rocks in a robe of clouds,
With a diadem of snow.
Around his waist are forests braced,
The Avalanche in his hand;
But ere it fall, that thundering ball
Must pause for my command.
The Glacier's cold and restless mass
Moves onward day by day;
But I am he who bids it pass,
Or with its ice delay.

I am the spirit of the place,
Could make the mountain bow
And quiver to his cavern'd base—
And what with me wouldst *Thou*?

Voice of the THIRD SPIRIT

In the blue depth of the waters,
Where the wave hath no strife,
Where the wind is a stranger,
And the sea-snake hath life,
Where the Mermaid is decking
Her green hair with shells;
Like the storm on the surface
Came the sound of thy spells;
O'er my calm Hall of Coral
The deep echo roll'd—
To the Spirit of Ocean
Thy wishes unfold!

FOURTH SPIRIT

Where the slumbering earthquake
Lies pillow'd on fire,
And the lakes of bitumen
Rise boilingly higher;
Where the roots of the Andes
Strike deep in the earth,
As their summits to heaven
Shoot soaringly forth;
I have quitted my birthplace,
Thy bidding to bide—
Thy spell hath subdued me,
Thy will be my guide!

FIFTH SPIRIT

I am the Rider of the wind,
The Stirrer of the storm;
The hurricane I left behind
Is yet with lightning warm;
To speed to thee, o'er shore and sea
I swept upon the blast:
The fleet I met sail'd well, and yet
'Twill sink ere night be past.

SIXTH SPIRIT

My dwelling is the shadow of the night,
Why doth thy magic torture me with light?

SEVENTH SPIRIT

The star which rules thy destiny
Was ruled, ere earth began, by me:
It was a world as fresh and fair
As e'er revolved round sun in air;
Its course was free and regular,
Space bosom'd not a lovelier star.
The hour arrived—and it became
A wandering mass of shapeless flame,
A pathless comet, and a curse,
The menace of the universe;
Still rolling on with innate force,
Without a sphere, without a course,
A bright deformity on high,
The monster of the upper sky!
And thou! beneath its influence born—
Thou worm! whom I obey and scorn—
Forced by a power (which is not thine,
And lent thee but to make thee mine)
For this brief moment to descend,
Where these weak spirits round thee bend
And parley with a thing like thee—
What wouldst thou, Child of Clay! with me?

The SEVEN SPIRITS

Earth, ocean, air, night, mountains, winds, thy star,
Are at thy beck and bidding, Child of Clay!
Before thee at thy quest their spirits are—
What wouldst thou with us, son of mortals—say?

Man. Forgetfulness——
First Spirit.   Of what—of whom—and why?
Man. Of that which is within me; read it there—
     Ye know it, and I cannot utter it.
Spirit. We can but give thee that which we possess:
     Ask of us subjects, sovereignty, the power
     O'er earth, the whole, or portion, or a sign
     Which shall control the elements, whereof
     We are the dominators, each and all,
     These shall be thine.
Man.   Oblivion, self-oblivion—
     Can ye not wring from out the hidden realms
     Ye offer so profusely what I ask?
Spirit. It is not in our essence, in our skill;
     But—thou mayst die.

Man.   Will death bestow it on me?

Spirit. We are immortal, and do not forget;
　We are eternal; and to us the past
　Is, as the future, present.　Art thou answer'd?

Man. Ye mock me—but the power which brought ye here
　Hath made you mine.　Slaves, scoff not at my will!
　The mind, the spirit, the Promethean spark,
　The lightning of my being, is as bright,
　Pervading, and far darting as your own,
　And shall not yield to yours, though coop'd in clay!
　Answer, or I will teach you what I am.

Spirit. We answer as we answer'd; our reply
　Is even in thine own words.

Man.   Why say ye so?

Spirit. If, as thou say'st, thine essence be as ours,
　We have replied in telling thee, the thing
　Mortals call death hath nought to do with us.

Man. I then have call'd ye from your realms in vain;
　Ye cannot, or ye will not, aid me.

Spirit.   Say;
　What we possess we offer; it is thine:
　Bethink ere thou dismiss us, ask again—
　Kingdom, and sway, and strength, and length of days——

Man. Accursed! what have I to do with days?
　They are too long already.—Hence—begone!

Spirit. Yet pause: being here, our will would do thee service;
　Bethink thee, is there then no other gift
　Which we can make not worthless in thine eyes?

Man. No, none: yet stay—one moment, ere we part—
　I would behold ye face to face.　I hear
　Your voices, sweet and melancholy sounds,
　As music on the waters; and I see
　The steady aspect of a clear large star;
　But nothing more.　Approach me as ye are,
　Or one, or all, in your accustom'd forms.

Spirit. We have no forms, beyond the elements
　Of which we are the mind and principle:
　But choose a form—in that we will appear.

Man. I have no choice; there is no form on earth
　Hideous or beautiful to me.　Let him,
　Who is most powerful of ye, take such aspect
　As unto him may seem most fitting—Come!

Seventh Spirit. [*Appearing in the shape of a beautiful female figure.*]
　Behold!

Man. Oh God! if it be thus, and *thou*
　Art not a madness and a mockery,

I yet might be most happy.   I will clasp thee,
And we again will be——   [*The figure vanishes.*
                         My heart is crush'd !
                                  [MANFRED *falls senseless.*

(*A Voice is heard in the Incantation which follows*)

      When the moon is on the wave,
      And the glow-worm in the grass,
      And the meteor on the grave,
      And the wisp on the morass;
      When the falling stars are shooting,
      And the answer'd owls are hooting,
      And the silent leaves are still
      In the shadow of the hill,
      Shall my soul be upon thine,
      With a power and with a sign.

      Though thy slumber may be deep,
      Yet thy spirit shall not sleep;
      There are shades which will not vanish,
      There are thoughts thou canst not banish;
      By a power to thee unknown,
      Thou canst never be alone,
      Thou art wrapt as with a shroud,
      Thou art gather'd in a cloud;
      And for ever shalt thou dwell
      In the spirit of this spell.

      Though thou seest me not pass by,
      Thou shalt feel me with thine eye
      As a thing that, though unseen,
      Must be near thee, and hath been,
      And when in that secret dread
      Thou hast turn'd around thy head,
      Thou shalt marvel I am not
      As thy shadow on the spot,
      And the power which thou dost feel,
      Shall be what thou must conceal.

      And a magic voice and verse
      Hath baptized thee with a curse;
      And a spirit of the air
      Hath begirt thee with a snare;
      In the wind there is a voice
      Shall forbid thee to rejoice;

And to thee shall Night deny
All the quiet of her sky;
And the day shall have a sun,
Which shall make thee wish it done.

From thy false tears I did distil
An essence which hath strength to kill;
From thy own heart I then did wring
The black blood in its blackest spring;
From thy own smile I snatch'd the snake,
For there it coil'd as in a brake;
From thy own lip I drew the charm
Which gave all these their chiefest harm;
In proving every poison known,
I found the strongest was thine own.

By thy cold breast and serpent smile,
By thy unfathom'd gulfs of guile,
By that most seeming virtuous eye,
By thy shut soul's hypocrisy;
By the perfection of thine art
Which pass'd for human thine own heart;
By thy delight in others' pain,
And by thy brotherhood of Cain,
I call upon thee! and compel
Thyself to be thy proper Hell!

And on thy head I pour the vial
Which doth devote thee to this trial;
Nor to slumber, nor to die,
Shall be in thy destiny;
Though thy death shall still seem near
To thy wish, but as a fear;
Lo! the spell now works around thee,
And the clankless chain hath bound thee;
O'er thy heart and brain together
Hath the word been pass'd—now wither!

SCENE II

*The Mountain of the Jungfrau.—Time, Morning.—*MANFRED *alone
upon the Cliffs*

Man. The spirits I have raised abandon me—
The spells which I have studied baffle me—
The remedy I reck'd of tortured me;
I lean no more on superhuman aid,

II—L 4⁸7

It hath no power upon the past, and for
The future, till the past be gulf'd in darkness,
It is not of my search.—My mother Earth!
And thou fresh breaking Day, and you, ye Mountains,
Why are ye beautiful? I cannot love ye.
And thou, the bright eye of the universe,
That openest above all, and unto all
Art a delight—thou shin'st not on my heart.
And you, ye crags, upon whose extreme edge
I stand, and on the torrent's brink beneath
Behold the tall pines dwindled as to shrubs
In dizziness of distance, when a leap,
A stir, a motion, even a breath, would bring
My breast upon its rocky bosom's bed
To rest for ever—wherefore do I pause?
I feel the impulse—yet I do not plunge;
I see the peril—yet do not recede;
And my brain reels—and yet my foot is firm:
There is a power upon me which withholds,
And makes it my fatality to live;
If it be life to wear within myself
This barrenness of spirit, and to be
My own soul's sepulchre, for I have ceased
To justify my deeds unto myself—
The last infirmity of evil. Ay,
Thou winged and cloud-cleaving minister,   [*An eagle passes.*
Whose happy flight is highest into heaven,
Well may'st thou swoop so near me—I should be
Thy prey, and gorge thine eaglets; thou art gone
Where the eye cannot follow thee; but thine
Yet pierces downward, onward, or above,
With a pervading vision.—Beautiful!
How beautiful is all this visible world!
How glorious in its action and itself!
But we, who name ourselves its sovereigns, we,
Half dust, half deity, alike unfit
To sink or soar, with our mix'd essence make
A conflict of its elements, and breathe
The breath of degradation and of pride,
Contending with low wants and lofty will,
Till our mortality predominates,
And men are—what they name not to themselves,
And trust not to each other. Hark! the note,
                    [*The Shepherd's pipe in the distance is heard.*
The natural music of the mountain reed—
For here the patriarchal days are not

A pastoral fable—pipes in the liberal air,
Mix'd with the sweet bells of the sauntering herd;
My soul would drink those echoes.—Oh, that I were
The viewless spirit of a lovely sound,
A living voice, a breathing harmony,
A bodiless enjoyment—born and dying
With the blest tone which made me!

Enter from below a CHAMOIS HUNTER.

Chamois Hunter.   Even so
This way the chamois leapt; her nimble feet
Have baffled me; my gains to-day will scarce
Repay my break-neck travail.—What is here?
Who seems not of my trade, and yet hath reach'd
A height which none even of our mountaineers,
Save our best hunters, may attain: his garb
Is goodly, his mien manly, and his air
Proud as a free-born peasant's, at this distance—
I will approach him nearer.
Man. [*Not perceiving the other.*] To be thus—
Grey-hair'd with anguish, like these blasted pines,
Wrecks of a single winter, barkless, branchless,
A blighted trunk upon a cursed root,
Which but supplies a feeling to decay—
And to be thus, eternally but thus,
Having been otherwise! Now furrow'd over
With wrinkles, plough'd by moments, not by years
And hours—all tortured into ages—hours
Which I outlive!—Ye toppling crags of ice!
Ye avalanches, whom a breath draws down
In mountainous o'erwhelming, come and crush me!
I hear ye momently above, beneath,
Crash with a frequent conflict; but ye pass,
And only fall on things that still would live;
On the young flourishing forest, or the hut
And the hamlet of the harmless villager.
C. Hun. The mists begin to rise from up the valley;
I'll warn him to descend, or he may chance
To lose at once his way and life together.
Man. The mists boil up around the glaciers; clouds
Rise curling fast beneath me, white and sulphury,
Like foam from the roused ocean of deep Hell,
Whose every wave breaks on a living shore,
Heap'd with the damn'd like pebbles.—I am giddy.

C. Hun. I must approach him cautiously; if near,
    A sudden step will startle him, and he
    Seems tottering already.

Man.   Mountains have fallen,
    Leaving a gap in the clouds, and with the shock
    Rocking their Alpine brethren; filling up
    The ripe green valleys with destruction's splinters;
    Damming the rivers with a sudden dash,
    Which crush'd the waters into mist, and made
    Their fountains find another channel—thus,
    Thus, in its old age, did Mount Rosenberg—
    Why stood I not beneath it?

C. Hun.   Friend! have a care,
    Your next step may be fatal!—for the love
    Of him who made you, stand not on that brink!

Man. [*Not hearing him.*] Such would have been for me a fitting
    tomb;
    My bones had then been quiet in their depth;
    They had not then been strewn upon the rocks
    For the wind's pastime—as thus —thus they shall be—
    In this one plunge.—Farewell, ye opening heavens!
    Look not upon me thus reproachfully—
    Ye were not meant for me—Earth! take these atoms!
    [*As* MANFRED *is in act to spring from the cliff, the* CHAMOIS
        HUNTER *seizes and retains him with a sudden grasp.*

C. Hun. Hold, madman!—though aweary of thy life,
    Stain not our pure vales with thy guilty blood—
    Away with me——I will not quit my hold.

Man. I am most sick at heart—nay, grasp me not—
    I am all feebleness—the mountains whirl
    Spinning around me——I grow blind——What art thou?

C. Hun. I'll answer that anon.—Away with me——
    The clouds grow thicker——there—now lean on me—
    Place your foot here—here, take this staff, and cling
    A moment to that shrub—now give me your hand,
    And hold fast by my girdle—softly—well—
    The Chalet will be gain'd within an hour—
    Come on, we'll quickly find a surer footing,
    And something like a pathway, which the torrent
    Hath wash'd since winter.—Come, 'tis bravely done—
    You should have been a hunter.—Follow me.
    [*As they descend the rocks with difficulty, the scene closes.*

ACT II

SCENE I

A Cottage among the Bernese Alps

MANFRED *and the* CHAMOIS HUNTER.

C. Hun. No, no—yet pause—thou must not yet go forth:
  Thy mind and body are alike unfit
  To trust each other, for some hours, at least;
  When thou art better, I will be thy guide—
  But whither?
Man.   It imports not: I do know
  My route full well, and need no further guidance.
C. Hun. Thy garb and gait bespeak thee of high lineage—
  One of the many chiefs, whose castled crags
  Look o'er the lower valleys—which of these
  May call thee lord? I only know their portals;
  My way of life leads me but rarely down
  To bask by the huge hearths of those old halls,
  Carousing with the vassals; but the paths,
  Which step from out our mountains to their doors,
  I know from childhood—which of these is thine?
Man. No matter.
C. Hun.   Well, sir, pardon me the question,
  And be of better cheer. Come, taste my wine;
  'Tis of ancient vintage; many a day
  'T has thawed my veins among our glaciers, now
  Let it do thus for thine—Come, pledge me fairly.
Man. Away, away! there's blood upon the brim!
  Will it then never—never sink in the earth?
C. Hun. What dost thou mean? thy senses wander from thee.
Man. I say 'tis blood—my blood! the pure warm stream
  Which ran in the veins of my fathers, and in ours
  When we were in our youth, and had one heart,
  And loved each other as we should not love,
  And this was shed: but still it rises up,
  Colouring the clouds, that shut me out from heaven,
  Where thou art not—and I shall never be.
C. Hun. Man of strange words, and some half-maddening sin,
  Which makes thee people vacancy, whate'er
  Thy dread and sufferance be, there's comfort yet—
  The aid of holy men, and heavenly patience——
Man. Patience and patience! Hence—that word was made
  For brutes of burthen, not for birds of prey;

Preach it to mortals of a dust like thine,—
I am not of thine order.

C. Hun.   Thanks to heaven!
I would not be of thine for the free fame
Of William Tell; but whatsoe'er thine ill
It must be borne, and these wild starts are useless.

Man. Do I not bear it?—Look on me—I live.

C. Hun. This is convulsion, and no healthful life.

Man. I tell thee, man! I have lived many years,
Many long years, but they are nothing now
To those which I must number: ages—ages—
Space and eternity—and consciousness,
With the fierce thirst of death—and still unslaked!

C. Hun. Why, on thy brow the seal of middle age
Hath scarce been set; I am thine elder far.

Man. Think'st thou existence doth depend on time?
It doth; but actions are our epochs: mine
Have made my days and nights imperishable,
Endless, and all alike, as sands on the shore,
Innumerable atoms; and one desert,
Barren and cold, on which the wild waves break,
But nothing rests, save carcasses and wrecks,
Rocks, and the salt-surf weeds of bitterness.

C. Hun. Alas! he's mad—but yet I must not leave him.

Man. I would I were—for then the things I see
Would be but a distemper'd dream.

C. Hun.   What is it
That thou dost see, or think thou look'st upon?

Man. Myself, and thee—a peasant of the Alps—
Thy humble virtues, hospitable home,
And spirit patient, pious, proud, and free;
Thy self-respect, grafted on innocent thoughts;
Thy days of health, and nights of sleep; thy toils,
By danger dignified, yet guiltless; hopes
Of cheerful old age and a quiet grave,
With cross and garland over its green turf,
And thy grandchildren's love for epitaph;
This do I see—and then I look within—
It matters not—my soul was scorch'd already!

C. Hun. And wouldst thou then exchange thy lot for mine?

Man. No, friend! I would not wrong thee nor exchange
My lot with living being: I can bear—
However wretchedly, 'tis still to bear—
In life what others could not brook to dream,
But perish in their slumber.

C. Hun.   And with this—

This cautious feeling for another's pain,
Canst thou be black with evil?—say not so.
Can one of gentle thoughts have wreak'd revenge
Upon his enemies?
Man.   Oh! no, no, no!
My injuries came down on those who loved me—
On those whom I best loved: I never quell'd
An enemy, save in my just defence—
But my embrace was fatal.
C. Hun.   Heaven give thee rest!
And penitence restore thee to thyself;
My prayers shall be for thee.
Man.   I need them not,
But can endure thy pity.   I depart—
'Tis time—farewell!—Here's gold, and thanks for thee—
No words—it is thy due.—Follow me not—
I know my path—the mountain peril's past:
And once again, I charge thee, follow not!   [*Exit* MANFRED.

SCENE II

A lower Valley in the Alps—A Cataract

Enter MANFRED.

It is not noon—the sunbow's rays[1] still arch
The torrent with the many hues of heaven,
And roll the sheeted silver's waving column
O'er the crag's headlong perpendicular,
And fling its lines of foaming light along,
And to and fro, like the pale courser's tail,
The Giant steed, to be bestrode by Death,
As told in the Apocalypse.   No eyes
But mine now drink this sight of loveliness;
I should be sole in this sweet solitude,
And with the Spirit of the place divide
The homage of these waters.—I will call her.
[MANFRED *takes some of the water into the palm of his hand, and
flings it into the air, muttering the adjuration.   After a
pause, the* WITCH OF THE ALPS *rises beneath the arch of
the sunbow of the torrent.*
Beautiful Spirit! with thy hair of light,
And dazzling eyes of glory, in whose form
The charms of earth's least mortal daughters grow

[1] This iris is formed by the rays of the sun over the lower part of the Alpine
torrents; it is exactly like a rainbow come down to pay a visit, and so close that
you may walk into it; this effect lasts till noon.

To an unearthly stature, in an essence
Of purer elements; while the hues of youth,—
Carnation'd like a sleeping infant's cheek,
Rock'd by the beating of her mother's heart,
Or the rose tints, which summer's twilight leaves
Upon the lofty glacier's virgin snow,
The blush of earth embracing with her heaven,—
Tinge thy celestial aspect, and make tame
The beauties of the sunbow which bends o'er thee.
Beautiful Spirit! in thy calm clear brow,
Wherein is glass'd serenity of soul,
Which of itself shows immortality,
I read that thou wilt pardon to a Son
Of Earth, whom the abstruser powers permit
At times to commune with them—if that he
Avail him of his spells—to call thee thus,
And gaze on thee a moment.

Witch.   Son of Earth!
I know thee, and the powers which give thee power;
I know thee for a man of many thoughts,
And deeds of good and ill, extreme in both,
Fatal and fated in thy sufferings.
I have expected this—what wouldst thou with me?

Man. To look upon thy beauty—nothing further.
The face of the earth hath madden'd me, and I
Take refuge in her mysteries, and pierce
To the abodes of those who govern her—
But they can nothing aid me.   I have sought
From them what they could not bestow, and now
I search no further.

Witch.   What could be the quest
Which is not in the power of the most powerful,
The rulers of the invisible?

Man.   A boon;
But why should I repeat it? 'twere in vain.

Witch. I know not that; let thy lips utter it.

Man. Well, though it torture me, 'tis but the same;
My pang shall find a voice.   From my youth upwards
My spirit walk'd not with the souls of men,
Nor look'd upon the earth with human eyes;
The thirst of their ambition was not mine,
The aim of their existence was not mine;
My joys, my griefs, my passions, and my powers,
Made me a stranger; though I wore the form,
I had no sympathy with breathing flesh,
Nor midst the creatures of clay that girded me

Was there but one who——but of her anon.
I said with men, and with the thoughts of men,
I held but slight communion; but instead,
My joy was in the Wilderness, to breathe
The difficult air of the iced mountain's top,
Where the birds dare not build, nor insect's wing
Flit o'er the herbless granite; or to plunge
Into the torrent, and to roll along
On the swift whirl of the new breaking wave
Of river-stream, or ocean, in their flow.
In these my early strength exulted; or
To follow through the night the moving moon,
The stars and their development; or catch
The dazzling lightnings till my eyes grew dim;
Or to look, list'ning, on the scatter'd leaves,
While Autumn winds were at their evening song.
These were my pastimes, and to be alone;
For if the beings, of whom I was one,—
Hating to be so,—cross'd me in my path,
I felt myself degraded back to them,
And was all clay again. And then I dived,
In my lone wanderings, to the caves of death,
Searching its cause in its effect; and drew
From wither'd bones, and skulls, and heap'd up dust,
Conclusions most forbidden. Then I pass'd
The nights of years in sciences untaught,
Save in the old time; and with time and toil,
And terrible ordeal, and such penance
As in itself hath power upon the air,
And spirits that do compass air and earth,
Space, and the peopled infinite, I made
Mine eyes familiar with Eternity,
Such as, before me, did the Magi, and
He who from out their fountain dwellings raised
Eros and Anteros,[1] at Gadara,
As I do thee;—and with my knowledge grew
The thirst of knowledge, and the power of joy
Of this most bright intelligence, until——
Witch. Proceed.
Man.   Oh! I but thus prolong'd my words,
Boasting these idle attributes, because
As I approach the core of my heart's grief—
But to my task. I have not named to thee
Father or mother, mistress, friend, or being,

[1] The philosopher Jamblicus. The story of the raising of Eros and Anteros may be found in his life by Eunapius.

With whom I wore the chain of human ties;
If I had such, they seem'd not such to me—
Yet there was one——

Witch.   Spare not thyself—proceed.

Man. She was like me in lineaments—her eyes,
Her hair, her features, all, to the very tone
Even of her voice, they said were like to mine;
But soften'd all, and temper'd into beauty;
She had the same lone thoughts and wanderings,
The quest of hidden knowledge, and a mind
To comprehend the universe: nor these
Alone, but with them gentler powers than mine,
Pity, and smiles, and tears—which I had not;
And tenderness—but that I had for her;
Humility—and that I never had.
Her faults were mine—her virtues were her own—
I loved her, and destroy'd her!

Witch.   With thy hand?

Man. Not with my hand, but heart—which broke her heart—
It gazed on mine, and wither'd. I have shed
Blood, but not hers—and yet her blood was shed—
I saw—and could not stanch it.

Witch.   And for this—
A being of the race thou dost despise,
The order which thine own would rise above,
Mingling with us and ours, thou dost forego
The gifts of our great knowledge, and shrink'st back
To recreant mortality——Away!

Man. Daughter of Air! I tell thee, since that hour—
But words are breath—look on me in my sleep,
Or watch my watchings—Come and sit by me!
My solitude is solitude no more,
But peopled with the Furies;—I have gnash'd
My teeth in darkness till returning morn,
Then cursed myself till sunset;—I have pray'd
For madness as a blessing—'tis denied me.
I have affronted death—but in the war
Of elements the waters shrunk from me,
And fatal things pass'd harmless—the cold hand
Of an all-pitiless demon held me back,
Back by a single hair, which would not break.
In fantasy, imagination, all
The affluence of my soul—which one day was
A Croesus in creation—I plunged deep,
But, like an ebbing wave, it dash'd me back
Into the gulf of my unfathom'd thought.

I plunged amidst mankind—Forgetfulness
I sought in all, save where 'tis to be found,
And that I have to learn—my sciences,
My long-pursued and superhuman art,
Is mortal here—I dwell in my despair—
And live—and live for ever.
Witch.   It may be
That I can aid thee.
Man.   To do this thy power
  Must wake the dead, or lay me low with them.
  Do so—in any shape—in any hour—
  With any torture—so it be the last.
Witch. That is not in my province; but if thou
  Wilt swear obedience to my will, and do
  My bidding, it may help thee to thy wishes.
Man. I will not swear—Obey! and whom? the spirits
  Whose presence I command, and be the slave
  Of those who served me—Never!
Witch.   Is this all?
  Hast thou no gentler answer?—Yet bethink thee,
  And pause ere thou rejectest.
Man.   I have said it.
Witch. Enough!—I may retire then—say!
Man.   Retire!
                    [*The* WITCH *disappears.*
Man. [*Alone.*] We are the fools of time and terror: Days
  Steal on us and steal from us; yet we live,
  Loathing our life, and dreading still to die.
  In all the days of this detested yoke—
  This vital weight upon the struggling heart,
  Which sinks with sorrow, or beats quick with pain,
  Or joy that ends in agony or faintness—
  In all the days of past and future, for
  In life there is no present, we can number
  How few—how less than few—wherein the soul
  Forbears to pant for death, and yet draws back
  As from a stream in winter, though the chill
  Be but a moment's. I have one resource
  Still in my science—I can call the dead,
  And ask them what it is we dread to be:
  The sternest answer can but be the Grave,
  And that is nothing—if they answer not—
  The buried Prophet answered to the Hag
  Of Endor; and the Spartan Monarch drew
  From the Byzantine maid's unsleeping spirit
  An answer and his destiny—he slew

That which he loved, unknowing what he slew,
And died unpardon'd—though he call'd in aid
The Phyxian Jove, and in Phigalia roused
The Arcadian Evocators to compel
The indignant shadow to depose her wrath,
Or fix her term of vengeance—she replied
In words of dubious import, but fulfill'd.
If I had never lived, that which I love
Had still been living; had I never loved,
That which I love would still be beautiful—
Happy and giving happiness.   What is she?
What is she now?—a sufferer for my sins—
A thing I dare not think upon—or nothing.
Within few hours I shall not call in vain—
Yet in this hour I dread the thing I dare:
Until this hour I never shrunk to gaze
On spirit, good or evil—now I tremble,
And feel a strange cold thaw upon my heart.
But I can act even what I most abhor,
And champion human fears.—The night approaches. [*Exit.*

SCENE III

The Summit of the Jungfrau Mountain

Enter FIRST DESTINY.

The moon is rising broad, and round, and bright;
And here on snows, where never human foot
Of common mortal trod, we nightly tread,
And leave no traces; o'er the savage sea,
The glassy ocean of the mountain ice,
We skim its rugged breakers, which put on
The aspect of a tumbling tempest's foam,
Frozen in a moment—a dead whirlpool's image:
And this most steep fantastic pinnacle,
The fretwork of some earthquake—where the clouds
Pause to repose themselves in passing by—
Is sacred to our revels, or our vigils;
Here do I wait my sisters, on our way
To the Hall of Arimanes, for to-night
Is our great festival—'tis strange they come not.

A Voice without, singing.

The Captive Usurper,
Hurl'd down from the throne,

Lay buried in torpor,
Forgotten and lone;
I broke through his slumbers,
I shiver'd his chain,
I leagued him with numbers—
He's Tyrant again!
With the blood of a million he'll answer my care,
With a nation's destruction—his flight and despair.

Second Voice, without.

The ship sail'd on, the ship sail'd fast,
But I left not a sail, and I left not a mast;
There is not a plank of the hull or the deck,
And there is not a wretch to lament o'er his wreck;
Save one, whom I held, as he swam, by the hair,
And he was a subject well worthy my care;
A traitor on land, and a pirate at sea—
But I saved him to wreak further havoc for me!

FIRST DESTINY, *answering.*

The city lies sleeping;
The morn, to deplore it,
May dawn on it weeping:
Sullenly, slowly,
The black plague flew o'er it—
Thousands lie lowly;
Tens of thousands shall perish—
The living shall fly from
The sick they should cherish;
But nothing can vanquish
The touch that they die from.
Sorrow and anguish,
And evil and dread,
Envelope a nation—
The blest are the dead,
Who see not the sight
Of their own desolation—
This work of a night—
This wreck of a realm—this deed of my doing—
For ages I've done, and shall still be renewing!

Enter the SECOND *and* THIRD DESTINIES.

The Three. Our hands contain the hearts of men,
   Our footsteps are their graves;
   We only give to take again
   The spirits of our slaves!

First Des. Welcome!—Where's Nemesis?
Second Des.   At some great work;
  But what I know not, for my hands were full.
Third Des. Behold she cometh.

Enter NEMESIS.

First Des.   Say, where hast thou been?
  My sisters and thyself are slow to-night.
Nem. I was detain'd repairing shatter'd thrones,
  Marrying fools, restoring dynasties,
  Avenging men upon their enemies,
  And making them repent their own revenge;
  Goading the wise to madness; from the dull
  Shaping out oracles to rule the world
  Afresh, for they were waxing out of date,
  And mortals dared to ponder for themselves,
  To weigh kings in the balance, and to speak
  Of freedom, the forbidden fruit.—Away!
  We have outstay'd the hour—mount we our clouds!
[Exeunt.

SCENE IV

The Hall of Arimanes—Arimanes on his Throne, a Globe of Fire,
surrounded by the Spirits

Hymn of the SPIRITS.

  Hail to our Master!—Prince of Earth and Air!
  Who walks the clouds and waters—in his hand
  The sceptre of the elements, which tear
  Themselves to chaos at his high command!
  He breatheth—and a tempest shakes the sea;
  He speaketh—and the clouds reply in thunder;
  He gazeth—from his glance the sunbeams flee;
  He moveth—earthquakes rend the world asunder.
  Beneath his footsteps the volcanoes rise;
  His shadow is the Pestilence; his path
  The comets herald through the crackling skies;
  And planets turn to ashes at his wrath.
  To him War offers daily sacrifice;
  To him Death pays his tribute; Life is his,
  With all its infinite of agonies—
  And his the spirit of whatever is!

Enter the DESTINIES and NEMESIS.

First Des. Glory to Arimanes! on the earth
  His power increaseth—both my sisters did
  His bidding, nor did I neglect my duty!

Second Des. Glory to Arimanes! we who bow
  The necks of men, bow down before his throne!
Third Des. Glory to Arimanes! we await
  His nod!
Nem.   Sovereign of Sovereigns! we are thine,
  And all that liveth, more or less, is ours,
  And most things wholly so; still to increase
  Our power, increasing thine, demands our care,
  And we are vigilant—Thy late commands
  Have been fulfill'd to the utmost.

Enter MANFRED.

A Spirit.   What is here?
  A mortal!—Thou most rash and fatal wretch,
  Bow down and worship!
Second Spirit.   I do know the man—
  A Magian of great power and fearful skill!
Third Spirit. Bow down and worship, slave!—What, know'st
    thou not
  Thine and our Sovereign?—Tremble, and obey!
All the Spirits. Prostrate thyself, and thy condemned clay,
  Child of the Earth! or dread the worst.
Man.   I know it;
  And yet ye see I kneel not.
Fourth Spirit.   'Twill be taught thee.
Man. 'Tis taught already;—many a night on the earth,
  On the bare ground, have I bow'd down my face,
  And strew'd my head with ashes; I have known
  The fulness of humiliation, for
  I sunk before my vain despair, and knelt
  To my own desolation.
Fifth Spirit.   Dost thou dare
  Refuse to Arimanes on his throne
  What the whole earth accords, beholding not
  The terror of his Glory?—Crouch! I say.
Man. Bid *him* bow down to that which is above him,
  The overruling Infinite—the Maker
  Who made him not for worship—let him kneel,
  And we will kneel together.
The Spirits.   Crush the worm!
  Tear him in pieces!—
First Des.   Hence! Avaunt!—he 's mine.
  Prince of the Powers invisible! This man
  Is of no common order, as his port
  And presence here denote; his sufferings

Have been of an immortal nature, like
Our own; his knowledge, and his powers and will,
As far as is compatible with clay,
Which clogs the ethereal essence, have been such
As clay hath seldom borne; his aspirations
Have been beyond the dwellers of the earth,
And they have only taught him what we know—
That knowledge is not happiness, and science
But an exchange of ignorance for that
Which is another kind of ignorance.
This is not all—the passions, attributes
Of earth and heaven, from which no power, nor being,
Nor breath from the worm upwards is exempt,
Have pierced his heart; and in their consequence
Made him a thing, which I, who pity not,
Yet pardon those who pity.   He is mine,
And thine, it may be—be it so, or not,
No other Spirit in this region hath
A soul like his—or power upon his soul.

Nem. What doth he here then?
First Des.   Let him answer that.
Man. Ye know what I have known; and without power
  I could not be amongst ye: but there are
  Powers deeper still beyond—I come in quest
  Of such, to answer unto what I seek.
Nem. What would'st thou?
Man.   Thou canst not reply to me.
  Call up the dead—my question is for them.
Nem. Great Arimanes, doth thy will avouch
  The wishes of this mortal?
Ari.   Yea.
Nem.   Whom wouldst thou
  Uncharnel?
Man.   One without a tomb—call up
  Astarte.

NEMESIS

Shadow! or Spirit!
Whatever thou art,
Which still doth inherit
The whole or a part
Of the form of thy birth,
Of the mould of thy clay,
Which return'd to the earth,
Re-appear to the day!
Bear what thou borest,

The heart and the form,
And the aspect thou worest
Redeem from the worm.
Appear!—Appear!—Appear!
Who sent thee there requires thee here!

[*The Phantom of* ASTARTE *rises and stands in the midst*

Man. Can this be death? there's bloom upon her cheek;
But now I see it is no living hue,
But a strange hectic—like the unnatural red
Which Autumn plants upon the perish'd leaf.
It is the same! Oh, God! that I should dread
To look upon the same—Astarte!—No,
I cannot speak to her—but bid her speak—
Forgive me or condemn me.

NEMESIS

By the power which hath broken
The grave which enthrall'd thee,
Speak to him who hath spoken,
Or those who have call'd thee!

Man.   She is silent,
And in that silence I am more than answered.
Nem. My power extends no further. Prince of air!
It rests with thee alone—command her voice.
Ari. Spirit—obey this sceptre!
Nem.   Silent still!
She is not of our order, but belongs
To the other powers. Mortal! thy quest is vain,
And we are baffled also.
Man.   Hear me, hear me—
Astarte! my beloved! speak to me:
I have so much endured—so much endure—
Look on me! the grave hath not changed thee more
Than I am changed for thee. Thou lovedst me
Too much, as I loved thee: we were not made
To torture thus each other, though it were
The deadliest sin to love as we have loved.
Say that thou loath'st me not—that I do bear
This punishment for both—that thou wilt be
One of the blessed—and that I shall die;
For hitherto all hateful things conspire
To bind me in existence—in a life
Which makes me shrink from immortality—
A future like the past. I cannot rest.
I know not what I ask, nor what I seek:

I feel but what thou art—and what I am;
And I would hear yet once before I perish
The voice which was my music—Speak to me!
For I have call'd on thee in the still night,
Startled the slumbering birds from the hush'd boughs,
And woke the mountain wolves, and made the caves
Acquainted with thy vainly echoed name,
Which answer'd me—many things answer'd me—
Spirits and men—but thou wert silent all.
Yet speak to me! I have outwatch'd the stars,
And gazed o'er heaven in vain in search of thee.
Speak to me! I have wander'd o'er the earth,
And never found thy likeness—Speak to me!
Look on the fiends around—they feel for me:
I fear them not, and feel for thee alone—
Speak to me! though it be in wrath;—but say—
I reck not what—but let me hear thee once—
This once—once more!

Phantom of Astarte. Manfred!
Man.   Say on, say on—
  I live but in the sound—it is thy voice!
Phan. Manfred!   To-morrow ends thine earthly ills.
  Farewell!
Man.   Yet one word more—am I forgiven?
Phan. Farewell!
Man.   Say, shall we meet again?
Phan. Farewell!
Man. One word for mercy!   Say thou lovest me.
Phan. Manfred!

                    [*The Spirit of* ASTARTE *disappears.*
Nem.   She's gone, and will not be recall'd;
  Her words will be fulfill'd.   Return to the earth.
A Spirit. He is convulsed—This is to be a mortal
  And seek the things beyond mortality.
Another Spirit. Yet, see, he mastereth himself, and makes
  His torture tributary to his will.
  Had he been one of us, he would have made
  An awful spirit.
Nem.   Hast thou further question
  Of our great sovereign, or his worshippers?
Man. None.
Nem.   Then for a time farewell.
Man. We meet then!   Where?   On the earth?—
  Even as thou wilt: and for the grace accorded
  I now depart a debtor.   Fare ye well!   [*Exit* MANFRED.
                    (*Scene closes.*)

ACT III

SCENE I

A Hall in the Castle of Manfred

MANFRED *and* HERMAN.

Man. What is the hour?
Her.   It wants but one till sunset,
  And promises a lovely twilight.
Man.   Say,
  Are all things so disposed of in the tower
  As I directed?
Her.   All, my lord, are ready:
  Here is the key and casket.
Man.   It is well:
  Thou may'st retire.

                                            [*Exit* HERMAN.

Man. [*Alone.*]   There is a calm upon me—
  Inexplicable stillness! which till now
  Did not belong to what I knew of life.
  If that I did not know philosophy
  To be of all our vanities the motliest,
  The merest word that ever fool'd the ear
  From out the schoolman's jargon, I should deem
  The golden secret, the sought 'Kalon,' found,
  And seated in my soul.   It will not last,
  But it is well to have known it, though but once:
  It hath enlarged my thoughts with a new sense,
  And I within my tablets would note down
  That there is such a feeling.   Who is there?

Re-enter HERMAN.

Her. My lord, the abbot of St. Maurice craves
  To greet your presence.

Enter the ABBOT OF ST. MAURICE.

Abbot.   Peace be with Count Manfred!
Man. Thanks, holy father! welcome to these walls;
  Thy presence honours them, and blesseth those
  Who dwell within them.
Abbot.   Would it were so, Count!—
  But I would fain confer with thee alone.
Man. Herman, retire.—What would my reverend quest?
Abbot. Thus, without prelude:—Age and zeal, my office,
  And good intent, must plead my privilege;
  Our near, though not acquainted neighbourhood,

May also be my herald.   Rumours ſtrange,
And of unholy nature, are abroad,
And busy with thy name; a noble name
For centuries: may he who bears it now
Transmit it unimpair'd!

Man.   Proceed,—I liſten.

Abbot. 'Tis said thou holdeſt converse with the things
Which are forbidden to the search of man;
That with the dwellers of the dark abodes,
The many evil and unheavenly spirits
Which walk the valley of the shade of death,
Thou communeſt.   I know that with mankind,
Thy fellows in creation, thou doſt rarely
Exchange thy thoughts, and that thy solitude
Is as an anchorite's, were it but holy.

Man. And what are they who do avouch these things?

Abbot. My pious brethren—the scared peasantry—
Even thy own vassals—who do look on thee
With moſt unquiet eyes.   Thy life's in peril.

Man. Take it.

Abbot.   I come to save, and not deſtroy—
I would not pry into thy secret soul;
But if these things be sooth, there ſtill is time
For penitence and pity: reconcile thee
With the true church, and through the church to heaven.

Man. I hear thee.   This is my reply: whate'er
I may have been, or am, doth reſt between
Heaven and myself.—I shall not choose a mortal
To be my mediator.   Have I sinn'd
Againſt your ordinances? prove and punish![1]

Abbot. My son! I did not speak of punishment,
But penitence and pardon;—with thyself
The choice of such remains—and for the laſt,
Our inſtitutions and our ſtrong belief

---

[1] [Thus far the text ſtands as originally penned: we subjoin the sequel of the scene as given in the firſt MS.:

   '*Abbot.* Then, hear and tremble!   For the headſtrong wretch
       Who in the mail of innate hardihood
       Would shield himself, and battle for his sins,
       There is the ſtake on earth, and beyond earth eternal——
   Man. Charity, moſt reverend father,
       Becomes thy lips so much more than this menace,
       That I would call thee back to it: but say,
       What wouldſt thou with me?
   Abbot.   It may be there are
       Things that would shake thee—but I keep them back,
       And give thee till to-morrow to repent,
       Then if thou doſt not all devote thyself

      To penance, and with gift of all thy lands
      To the monastery——

Man.   I understand thee,—well!

Abbot. Expect no mercy; I have warned thee.

Man. [*Opening the casket.*]   Stop—
There is a gift for thee within this casket.

      [MANFRED *opens the casket, strikes a light, and burns some incense.*
Ho! Ashtaroth!

  The DEMON ASHTAROTH *appears, singing as follows :*
The raven sits
  On the raven-stone,[1]
And his black wing flits
  O'er the milk-white bone;
To and fro, as the night-winds blow,
The carcass of the assassin swings;
And there alone, on the raven-stone,
The raven flaps his dusky wings.

The fetters creak—and his ebon beak
  Croaks to the close of the hollow sound;
And this is the tune, by the light of the moon,
  To which the witches dance their round—
Merrily, merrily, cheerily, cheerily,
Merrily, speeds the ball:
The dead in their shrouds, and the demons in clouds,
Flock to the witches' carnival.

Abbot. I fear thee not—hence—hence—
  Avaunt thee, evil one !—help, ho ! without there !

Man. Convey this man to the Shreckhorn—to its peak—
To its extremest peak—watch with him there
From now till sunrise; let him gaze, and know
He ne'er again will be so near to heaven.
But harm him not; and, when the morrow breaks,
Set him down safe in his cell—away with him !

Ash. Had I not better bring his brethren too,
Convent and all, to bear him company?

Man. No, this will serve for the present. Take him up.

Ash. Come, friar ! now an exorcism or two,
And we shall fly the lighter.

   [ASHTAROTH *disappears with the* ABBOT, *singing as follows :*
A prodigal son, and a maid undone,
  And a widow re-wedded within the year;
And a worldly monk, and a pregnant nun,
  Are things which every day appear.

          MANFRED *alone.*

Man. Why would this fool break in on me, and force
My art to pranks fantastical?—no matter,
It was not of my seeking. My heart sickens,
And weighs a fix'd foreboding on my soul:
But it is calm—calm as a sullen sea
After the hurricane; the winds are still,
But the cold waves swell high and heavily,
And there is danger in them. Such a rest
Is no repose. My life hath been a combat,
And every thought a wound, till I am scarr'd
In the immortal part of me.—What now?']

---

[1] Raven-stone (Rabenstein), a translation of the German word for the gibbet, which in Germany and Switzerland is permanent, and made of stone.

Hath given me power to smooth the path from sin
To higher hope and better thoughts; the first
I leave to heaven,—'Vengeance is mine alone!'
So saith the Lord, and with all humbleness
His servant echoes back the awful word.

Man. Old man! there is no power in holy men,
Nor charm in prayer—nor purifying form
Of penitence—nor outward look—nor fast—
Nor agony—nor, greater than all these,
The innate tortures of that deep despair,
Which is remorse without the fear of hell,
But all in all sufficient to itself
Would make a hell of heaven—can exorcise
From out the unbounded spirit the quick sense
Of its own sins, wrongs, sufferance, and revenge.
Upon itself; there is no future pang
Can deal that justice on the self-condemn'd
He deals on his own soul.

Abbot.   All this is well;
For this will pass away, and be succeeded
By an auspicious hope, which shall look up
With calm assurance to that blessed place,
Which all who seek may win, whatever be
Their earthly terrors, so they be atoned:
And the commencement of atonement is
The sense of its necessity.—Say on—
And all our church can teach thee shall be taught;
And all we can absolve thee shall be pardon'd.

Man. When Rome's sixth emperor was near his last,
The victim of a self-inflicted wound,
To shun the torments of a public death
From senates once his slaves, a certain soldier,
With show of loyal pity, would have stanch'd
The gushing throat with his officious robe;
The dying Roman thrust him back, and said—
Some empire still in his expiring glance,
'It is too late—is this fidelity?'

Abbot. And what of this?

Man.   I answer with the Roman—
'It is too late!'

Abbot.   It never can be so,
To reconcile thyself with thy own soul,
And thy own soul with heaven.   Hast thou no hope?
'Tis strange—even those who do despair above,
Yet shape themselves some fantasy on earth,
To which frail twig they cling, like drowning men.

Man. Ay—father! I have had those earthly visions
    And noble aspirations in my youth,
    To make my own the mind of other men,
    The enlightener of nations; and to rise
    I knew not whither—it might be to fall;
    But fall, even as the mountain cataract,
    Which having leapt from its more dazzling height,
    Even in the foaming strength of its abyss,
    (Which casts up misty columns that become
    Clouds raining from the re-ascended skies,)
    Lies low but mighty still.—But this is past,
    My thoughts mistook themselves.
Abbot.   And wherefore so?
Man. I could not tame my nature down; for he
    Must serve who fain would sway—and soothe—and sue—
    And watch all time—and pry into all place—
    And be a living lie—who would become
    A mighty thing amongst the mean, and such
    The mass are; I disdain'd to mingle with
    A herd, though to be leader—and of wolves.
    The lion is alone, and so am I.
Abbot. And why not live and act with other men?
Man. Because my nature was averse from life;
    And yet not cruel; for I would not make,
    But find a desolation:—like the wind,
    The red-hot breath of the most lone Simoom,
    Which dwells but in the desert, and sweeps o'er
    The barren sands which bear no shrubs to blast,
    And revels o'er their wild and arid waves,
    And seeketh not, so that it is not sought,
    But being met is deadly; such hath been
    The course of my existence; but there came
    Things in my path which are no more.
Abbot.   Alas!
    I 'gin to fear that thou art past all aid
    From me and from my calling; yet so young,
    I still would——
Man.   Look on me! there is an order
    Of mortals on the earth, who do become
    Old in their youth, and die ere middle age,
    Without the violence of warlike death;
    Some perishing of pleasure—some of study—
    Some worn with toil—some of mere weariness,—
    Some of disease—and some insanity—
    And some of wither'd, or of broken hearts;
    For this last is a malady which slays

More than are numbered in the lists of Fate,
Taking all shapes, and bearing many names.
Look upon me! for even of all these things
Have I partaken; and of all these things,
One were enough; then wonder not that I
Am what I am, but that I ever was,
Or having been, that I am still on earth.
Abbot. Yet, hear me still——
Man.   Old man! I do respect
Thine order, and revere thy years; I deem
Thy purpose pious, but it is in vain:
Think me not churlish; I would spare thyself,
Far more than me, in shunning at this time
All further colloquy—and so—farewell.   [*Exit* MANFRED.
Abbot. This should have been a noble creature: he
Hath all the energy which would have made
A goodly frame of glorious elements,
Had they been wisely mingled; as it is,
It is an awful chaos—light and darkness—
And mind and dust—and passions and pure thoughts
Mix'd, and contending without end or order,
All dormant or destructive: he will perish,
And yet he must not; I will try once more,
For such are worth redemption; and my duty
Is to dare all things for a righteous end.
I 'll follow him—but cautiously, though surely. [*Exit* ABBOT.

SCENE II

Another Chamber

MANFRED *and* HERMAN.

Her. My lord, you bade me wait on you at sunset:
He sinks behind the mountain.
Man.   Doth he so?
I will look on him.
                    MANFRED *advances to the Window of the Hall.*
                    Glorious Orb! the idol
Of early nature, and the vigorous race
Of undiseased mankind, the giant sons
Of the embrace of angels, with a sex
More beautiful than they, which did draw down
The erring spirits who can ne'er return.—
Most glorious orb! that wert a worship, ere

The mystery of thy making was reveal'd!
Thou earliest minister of the Almighty,
Which gladden'd, on their mountain tops, the hearts
Of the Chaldean shepherds, till they pour'd
Themselves in orisons!   Thou material God!
And representative of the Unknown—
Who chose thee for his shadow!   Thou chief star!
Centre of many stars! which mak'st our earth
Endurable, and temperest the hues
And hearts of all who walk within thy rays!
Sire of the seasons!   Monarch of the climes,
And those who dwell in them! for near or far,
Our inborn spirits have a tint of thee
Even as our outward aspects;—thou dost rise,
And shine, and set in glory.   Fare thee well!
I ne'er shall see thee more.   As my first glance
Of love and wonder was for thee, then take
My latest look: thou wilt not beam on one
To whom the gifts of life and warmth have been
Of a more fatal nature.   He is gone:
I follow.   [*Exit* MANFRED.

SCENE III

*The Mountains—The Castle of Manfred at some distance—A Terrace
before a Tower.—Time, Twilight*

HERMAN, MANUEL, *and other Dependants of* MANFRED.

Her. 'Tis strange enough; night after night, for years,
   He hath pursued long vigils in this tower,
   Without a witness.   I have been within it,—
   So have we all been oft-times; but from it,
   Or its contents, it were impossible
   To draw conclusions absolute, of aught
   His studies tend to.   To be sure, there is
   One chamber where none enter: I would give
   The fee of what I have to come these three years,
   To pore upon its mysteries.
Manuel.   'Twere dangerous;
   Content thyself with what thou know'st already.
Her. Ah! Manuel! thou art elderly and wise,
   And couldst say much; thou hast dwelt within the castle—
   How many years is 't?
Manuel.   Ere Count Manfred's birth,
   I served his father, whom he nought resembles.
Her. There be more sons in like predicament.
   But wherein do they differ?

Manuel.   I speak not
   Of features or of form, but mind and habits;
   Count Sigismund was proud,—but gay and free,—
   A warrior and a reveller; he dwelt not
   With books and solitude, nor made the night
   A gloomy vigil, but a festal time,
   Merrier than day; he did not walk the rocks
   And forests like a wolf, nor turn aside
   From men and their delights.
Her.   Beshrew the hour,
   But those were jocund times! I would that such
   Would visit the old walls again; they look
   As if they had forgotten them.
Manuel.   These walls
   Must change their chieftain first. Oh! I have seen
   Some strange things in them, Herman.
Her.   Come, be friendly;
   Relate me some to while away our watch:
   I've heard thee darkly speak of an event
   Which happen'd hereabouts, by this same tower.
Manuel. That was a night indeed! I do remember
   'Twas twilight, as it may be now, and such
   Another evening;—yon red cloud, which rests
   On Eigher's pinnacle, so rested then,—
   So like that it might be the same; the wind
   Was faint and gusty, and the mountain snows
   Began to glitter with the climbing moon;
   Count Manfred was, as now, within his tower,—
   How occupied, we knew not, but with him
   The sole companion of his wanderings
   And watchings—her, whom of all earthly things
   That lived, the only thing he seem'd to love,—
   As he, indeed, by blood was bound to do,
   The lady Astarte, his——
                         Hush! who comes here?

Enter the ABBOT.

Abbot. Where is your master?
Her.   Yonder in the tower.
Abbot. I must speak with him.
Manuel.   'Tis impossible;
   He is most private, and must not be thus
   Intruded on.
Abbot.   Upon myself I take
   The forfeit of my fault, if fault there be—
   But I must see him.

Her.   Thou hast seen him once
  This eve already.
Abbot.   Herman! I command thee,
  Knock, and apprise the Count of my approach.
Her. We dare not.
Abbot.   Then it seems I must be herald
  Of my own purpose.
Manuel.   Reverend father, stop—
  I pray you pause.
Abbot.   Why so?
Manuel.   But step this way,
  And I will tell you further.   [*Exeunt.*

SCENE IV

Interior of the Tower

MANFRED *alone.*

The stars are forth, the moon above the tops
Of the snow-shining mountains.—Beautiful!
I linger yet with Nature, for the night
Hath been to me a more familiar face
Than that of man; and in her starry shade
Of dim and solitary loveliness,
I learn'd the language of another world.
I do remember me, that in my youth,
When I was wandering,—upon such a night
I stood within the Coliseum's wall,
Midst the chief relics of almighty Rome;
The trees which grew along the broken arches
Waved dark in the blue midnight, and the stars
Shone through the rents of ruin; from afar
The watchdog bay'd beyond the Tiber; and
More near from out the Caesars' palace came
The owl's long cry, and, interruptedly,
Of distant sentinels the fitful song
Begun and died upon the gentle wind.
Some cypresses beyond the time-worn breach
Appear'd to skirt the horizon, yet they stood
Within a bowshot—Where the Caesars dwelt,
And dwell the tuneless birds of night, amidst
A grove which springs through levell'd battlements,
And twines its roots with the imperial hearths,
Ivy usurps the laurel's place of growth;—
But the gladiators' bloody Circus stands,
A noble wreck in ruinous perfection!

While Caesar's chambers, and the Augustan halls,
Grovel on earth in indistinct decay.—
And thou didst shine, thou rolling moon, upon
All this, and cast a wide and tender light,
Which soften'd down the hoar austerity
Of rugged desolation, and fill'd up,
As 'twere anew, the gaps of centuries;
Leaving that beautiful which still was so,
And making that which was not, till the place
Became religion, and the heart ran o'er
With silent worship of the great of old!—
The dead, but sceptred sovereigns, who still rule
Our spirits from their urns.—

                   'Twas such a night!
'Tis strange that I recall it at this time;
But I have found our thoughts take wildest flight
Even at the moment when they should array
Themselves in pensive order.

Enter the ABBOT.

Abbot.   My good lord!
I crave a second grace for this approach;
But yet let not my humble zeal offend
By its abruptness—all it hath of ill
Recoils on me; its good in the effect
May light upon your head—could I say *heart*—
Could I touch *that*, with words or prayers, I should
Recall a noble spirit which hath wander'd;
But is not yet all lost.
Man.   Thou know'st me not;
My days are number'd, and my deeds recorded:
Retire, or 'twill be dangerous—Away!
Abbot. Thou dost not mean to menace me?
Man.   Not I;
I simply tell thee peril is at hand,
And would preserve thee.
Abbot.   What dost thou mean?
Man.   Look there!
What dost thou see?
Abbot.   Nothing.
Man.   Look there, I say,
And steadfastly;—now tell me what thou seest?
Abbot. That which should shake me,—but I fear it not—
I see a dusk and awful figure rise,
Like an infernal dog, from out the earth;

His face wrapt in a mantle, and his form
Robed as with angry clouds: he stands between
Thyself and me—but I do fear him not.

Man. Thou hast no cause—he shall not harm thee—but
His sight may shock thine old limbs into palsy.
I say to thee—Retire!

Abbot.   And I reply—
Never—till I have battled with this fiend:—
What doth he here?

Man.   Why—ay—what doth he here?—
I did not send for him,—he is unbidden.

Abbot. Alas! lost mortal! what with guests like these
Hast thou to do? I tremble for thy sake:
Why doth he gaze on thee, and thou on him?
Ah! he unveils his aspect: on his brow
The thunder-scars are graven; from his eye
Glares forth the immortality of hell—
Avaunt!——

Man.   Pronounce—what is thy mission?

Spirit.   Come!

Abbot. What art thou, unknown being? answer!—speak!

Spirit. The genius of this mortal.—Come! 'tis time.

Man. I am prepared for all things, but deny
The power which summons me. Who sent thee here?

Spirit. Thou 'lt know anon—Come! come!

Man.   I have commanded
Things of an essence greater far than thine,
And striven with thy masters. Get thee hence!

Spirit. Mortal! thine hour is come—Away! I say.

Man. I knew, and know my hour is come, but not
To render up my soul to such as thee:
Away! I 'll die as I have lived—alone.

Spirit. Then I must summon up my brethren.—Rise!

[*Other Spirits rise up.*

Abbot. Avaunt! ye evil ones!—Avaunt! I say,—
Ye have no power where piety hath power,
And I do charge thee in the name——

Spirit.   Old man!
We know ourselves, our mission, and thine order;
Waste not thy holy words on idle uses,
It were in vain: this man is forfeited.
Once more I summon him—Away! away!

Man. I do defy ye,—though I feel my soul
Is ebbing from me, yet I do defy ye;
Nor will I hence, while I have earthly breath
To breathe my scorn upon ye—earthly strength

To wrestle, though with spirits; what ye take
Shall be ta'en limb by limb.
Spirit.   Reluctant mortal!
    Is this the Magian who would so pervade
    The world invisible, and make himself
    Almost our equal?—Can it be that thou
    Art thus in love with life? the very life
    Which made thee wretched!
Man.   Thou false fiend, thou liest!
    My life is in its last hour,—*that* I know,
    Nor would redeem a moment of that hour;
    I do not combat against death, but thee
    And thy surrounding angels; my past power
    Was purchased by no compact with thy crew,
    But by superior science, penance, daring
    And length of watching, strength of mind, and skill
    In knowledge of our fathers—when the earth
    Saw men and spirits walking side by side,
    And gave ye no supremacy: I stand
    Upon my strength—I do defy—deny—
    Spurn back, and scorn ye!—
Spirit.   But thy many crimes
    Have made thee——
Man.   What are they to such as thee?
    Must crimes be punish'd but by other crimes,
    And greater criminals?—Back to thy hell!
    Thou hast no power upon me, *that* I feel;
    Thou never shalt possess me, *that* I know:
    What I have done is done; I bear within
    A torture which could nothing gain from thine:
    The mind which is immortal makes itself
    Requital for its good or evil thoughts—
    Is its own origin of ill and end—
    And its own place and time—its innate sense,
    When stripp'd of this mortality, derives
    No colour from the fleeting things without;
    But is absorbed in sufferance or in joy,
    Born from the knowledge of its own desert.
    Thou didst not tempt me, and thou couldst not tempt me;
    I have not been thy dupe, nor am thy prey—
    But was my own destroyer, and will be
    My own hereafter.—Back, ye baffled fiends!
    The hand of death is on me—but not yours!
                                    [*The Demons disappear.*
Abbot. Alas! how pale thou art—thy lips are white—
    And thy breast heaves—and in thy gasping throat

The accents rattle—Give thy prayers to Heaven—
Pray—albeit but in thought,—but die not thus.

Man. 'Tis over—my dull eyes can fix thee not;
But all things swim around me, and the earth
Heaves as it were beneath me.   Fare thee well—
Give me thy hand.

Abbot.   Cold—cold—even to the heart—
But yet one prayer—Alas! how fares it with thee?

Man. Old man! 'tis not so difficult to die.

[MANFRED *expires.*

Abbot. He's gone—his soul hath ta'en its earthless flight—
Whither?   I dread to think—but he is gone.

MARINO FALIERO

DOGE OF VENICE

AN HISTORICAL TRAGEDY IN FIVE ACTS [1]

Dux inquieti turbidus Adriae.

HORACE.

[1] [On the original MS. sent from Ravenna, Lord Byron has written: 'Begun April 4th, 1820 — completed July 16th, 1820 — finished copying August 16th–17th, 1820; the which copying makes ten times the toil of composing, considering the weather—thermometer 90 in the shade—and my domestic duties.']

LORD BYRON finished this tragedy on 16th July 1820. He at the time intended to keep it by him for six years before sending it to the press; but resolutions of this kind are, in modern days, very seldom adhered to. It was published in the end of the same year; and, to the poet's great disgust, and in spite of his urgent and repeated remonstrances, was produced on the stage of Drury Lane Theatre early in 1821.

PREFACE

THE conspiracy of the Doge Marino Faliero is one of the most remarkable events in the annals of the most singular government, city, and people of modern history. It occurred in the year 1355. Everything about Venice is, or was, extraordinary—her aspect is like a dream, and her history is like a romance. The story of this Doge is to be found in all her Chronicles, and particularly detailed in the *Lives of the Doges*, by Marin Sanuto. It is simply and clearly related, and is perhaps more dramatic in itself than any scenes which can be founded upon the subject.

Marino Faliero appears to have been a man of talents and of courage. I find him commander-in-chief of the land forces at the siege of Zara, where he beat the king of Hungary and his army of eighty thousand men, killing eight thousand men, and keeping the besieged at the same time in check; an exploit to which I know none similar in history, except that of Caesar at Alesia, and of Prince Eugene at Belgrade. He was afterwards commander of the fleet in the same war. He took Capo d'Istria. He was ambassador at Genoa and Rome,—at which last he received the news of his election to the dukedom; his absence being a proof that he sought it by no intrigue, since he was apprised of his predecessor's death and his own succession at the same moment. But he appears to have been of an ungovernable temper. A story is told by Sanuto, of his having, many years before, when podestà and captain at Treviso, boxed the ears of the bishop, who was somewhat tardy in bringing the host. For this, honest Sanuto 'saddles him with judgment,' as Thwackum did Square; but he does not tell us whether he was punished or rebuked by the Senate for this outrage at the time of its commission. He seems, indeed, to have been afterwards at peace with the church, for we find him ambassador at Rome, and invested with the fief of Val di Marino, in the march of Treviso, and with the title of Count, by Lorenzo Count-bishop of Ceneda. For these facts my authorities are Sanuto, Vettor Sandi, Andrea Navagero, and the account of the siege of Zara, first published by the indefatigable Abate Morelli, in his *Monumenti Veneziani di varia Letteratura*, printed in 1796, all of which I have looked over in the original language. The moderns, Darù, Sismondi, and Laugier, nearly agree with the ancient chroniclers. Sismondi attributes the conspiracy to his *jealousy*; but I find this nowhere asserted by the national

historians.   Vettor Sandi, indeed, says that 'altri scrissero che
. . . dalla gelosa suspizion di esso Doge siasi fatto (Michel
Steno) staccar con violenza,' etc. etc.; but this appears to have
been by no means the general opinion, nor is it alluded to by
Sanuto or by Navagero; and Sandi himself adds, a moment
after, that 'per altre Veneziane memorie traspiri, che non il
solo desiderio di vendetta lo dispose alla congiura ma anche la
innata abituale ambizion sua, per cui arrivava a farsi principe
independente.'   The first motive appears to have been excited
by the gross affront of the words written by Michel Steno on
the ducal chair, and by the light and inadequate sentence of the
Forty on the offender, who was one of their 'tre Capi.'   The
attentions of Steno himself appear to have been directed towards
one of her damsels, and not to the 'Dogaressa' herself, against
whose fame not the slightest insinuation appears, while she is
praised for her beauty, and remarked for her youth.   Neither
do I find it asserted (unless the hint of Sandi be an assertion),
that the Doge was actuated by jealousy of his wife; but rather
by respect for her, and for his own honour, warranted by his
past services and present dignity.

I know not that the historical facts are alluded to in English,
unless by Dr. Moore in his *View of Italy.*   His account is false
and flippant, full of stale jests about old men and young
wives, and wondering at so great an effect from so slight a cause.
How so acute and severe an observer of mankind as the author
of *Zuluco* could wonder at this is inconceivable.   He knew that
a basin of water spilt on Mrs. Masham's gown deprived the
Duke of Marlborough of his command, and led to the inglorious
peace of Utrecht—that Louis XIV was plunged into the most
desolating wars, because his minister was nettled at his finding
fault with a window, and wished to give him another occupa-
tion—that Helen lost Troy—that Lucretia expelled the Tarquins
from Rome—and that Cava brought the Moors to Spain—that
an insulted husband led the Gauls to Clusium, and thence to
Rome—that a single verse of Frederick II of Prussia on the
Abbé de Bernis, and a jest on Madame de Pompadour, led to the
battle of Rosbach—that the elopement of Dearbhorgil with
Mac Murchad conducted the English to the slavery of Ireland—
that a personal pique between Maria Antoinette and the Duke
of Orleans precipitated the first expulsion of the Bourbons—
and, not to multiply instances, that Commodus, Domitian, and
Caligula fell victims not to their public tyranny, but to private
vengeance—and that an order to make Cromwell disembark
from the ship in which he would have sailed to America destroyed both king and commonwealth. After these instances, on
the least reflection, it is indeed extraordinary in Dr. Moore to

seem surprised that a man used to command, who had served
and swayed in the most important offices, should fiercely resent,
in a fierce age, an unpunished affront, the grossest that can be
offered to a man, be he prince or peasant.   The age of Faliero
is little to the purpose, unless to favour it—

> The young man's wrath is like straw on fire,
> *But like red-hot steel is the old man's ire.*

> Young men soon give and soon forget affronts,
> Old age is slow at both.

Laugier's reflections are more philosophical: 'Tale fù il
fine ignominioso di un' uomo, che la sua nascità, la sua
età, il suo carattere dovevano tener lontano dalle passioni
produttrici di grandi delitti.   I suoi *talenti* per lungo tempo
esercitati ne' maggiori impieghi, la sua capacità sperimentata
ne' governi e nelle ambasciate, gli avevano acquistato la stima
e la fiducia de' cittadini, ed avevano uniti i suffragj per collo-
carlo alla testa della republica.   Innalzato ad un grado che
terminava gloriosamente la sua vita, il risentimento di un'
ingiuria leggiera insinuò nel suo cuore tal veleno che bastò a
corrompere le antiche sue qualità, e a condurlo al termine dei
scellerati; serio esempio, che prova *non esservi età, in cui la
prudenza umana sia sicura, e che nell' uomo restano sempre passioni
capaci a disonorarlo, quando non invigili sopra se stesso.*' [1]
Where did Dr. Moore find that Marino Faliero begged his
life?   I have searched the chroniclers, and find nothing of the
kind; it is true that he avowed all.   He was conducted to the
place of torture, but there is no mention made of any application
for mercy on his part; and the very circumstance of their
having taken him to the rack seems to argue anything but his
having shown a want of firmness, which would doubtless have
been also mentioned by those minute historians, who by no
means favour him; such, indeed, would be contrary to his
character as a soldier, to the age in which he lived, and *at* which
he died, as it is to the truth of history.   I know no justification,
at any distance of time, for calumniating an historical character:
surely truth belongs to the dead, and to the unfortunate; and
they who have died upon a scaffold have generally had faults
enough of their own, without attributing to them that which
the very incurring of the perils which conducted them to their
violent death renders, of all others, the most improbable.   The
black veil which is painted over the place of Marino Faliero
amongst the Doges, and the Giants' Staircase where he was

[1] Laugier, *Histoire de la République de Venise*, Italian translation, vol. iv, p. 30.

crowned, and discrowned, and decapitated, struck forcibly upon
my imagination; as did his fiery character and strange story.
I went, in 1819, in search of his tomb more than once to the
church San Giovanni e San Paolo; and, as I was standing
before the monument of another family, a priest came up to me
and said: 'I can show you finer monuments than that.' I told
him that I was in search of that of the Faliero family, and
particularly of the Doge Marino's. 'Oh,' said he, 'I will show
it you'; and conducting me to the outside, pointed out a
sarcophagus in the wall with an illegible inscription. He said
that it had been in a convent adjoining, but was removed after
the French came, and placed in its present situation; that he
had seen the tomb opened at its removal; there were still some
bones remaining, but no positive vestige of the decapitation.
The equestrian statue of which I have made mention in the third
act as before that church is not, however, of a Faliero, but of
some other now obsolete warrior, although of a later date.
There were two other Doges of this family prior to Marino;
Ordelafo, who fell in battle at Zara in 1117 (where his descendant afterwards conquered the Huns), and Vital Faliero, who
reigned in 1082. The family, originally from Fano, was of the
most illustrious in blood and wealth in the city of once most the
wealthy and still the most ancient families in Europe. The
length I have gone into on this subject will show the interest I
have taken in it. Whether I have succeeded or not in the
tragedy, I have at least transferred into our language an
historical fact worthy of commemoration.

It is now four years that I have meditated this work; and
before I had sufficiently examined the records, I was rather
disposed to have made it turn on a jealousy in Faliero. But,
perceiving no foundation for this in historical truth, and aware
that jealousy is an exhausted passion in the drama, I have
given it a more historical form. I was, besides, well advised
by the late Matthew Lewis on that point, in talking with him
of my intention at Venice in 1817. 'If you make him jealous,'
said he, 'recollect that you have to contend with established
writers, to say nothing of Shakespeare, and an exhausted
subject; stick to the old fiery Doge's natural character, which
will bear you out, if properly drawn; and make your plot as
regular as you can.' Sir William Drummond gave me nearly
the same counsel. How far I have followed these instructions,
or whether they have availed me, is not for me to decide. I
have had no view to the stage; in its present state it is, perhaps,
not a very exalted object of ambition; besides, I have been too
much behind the scenes to have thought it so at any time. And
I cannot conceive of any man of irritable feeling putting himsel

at the mercies of an audience. The sneering reader, and the loud critic, and the tart review, are scattered and distant calamities; but the trampling of an intelligent or of an ignorant audience on a production which, be it good or bad, has been a mental labour to the writer, is a palpable and immediate grievance, heightened by a man's doubt of their competency to judge, and his certainty of his own imprudence in electing them his judges. Were I capable of writing a play which could be deemed stage-worthy, success would give me no pleasure, and failure great pain. It is for this reason that, even during the time of being one of the committee of one of the theatres, I never made the attempt, and never will. But surely there is dramatic power somewhere, where Joanna Baillie, and Milman, and John Wilson exist. The *City of the Plague* and the *Fall of Jerusalem* are full of the best *materiel* for tragedy that has been seen since Horace Walpole, except passages of *Ethwald* and *De Montfort*. It is the fashion to underrate Horace Walpole; firstly, because he was a nobleman, and secondly, because he was a gentleman; but, to say nothing of the composition of his incomparable letters, and of the *Castle of Otranto*, he is the *Ultimus Romanorum*, the author of the *Mysterious Mother*, a tragedy of the highest order, and not a puling love-play. He is the father of the first romance and of the last tragedy in our language, and surely worthy of a higher place than any living writer, be he who he may.

In speaking of the drama of *Marino Faliero*, I forgot to mention, that the desire of preserving, though still too remote, a nearer approach to unity than the irregularity, which is the reproach of the English theatrical compositions, permits, has induced me to represent the conspiracy as already formed, and the Doge acceding to it; whereas, in fact, it was of his own preparation and that of Israel Bertuccio. The other characters (except that of the Duchess), incidents, and almost the time, which was wonderfully short for such a design in real life, are strictly historical, except that all the consultations took place in the palace. Had I followed this, the unity would have been better preserved; but I wished to produce the Doge in the full assembly of the conspirators, instead of monotonously placing him always in dialogue with the same individuals.

DRAMATIS PERSONAE

MEN

MARINO FALIERO, *Doge of Venice.*
BERTUCCIO FALIERO, *Nephew of the Doge.*
LIONI, *a Patrician and Senator.*
BENINTENDE, *Chief of the Council of Ten.*
MICHEL STENO, *One of the three Capi of the Forty.*
ISRAEL BERTUCCIO, *Chief of the Arsenal*
PHILIP CALENDARO   } *Conspirators.*
DAGOLINO
BERTRAM
Signor of the Night { *'Signore di Notte,' one of the Officers belonging to the Republic.*
First Citizen.
Second Citizen.
Third Citizen.
VINCENZO
PIETRO   } *Officers belonging to the Ducal Palace.*
BATTISTA
Secretary of the Council of Ten.
Guards, Conspirators, Citizens, the Council of Ten, The Giunta, etc.

WOMEN

ANGIOLINA, *Wife to the Doge.*
MARIANNA, *her Friend.*
Female Attendants, etc.

Scene: VENICE—in the year 1355

MARINO FALIERO

ACT I

SCENE I

An Antechamber in the Ducal Palace

PIETRO *speaks, in entering, to* BATTISTA.

Pie. Is not the messenger return'd?
Bat.   Not yet;
  I have sent frequently, as you commanded,
  But still the Signory is deep in council,
  And long debate on Steno's accusation.
Pie. Too long—at least so thinks the Doge.
Bat.   How bears he
  These moments of suspense?
Pie.   With struggling patience.
  Placed at the ducal table, cover'd o'er
  With all the apparel of the state; petitions,
  Despatches, judgments, acts, reprieves, reports,
  He sits as rapt in duty; but whene'er
  He hears the jarring of a distant door,
  Or aught that intimates a coming step,
  Or murmur of a voice, his quick eye wanders,
  And he will start up from his chair, then pause,
  And seat himself again, and fix his gaze
  Upon some edict; but I have observed
  For the last hour he has not turn'd a leaf.
Bat. 'Tis said he is much moved,—and doubtless 'twas
  Foul scorn in Steno to offend so grossly.
Pie. Ay, if a poor man: Steno 's a patrician,
  Young, galliard, gay, and haughty.
Bat.   Then you think
  He will not be judged hardly?
Pie.   'Twere enough
  He be judged justly; but 'tis not for us
  To anticipate the sentence of the Forty.
Bat. And here it comes.—What news, Vincenzo?

Enter VINCENZO.

Vin.   'Tis
Decided; but as yet his doom 's unknown:
I saw the president in act to seal
The parchment which will bear the Forty's judgment
Unto the Doge, and hasten to inform him.   [*Exeunt.*

SCENE II

The Ducal Chamber

MARINO FALIERO, *Doge; and his Nephew,*

BERTUCCIO FALIERO.

Ber. F. It cannot be but they will do you justice.
Doge. Ay, such as the Avogadori did,
Who sent up my appeal unto the Forty
To try him by his peers, his own tribunal.
Ber. F. His peers will scarce protect him; such an act
Would bring contempt on all authority.
Doge. Know you not Venice? Know you not the Forty?
But we shall see anon.
Ber. F. [*Addressing* VINCENZO, *then entering.*]
                                        How now—what tidings?
Vin. I am charged to tell his highness that the court
Has pass'd its resolution, and that, soon
As the due forms of judgment are gone through,
The sentence will be sent up to the Doge;
In the mean time the Forty doth salute
The Prince of the Republic, and entreat
His acceptation of their duty.
Doge.   Yes—
They are wondrous dutiful, and ever humble.
Sentence is pass'd, you say?
Vin.   It is, your highness:
The president was sealing it, when I
Was call'd in, that no moment might be lost
In forwarding the intimation due
Not only to the Chief of the Republic,
But the complainant, both in one united.
Ber. F. Are you aware, from aught you have perceived,
Of their decision?
Vin.   No, my lord; you know
The secret custom of the courts in Venice.
Ber. F. True; but there still is something given to guess,
Which a shrewd gleaner and quick eye would catch at;
A whisper, or a murmur, or an air

More or less solemn spread o'er the tribunal.
The Forty are but men—most worthy men,
And wise, and just, and cautious—this I grant—
And secret as the grave to which they doom
The guilty; but with all this, in their aspects—
At least in some, the juniors of the number—
A searching eye, an eye like yours, Vincenzo,
Would read the sentence ere it was pronounced.

Vin. My lord, I came away upon the moment,
And had no leisure to take note of that
Which pass'd among the judges, even in seeming;
My station near the accused too, Michel Steno,
Made me—

Doge. [*Abruptly.*] And how look'd *he*? deliver that.

Vin. Calm, but not overcast, he stood resign'd
To the decree, whate'er it were;—but lo!
It comes, for the perusal of his highness.

Enter the SECRETARY *of the* Forty.

Sec. The high tribunal of the Forty sends
Health and respect to the Doge Faliero,
Chief magistrate of Venice, and requests
His highness to peruse and to approve
The sentence pass'd on Michel Steno, born
Patrician, and arraign'd upon the charge
Contain'd, together with its penalty,
Within the rescript which I now present.

Doge. Retire, and wait without.

[*Exeunt* SECRETARY *and* VINCENZO.
                                    Take thou this paper:
The misty letters vanish from my eyes;
I cannot fix them.

Ber. F.   Patience, my dear uncle:
Why do you tremble thus?—nay, doubt not, all
Will be as could be wish'd.

Doge.   Say on.

Ber. F. [*Reading.*]   'Decreed
In council, without one dissenting voice,
That Michel Steno, by his own confession,
Guilty on the last night of Carnival
Of having graven on the ducal throne
The following words——' [1]

Doge.   Wouldst thou repeat them?
Wouldst *thou* repeat them—*thou*, a Faliero,

[1] ['Marin Faliero, dalla bella moglie—altri la gode, ed egli la mantiene.'—
SANUTO.]

Harp on the deep dishonour of our house,
Dishonour'd in its chief—that chief the prince
Of Venice, first of cities?—To the sentence.

Ber. F. Forgive me, my good lord; I will obey—
[*Reads.*] 'That Michel Steno be detain'd a month
In close arrest.'

Doge.   Proceed.

Ber. F.   My lord, 'tis finished.

Doge. How, say you?—finish'd! Do I dream?—'tis false—
Give me the paper—   [*Snatches the paper and reads.*
               —''Tis decreed in council
That Michel Steno'——Nephew, thine arm!

Ber. F.   Nay,
Cheer up, be calm; this transport is uncall'd for—
Let me seek some assistance.

Doge.   Stop, sir—Stir not—
'Tis past.

Ber. F.   I cannot but agree with you
The sentence is too slight for the offence—
It is not honourable in the Forty
To affix so slight a penalty to that
Which was a foul affront to you, and even
To them, as being your subjects; but 'tis not
Yet without remedy: you can appeal
To them once more, or to the Avogadori,
Who, seeing that true justice is withheld,
Will now take up the cause they once declined,
And do you right upon the bold delinquent.
Think you not thus, good uncle? why do you stand
So fix'd? You heed me not:—I pray you, hear me!

Doge. [*Dashing down the ducal bonnet, and offering to trample upon
     it, exclaims, as he is withheld by his nephew.*]
Oh! that the Saracen were in Saint Mark's!
Thus would I do him homage.

Ber. F.   For the sake
Of Heaven and all its saints, my lord——

Doge.   Away!
Oh, that the Genoese were in the port!
Oh, that the Huns whom I o'erthrew at Zara
Were ranged around the palace!

Ber. F.   'Tis not well
In Venice' Duke to say so.

Doge.   Venice' Duke!
Who now is Duke of Venice? let me see him,
That he may do me right.

Ber. F.   If you forget
    Your office, and its dignity and duty,
    Remember that of man, and curb this passion.
    The Duke of Venice——
Doge. [*Interrupting him.*]   There is no such thing—
    It is a word—nay, worse—a worthless by-word:
    The most despised, wrong'd, outraged, helpless wretch.
    Who begs his bread, if 'tis refused by one,
    May win it from another kinder heart;
    But he, who is denied his right by those
    Whose place it is to do no wrong, is poorer
    Than the rejected beggar—he 's a slave—
    And that am I, and thou, and all our house,
    Even from this hour; the meanest artisan
    Will point the finger, and the haughty noble
    May spit upon us:—where is our redress?
Ber. F. The law, my prince?——
Doge. [*Interrupting him.*]   You see what it has done—
    I ask'd no remedy but from the law—
    I sought no vengeance but redress by law—
    I call'd no judges but those named by law—
    As sovereign, I appeal'd unto my subjects,
    The very subjects who had made me sovereign,
    And gave me thus a double right to be so.
    The rights of place and choice, of birth and service,
    Honours and years, these scars, these hoary hairs,
    The travel, toil, the perils, the fatigues,
    The blood and sweat of almost eighty years,
    Were weigh'd i' the balance, 'gainst the foulest stain.
    The grossest insult, most contemptuous crime
    Of a rank, rash patrician—and found wanting!
    And this is to be borne!
Ber. F.   I say not that:—
    In case your fresh appeal should be rejected,
    We will find other things to make all even.
Doge. Appeal again! art thou my brother's son?
    A scion of the house of Faliero?
    The nephew of a Doge? and of that blood
    Which hath already given three dukes to Venice?
    But thou say'st well—we must be humble now.
Ber. F. My princely uncle! you are too much moved:—
    I grant it was a gross offence, and grossly
    Left without fitting punishment: but still
    This fury doth exceed the provocation,
    Or any provocation: if we are wrong'd,
    We will ask justice; if it be denied,

We 'll take it; but may do all this in calmness—
Deep Vengeance is the daughter of deep Silence.
I have yet scarce a third part of your years,
I love our house, I honour you, its chief,
The guardian of my youth, and its instructor—
But though I understand your grief, and enter
In part of your disdain, it doth appal me
To see your anger, like our Adrian waves,
O'ersweep all bounds, and foam itself to air.

Doge. I tell thee—*must* I tell thee—what thy father
Would have required no words to comprehend?
Hast thou no feeling save the external sense
Of torture from the touch? hast thou no soul—
No pride—no passion—no deep sense of honour?

Ber. F. 'Tis the first time that honour has been doubted,
And were the last, from any other sceptic.

Doge. You know the full offence of this born villain,
This creeping coward, rank, acquitted felon,
Who threw his sting into a poisonous libel,
And on the honour of—Oh God!—my wife,
The nearest, dearest part of all men's honour,
Left a base slur to pass from mouth to mouth
Of loose mechanics, with all coarse foul comments,
And villainous jests, and blasphemies obscene;
While sneering nobles, in more polish'd guise,
Whisper'd the tale, and smiled upon the lie
Which made me look like them—a courteous wittol,
Patient—ay, proud, it may be, of dishonour.

Ber. F. But still it was a lie—you knew it false
And so did all men.

Doge.   Nephew, the high Roman
Said, 'Caesar's wife must not even be suspected,'
And put her from him.

Ber. F.   True—but in those days——

Doge. What is it that a Roman would not suffer,
That a Venetian prince must bear? Old Dandolo
Refused the diadem of all the Caesars,
And wore the ducal cap I trample on,
Because 'tis now degraded.

Ber. F.   'Tis even so.

Doge. It is—it is;—I did not visit on
The innocent creature thus most vilely slander'd
Because she took an old man for her lord,
For that he had been long her father's friend
And patron of her house, as if there were
No love in woman's heart but lust of youth

And beardless faces;—I did not for this
Visit the villain's infamy on her,
But craved my country's justice on his head.
The justice due unto the humblest being
Who hath a wife whose faith is sweet to him,
Who hath a home whose hearth is dear to him,
Who hath a name whose honour's all to him,
When these are tainted by the accursing breath
Of calumny and scorn.

Ber. F.   And what redress
Did you expect as his fit punishment?

Doge. Death! Was I not the sovereign of the State—
Insulted on his very throne, and made
A mockery to the men who should obey me?
Was I not injured as a husband? scorn'd
As man? reviled, degraded, as a prince?
Was not offence like his a complication
Of insult and of treason?—and he lives!
Had he instead of on the Doge's throne
Stamp'd the same brand upon a peasant's stool,
His blood had gilt the threshold; for the carle
Had stabb'd him on the instant.

Ber. F.   Do not doubt it,
He shall not live till sunset—leave to me
The means, and calm yourself.

Doge.   Hold, nephew: this
Would have sufficed but yesterday; at present
I have no further wrath against this man.

Ber. F. What mean you? is not the offence redoubled
By this most rank—I will not say—acquittal;
For it is worse, being full acknowledgment
Of the offence, and leaving it unpunish'd?

Doge. It is *redoubled*, but not now by him:
The Forty hath decreed a month's arrest—
We must obey the Forty.

Ber. F.   Obey *them*!
Who have forgot their duty to the sovereign?

Doge. Why, yes;—boy, you perceive it then at last:
Whether as fellow citizen who sues
For justice, or as sovereign who commands it,
They have defrauded me of both my rights
(For here the sovereign is a citizen);
But, notwithstanding, harm not thou a hair
Of Steno's head—he shall not wear it long.

Ber. F. Not twelve hours longer, had you left to me
The mode and means: if you had calmly heard me,

I never meant this miscreant should escape,
But wish'd you to suppress such gusts of passion,
That we more surely might devise together
His taking off.
Doge.   No, nephew, he must live;
At least, just now—a life so vile as his
Were nothing at this hour; in th' olden time
Some sacrifices ask'd a single victim,
Great expiations had a hecatomb.
Ber. F. Your wishes are my law: and yet I fain
Would prove to you how near unto my heart
The honour of our house must ever be.
Doge. Fear not; you shall have time and place of proof:
But be thou not too rash, as I have been.
I am ashamed of my own anger now;
I pray you, pardon me.
Ber. F.   Why that's my uncle!
The leader, and the statesman, and the chief
Of commonwealths, and sovereign of himself!
I wonder'd to perceive you so forget
All prudence in your fury at these years,
Although the cause——
Doge.   Ay, think upon the cause—
Forget it not:—When you lie down to rest,
Let it be black among your dreams; and when
The morn returns, so let it stand between
The sun and you, as an ill-omen'd cloud
Upon a summer-day of festival:
So will it stand to me;—but speak not, stir not,—
Leave all to me;—we shall have much to do,
And you shall have a part.—But now retire,
'Tis fit I were alone.
Ber. F. [*Taking up and placing the ducal bonnet on the table.*]
            Ere I depart,
I pray you to resume what you have spurn'd,
Till you can change it haply for a crown.
And now I take my leave, imploring you
In all things to rely upon my duty
As doth become your near and faithful kinsman,
And not less loyal citizen and subject.
            [*Exit* BERTUCCIO FALIERO.
Doge. [*Solus.*] Adieu, my worthy nephew.—Hollow bauble!
            [*Taking up the ducal cap.*
Beset with all the thorns that line a crown,
Without investing the insulted brow
With the all-swaying majesty of kings;

Thou idle, gilded, and degraded toy,
Let me resume thee as I would a vizor. [Puts it on.
How my brain aches beneath thee! and my temples
Throb feverish under thy dishonest weight.
Could I not turn thee to a diadem?
Could I not shatter the Briarean sceptre
Which in this hundred-handed senate rules,
Making the people nothing, and the prince
A pageant? In my life I have achieved
Tasks not less difficult—achieved for them,
Who thus repay me!—Can I not requite them?
Oh for one year! Oh! but for even a day
Of my full youth, while yet my body served
My soul as serves the generous steed his lord,
I would have dash'd amongst them, asking few
In aid to overthrow these swoln patricians;
But now I must look round for other hands
To serve this hoary head;—but it shall plan
In such a sort as will not leave the task
Herculean, though as yet 'tis but a chaos
Of darkly brooding thoughts: my fancy is
In her first work, more nearly to the light
Holding the sleeping images of things
For the selection of the pausing judgment.—
The troops are few in——

Enter VINCENZO.

Vin.   There is one without
Craves audience of your highness.
Doge.   I'm unwell—
I can see no one, not even a patrician—
Let him refer his business to the council.
Vin. My lord, I will deliver your reply;
It cannot much import—he's a plebeian,
The master of a galley, I believe.
Doge. How! did you say the patron of a galley?
That is—I mean—a servant of the state:
Admit him, he may be on public service. [*Exit* VINCENZO.
Doge. [*Solus.*] This patron may be sounded; I will try him.
I know the people to be discontented:
They have cause, since Sapienza's adverse day,
When Genoa conquer'd: they have further cause,
Since they are nothing in the state, and in
The city worse than nothing—mere machines,
To serve the nobles' most patrician pleasure.
The troops have long arrears of pay, oft promised,

And murmur deeply—any hope of change
Will draw them forward: they shall pay themselves
With plunder:—but the priests—I doubt the priesthood
Will not be with us; they have hated me
Since that rash hour, when, madden'd with the drone,
I smote the tardy bishop at Treviso,
Quickening his holy march; yet, ne'ertheless,
They may be won, at least their chief at Rome,
By some well-timed concessions; but, above
All things, I must be speedy: at my hour
Of twilight little light of life remains.
Could I free Venice, and avenge my wrongs,
I had lived too long, and willingly would sleep
Next moment with my sires; and, wanting this,
Better that sixty of my fourscore years
Had been already where—how soon, I care not—
The whole must be extinguish'd;—better that
They ne'er had been, than drag me on to be
The thing these arch-oppressors fain would make me.
Let me consider—of efficient troops
There are three thousand posted at——

Enter VINCENZO *and* ISRAEL BERTUCCIO.

Vin.   May it please
  Your highness, the same patron whom I spake of
  Is here to crave your patience.
Doge.   Leave the chamber,
Vincenzo.—   [*Exit* VINCENZO.
              Sir, you may advance—what would you?
I. Ber. Redress.
Doge.   Of whom?
I. Ber.   Of God and the Doge.
Doge. Alas! my friend, you seek it of the twain
  Of least respect and interest in Venice.
  You must address the council.
I. Ber.   'Twere in vain;
  For he who injured me is one of them.
Doge. There's blood upon thy face—how came it there?
I. Ber. 'Tis mine, and not the first I've shed for Venice,
  But the first shed by a Venetian hand:
  A noble smote me.
Doge.   Doth he live?
I. Ber.   Not long—
  But for the hope I had and have, that you,
  My prince, yourself a soldier, will redress
  Him, whom the laws of discipline and Venice

Permit not to protect himself;—if not—
I say no more.

Doge.   But something you would do—
Is it not so?

I. Ber.   I am a man, my lord.

Doge. Why so is he who smote you.

I. Ber.   He is call'd so;
Nay, more, a noble—at least, in Venice:
But since he hath forgotten that I am one,
And treats me like a brute, the brute may turn—
'Tis said the worm will.

Doge.   Say—his name and lineage?

I. Ber. Barbaro.

Doge.   What was the cause? or the pretext?

I. Ber. I am the chief of the arsenal,[1] employ'd
At present in repairing certain galleys
But roughly used by the Genoese last year.
This morning comes the noble Barbaro
Full of reproof, because our artisans
Had left some frivolous order of his house,
To execute the state's decree; I dared
To justify the men—he raised his hand;—
Behold my blood! the first time it e'er flow'd
Dishonourably.

Doge.   Have you long time served?

I. Ber. So long as to remember Zara's siege,
And fight beneath the chief who beat the Huns there,
Sometime my general, now the Doge Faliero.—

Doge. How! are we comrades?—the state's ducal robes
Sit newly on me, and you were appointed
Chief of the arsenal ere I came from Rome;
So that I recognized you not. Who placed you?

I. Ber. The late Doge; keeping still my old command
As patron of a galley: my new office
Was given as the reward of certain scars
(So was your predecessor pleased to say):
I little thought his bounty would conduct me
To his successor as a helpless plaintiff;
At least, in such a cause.

Doge.   Are you much hurt?

---

[1] [This officer was chief of the artisans of the arsenal, and commanded the Bucentaur, for the safety of which, even if an accidental storm should arise, he was responsible with his life. He mounted guard at the ducal palace during an interregnum, and bore the red standard before the new Doge on his inauguration; for which service his perquisites were the ducal mantle, and the two silver basins from which the Doge scattered the regulated pittance which he was permitted to throw among the people.—*Amelot de la Houssaye*, 79.]

I. Ber. Irreparably in my self-esteem.

Doge. Speak out; fear nothing: being stung at heart,
  What would you do to be revenged on this man?

I. Ber. That which I dare not name, and yet will do.

Doge. Then wherefore came you here?

I. Ber.   I come for justice,
  Because my general is Doge, and will not
  See his old soldier trampled on.   Had any,
  Save Faliero, fill'd the ducal throne,
  This blood had been wash'd out in other blood.

Doge. You come to me for justice—unto *me*!
  The Doge of Venice, and I cannot give it;
  I cannot even obtain it—'twas denied
  To me most solemnly an hour ago!

I. Ber. How says your highness?

Doge.   Steno is condemned
  To a month's confinement.

I. Ber.   What! the same who dared
  To stain the ducal throne with those foul words,
  That have cried shame to every ear in Venice?

Doge. Ay, doubtless they have echo'd o'er the arsenal,
  Keeping due time with every hammer's clink
  As a good jest to jolly artisans;
  Or making chorus to the creaking oar,
  In the vile tune of every galley-slave,
  Who, as he sung the merry stave, exulted
  He was not a shamed dotard like the Doge.

I. Ber. Is't possible? a month's imprisonment!
  No more for Steno?

Doge.   You have heard the offence,
  And now you know his punishment; and then
  You ask redress of *me*!   Go to the Forty,
  Who pass'd the sentence upon Michel Steno;
  They'll do as much by Barbaro, no doubt.

I. Ber. Ah! dared I speak my feelings!

Doge.   Give them breath.
  Mine have no further outrage to endure.

I. Ber. Then, in a word, it rests but on your word
  To punish and avenge—I will not say
  My petty wrong, for what is a mere blow,
  However vile, to such a thing as I am?—
  But the base insult done your state and person.

Doge. You overrate my power, which is a pageant.
  This cap is not the monarch's crown; these robes
  Might move compassion, like a beggar's rags;
  Nay, more, a beggar's are his own, and these

But lent to the poor puppet, who must play
Its part with all its empire in this ermine.
I. Ber. Wouldst thou be king?
Doge.   Yes—of a happy people.
I. Ber. Wouldst thou be sovereign lord of Venice? [1]
Doge.   Ay,
If that the people shared that sovereignty.
So that nor they nor I were further slaves
To this o'ergrown aristocratic Hydra,
The poison'd heads of whose envenom'd body
Have breathed a pestilence upon us all.
I. Ber. Yet, thou wast born, and still hast lived, patrician.
Doge. In evil hour was I so born; my birth
Hath made me Doge to be insulted: but
I lived and toil'd a soldier and a servant
Of Venice and her people, not the senate;
Their good and my own honour were my guerdon.
I have fought and bled; commanded, ay, and conquered;
Have made and marr'd peace oft in embassies,
As it might chance to be our country's vantage;
Have traversed land and sea in constant duty,
Through almost sixty years, and still for Venice,
My fathers' and my birthplace, whose dear spires,
Rising at distance o'er the blue Lagoon,
It was reward enough for me to view
Once more; but not for any knot of men,
Nor sect, nor faction, did I bleed or sweat!
But would you know why I have done all this?
Ask of the bleeding pelican why she
Hath ripp'd her bosom?   Had the bird a voice,
She 'd tell thee 'twas for *all* her little ones.
I. Ber. And yet they made thee duke.

---

[1] ['Upon this the admiral answered: "My Lord Duke, if you would wish to make yourself a prince, and to cut all those cuckoldy gentlemen to pieces, I have the heart, if you do but help me, to make you prince of all this state; and then you may punish them all." Hearing this, the duke said:—"How can such a matter be brought about?" and so they discoursed thereon.' Such is Sanuto's narrative, and we have nothing more certain to offer. It is not easy to say whence he obtained his intelligence. If such a conversation as that which he relates really did occur, it must have taken place without the presence of witnesses, and therefore could be disclosed only by one of the parties. It is far more likely that the chronicler is relating that which he *supposed*, than that which he *knew*; and, as it must be admitted that the interview with the admiral of the arsenal occurred, and that immediately after it the Doge was found linked with the daring band of which that officer was chief, there is no violation of probability in granting that some such conversation took place; and that the train was ignited by this collision of two angry spirits.—*Sketches of Venetian History*.]

Doge.   *They made* me so;
   I sought it not, the flattering fetters met me
   Returning from my Roman embassy,
   And never having hitherto refused
   Toil, charge, or duty for the state, I did not,
   At these late years, decline what was the highest
   Of all in seeming, but of all most base
   In what we have to do and to endure:
   Bear witness for me thou, my injured subject,
   When I can neither right myself nor thee.
I. Ber. You shall do both, if you possess the will;
   And many thousands more not less oppress'd,
   Who wait but for a signal—will you give it?
Doge. You speak in riddles.
I. Ber.   Which shall soon be read
   At peril of my life; if you disdain not
   To lend a patient ear.
Doge.   Say on.
I. Ber.   Not thou,
   Nor I alone, are injured and abused,
   Contemn'd and trampled on; but the whole people
   Groan with the strong conception of their wrongs:
   The foreign soldiers in the senate's pay
   Are discontented for their long arrears;
   The native mariners, and civic troops,
   Feel with their friends; for who is he amongst them
   Whose brethren, parents, children, wives, or sisters,
   Have not partook oppression, or pollution,
   From the patricians? And the hopeless war
   Against the Genoese, which is still maintain'd
   With the plebeian blood, and treasure wrung
   From their hard earnings, has inflamed them further:
   Even now—but, I forget that speaking thus,
   Perhaps I pass the sentence of my death!
Doge. And suffering what thou hast done—fear'st thou death?
   Be silent then, and live on, to be beaten
   By those for whom thou hast bled.
I. Ber.   No, I will speak
   At every hazard; and if Venice' Doge
   Should turn delator, be the shame on him,
   And sorrow too; for he will lose far more
   Than I.
Doge.   From me fear nothing; out with it!
I. Ber. Know then, that there are met and sworn in secret
   A band of brethren, valiant hearts and true;
   Men who have proved all fortunes, and have long

Grieved over that of Venice, and have right
To do so; having served her in all climes,
And having rescued her from foreign foes,
Would do the same from those within her walls.
They are not numerous, nor yet too few
For their great purpose; they have arms, and means,
And hearts, and hopes, and faith, and patient courage.

Doge. For what then do they pause?

I. Ber.   An hour to strike.

Doge. [*Aside.*] Saint Mark's shall strike that hour!

I. Ber.   I have now placed
My life, my honour, all my earthly hopes
Within thy power, but in the firm belief
That injuries like ours, sprung from one cause,
Will generate one vengeance: should it be so,
Be our chief now—our sovereign hereafter.

Doge. How many are ye?

I. Ber.   I 'll not answer that
Till I am answer'd.

Doge.   How, sir! do you menace?

I. Ber. No; I affirm. I have betray'd myself;
But there 's no torture in the mystic wells
Which undermine your palace, nor in those
Not less appalling cells, the 'leaden roofs,'
To force a single name from me of others.
The Pozzi and the Piombi were in vain;
They might wring blood from me, but treachery never.
And I would pass the fearful 'Bridge of Sighs.'
Joyous that mine must be the last that e'er
Would echo o'er the Stygian wave which flows
Between the murderers and the murder'd, washing
The prison and the palace walls: there are
Those who would live to think on 't, and avenge me.

Doge. If such your power and purpose, why come here
To sue for justice, being in the course
To do yourself due right?

I. Ber.   Because the man,
Who claims protection from authority,
Showing his confidence and his submission
To that authority, can hardly be
Suspected of combining to destroy it.
Had I sate down too humbly with this blow,
A moody brow and mutter'd threats had made me
A mark'd man to the Forty's inquisition;
But loud complaint, however angrily
It shapes its phrase, is little to be fear'd,

And less distrusted.   But, besides all this,
I had another reason.

Doge.   What was that?

I. Ber. Some rumours that the Doge was greatly moved
By the reference of the Avogadori
Of Michel Steno's sentence to the Forty
Had reach'd me.   I had served you, honour'd you,
And felt that you were dangerously insulted,
Being of an order of such spirits, as
Requite tenfold both good and evil: 'twas
My wish to prove and urge you to redress.
Now you know all; and that I speak the truth,
My peril be the proof.

Doge.   You have deeply ventured;
But all must do so who would greatly win:
Thus far I 'll answer you—your secret 's safe.

I. Ber. And is this all?

Doge.   Unless with all intrusted,
What would you have me answer?

I. Ber.   I would have you
Trust him who leaves his life in trust with you.

Doge. But I must know your plan, your names, and numbers;
The last may then be doubled, and the former
Matur'd and strengthen'd.

I. Ber.   We're enough already;
You are the sole ally we covet now.

Doge. But bring me to the knowledge of your chiefs.

I. Ber. That shall be done upon your formal pledge
To keep the faith that we will pledge to you.

Doge. When? where?

I. Ber.   This night I 'll bring to your apartment
Two of the principals; a greater number
Were hazardous.

Doge.   Stay, I must think of this.
What if I were to trust myself amongst you,
And leave the palace?

I. Ber.   You must come alone.

Doge. With but my nephew.

I. Ber.   Not were he your son.

Doge. Wretch! darest thou name my son?   He died in arms
At Sapienza for this faithless state.
Oh! that he were alive, and I in ashes!
Or that he were alive ere I be ashes!
I should not need the dubious aid of strangers.

I. Ber. Not one of all those strangers whom thou doubtest,
　　But will regard thee with a filial feeling,
　　So that thou keep'st a father's faith with them.
Doge. The die is cast.　Where is the place of meeting?
I. Ber. At midnight I will be alone and mask'd
　　Where'er your highness pleases to direct me,
　　To wait your coming, and conduct you where
　　You shall receive our homage, and pronounce
　　Upon our project.
Doge.　　　　　　　　At what hour arises
　　The moon?
I. Ber. Late, but the atmosphere is thick and dusky,
　　'Tis the sirocco.
Doge.　　　　　　　At the midnight hour, then,
　　Near to the church where sleep my sires;[1] the same,
　　Twin-named from the apostles John and Paul:
　　A gondola, with one oar only, will
　　Lurk in the narrow channel which glides by.
　　Be there.
I. Ber.　　　I will not fail.
Doge.　　　　　　　　　And now retire——
I. Ber. In the full hope your highness will not falter
　　In your great purpose.　Prince, I take my leave.
　　　　　　　　　　　　　　　[*Exit* ISRAEL BERTUCCIO.
Doge. [*Solus.*] At midnight, by the church Saints John and Paul,
　　Where sleep my noble fathers, I repair—
　　To what? to hold a council in the dark
　　With common ruffians leagued to ruin states!
　　And will not my great sires leap from the vault,
　　Where lie two doges who preceded me,
　　And pluck me down amongst them?　Would they could!
　　For I should rest in honour with the honour'd.
　　Alas! I must not think of them, but those
　　Who have made me thus unworthy of a name
　　Noble and brave as aught of consular
　　On Roman marbles; but I will redeem it
　　Back to its antique lustre in our annals,

---

[1] The Doges were all buried in St. Mark's *before* Faliero.　It is singular that
when his predecessor, Andrea Dandolo, died, the Ten made a law that all the
future Doges should be buried with their families in their own churches—one
would think, by a kind of presentiment.　So that all that is said of his *ancestral
Doges*, as buried at St. John's and Paul's, is altered from the fact, they being in
St. Mark's.　Make a note of this, and put *Editor* as the subscription to it.
As I make such pretensions to accuracy, I should not like to be twitted even
with such trifles on that score.　Of the play they may say what they please,
but not so of my costume and *dram. pers.*—they having been real existences.—
Letter, Oct. 1820.

By sweet revenge on all that's base in Venice,
And freedom to the rest, or leave it black
To all the glowing calumnies of time,
Which never spare the fame of him who fails,
But try the Caesar, or the Catiline,
By the true touchstone of desert—success.

ACT II

SCENE I

An Apartment in the Ducal Palace

ANGIOLINA (*wife of the* DOGE) *and* MARIANNA.

Ang. What was the Doge's answer?
Mar.   That he was
  That moment summon'd to a conference;
  But 'tis by this time ended. I perceived
  Not long ago the senators embarking;
  And the last gondola may now be seen
  Gliding into the throng of barks which stud
  The glittering waters.
Ang.   Would he were return'd!
  He has been much disquieted of late;
  And Time, which has not tamed his fiery spirit
  Nor yet enfeebled even his mortal frame,
  Which seems to be more nourished by a soul
  So quick and restless that it would consume
  Less hardy clay—Time has but little power
  On his resentments or his griefs. Unlike
  To other spirits of his order, who,
  In the first burst of passion, pour away
  Their wrath or sorrow, all things wear in him
  An aspect of eternity: his thoughts,
  His feelings, passions, good or evil, all
  Have nothing of old age; and his bold brow
  Bears but the scars of mind, the thoughts of years,
  Not their decrepitude: and he of late
  Has been more agitated than his wont.
  Would he were come! for I alone have power
  Upon his troubled spirit.
Mar.   It is true,
  His highness has of late been greatly moved
  By the affront of Steno, and with cause:
  But the offender doubtless even now
  Is doom'd to expiate his rash insult with

Such chastisement as will enforce respect
To female virtue, and to noble blood.
Ang. 'Twas a gross insult; but I heed it not
For the rash scorner's falsehood in itself,
But for the effect, the deadly deep impression
Which it has made upon Faliero's soul,
The proud, the fiery, the austere—austere
To all save me: I tremble when I think
To what it may conduct.
Mar.   Assuredly
The Doge cannot suspect you?
Ang.   Suspect *me* !
Why Steno dared not: when he scrawl'd his lie,
Grovelling by stealth in the moon's glimmering light,
His own still conscience smote him for the act,
And every shadow on the walls frown'd shame
Upon his coward calumny.
Mar.   'Twere fit
He should be punished grievously.
Ang.   He is so.
Mar. What ! is the sentence pass'd? is he condemn'd?
Ang. I know not that, but he has been detected.
Mar. And deem you this enough for this foul scorn?
Ang. I would not be a judge in my own cause,
Nor do I know what sense of punishment
May reach the soul of ribalds such as Steno;
But if his insults sink no deeper in
The minds of the inquisitors than they
Have ruffled mine, he will, for all acquittance,
Be left to his own shamelessness or shame.
Mar. Some sacrifice is due to slander'd virtue.
Ang. Why, what is virtue if it needs a victim?
Or if it must depend upon men's words?
The dying Roman said, ''twas but a name':
It were indeed no more, if human breath
Could make or mar it.
Mar.   Yet full many a dame,
Stainless and faithful, would feel all the wrong
Of such a slander; and less rigid ladies,
Such as abound in Venice, would be loud
And all-inexorable in their cry
For justice.
Ang.   This but proves it is the name
And not the quality they prize: the first
Have found it a hard task to hold their honour,
If they require it to be blazon'd forth;

And those who have not kept it, seek its seeming
As they would look out for an ornament
Of which they feel the want, but not because
They think it so; they live in others' thoughts,
And would seem honest as they must seem fair.

Mar. You have strange thoughts for a patrician dame.

Ang. And yet they were my father's; with his name,
　The sole inheritance he left.

Mar.　　　　　　　　You want none;
Wife to a prince, the chief of the Republic.

Ang. I should have sought none though a peasant's bride,
　But feel not less the love and gratitude
　Due to my father, who bestow'd my hand
　Upon his early, tried, and trusted friend,
　The Count Val di Marino, now our Doge.

Mar. And with that hand did he bestow your heart?

Ang. He did so, or it had not been bestow'd.

Mar. Yet this strange disproportion in your years,
　And, let me add, disparity of tempers,
　Might make the world doubt whether such an union
　Could make you wisely, permanently happy.

Ang. The world will think with worldlings; but my heart
　Has still been in my duties, which are many,
　But never difficult.

Mar.　　　　　　　And do you love him?

Ang. I love all noble qualities which merit
　Love, and I loved my father, who first taught me
　To single out what we should love in others,
　And to subdue all tendency to lend
　The best and purest feelings of our nature
　To baser passions.　He bestow'd my hand
　Upon Faliero: he had known him noble,
　Brave, generous; rich in all the qualities
　Of soldier, citizen, and friend; in all
　Such have I found him as my father said.
　His faults are those that dwell in the high bosoms
　Of men who have commanded; too much pride,
　And the deep passions fiercely foster'd by
　The uses of patricians, and a life
　Spent in the storms of state and war; and also
　From the quick sense of honour, which becomes
　A duty to a certain sign, a vice
　When overstrain'd, and this I fear in him.
　And then he has been rash from his youth upwards,
　Yet temper'd by redeeming nobleness
　In such sort, that the wariest of republics

Has lavish'd all its chief employs upon him,
From his first fight to his last embassy,
From which on his return the dukedom met him.

Mar. But previous to this marriage, had your heart
Ne'er beat for any of the noble youth,
Such as in years had been more meet to match
Beauty like yours? or since have you ne'er seen
One, who, if your fair hand were still to give,
Might now pretend to Loredano's daughter?

Ang. I answer'd your first question when I said
I married.

Mar. And the second?

Ang. Needs no answer.

Mar. I pray you pardon, if I have offended.

Ang. I feel no wrath, but some surprise: I knew not
That wedded bosoms could permit themselves
To ponder upon what they *now* might choose,
Or aught save their past choice.

Mar. 'Tis their past choice
That far too often makes them deem they would
Now choose more wisely, could they cancel it.

Ang. It may be so. I knew not of such thoughts.

Mar. Here comes the Doge—shall I retire?

Ang. It may
Be better you should quit me; he seems rapt
In thought.—How pensively he takes his way!
[*Exit* MARIANNA.

Enter the DOGE *and* PIETRO.

Doge. [*Musing.*] There is a certain Philip Calendaro
Now in the arsenal, who holds command
Of eighty men, and has great influence
Besides on all the spirits of his comrades:
This man, I hear, is bold and popular,
Sudden and daring, and yet secret; 'twould
Be well that he were won: I needs must hope
That Israel Bertuccio has secured him,
But fain would be——

Pie. My lord, pray pardon me
For breaking in upon your meditation;
The Senator Bertuccio, your kinsman,
Charged me to follow and inquire your pleasure
To fix an hour when he may speak with you.

Doge. At sunset.—Stay a moment—let me see—
Say in the second hour of night. [*Exit* PIETRO.

Ang. My lord!

Doge. My dearest child, forgive me—why delay
　　So long approaching me?—I saw you not.
Ang. You were absorb'd in thought, and he who now
　　Has parted from you might have words of weight
　　To bear you from the senate.
Doge.　　　　　　　　　　From the senate?
Ang. I would not interrupt him in his duty
　　And theirs.
Doge.　　　　The senate's duty! you mistake;
　　'Tis we who owe all service to the senate.
Ang. I thought the Duke had held command in Venice.
Doge. He shall.—But let that pass.—We will be jocund.
　　How fares it with you? have you been abroad?
　　The day is overcast, but the calm wave
　　Favours the gondolier's light skimming oar;
　　Or have you held a levee of your friends?
　　Or has your music made you solitary?
　　Say—is there aught that you would will within
　　The little sway now left the Duke? or aught
　　Of fitting splendour, or of honest pleasure,
　　Social or lonely, that would glad your heart,
　　To compensate for many a dull hour, wasted
　　On an old man oft moved with many cares?
　　Speak, and 'tis done.
Ang.　　　　　　You 're ever kind to me.
　　I have nothing to desire, or to request,
　　Except to see you oftener and calmer.
Doge. Calmer?
Ang.　　　　Ay, calmer, my good lord. Ah, why
　　Do you still keep apart, and walk alone,
　　And let such strong emotions stamp your brow,
　　As not betraying their full import, yet
　　Disclose too much?
Doge.　　　　　Disclose too much!—of what?
　　What is there to disclose?
Ang.　　　　　　　A heart so ill
　　At ease.
Doge.　　　'Tis nothing, child.—But in the state
　　You know what daily cares oppress all those
　　Who govern this precarious commonwealth;
　　Now suffering from the Genoese without,
　　And malcontents within—'tis this which makes me
　　More pensive and less tranquil than my wont.
Ang. Yet this existed long before, and never
　　Till in these late days did I see you thus.
　　Forgive me; there is something at your heart

More than the mere discharge of public duties,
Which long use and a talent like to yours
Have render'd light, nay, a necessity,
To keep your mind from stagnating. 'Tis not
In hostile states, nor perils, thus to shake you;
You, who have stood all storms and never sunk,
And climb'd up to the pinnacle of power
And never fainted by the way, and stand
Upon it, and can look down steadily
Along the depth beneath, and ne'er feel dizzy.
Were Genoa's galleys riding in the port,
Were civil fury raging in Saint Mark's,
You are not to be wrought on, but would fall,
As you have risen, with an unalter'd brow—
Your feelings now are of a different kind;
Something has stung your pride, not patriotism.

Doge. Pride! Angiolina? Alas! none is left me.

Ang. Yes—the same sin that overthrew the angels,
And of all sins most easily besets
Mortals the nearest to the angelic nature:
The vile are only vain; the great are proud.

Doge. I *had* the pride of honour, of *your* honour,
Deep at my heart—— But let us change the theme.

Ang. Ah no!—As I have ever shared your kindness
In all things else, let me not be shut out
From your distress: were it of public import,
You know I never sought, would never seek
To win a word from you; but feeling now
Your grief is private, it belongs to me
To lighten or divide it. Since the day
When foolish Steno's ribaldry detected
Unfix'd your quiet, you are greatly changed,
And I would soothe you back to what you were.

Doge. To what I was!—Have you heard Steno's sentence?

Ang. No.

Doge. A month's arrest.

Ang. Is it not enough?

Doge. Enough!—yes, for a drunken galley slave,
Who, stung by stripes, may murmur at his master;
But not for a deliberate false, cool villain,
Who stains a lady's and a prince's honour
Even on the throne of his authority.

Ang. There seems to me enough in the conviction
Of a patrician guilty of a falsehood:
All other punishment were light unto
His loss of honour.

Doge.   Such men have no honour;
  They have but their vile lives—and these are spared.
Ang. You would not have him die for this offence?
Doge. Not *now*:—being still alive, I'd have him live
  Long as *he* can; he has ceased to merit death;
  The guilty saved hath damn'd his hundred judges,
  And he is pure, for now his crime is theirs.
Ang. Oh! had this false and flippant libeller
  Shed his young blood for his absurd lampoon,
  Ne'er from that moment could this breast have known
  A joyous hour, or dreamless slumber more.
Doge. Does not the law of Heaven say blood for blood?
  And he who *taints* kills more than he who sheds it.
  Is it the *pain* of blows, or *shame* of blows,
  That makes such deadly to the sense of man?
  Do not the laws of man say blood for honour?
  And, less than honour, for a little gold?
  Say not the laws of nations blood for treason?
  Is 't nothing to have fill'd these veins with poison
  For their once healthful current? is it nothing
  To have stain'd your name and mine—the noblest names?
  Is 't nothing to have brought into contempt
  A prince before his people? to have fail'd
  In the respect accorded by mankind
  To youth in woman, and old age in man?
  To virtue in your sex, and dignity
  In ours?—But let them look to it who have saved him.
Ang. Heaven bids us to forgive our enemies.
Doge. Doth Heaven forgive her own?   Is Satan saved
  From wrath eternal?
Ang.   Do not speak thus wildly—
  Heaven will alike forgive you and your foes.
Doge. Amen!   May Heaven forgive them!
Ang.   And will you?
Doge. Yes, when they are in heaven!
Ang.   And not till then?
Doge. What matters my forgiveness? an old man's,
  Worn out, scorned, spurn'd, abused; what matters then
  My pardon more than my resentment, both
  Being weak and worthless?   I have lived too long.—
  But let us change the argument.—My child!
  My injured wife, the child of Loredano,
  The brave, the chivalrous, how little deem'd
  Thy father, wedding thee unto his friend,
  That he was linking thee to shame!—Alas!
  Shame without sin, for thou art faultless.   Hadst thou

But had a different husband, *any* husband
In Venice save the Doge, this blight, this brand,
This blasphemy had never fallen upon thee.
So young, so beautiful, so good, so pure,
To suffer this, and yet be unavenged!

Ang. I am too well avenged, for you still love me,
And trust, and honour me; and all men know
That you are just, and I am true: what more
Could I require, or you command?

Doge.   'Tis well,
And may be better; but whate'er betide,
Be thou at least kind to my memory.

Ang. Why speak you thus?

Doge.   It is no matter why;
But I would still, whatever others think,
Have your respect both now and in my grave.

Ang. Why should you doubt it? has it ever fail'd?

Doge. Come hither, child; I would a word with you.
Your father was my friend, unequal fortune
Made him my debtor for some courtesies
Which bind the good more firmly: when, oppress'd
With his last malady, he will'd our union,
It was not to repay me, long repaid
Before by his great loyalty in friendship;
His object was to place your orphan beauty
In honourable safety from the perils,
Which, in this scorpion nest of vice, assail
A lonely and undower'd maid. I did not
Think with him, but would not oppose the thought
Which soothed his death-bed.

Ang.   I have not forgotten
The nobleness with which you bade me speak
If my young heart held any preference
Which would have made me happier; nor your offer
To make my dowry equal to the rank
Of aught in Venice, and forego all claim
My father's last injunction gave you.

Doge.   Thus,
'Twas not a foolish dotard's vile caprice,
Nor the false edge of aged appetite,
Which made me covetous of girlish beauty,
And a young bride: for in my fieriest youth
I sway'd such passions; nor was this my age
Infected with that leprosy of lust
Which taints the hoariest years of vicious men,
Making them ransack to the very last

The dregs of pleasure for their vanish'd joys;
Or buy in selfish marriage some young victim,
Too helpless to refuse a state that 's honest,
Too feeling not to know herself a wretch.
Our wedlock was not of this sort; you had
Freedom from me to choose, and urged in answer
Your father's choice.

Ang.   I did so; I would do so
In face of earth and heaven; for I have never
Repented for my sake; sometimes for yours,
In pondering o'er your late disquietudes.

Doge. I knew my heart would never treat you harshly;
I knew my days could not disturb you long;
And then the daughter of my earliest friend,
His worthy daughter, free to choose again,
Wealthier and wiser, in the ripest bloom
Of womanhood, more skilful to select
By passing these probationary years
Inheriting a prince's name and riches,
Secured, by the short penance of enduring
An old man for some summers, against all
That law's chicane or envious kinsmen might
Have urged against her right; my best friend's child
Would choose more fitly in respect of years,
And not less truly in a faithful heart.

Ang. My lord, I look'd but to my father's wishes,
Hallow'd by his last words, and to my heart
For doing all its duties, and replying
With faith to him with whom I was affianced.
Ambitious hopes ne'er cross'd my dreams; and should
The hour you speak of come, it will be seen so.

Doge. I do believe you; and I know you true:
For love, romantic love, which in my youth
I knew to be illusion, and ne'er saw
Lasting, but often fatal, it had been
No lure for me, in my most passionate days,
And could not be so now, did such exist.
But such respect, and mildly paid regard
As a true feeling for your welfare, and
A free compliance with all honest wishes;
A kindness to your virtues, watchfulness
Not shown, but shadowing o'er such little failings
As youth is apt in, so as not to check
Rashly, but win you from them ere you knew
You had been won, but thought the change your choice;
A pride not in your beauty, but your conduct,—

A trust in you—a patriarchial love,
And not a doting homage—friendship, faith—
Such estimation in your eyes as these
Might claim, I hoped for.
Ang.   And have ever had.
Doge. I think so. For the difference in our years
    You knew it, choosing me, and chose; I trusted
    Not to my qualities, nor would have faith
    In such, nor outward ornaments of nature,
    Were I still in my five and twentieth spring;
    I trusted to the blood of Loredano
    Pure in your veins; I trusted to the soul
    God gave you—to the truths your father taught you—
    To your belief in heaven—to your mild virtues—
    To your own faith and honour, for my own.
Ang. You have done well.—I thank you for that trust,
    Which I have never for one moment ceased
    To honour you the more for.
Doge.   Where is honour,
    Innate and precept-strengthen'd, 'tis the rock
    Of faith connubial; where it is not—where
    Light thoughts are lurking, or the vanities
    Of worldly pleasure rankle in the heart,
    Or sensual throbs convulse it, well I know
    'Twere hopeless for humanity to dream
    Of honesty in such infected blood,
    Although 'twere wed to him it covets most:
    An incarnation of the poet's god
    In all his marble-chisell'd beauty, or
    The demi-deity, Alcides, in
    His majesty of superhuman manhood,
    Would not suffice to bind where virtue is not;
    It is consistency which forms and proves it:
    Vice cannot fix, and virtue cannot change.
    The once fall'n woman must for ever fall;
    For vice must have variety, while virtue
    Stands like the sun, and all which rolls around
    Drinks life, and light, and glory from her aspect.
Ang. And seeing, feeling thus this truth in others,
    (I pray you pardon me;) but wherefore yield you
    To the most fierce of fatal passions, and
    Disquiet your great thoughts with restless hate
    Of such a thing as Steno?
Doge.   You mistake me.
    It is not Steno who could move me thus;
    Had it been so, he should——but let that pass.

Ang. What is 't you feel so deeply, then, even now?

Doge. The violated majesty of Venice,
  At once insulted in her lord and laws.

Ang. Alas! why will you thus consider it?

Doge. I have thought on 't till——but let me lead you back
  To what I urged; all these things being noted,
  I wedded you; the world then did me justice
  Upon the motive, and my conduct proved
  They did me right, while yours was all to praise:
  You had all freedom, all respect, all trust
  From me and mine; and, born of those who made
  Princes at home, and swept kings from their thrones
  On foreign shores, in all things you appear'd
  Worthy to be our first of native dames.

Ang. To what does this conduct?

Doge.   To thus much – that
  A miscreant's angry breath may blast it all—
  A villain, whom for his unbridled bearing,
  Even in the midst of our great festival,
  I caused to be conducted forth, and taught
  How to demean himself in ducal chambers;
  A wretch like this may leave upon the wall
  The blighting venom of his sweltering heart,
  And this shall spread itself in general poison;
  And woman's innocence, man's honour, pass
  Into a by-word; and the doubly felon
  (Who first insulted virgin modesty
  By a gross affront to your attendant damsels
  Amidst the noblest of our dames in public)
  Requite himself for his most just expulsion
  By blackening publicly his sovereign's consort,
  And be absolved by his upright compeers.

Ang. But he has been condemn'd into captivity.

Doge. For such as him a dungeon were acquittal;
  And his brief term of mock-arrest will pass
  Within a palace.   But I 've done with him;
  The rest must be with you.

Ang.   With me, my lord?

Doge. Yes, Angiolina.   Do not marvel; I
  Have let this prey upon me till I feel
  My life cannot be long; and fain would have you
  Regard the injunctions you will find within
  This scroll. [*Giving her a paper.*]——Fear not; they are for your
    advantage:
  Read them hereafter at the fitting hour.

Ang. My lord, in life, and after life, you shall
  Be honour'd still by me: but may your days
  Be many yet—and happier than the present!
  This passion will give way, and you will be
  Serene, and what you should be—what you were.

Doge. I will be what I should be, or be nothing;
  But never more—oh! never, never more,
  O'er the few days or hours which yet await
  The blighted old age of Faliero, shall
  Sweet Quiet shed her sunset! Never more
  Those summer shadows rising from the past
  Of a not ill-spent nor inglorious life,
  Mellowing the last hours as the night approaches,
  Shall soothe me to my moment of long rest.
  I had but little more to ask, or hope,
  Save the regards due to the blood and sweat,
  And the soul's labour through which I had toil'd
  To make my country honour'd. As her servant—
  Her servant, though her chief—I would have gone
  Down to my fathers with a name serene
  And pure as theirs; but this has been denied me.—
  Would I had died at Zara!

Ang.   There you saved
  The state; then live to save her still. A day,
  Another day like that would be the best
  Reproof to them, and sole revenge for you.

Doge. But one such day occurs within an age;
  My life is little less than one, and 'tis
  Enough for Fortune to have granted *once*,
  That which scarce one more favour'd citizen
  May win in many states and years. But why
  Thus speak I? Venice has forgot that day—
  Then why should I remember it?—Farewell,
  Sweet Angiolina! I must to my cabinet;
  There's much for me to do—and the hour hastens.

Ang. Remember what you were.

Doge.   It were in vain!
  Joy's recollection is no longer joy,
  While Sorrow's memory is a sorrow still.

Ang. At least, whate'er may urge, let me implore
  That you will take some little pause of rest;
  Your sleep for many nights has been so turbid,
  That it had been relief to have awaked you,
  Had I not hoped that Nature would o'erpower
  At length the thoughts which shook your slumbers thus.

An hour of reſt will give you to your toils
With fitter thoughts and freshen'd strength.

Doge.   I cannot—
I muſt not, if I could; for never was
Such reason to be watchful: yet a few—
Yet a few days and dream-perturbed nights
And I shall slumber well—but where?—no matter.
Adieu, my Angiolina.

Ang.   Let me be
An inſtant—yet an inſtant your companion!
I cannot bear to leave you thus.

Doge.   Come then,
My gentle child—forgive me; thou wert made
For better fortunes than to share in mine,
Now darkling in their close toward the deep vale
Where Death sits robed in his all-sweeping shadow.
When I am gone—it may be sooner than
Even these years warrant, for there is that ſtirring
Within, above, around, that in this city
Will make the cemeteries populous
As e'er they were by peſtilence or war,—
When I *am* nothing, let that which I *was*
Be ſtill sometimes a name on thy sweet lips,
A shadow in thy fancy, of a thing
Which would not have thee mourn it, but remember;—
Let us begone, my child—the time is pressing.   [*Exeunt.*

SCENE II

A retired Spot near the Arsenal

ISRAEL BERTUCCIO *and* PHILIP CALENDARO.

Cal. How sped you, Israel, in your late complaint?
I. Ber. Why, well.
Cal.   Is 't possible! will he be punish'd?
I. Ber.   Yes.
Cal. With what? a mulċt or an arreſt?
I. Ber.   With death!—
Cal. Now you rave, or muſt intend revenge,
Such as I counsell'd you, with your own hand.
I. Ber. Yes; and for one sole draught of hate, forego
The great redress we meditate for Venice,
And change a life of hope for one of exile;
Leaving one scorpion crush'd, and thousands ſtinging
My friends, my family, my countrymen!
No, Calendaro; these same drops of blood,

Shed shamefully, shall have the whole of his
For their requital——But not only his;
We will not strike for private wrongs alone:
Such are for selfish passions and rash men,
But are unworthy a tyrannicide.

Cal. You have more patience than I care to boast.
Had I been present when you bore this insult,
I must have slain him, or expired myself
In the vain effort to repress my wrath.

I. Ber. Thank Heaven, you were not—all had else been marr'd:
As 'tis, our cause looks prosperous still.

Cal.   You saw
The Doge—what answer gave he?

I. Ber.   That there was
No punishment for such as Barbaro.

Cal. I told you so before, and that 'twas idle
To think of justice from such hands.

I. Ber.   At least,
It lull'd suspicion, showing confidence.
Had I been silent, not a sbirro but
Had kept me in his eye, as meditating
A silent, solitary, deep revenge.

Cal. But wherefore not address you to the Council?
The Doge is a mere puppet, who can scarce
Obtain right for himself.   Why speak to him?

I. Ber. You shall know that hereafter.

Cal.   Why not now?

I. Ber. Be patient but till midnight.   Get your musters,
And bid our friends prepare their companies:—
Set all in readiness to strike the blow,
Perhaps in a few hours; we have long waited
For a fit time—that hour is on the dial,
It may be, of to-morrow's sun: delay
Beyond may breed us double danger.   See
That all be punctual at our place of meeting,
And arm'd, excepting those of the Sixteen,
Who will remain among the troops to wait
The signal.

Cal.   These brave words have breathed new life
Into my veins; I am sick of these protracted
And hesitating councils: day on day
Crawl'd on, and added but another link
To our long fetters, and some fresher wrong
Inflicted on our brethren or ourselves,
Helping to swell our tyrants' bloated strength.
Let us but deal upon them, and I care not

For the result, which must be death or freedom!
  I 'm weary to the heart of finding neither.
I. Ber. We will be free in life or death! the grave
  Is chainless. Have you all the musters ready?
  And are the sixteen companies completed
  To sixty?
Cal.   All save two, in which there are
  Twenty-five wanting to make up the number.
I. Ber. No matter; we can do without. Whose are they?
Cal. Bertram's and old Soranzo's, both of whom
  Appear less forward in the cause than we are.
I. Ber. Your fiery nature makes you deem all those
  Who are not restless cold: but there exists
  Oft in concentrated spirits not less daring
  Than in more loud avengers. Do not doubt them.
Cal. I do not doubt the elder; but in Bertram
  There is a hesitating softness, fatal
  To enterprise like ours: I 've seen that man
  Weep like an infant o'er the misery
  Of others, heedless of his own, though greater;
  And in a recent quarrel I beheld him
  Turn sick at sight of blood, although a villain's.
I. Ber. The truly brave are soft of heart and eyes,
  And feel for what their duty bids them do.
  I have known Bertram long; there doth not breathe
  A soul more full of honour.
Cal.   It may be so:
  I apprehend less treachery than weakness;
  Yet as he has no mistress, and no wife
  To work upon his milkiness of spirit,
  He may go through the ordeal; it is well
  He is an orphan, friendless save in us:
  A woman or a child had made him less
  Than either in resolve.
I. Ber.   Such ties are not
  For those who are call'd to the high destinies
  Which purify corrupted commonwealths;
  We must forget all feelings save the *one*—
  We must resign all passions save our purpose—
  We must behold no object save our country—
  And only look on death as beautiful,
  So that the sacrifice ascend to heaven,
  And draw down freedom on her evermore.
Cal. But if we fail——
I. Ber.   They never fail who die
  In a great cause: the block may soak their gore;

Their heads may sodden in the sun; their limbs
Be strung to city gates and castle walls—
But still their spirit walks abroad.   Though years
Elapse, and others share as dark a doom,
They but augment the deep and sweeping thoughts
Which overpower all others, and conduct
The world at last to freedom: What were we,
If Brutus had not lived?   He died in giving
Rome liberty, but left a deathless lesson—
A name which is a virtue, and a soul
Which multiplies itself throughout all time
When wicked men wax mighty, and a state
Turns servile: he and his high friend were styled
'The last of Romans!'   Let us be the first
Of true Venetians, sprung from Roman sires.

Cal. Our fathers did not fly from Attila
Into these isles, where palaces have sprung
On banks redeem'd from the rude ocean's ooze,
To own a thousand despots in his place.
Better bow down before the Hun, and call
A Tartar lord, than these swoln silkworms masters!
The first at least was man, and used his sword
As sceptre: these unmanly creeping things
Command our swords, and rule us with a word
As with a spell.

I. Ber.   It shall be broken soon.
You say that all things are in readiness:
To-day I have not been the usual round,
And why thou knowest; but thy vigilance
Will better have supplied my care: these orders
In recent council to redouble now
Our efforts to repair the galleys, have
Lent a fair colour to the introduction
Of many of our cause into the arsenal,
As new artificers for their equipment,
Or fresh recruits obtain'd in haste to man
The hoped-for fleet.—Are all supplied with arms?

Cal. All who were deem'd trustworthy: there are some
Whom it were well to keep in ignorance
Till it be time to strike, and then supply them;
When in the heat and hurry of the hour
They have no opportunity to pause,
But needs must on with those who will surround them.

I. Ber. You have said well.   Have you remark'd all such?

Cal. I've noted most; and caused the other chiefs
To use like caution in their companies.

As far as I have seen, we are enough
To make the enterprise secure, if 'tis
Commenced to-morrow; but, till 'tis begun,
Each hour is pregnant with a thousand perils.

I. Ber. Let the Sixteen meet at the wonted hour.
Except Soranzo, Nicoletto Blondo,
And Marco Giuda, who will keep their watch
Within the arsenal, and hold all ready
Expectant of the signal we will fix on.

Cal. We will not fail.

I. Ber.   Let all the rest be there;
I have a stranger to present to them.

Cal. A stranger! doth he know the secret?

I. Ber.   Yes.

Cal. And have you dared to peril your friends' lives
On a rash confidence in one we know not?

I. Ber. I have risk'd no man's life except my own—
Of that be certain: he is one who may
Make our assurance doubly sure, according
His aid; and if reluctant, he no less
Is in our power: he comes alone with me,
And cannot 'scape us; but he will not swerve.

Cal. I cannot judge of this until I know him:
Is he one of our order?

I. Ber.   Ay, in spirit,
Although a child of greatness; he is one
Who would become a throne, or overthrow one—
One who has done great deeds, and seen great changes;
No tyrant, though bred up to tyranny;
Valiant in war, and sage in council; noble
In nature, although haughty; quick, yet wary:
Yet for all this, so full of certain passions,
That if once stirr'd and baffled, as he has been
Upon the tenderest points, there is no Fury
In Grecian story like to that which wrings
His vitals with her burning hands, till he
Grows capable of all things for revenge;
And add too, that his mind is liberal,
He sees and feels the people are oppress'd,
And shares their sufferings. Take him all in all,
We have need of such, and such have need of us.

Cal. And what part would you have him take with us?

I. Ber. It may be, that of chief.

Cal.   What! and resign
Your own command as leader?

I. Ber.   Even so.
    My object is to make your cause end well,
    And not to push myself to power. Experience,
    Some skill, and your own choice, had marked me out
    To act in trust as your commander, till
    Some worthier should appear: if I have found such
    As you yourselves shall own more worthy, think you
    That I would hesitate from selfishness,
    And, covetous of brief authority,
    Stake our deep interest on my single thoughts,
    Rather than yield to one above me in
    All leading qualities? No, Calendaro,
    Know your friend better; but you all shall judge.—
    Away! and let us meet at the fix'd hour.
    Be vigilant, and all will yet go well.
Cal. Worthy Bertuccio, I have known you ever
    Trusty and brave, with head and heart to plan
    What I have still been prompt to execute.
    For my own part, I seek no other chief;
    What the rest will decide I know not, but
    I am with you, as I have ever been,
    In all our undertakings. Now farewell,
    Until the hour of midnight sees us meet.   [*Exeunt.*

ACT III

SCENE I

*Scene, the Space between the Canal and the Church of San Giovanni
e San Paolo. An equestrian Statue before it.—A Gondola lies in
the Canal at some distance.*

Enter the DOGE alone, disguised.

Doge. [*Solus.*] I am before the hour, the hour, whose voice,
    Pealing into the arch of night, might strike
    These palaces with ominous tottering,
    And rock their marbles to the corner-stone,
    Waking the sleepers from some hideous dream
    Of indistinct but awful augury
    Of that which will befall them. Yes, proud city!
    Thou must be cleansed of the black blood which makes thee
    A lazar-house of tyranny: the task
    Is forced upon me, I have sought it not;
    And therefore was I punish'd, seeing this
    Patrician pestilence spread on and on,

Until at length it smote me in my slumbers,
And I am tainted, and must wash away
The plague-spots in the healing wave.   Tall fane!
Where sleep my fathers, whose dim statues shadow
The floor which doth divide us from the dead,
Where all the pregnant hearts of our cold blood,
Moulder'd into a mite of ashes, hold
In one shrunk heap what once made many heroes,
When what is now a handful shook the earth—
Fane of the tutelar saints who guard our house!
Vault where two Doges rest—my sires! who died
The one of toil, the other in the field,
With a long race of other lineal chiefs
And sages, whose great labours, wounds, and state
I have inherited,—let the graves gape,
Till all thine aisles be peopled with the dead,
And pour them from thy portals to gaze on me!
I call them up, and them and thee to witness
What it hath been which put me to this task—
Their pure high blood, their blazon-roll of glories,
Their mighty name dishonour'd all *in* me,
Not *by* me, but by the ungrateful nobles
We fought to make our equals, not our lords:—
And chiefly thou, Ordelafo the brave,
Who perish'd in the field, where I since conquer'd,
Battling at Zara, did the hecatombs
Of thine and Venice' foes, there offer'd up
By thy descendant, merit such acquittance?
Spirits! smile down upon me, for my cause
Is yours, in all life now can be of yours,—
Your fame, your name, all mingled up in mine,
And in the future fortunes of our race!
Let me but prosper, and I make this city
Free and immortal, and our house's name
Worthier of what you were, now and hereafter!

Enter ISRAEL BERTUCCIO

I. Ber. Who goes there?
Doge.   A friend to Venice.
I. Ber.   'Tis he.
     Welcome, my lord,—you are before the time.
Doge. I am ready to proceed to your assembly.
I. Ber. Have with you.—I am proud and pleased to see
     Such confident alacrity.   Your doubts
     Since our last meeting, then, are all dispell'd?

Doge. Not so—but I have set my little left
　　Of life upon this cast: the die was thrown
　　When I first listened to your treason.—Start not!
　　That is the word; I cannot shape my tongue
　　To syllable black deeds into smooth names,
　　Though I be wrought on to commit them. When
　　I heard you tempt your sovereign, and forbore
　　To have you dragg'd to prison, I became
　　Your guiltiest accomplice: now you may
　　If it so please you, do as much by me.

I. Ber. Strange words, my lord, and most unmerited;
　　I am no spy, and neither are we traitors.

Doge. *We—We!*—no matter—you have earn'd the right
　　To talk of *us.*—But to the point.—If this
　　Attempt succeeds, and Venice, render'd free
　　And flourishing, when we are in our graves,
　　Conducts her generations to our tombs,
　　And makes her children with their little hands
　　Strew flowers o'er her deliverers' ashes, then
　　The consequence will sanctify the deed,
　　And we shall be like the two Bruti in
　　The annals of hereafter; but if not,
　　If we should fail, employing bloody means
　　And secret plot, although to a good end,
　　Still we are traitors, honest Israel;—thou
　　No less than he who was thy sovereign
　　Six hours ago, and now thy brother rebel.

I. Ber. 'Tis not the moment to consider thus,
　　Else I could answer.—Let us to the meeting,
　　Or we may be observed in lingering here.

Doge. We *are* observed, and have been.

I. Ber. 　　　　　　　　　　We observed!
　　Let me discover—and this steel——

Doge. 　　　　　　　　　　　　　Put up;
　　Here are no human witnesses: look there—
　　What see you?

I. Ber. 　　　　Only a tall warrior's statue
　　Bestriding a proud steed, in the dim light
　　Of the dull moon.

Doge. 　　　　That warrior was the sire
　　Of my sire's fathers, and that statue was
　　Decreed to him by the twice rescued city:—
　　Think you that he looks down on us or no?

I. Ber. My lord, these are mere fantasies; there are
　　No eyes in marble.

Doge.   But there are in Death.
I tell thee, man, there is a spirit in
Such things that acts and sees, unseen, though felt;
And, if there be a spell to stir the dead,
'Tis in such deeds as we are now upon.
Deem'st thou the souls of such a race as mine
Can rest, when he, their last descendant chief,
Stands plotting on the brink of their pure graves
With stung plebeians?
I. Ber.   It had been as well
To have ponder'd this before,—ere you embark'd
In our great enterprise.—Do you repent?
Doge. No, but I *feel*, and shall do to the last.
I cannot quench a glorious life at once,
Nor dwindle to the thing I now must be,
And take men's lives by stealth, without some pause:
Yet doubt me not; it is this very feeling,
And knowing *what* has wrung me to be thus,
Which is your best security.   There 's not
A roused mechanic in your busy plot
So wrong'd as I, so fall'n, so loudly call'd
To his redress: the very means I am forced
By these fell tyrants to adopt is such,
That I abhor them doubly for the deeds
Which I must do to pay them back for theirs.
I. Ber. Let us away—hark—the hour strikes.
Doge.   On—on—
It is our knell, or that of Venice—On.
I. Ber. Say, rather, 'tis her freedom's rising peal
Of triumph.—This way—we are near the place.   [*Exeunt.*

SCENE II

The House where the Conspirators meet

DAGOLINO, DORO, BERTRAM, FEDELE TREVISANO, CALEN-
DARO, ANTONIO DELLE BENDE, *etc. etc.*

Cal. [*Entering.*] Are all here?
Dag.   All with you; except the three
On duty, and our leader Israel,
Who is expected momently.
Cal.   Where 's Bertram?
Ber. Here!
Cal.   Have you not been able to complete
The number wanting in your company?

Ber. I had mark'd out some: but I have not dared
    To trust them with the secret, till assured
    That they were worthy faith.
Cal.   There is no need
    Of trusting to their faith: *who*, save ourselves
    And our more chosen comrades, is aware
    Fully of our intent? they think themselves
    Engaged in secret to the Signory,
    To punish some more dissolute young nobles
    Who have defied the law in their excesses;
    But once drawn up, and their new swords well-flesh'd
    In the rank hearts of the more odious senators,
    They will not hesitate to follow up
    Their blow upon the others, when they see
    The example of their chiefs, and I for one
    Will set them such, that they for very shame
    And safety will not pause till all have perished.
Ber. How say you? *all!*
Cal.   Whom wouldst thou spare?
Ber.   *I spare?*
    I have no power to spare. I only question'd,
    Thinking that even amongst these wicked men
    There might be some, whose age and qualities
    Might mark them out for pity.
Cal.   Yes, such pity
    As when the viper hath been cut to pieces,
    The separate fragments quivering in the sun,
    In the last energy of venomous life,
    Deserve and have. Why, I should think as soon
    Of pitying some particular fang which made
    One in the jaw of the swoln serpent, as
    Of saving one of these: they form but links
    Of one long chain; one mass, one breath, one body;
    They eat, and drink, and live, and breed together,
    Revel, and lie, oppress, and kill in concert,—
    So let them die as *one!*
Dag.   Should *one* survive,
    He would be dangerous as the whole; it is not
    Their number, be it tens or thousands, but
    The spirit of this aristocracy
    Which must be rooted out; and if there were
    A single shoot of the old tree in life,
    'Twould fasten in the soil, and spring again
    To gloomy verdure and to bitter fruit.
    Bertram, we must be firm!

Cal.   Look to it well,
  Bertram; I have an eye upon thee.
Ber.   Who
    Distrusts me?
Cal.   Not I; for if I did so,
  Thou wouldst not now be there to talk of trust:
  It is **thy** softness, not thy want of faith,
  Which makes thee to be doubted.
Ber.   You should know
  Who hear me, who and what I am; a man
  Roused like yourselves to overthrow oppression;
  A kind man, I am apt to think, as some
  Of you have found me; and if brave or no,
  You, Calendaro, can pronounce, who have seen me
  Put to the proof; or, if you should have doubts,
  I'll clear them on your person!
Cal.   You are welcome,
  When once our enterprise is o'er, which must not
  Be interrupted by a private brawl.
Ber. I am no brawler; but can bear myself
  As far among the foe as any he
  Who hears me; else why have I been selected
  To be of your chief comrades? but no less
  I own my natural weakness; I have not
  Yet learn'd to think of indiscriminate murder
  Without some sense of shuddering; and the sight
  Of blood which spouts through hoary scalps is not
  To me a thing of triumph, nor the death
  Of man surprised a glory. Well—too well
  I know that we must do such things on those
  Whose acts have raised up such avengers; but
  If there were some of these who could be saved
  From out this sweeping fate, for our own sakes
  And for our honour, to take off some stain
  Of massacre, which else pollutes it wholly,
  I had been glad; and see no cause in this
  For sneer, nor for suspicion!
Dag.   Calm thee, Bertram;
  For we suspect thee not, and take good heart.
  It is the cause, and not our will, which asks
  Such actions from our hands; we'll wash away
  All stains in Freedom's fountain!

Enter ISRAEL BERTUCCIO, *and the* DOGE, *disguised.*

Dag.   Welcome, Israel.

Consp. Most welcome.—Brave Bertuccio, thou art late—
    Who is this stranger?
Cal.   It is time to name him.
    Our comrades are even now prepared to greet him
    In brotherhood, as I have made it known
    That thou wouldst add a brother to our cause,
    Approved by thee, and thus approved by all,
    Such is our trust in all thine actions.   Now
    Let him unfold himself.
I. Ber.   Stranger, step forth!
                            [*The* DOGE *discovers himself.*

Consp. To arms!—we are betray'd—it is the Doge!
    Down with them both! our traitorous captain, and
    The tyrant he hath sold us to.
Cal. [*Drawing his sword.*]   Hold! hold!
    Who moves a step against them dies.   Hold! hear
    Bertuccio—What! are you appall'd to see
    A lone, unguarded, weaponless old man
    Amongst you?—Israel, speak! what means this mystery?
I. Ber. Let them advance and strike at their own bosoms,
    Ungrateful suicides! for on our lives
    Depend their own, their fortunes, and their hopes.
Doge. Strike!—If I dreaded death, a death more fearful
    Than any your rash weapons can inflict,
    I should not now be here:—Oh, noble Courage!
    The eldest born of Fear, which makes you brave
    Against this solitary hoary head!
    See the bold chiefs, who would reform a state
    And shake down senates, mad with wrath and dread
    At sight of one patrician!—Butcher me,
    You can; I care not.—Israel, are these men
    The mighty hearts you spoke of? look upon them!
Cal. Faith! he hath shamed us, and deservedly.
    Was this your trust in your true chief Bertuccio,
    To turn your swords against him and his guest?
    Sheathe them, and hear him.
I. Ber.   I disdain to speak.
    They might and must have known a heart like mine
    Incapable of treachery; and the power
    They gave me to adopt all fitting means
    To further their design was ne'er abused.
    They might be certain that whoe'er was brought
    By me into this council had been led
    To take his choice—as brother, or as victim.
Doge. And which am I to be? your actions leave
    Some cause to doubt the freedom of the choice.

I. Ber. My lord, we would have perish'd here together,
    Had these rash men proceeded; but, behold,
    They are ashamed of that mad moment's impulse,
    And droop their heads; believe me, they are such
    As I described them.—Speak to them.

Cal.   Ay, speak;
    We are all listening in wonder.

I. Ber. [*Addressing the Conspirators.*] You are safe,
    Nay, more, almost triumphant—listen then,
    And know my words for truth.

Doge.   You see me here,
    As one of you hath said, an old, unarm'd,
    Defenceless man; and yesterday you saw me
    Presiding in the hall of ducal state,
    Apparent sovereign of our hundred isles,
    Robed in official purple, dealing out
    The edicts of a power which is not mine,
    Nor yours, but of our masters—the patricians.
    Why I was there you know, or think you know;
    Why I am *here*, he who hath been most wrong'd,
    He who among you hath been most insulted,
    Outraged and trodden on, until he doubt
    If he be worm or no, may answer for me,
    Asking of his own heart what brought him here?
    You know my recent story, all men know it,
    And judge of it far differently from those
    Who sate in judgment to heap scorn on scorn.
    But spare me the recital—it is here,
    Here at my heart the outrage—but my words,
    Already spent in unavailing plaints,
    Would only show my feebleness the more,
    And I come here to strengthen even the strong,
    And urge them on to deeds, and not to war
    With woman's weapons; but I need not urge you.
    Our private wrongs have sprung from public vices
    In this—I cannot call it commonwealth
    Nor kingdom, which hath neither prince nor people,
    But all the sins of the old Spartan state
    Without its virtues—temperance and valour.
    The Lords of Lacedaemon were true soldiers,
    But ours are Sybarites, while we are Helots,
    Of whom I am the lowest, most enslaved;
    Although dress'd out to head a pageant, as
    The Greeks of yore made drunk their slaves to form
    A pastime for their children. You are met
    To overthrow this monster of a state,

This mockery of a government, this spectre,
Which must be exorcised with blood,—and then
We will renew the times of truth and justice,
Condensing in a fair free commonwealth
Not rash equality but equal rights,
Proportion'd like the columns to the temple,
Giving and taking strength reciprocal,
And making firm the whole with grace and beauty,
So that no part could be removed without
Infringement of the general symmetry.
In operating this great change, I claim
To be one of you—if you trust in me;
If not, strike home,—my life is compromised,
And I would rather fall by freemen's hands
Than live another day to act the tyrant
As delegate of tyrants: such I am not,
And never have been—read it in our annals;
I can appeal to my past government
In many lands and cities; they can tell you
If I were an oppressor, or a man
Feeling and thinking for my fellow men.
Haply had I been what the senate sought,
A thing of robes and trinkets, dizen'd out
To sit in state as for a sovereign's picture;
A popular scourge, a ready sentence-signer,
A stickler for the Senate and 'the Forty,'
A sceptic for all measures which had not
The sanction of 'the Ten,' a council-fawner,
A tool, a fool, a puppet,—they had ne'er
Foster'd the wretch who stung me. What I suffer
Has reach'd me through my pity for the people;
That many know, and they who know not yet
Will one day learn: meantime I do devote,
Whate'er the issue, my last days of life—
My present power such as it is, not that
Of Doge, but of a man who has been great
Before he was degraded to a Doge,
And still has individual means and mind;
I stake my fame (and I had fame)—my breath—
(The least of all, for its last hours are nigh)
My heart, my hope, my soul, upon this cast!
Such as I am, I offer me to you
And to your chiefs, accept me or reject me,
A Prince who fain would be a citizen
Or nothing, and who has left his throne to be so.
Cal. Long live Faliero!—Venice shall be free!

Consp. Long live Faliero!
I. Ber.   Comrades! did I well?
  Is not this man a host in such a cause?
Doge. This is no time for eulogies, nor place
  For exultation. Am I one of you?
Cal. Ay, and the first amongst us, as thou hast been
  Of Venice—be our general and chief.
Doge. Chief!—general!—I was general at Zara,
  And chief in Rhodes and Cyprus, prince in Venice:
  I cannot stoop——that is, I am not fit
  To lead a band of——patriots: when I lay
  Aside the dignities which I have borne,
  'Tis not to put on others, but to be
  Mate to my fellows—but now to the point:
  Israel has stated to me your whole plan—
  'Tis bold, but feasible if I assist it,
  And must be set in motion instantly.
Cal. E'en when thou wilt. Is it not so, my friends?
  I have disposed all for a sudden blow;
  When shall it be then?
Doge.   At sunrise.
Ber.   So soon?
Doge. So soon?—so late—each hour accumulates
  Peril on peril, and the more so now
  Since I have mingled with you;—know you not
  The Council, and 'the Ten'? the spies, the eyes
  Of the patricians dubious of their slaves,
  And now more dubious of the prince they have made one?
  I tell you, you must strike, and suddenly,
  Full to the Hydra's heart—its heads will follow.
Cal. With all my soul and sword, I yield assent;
  Our companies are ready, sixty each,
  And all now under arms by Israel's order;
  Each at their different place of rendezvous,
  And vigilant, expectant of some blow;
  Let each repair for action to his post!
  And now, my lord, the signal?
Doge.   When you hear
  The great bell of Saint Mark's, which may not be
  Struck without special order of the Doge
  (The last poor privilege they leave their prince),
  March on Saint Mark's!
I. Ber.   And there?—
Doge.   By different routes
  Let your march be directed, every sixty
  Entering a separate avenue, and still

Upon the way let your cry be of war
And of the Genoese fleet, by the first dawn
Discern'd before the port; form round the palace,
Within whose court will be drawn out in arms
My nephew and the clients of our house,
Many and martial; while the bell tolls on,
Shout ye, 'Saint Mark!—the foe is on our waters!'

Cal. I see it now—but on, my noble lord.

Doge. All the patricians flocking to the Council,
(Which they dare not refuse, at the dread signal
Pealing from out their patron saint's proud tower,)
Will then be gather'd in unto the harvest,
And we will reap them with the sword for sickle.
If some few should be tardy or absent them,
'Twill be but to be taken faint and single,
When the majority are put to rest.

Cal. Would that the hour were come! we will not scotch,
But kill.

Ber.   Once more, sir, with your pardon, I
Would now repeat the question which I ask'd
Before Bertuccio added to our cause
This great ally who renders it more sure,
And therefore safer, and as such admits
Some dawn of mercy to a portion of
Our victims—must all perish in this slaughter?

Cal. All who encounter me and mine, be sure,
The mercy they have shown, I show.

Consp.   All! all!
Is this a time to talk of pity? when
Have they e'er shown, or felt, or feign'd it?

I. Ber.   Bertram,
This false compassion is a folly, and
Injustice to thy comrades and thy cause!
Dost thou not see, that if we single out
Some for escape, they live but to avenge
The fallen? and how distinguish now the innocent
From out the guilty? all their acts are *one*—
A single emanation from one body,
Together knit for our oppression! 'Tis
Much that we let their children live; I doubt
If all of these even should be set apart:
The hunter may reserve some single cub
From out the tiger's litter, but who e'er
Would seek to save the spotted sire or dam,
Unless to perish by their fangs? however,

I will abide by Doge Faliero's counsel:
Let him decide if any should be saved.

Doge. Ask me not—tempt me not with such a question—
Decide yourselves.

I. Ber.   You know their private virtues
Far better than we can, to whom alone
Their public vices, and most foul oppression,
Have made them deadly; if there be amongst them
One who deserves to be repeal'd, pronounce.

Doge. Dolfino's father was my friend, and Lando
Fought by my side, and Marc Cornaro shared
My Genoese embassy: I saved the life
Of Veniero—shall I save it twice?
Would that I could save them and Venice also!
All these men, or their fathers, were my friends
Till they became my subjects, then fell from me
As faithless leaves drop from the o'erblown flower,
And left me a lone blighted thorny stalk,
Which, in its solitude, can shelter nothing;
So, as they let me wither, let them perish!

Cal. They cannot co-exist with Venice' freedom!

Doge. Ye, though you know and feel our mutual mass
Of many wrongs, even ye are ignorant
What fatal poison to the springs of life,
To human ties, and all that's good and dear,
Lurks in the present institutes of Venice:
All these men were my friends; I loved them, they
Requited honourably my regards;
We served and fought; we smiled and wept in concert;
We revell'd or we sorrow'd side by side;
We made alliances of blood and marriage;
We grew in years and honours fairly,—till
Their own desire, not my ambition, made
Them choose me for their prince, and then farewell!
Farewell all social memory! all thoughts
In common! and sweet bonds which link old friendships,
When the survivors of long years and actions,
Which now belong to history, soothe the days
Which yet remain by treasuring each other,
And never meet, but each beholds the mirror
Of half a century on his brother's brow,
And sees a hundred beings, now in earth,
Flit round them whispering of the days gone by,
And seeming not all dead, as long as two
Of the brave, joyous, reckless, glorious band,
Which once were one and many, still retain

A breath to sigh for them, a tongue to speak
Of deeds that else were silent, save on marble——
Oime! Oime!—and must I do this deed?

I. Ber. My lord, you are much moved: it is not now
That such things must be dwelt upon.

Doge.   Your patience
A moment—I recede not: mark with me
The gloomy vices of this government.
From the hour that made me Doge, the *Doge* THEY *made* me—
Farewell the past! I died to all that had been,
Or rather they to me: no friends, no kindness,
No privacy of life—all were cut off:
They came not near me, such approach gave umbrage;
They could not love me, such was not the law;
They thwarted me, 'twas the state's policy;
They baffled me, 'twas a patrician's duty;
They wrong'd me, for such was to right the state;
They could not right me, that would give suspicion;
So that I was a slave to my own subjects;
So that I was a foe to my own friends;
Begirt with spies for guards—with robes for power—
With pomp for freedom—gaolers for a council—
Inquisitors for friends—and hell for life!
I had one only fount of quiet left,
And *that* they poison'd! My pure household gods
Were shiver'd on my hearth, and o'er their shrine
Sate grinning Ribaldry and sneering Scorn.

I. Ber. You have been deeply wrong'd, and now shall be
Nobly avenged before another night.

Doge. I had borne all—it hurt me, but I bore it—
Till this last running over of the cup
Of bitterness—until this last loud insult,
Not only unredress'd, but sanction'd; then,
And thus, I cast all further feelings from me—
The feelings which they crush'd for me, long, long
Before, even in their oath of false allegiance!
Even in that very hour and vow, they abjured
Their friend and made a sovereign, as boys make
Playthings, to do their pleasure—and be broken!
I from that hour have seen but senators
In dark suspicious conflict with the Doge,
Brooding with him in mutual hate and fear;
They dreading he should snatch the tyranny
From out their grasp, and he abhorring tyrants.
To me, then, these men have no *private* life,
Nor claim to ties they have cut off from others;

As senators for arbitrary acts
Amenable, I look on them—as such
Let them be dealt upon.

Cal.   And now to action!
Hence, brethren, to our posts, and may this be
The last night of mere words: I'd fain be doing!
Saint Mark's great bell at dawn shall find me wakeful!

I. Ber. Disperse then to your posts: be firm and vigilant;
Think on the wrongs we bear, the rights we claim.
This day and night shall be the last of peril!
Watch for the signal, and then march. I go
To join my band; let each be prompt to marshal
His separate charge: the Doge will now return
To the palace to prepare all for the blow.
We part to meet in freedom and in glory!

Cal. Doge, when I greet you next, my homage to you
Shall be the head of Steno on this sword!

Doge. No; let him be reserved unto the last,
Nor turn aside to strike at such a prey,
Till nobler game is quarried: his offence
Was a mere ebullition of the vice,
The general corruption generated
By the foul aristocracy: he could not—
He dared not in more honourable days
Have risk'd it. I have merged all private wrath
Against him in the thought of our great purpose.
A slave insults me—I require his punishment
From his proud master's hands; if he refuse it,
The offence grows his, and let him answer it.

Cal. Yet, as the immediate cause of the alliance
Which consecrates our undertaking more,
I owe him such deep gratitude, that fain
I would repay him as he merits; may I?

Doge. You would but lop the hand, and I the head;
You would but smite the scholar, I the master;
You would but punish Steno, I the senate.
I cannot pause on individual hate,
In the absorbing, sweeping, whole revenge,
Which, like the sheeted fire from heaven, must blast
Without distinction, as it fell of yore,
Where the Dead Sea hath quench'd two cities' ashes.

I. Ber. Away, then, to your posts! I but remain
A moment to accompany the Doge
To our late place of tryst, to see no spies
Have been upon the scout, and thence I hasten
To where my allotted band is under arms.

Cal. Farewell, then,—until dawn!
I. Ber.   Success go with you!
Consp. We will not fail—Away!   My lord, farewell!
      [*The Conspirators salute the* DOGE *and* ISRAEL BERTUCCIO,
         and retire, headed by PHILIP CALENDARO. *The* DOGE *and*
         ISRAEL BERTUCCIO *remain.*
I. Ber. We have them in the toil—it cannot fail!
  Now thou 'rt indeed a sovereign, and wilt make
  A name immortal greater than the greatest:
  Free citizens have struck at kings ere now;
  Caesars have fallen, and even patrician hands
  Have crush'd dictators, as the popular steel
  Has reach'd patricians: but, until this hour,
  What prince has plotted for his people's freedom?
  Or risk'd a life to liberate his subjects?
  For ever, and for ever, they conspire
  Against the people, to abuse their hands
  To chains, but laid aside to carry weapons
  Against the fellow nations, so that yoke
  On yoke, and slavery and death may whet,
  Not glut, the never-gorged Leviathan!
  Now, my lord, to our enterprise;—'tis great,
  And greater the reward; why stand you rapt?
  A moment back, and you were all impatience!
Doge. And is it then decided! must they die?
I. Ber. Who?
Doge.   My own friends by blood and courtesy,
  And many deeds and days—the senators?
I. Ber. You pass'd their sentence, and it is a just one.
Doge. Ay, so it seems, and so it is to *you*;
  You are a patriot, plebeian Gracchus—
  The rebels' oracle, the people's tribune—
  I blame you not—you act in your vocation;
  They smote you, and oppress'd you, and despised you;
  So they have *me*: but *you* ne'er spake with them;
  You never broke their bread, nor shared their salt;
  You never had their wine-cup at your lips;
  You grew not up with them, nor laugh'd, nor wept,
  Nor held a revel in their company;
  Ne'er smiled to see them smile, nor claim'd their smile
  In social interchange for yours, nor trusted
  Nor wore them in your heart of hearts, as I have;
  These hairs of mine are grey, and so are theirs,
  The elders of the council: I remember
  When all our locks were like the raven's wing,
  As we went forth to take our prey around

The isles wrung from the false Mahometan;
And can I see them dabbled o'er with blood?
Each ſtab to them will seem my suicide.
I. Ber. Doge! Doge! this vacillation is unworthy
A child; if you are not in second childhood,
Call back your nerves to your own purpose, nor
Thus shame yourself and me.   By heavens! I'd rather
Forego even now, or fail in our intent,
Than see the man I venerate subside
From high resolves into such shallow weakness!
You have seen blood in battle, shed it, both
Your own and that of others; can you shrink then
From a few drops from veins of hoary vampires,
Who but give back what they have drain'd from millions?
Doge. Bear with me!   Step by ſtep, and blow on blow,
I will divide with you; think not I waver:
Ah! no; it is the *certainty* of all
Which I muſt do doth make me tremble thus.
But let these laſt and lingering thoughts have way
To which you only and the night are conscious,
And both regardless; when the hour arrives,
'Tis mine to sound the knell, and ſtrike the blow,
Which shall unpeople many palaces,
And hew the higheſt genealogic trees
Down to the earth, strew'd with their bleeding fruit,
And crush their blossoms into barrenness:
This will I—muſt I—have I sworn to do,
Nor aught can turn me from my deſtiny;
But ſtill I quiver to behold what I
Muſt be, and think what I have been!   Bear witʰ ne.
I. Ber. Re-man your breaſt; I feel no such remorse,
I underſtand it not: why should you change?
You acted, and you act, on your free will.
Doge. Ay, there it is—*you* feel not, nor do I,
Else I should ſtab thee on the spot, to save
A thousand lives, and, killing, do no murder;
You *feel* not—*you* go to this butcher-work
As if these high-born men were ſteers for shambles!
When all is over, you 'll be free and merry
And calmly wash those hands incarnadine;
But I, outgoing thee and all thy fellows
In this surpassing massacre, shall be,
Shall see and feel—oh God! oh God! 'tis true
And thou doſt well to answer that it was
'My own free will and act,' and yet you err,
For I *will* do this!   Doubt not—fear not; I

Will be your most unmerciful accomplice!
And yet I act no more on my free will,
Nor my own feelings—both compel me back;
But there is *hell* within me and around,
And like the demon who believes and trembles
Must I abhor and do.   Away! away!
Get thee unto thy fellows, I will hie me
To gather the retainers of our house.
Doubt not, Saint Mark's great bell shall wake all Venice,
Except her slaughter'd senate: ere the sun
Be broad upon the Adriatic there
Shall be the voice of weeping, which shall drown
The roar of waters in the cry of blood!
I am resolved—come on.

I. *Ber.*   With all my soul!
Keep a firm rein upon these bursts of passion;
Remember what these men have dealt to thee,
And that this sacrifice will be succeeded
By ages of prosperity and freedom
To this unshackled city: a true tyrant
Would have depopulated empires, nor
Have felt the strange compunction which hath wrung you
To punish a few traitors to the people.
Trust me, such were a pity more misplaced
Than the late mercy of the state to Steno.

Doge. Man, thou hast struck upon the chord which jars
All nature from my heart.   Hence to our task!   [*Exeunt.*

ACT IV

SCENE I

Palazzo of the Patrician LIONI. LIONI *laying aside the mask and
cloak which the Venetian Nobles wore in public, attended by a
Domestic.*

Lioni. I will to rest, right weary of this revel.
The gayest we have held for many moons,
And yet, I know not why, it cheer'd me not;
There came a heaviness across my heart,
Which, in the lightest movement of the dance,
Though eye to eye, and hand in hand united
Even with the lady of my love, oppress'd me,
And through my spirit chill'd my blood, until
A damp like death rose o'er my brow; I strove
To laugh the thought away, but 'twould not be;

Through all the music ringing in my ears
A knell was sounding as distinct and clear,
Though low and far, as e'er the Adrian wave
Rose o'er the city's murmur in the night,
Dashing against the outward Lido's bulwark:
So that I left the festival before
It reach'd its zenith, and will woo my pillow
For thoughts more tranquil, or forgetfulness.
Antonio, take my mask and cloak, and light
The lamp within my chamber.

Ant.   Yes, my lord:
Command you no refreshment?

Lioni.   Nought, save sleep,
Which will not be commanded.   Let me hope it,
                                        [*Exit* ANTONIO
Though my breast feels too anxious; I will try
Whether the air will calm my spirits: 'tis
A goodly night; the cloudy wind which blew
From the Levant hath crept into its cave,
And the broad moon has brighten'd.   What a stillness!
                                 [*Goes to an open lattice.*
And what a contrast with the scene I left,
Where the tall torches' glare, and silver lamps'
More pallid gleam along the tapestried walls,
Spread over the reluctant gloom which haunts
Those vast and dimly-latticed galleries
A dazzling mass of artificial light,
Which show'd all things, but nothing as they were.
There Age essaying to recall the past,
After long striving for the hues of youth
At the sad labour of the toilet, and
Full many a glance at the too faithful mirror,
Prank'd forth in all the pride of ornament,
Forgot itself, and trusting to the falsehood
Of the indulgent beams, which show, yet hide,
Believed itself forgotten, and was fool'd.
There Youth, which needed not, nor thought of such
Vain adjuncts, lavish'd its true bloom, and health,
And bridal beauty, in the unwholesome press
Of flush'd and crowded wassailers, and wasted
Its hours of rest in dreaming this was pleasure,
And so shall waste them till the sunrise streams
On sallow cheeks and sunken eyes, which should not
Have worn this aspect yet for many a year.
The music, and the banquet, and the wine—
The garlands, the rose odours, and the flowers—

The sparkling eyes, and flashing ornaments—
The white arms and the raven hair—the braids
And bracelets; swanlike bosoms, and the necklace,
An India in itself, yet dazzling not
The eye like what it circled; the thin robes,
Floating like light clouds 'twixt our gaze and heaven;
The many-twinkling feet so small and sylphlike,
Suggesting the more secret symmetry
Of the fair forms which terminate so well—
All the delusion of the dizzy scene,
Its false and true enchantments—art and nature,
Which swam before my giddy eyes, that drank
The sight of beauty as the parch'd pilgrim's
On Arab sands the false mirage, which offers
A lucid lake to his eluded thirst,
Are gone.—Around me are the stars and waters—
Worlds mirror'd in the ocean, goodlier sight
Than torches glared back by a gaudy glass;
And the great element, which is to space
What ocean is to earth, spreads its blue depths,
Soften'd with the first breathings of the spring;
The high moon sails upon her beauteous way,
Serenely smoothing o'er the lofty walls
Of those tall piles and sea-girt palaces,
Whose porphyry pillars, and whose costly fronts,
Fraught with the orient spoil of many marbles,
Like altars ranged along the broad canal,
Seem each a trophy of some mighty deed
Rear'd up from out the waters, scarce less strangely
Than those more massy and mysterious giants
Of architecture, those Titanian fabrics,
Which point in Egypt's plains to times that have
No other record.   All is gentle: nought
Stirs rudely; but, congenial with the night,
Whatever walks is gliding like a spirit.
The tinklings of some vigilant guitars
Of sleepless lovers to a wakeful mistress,
And cautious opening of the casement, showing
That he is not unheard; while her young hand,
Fair as the moonlight of which it seems part,
So delicately white, it trembles in
The act of opening the forbidden lattice,
To let in love through music, makes his heart
Thrill like his lyre-strings at the sight; the dash
Phosphoric of the oar, or rapid twinkle
Of the far lights of skimming gondolas,

And the responsive voices of the choir
Of boatmen answering back with verse for verse;
Some dusky shadow checkering the Rialto;
Some glimmering palace roof, or tapering spire,
Are all the sights and sounds which here pervade
The ocean-born and earth-commanding city—
How sweet and soothing is this hour of calm!
I thank thee, Night! for thou hast chased away
Those horrid bodements which, amidst the throng,
I could not dissipate: and with the blessing
Of thy benign and quiet influence,
Now will I to my couch, although to rest
Is almost wronging such a night as this——

       [*A knocking is heard from without.*

Hark! what is that? or who at such a moment?

Enter ANTONIO.

Ant. My lord, a man without, on urgent business,
 Implores to be admitted.
Lioni.   Is he a stranger?
Ant. His face is muffled in his cloak, but both
 His voice and gestures seem familiar to me;
 I craved his name, but this he seem'd reluctant
 To trust, save to yourself; most earnestly
 He sues to be permitted to approach you.
Lioni. 'Tis a strange hour, and a suspicious bearing!
 And yet there is slight peril: 'tis not in
 Their houses noble men are struck at; still,
 Although I know not that I have a foe
 In Venice, 'twill be wise to use some caution.
 Admit him, and retire; but call up quickly
 Some of thy fellows, who may wait without.—
 Who can this man be?—

    [*Exit* ANTONIO, *and returns with* BERTRAM *muffled.*
Ber.   My good lord Lioni,
 I have no time to lose, nor thou—dismiss
 This menial hence; I would be private with you.
Lioni. It seems the voice of Bertram—Go, Antonio.

            [*Exit* ANTONIO.
 Now, stranger, what would you at such an hour?
Ber. [*Discovering himself*]. A boon, my noble patron; you have granted
 Many to your poor client, Bertram; add
 This one, and make him happy.
Lioni.   Thou hast known me

From boyhood, ever ready to assist thee
In all fair objects of advancement, which
Beseem one of thy station; I would promise
Ere thy request was heard, but that the hour,
Thy bearing, and this strange and hurried mode
Of suing, gives me to suspect this visit
Hath some mysterious import—but say on—
What has occurred, some rash and sudden broil?—
A cup too much, a scuffle, and a stab?—
Mere things of every day; so that thou hast not
Spilt noble blood, I guarantee thy safety;
But then thou must withdraw, for angry friends
And relatives, in the first burst of vengeance,
Are things in Venice deadlier than the laws.

Ber. My lord, I thank you; but——

Lioni.   But what? You have not
Raised a rash hand against one of our order?
If so, withdraw and fly, and own it not;
I would not slay—but then I must not save thee!
He who has shed patrician blood——

Ber.   I come
To save patrician blood, and not to shed it!
And thereunto I must be speedy, for
Each minute lost may lose a life; since Time
Has changed his slow scythe for the two-edged sword,
And is about to take, instead of sand,
The dust from sepulchres to fill his hour-glass!—
Go not *thou* forth to-morrow!

Lioni.   Wherefore not?—
What means this menace?

Ber.   Do not seek its meaning,
But do as I implore thee;—stir not forth,
Whate'er be stirring; though the roar of crowds—
The cry of women, and the shrieks of babes—
The groans of men—the clash of arms—the sound
Of rolling drum, shrill trump, and hollow bell,
Peal in one wide alarum!—Go not forth
Until the tocsin's silent, nor even then
Till I return!

Lioni.   Again, what does this mean?

Ber. Again, I tell thee, ask not: but by all
Thou holdest dear on earth or heaven—by all
The souls of thy great fathers, and thy hope
To emulate them, and to leave behind
Descendants worthy both of them and thee—
By all thou hast of bless'd in hope or memory—

By all thou hast to fear here or hereafter—
By all the good deeds thou hast done to me,
Good I would now repay with greater good,
Remain within—trust to thy household gods,
And to my word for safety, if thou dost
As I now counsel—but if not, thou art lost!

Lioni. I am indeed already lost in wonder;
Surely thou ravest! what have *I* to dread?
Who are my foes? or if there be such, *why*
Art *thou* leagued with them?—*thou*! or if so leagued,
Why comest thou to tell me at this hour,
And not before?

Ber.   I cannot answer this.
Wilt thou go forth despite of this true warning?

Lioni. I was not born to shrink from idle threats,
The cause of which I know not: at the hour
Of council, be it soon or late, I shall not
Be found among the absent.

Ber.   Say not so!
Once more, art thou determined to go forth?

Lioni. I am.   Nor is there aught which shall impede me!

Ber. Then Heaven have mercy on thy soul!—Farewell! [*Going*

Lioni. Stay—there is more in this than my own safety
Which makes me call thee back; we must not part thus:
Bertram, I have known thee long.

Ber.   From childhood, signor,
You have been my protector: in the days
Of reckless infancy, when rank forgets,
Or, rather, is not yet taught to remember
Its cold prerogative, we play'd together;
Our sports, our smiles, our tears, were mingled oft;
My father was your father's client, I
His son's scarce less than foster-brother; years
Saw us together—happy, heart-full hours!
Oh God! the difference 'twixt those hours and this!

Lioni. Bertram, 'tis thou who hast forgotten them.

Ber. Nor now, nor ever; whatsoe'er betide,
I would have saved you: when to manhood's growth
We sprung, and you, devoted to the state,
As suits your station, the more humble Bertram
Was left unto the labours of the humble,
Still you forsook me not; and if my fortunes
Have not been towering, 'twas no fault of him
Who ofttimes rescued and supported me
When struggling with the tides of circumstance,
Which bear away the weaker: noble blood

Ne'er mantled in a nobler heart than thine
Has proved to me, the poor plebeian Bertram.
Would that thy fellow senators were like thee!

Lioni. Why, what hast thou to say against the senate?

Ber. Nothing.

Lioni.　　　　　I know that there are angry spirits
And turbulent mutterers of stifled treason,
Who lurk in narrow places, and walk out
Muffled to whisper curses to the night;
Disbanded soldiers, discontented ruffians,
And desperate libertines who brawl in taverns;
Thou herdest not with such: 'tis true, of late
I have lost sight of thee, but thou wert wont
To lead a temperate life, and break thy bread
With honest mates, and bear a cheerful aspect.
What hath come to thee? in thy hollow eye
And hueless cheek, and thine unquiet motions,
Sorrow and shame and conscience seem at war
To waste thee.

Ber.　　　　　Rather shame and sorrow light
On the accursed tyranny which rides
The very air in Venice, and makes men
Madden as in the last hours of the plague
Which sweeps the soul deliriously from life!

Lioni. Some villains have been tampering with thee, Bertram;
This is not thy old language, nor own thoughts;
Some wretch has made thee drunk with disaffection:
But thou must not be lost so; thou *wert* good
And kind, and art not fit for such base acts
As vice and villainy would put thee to:
Confess—confide in me—thou know'st my nature—
What is it thou and thine are bound to do,
Which should prevent thy friend, the only son
Of him who was a friend unto thy father,
So that our good-will is a heritage
We should bequeath to our posterity
Such as ourselves received it, or augmented;
I say, what is it thou must do, that I
Should deem thee dangerous, and keep the house
Like a sick girl?

Ber.　　　　　Nay, question me no further:
I must be gone.——

Lioni.　　　　　And I be murder'd!—say,
Was it not thus thou said'st, my gentle Bertram?

Ber. Who talks of murder? what said I of murder?—
'Tis false! I did not utter such a word.

Lioni. Thou didst not; but from out thy wolfish eye,
  So changed from what I knew it, there glares forth
  The gladiator.   If *my* life 's thine object,
  Take it—I am unarm'd,—and then away!
  I would not hold my breath on such a tenure
  As the capricious mercy of such things
  As thou and those who have set thee to thy task-work.
Ber. Sooner than spill thy blood, I peril mine;
  Sooner than harm a hair of thine, I place
  In jeopardy a thousand heads, and some
  As noble, nay, even nobler than thine own.
Lioni. Ay, is it even so?   Excuse me, Bertram;
  I am not worthy to be singled out
  From such exalted hecatombs—who are they
  That *are* in danger, and that *make* the danger?
Ber. Venice, and all that she inherits, are
  Divided like a house against itself,
  And so will perish ere to-morrow's twilight!
Lioni. More mysteries, and awful ones!   But now,
  Or thou, or I, or both, it may be, are
  Upon the verge of ruin; speak once out,
  And thou art safe and glorious: for 'tis more
  Glorious to save than slay, and slay i' the dark too—
  Fie, Bertram! that was not a craft for thee!
  How would it look to see upon a spear
  The head of him whose heart was open to thee,
  Borne by thy hand before the shuddering people?
  And such may be my doom; for here I swear,
  Whate'er the peril or the penalty
  Of thy denunciation, I go forth,
  Unless thou dost detail the cause, and show
  The consequence of all which led thee here!
Ber. Is there no way to save thee? minutes fly,
  And thou art lost!—*thou!* my sole benefactor,
  The only being who was constant to me
  Through every change.   Yet, make me not a traitor!
  Let me save thee—but spare my honour!
Lioni.   Where
  Can lie the honour in a league of murder?
  And who are traitors save unto the state?
Ber. A league is still a compact, and more binding
  In honest hearts when words must stand for law;
  And in my mind, there is no traitor like
  He whose domestic treason plants the poniard
  Within the breast which trusted to his truth.
Lioni. And who will strike the steel to mine?

Ber.   Not I;
I could have wound my soul up to all things
Save this.   *Thou* must not die! and think how dear
Thy life is, when I risk so many lives,
Nay, more, the life of lives, the liberty
Of future generations, *not* to be
The assassin thou miscall'st me;—once, once more
I do adjure thee, pass not o'er thy threshold!
Lioni. It is in vain—this moment I go forth.
Ber. Then perish Venice rather than my friend!
I will disclose—ensnare—betray—destroy—
Oh, what a villain I become for thee!
Lioni. Say, rather thy friend's saviour and the state's!—
Speak—pause not—all rewards, all pledges for
Thy safety and thy welfare; wealth such as
The state accords her worthiest servants; nay,
Nobility itself I guarantee thee,
So that thou art sincere and penitent.
Ber. I have thought again: it must not be—I love thee—
Thou knowest it—that I stand here is the proof,
Not least though last; but having done my duty
By thee, I now must do it by my country!
Farewell—we meet no more in life!—farewell!
Lioni. What, ho!—Antonio—Pedro—to the door!
See that none pass—arrest this man!——

Enter ANTONIO *and other armed Domestics, who seize* BERTRAM.

Lioni. [*Continues.*]   Take care
He hath no harm; bring me my sword and cloak,
And man the gondola with four oars—quick—
                                          [*Exit* ANTONIO.
We will unto Giovanni Gradenigo's,
And send for Marc Cornaro:—fear not, Bertram;
This needful violence is for thy safety,
No less than for the general weal.
Ber.   Where wouldst thou
Bear me a prisoner?
Lioni.   Firstly to 'the Ten';
Next to the Doge.
Ber.   To the Doge?
Lioni.   Assuredly;
Is he not chief of the state?
Ber.   Perhaps at sunrise—
Lioni. What mean you?—but we 'll know anon.
Ber.   Art sure?

Lioni. Sure as all gentle means can make; and if
    They fail, you know 'the Ten' and their tribunal,
    And that Saint Mark's has dungeons, and the dungeons
    A rack.
Ber.   Apply it then before the dawn
    Now hastening into heaven.—One more such word,
    And you shall perish piecemeal, by the death
    You think to doom to me.

Re-enter ANTONIO.

Ant.   The bark is ready,
    My lord, and all prepared.
Lioni.   Look to the prisoner.
    Bertram, I'll reason with thee as we go
    To the Magnifico's, sage Gradenigo.   *[Exeunt.*

SCENE II

The Ducal Palace—The Doge's Apartment

The DOGE and his nephew, BERTUCCIO FALIERO.

Doge. Are all the people of our house in muster?
Ber. F. They are array'd, and eager for the signal,
    Within our palace precincts at San Polo.[1]
    I come for your last orders.
Doge.   It had been
    As well had there been time to have got together,
    From my own fief, Val di Marino, more
    Of our retainers—but it is too late.
Ber. F. Methinks, my lord, 'tis better as it is:
    A sudden swelling of our retinue
    Had waked suspicion; and, though fierce and trusty,
    The vassals of that district are too rude
    And quick in quarrel to have long maintain'd
    The secret discipline we need for such
    A service, till our foes are dealt upon.
Doge. True; but when once the signal has been given,
    These are the men for such an enterprise;
    These city slaves have all their private bias,
    Their prejudice *against* or *for* this noble,
    Which may induce them to o'erdo or spare
    Where mercy may be madness; the fierce peasants,
    Serfs of my county of Val di Marino,
    Would do the bidding of their lord without
    Distinguishing for love or hate his foes;

[1] The Doge's family palace.

Alike to them Marcello or Cornaro,
A Gradenigo or a Foscari;
They are not used to start at those vain names,
Nor bow the knee before a civic senate;
A chief in armour is their Suzerain,
And not a thing in robes.
Ber. F.   We are enough;
And for the dispositions of our clients
Against the senate I will answer.
Doge.   Well,
The die is thrown; but for a warlike service,
Done in the field, commend me to my peasants:
They made the sun shine through the host of Huns
When sallow burghers slunk back to their tents,
And cower'd to hear their own victorious trumpet.
If there be small resistance, you will find
These citizens all lions, like their standard;
But if there 's much to do, you'll wish with me,
A band of iron rustics at our backs.
Ber. F. Thus thinking, I must marvel you resolve
To strike the blow so suddenly.
Doge.   Such blows
Must be struck suddenly or never.   When
I had o'ermaster'd the weak false remorse
Which yearn'd about my heart, too fondly yielding
A moment to the feelings of old days,
I was most fain to strike; and, firstly, that
I might not yield again to such emotions;
And, secondly, because of all these men,
Save Israel and Philip Calendaro,
I know not well the courage or the faith:
To-day might find 'mongst them a traitor to us,
As yesterday a thousand to the senate;
But once in, with their hilts hot in their hands,
They must *on* for their own sakes; one stroke struck,
And the mere instinct of the first-born Cain,
Which ever lurks somewhere in human hearts,
Though circumstance may keep it in abeyance,
Will urge the rest on like to wolves; the sight
Of blood to crowds begets the thirst of more,
As the first wine-cup leads to the long revel;
And you will find a harder task to quell
Than urge them when they *have* commenced, but *till*
That moment, a mere voice, a straw, a shadow,
Are capable of turning them aside.—
How goes the night?

Ber. F.   Almost upon the dawn.
Doge. Then it is time to strike upon the bell.
  Are the men posted?
Ber. F.   By this time they are;
  But they have orders not to strike, until
  They have command from you through me in person.
Doge. 'Tis well.—Will the morn never put to rest
  These stars which twinkle yet o'er all the heavens?
  I am settled and bound up, and being so,
  The very effort which it cost me to
  Resolve to cleanse this commonwealth with fire,
  Now leaves my mind more steady.   I have wept,
  And trembled at the thought of this dread duty;
  But now I have put down all idle passion,
  And look the growing tempest in the face,
  As doth the pilot of an admiral galley:
  Yet (wouldst thou think it, kinsman?) it hath been
  A greater struggle to me, than when nations
  Beheld their fate merged in the approaching fight,
  Where I was leader of a phalanx, where
  Thousands were sure to perish—Yes, to spill
  The rank polluted current from the veins
  Of a few bloated despots needed more
  To steel me to a purpose such as made
  Timoleon immortal, than to face
  The toils and dangers of a life of war.
Ber. F. It gladdens me to see your former wisdom
  Subdue the furies which so wrung you ere
  You were decided.
Doge.   It was ever thus
  With me; the hour of agitation came
  In the first glimmerings of a purpose, when
  Passion had too much room to sway; but in
  The hour of action I have stood as calm
  As were the dead who lay around me: this
  They knew who made me what I am, and trusted
  To the subduing power which I preserved
  Over my mood, when its first burst was spent.
  But they were not aware that there are things
  Which make revenge a virtue by reflection,
  And not an impulse of mere anger; though
  The laws sleep, justice wakes, and injured souls
  Oft do a public right with private wrong,
  And justify their deeds unto themselves.—
  Methinks the day breaks—is it not so? look,
  Thine eyes are clear with youth;—the air puts on

A morning freshness, and, at least to me,
The sea looks greyer through the lattice.
Ber. F.   True,
The morn is dappling in the sky.
Doge.   Away then!
See that they strike without delay, and with
The first toll from Saint Mark's, march on the palace
With all our house's strength; here I will meet you—
The Sixteen and their companies will move
In separate columns at the self-same moment—
Be sure you post yourself at the great gate:
I would not trust 'the Ten' except to us—
The rest, the rabble of patricians, may
Glut the more careless swords of those leagued with us.
Remember that the cry is still 'Saint Mark!
The Genoese are come—ho! to the rescue!
Saint Mark and Liberty!'—Now—now to action!
Ber. F. Farewell then, noble uncle, we will meet
In freedom and true sovereignty, or never!
Doge. Come hither, my Bertuccio—one embrace—
Speed, for the day grows broader—Send me soon
A messenger to tell me how all goes
When you rejoin our troops, and then sound—sound
The storm-bell from Saint Mark's!
                                   [*Exit* BERTUCCIO FALIERO
Doge. [*Solus.*]   He is gone,
And on each footstep moves a life.—'Tis done.
Now the destroying angel hovers o'er
Venice, and pauses ere he pours the vial,
Even as the eagle overlooks his prey,
And for a moment, poised in middle air,
Suspends the motion of his mighty wings,
Then swoops with his unerring beak.—Thou day!
That slowly walk'st the waters! march—march on—
I would not smite i' the dark, but rather see
That no stroke errs.   And you, ye blue sea-waves!
I have seen you dyed ere now, and deeply too,
With Genoese, Saracen, and Hunnish gore,
While that of Venice flow'd too, but victorious;
Now thou must wear an unmix'd crimson; no
Barbaric blood can reconcile us now
Unto that horrible incarnadine,
But friend or foe will roll in civic slaughter.
And have I lived to fourscore years for this?
I, who was named Preserver of the City?
I, at whose name the million's caps were flung

Into the air, and cries from tens of thousands
Rose up, imploring Heaven to send me blessings,
And fame, and length of days—to see this day?
But this day, black within the calendar,
Shall be succeeded by a bright millennium.
Doge Dandolo survived to ninety summers
To vanquish empires, and refuse their crown;
I will resign a crown, and make the state
Renew its freedom—but oh! by what means?
The noble end must justify them. What
Are a few drops of human blood? 'tis false,
The blood of tyrants is not human; they,
Like to incarnate Molochs, feed on ours,
Until 'tis time to give them to the tombs
Which they have made so populous.—Oh world!
Oh men! what are ye, and our best designs,
That we must work by crime to punish crime?
And slay as if Death had but this one gate,
When a few years would make the sword superfluous?
And I, upon the verge of th' unknown realm,
Yet send so many heralds on before me?—
I must not ponder this.   [A pause.
                    Hark! was there not
A murmur as of distant voices, and
The tramp of feet in martial unison?
What phantoms even of sound our wishes raise!
It cannot be—the signal hath not rung—
Why pauses it? My nephew's messenger
Should be upon his way to me, and he
Himself perhaps even now draws grating back
Upon its ponderous hinge the steep tower portal,
Where swings the sullen huge oracular bell,
Which never knells but for a princely death,
Or for a state in peril, pealing forth
Tremendous bodements; let it do its office,
And be this peal its awfullest and last
Sound till the strong tower rock!—What! silent still?
I would go forth, but that my post is here,
To be the centre of re-union to
The oft discordant elements which form
Leagues of this nature, and to keep compact
The wavering of the weak, in case of conflict;
For if they should do battle, 'twill he here,
Within the palace, that the strife will thicken:
Then here must be my station, as becomes
The master-mover.——Hark! he comes—he comes,

My nephew, brave Bertuccio's messenger.—
What tidings? Is he marching? hath he sped?—
They here!—all 's lost—yet will I make an effort.
    Enter a SIGNOR OF THE NIGHT, *with Guards, etc. etc.*

Sig. Doge, I arrest thee of high treason!
Doge.   Me!
  Thy prince, of treason?—Who are they that dare
  Cloak their own treason under such an order?
Sig. [*Showing his order.*] Behold my order from the assembled
    Ten.
Doge. And *where* are they, and *why* assembled? no
  Such council can be lawful, till the prince
  Preside there, and that duty 's mine: on thine
  I charge thee, give me way, or marshal me
  To the Council chamber.
Sig.   Duke! it may not be:
  Nor are they in the wonted Hall of Council,
  But sitting in the convent of Saint Saviour's.
Doge. You dare to disobey me, then?
Sig.   I serve
  The state, and needs must serve it faithfully;
  My warrant is the will of those who rule it.
Doge. And till that warrant has my signature
  It is illegal, and, as *now* applied,
  Rebellious. Hast thou weigh'd well thy life's worth,
  That thus you dare assume a lawless function?
Sig. 'Tis not my office to reply, but act—
  I am placed here as guard upon thy person,
  And not as judge to hear or to decide.
Doge. [*Aside.*] I must gain time. So that the storm-bell sound
  All may be well yet.—Kinsman, speed—speed—speed!—
  Our fate is trembling in the balance, and
  Woe to the vanquish'd! be they prince and people,
  Or slaves and senate—
              [*The great bell of Saint Mark's tolls.*
            Lo! it sounds—it tolls!
[*Aloud.*] Hark, Signor of the Night! and you, ye hirelings,
  Who wield your mercenary staves in fear,
  It is your knell—Swell on, thou lusty peal!
  Now, knaves, what ransom for your lives?
Sig.   Confusion!
  Stand to your arms and guard the door—all 's lost
  Unless that fearful bell be silenced soon.
  The officer hath miss'd his path or purpose,
  And met some unforeseen and hideous obstacle.
  Anselmo, with thy company proceed
  II—* O 487

Straight to the tower; the rest remain with me.

[*Exit part of the Guard.*

Doge. Wretch! if thou wouldst have thy vile life, implore it;
It is not now a lease of sixty seconds.
Ay, send thy miserable ruffians forth;
They never shall return.

Sig.   So let it be!
They die then in their duty, as will I.

Doge. Fool! the high eagle flies at nobler game
Than thou and thy base myrmidons,—live on,
So thou provok'st not peril by resistance,
And learn (if souls so much obscured can bear
To gaze upon the sunbeams) to be free.

Sig. And learn thou to be captive. It hath ceased,

[*The bell ceases to toll.*

The traitorous signal, which was to have set
The bloodhound mob on their patrician prey—
The knell hath rung, but it is not the senate's!

Doge. [*After a pause.*] All 's silent, and all 's lost!

Sig.   Now, Doge, denounce me
As rebel slave of a revolted council!
Have I not done my duty?

Doge.   Peace, thou thing!
Thou hast done a worthy deed, and earn'd the price
Of blood, and they who use thee will reward thee.
But thou wert sent to watch, and not to prate,
As thou said'st even now—then do thine office,
But let it be in silence, as behoves thee,
Since, though thy prisoner, I am thy prince.

Sig. I did not mean to fail in the respect
Due to your rank: in this I shall obey you.

Doge. [*Aside.*] There now is nothing left me save to die;
And yet how near success! I would have fallen,
And proudly, in the hour of triumph, but
To miss it thus!——

Enter other SIGNORS OF THE NIGHT, *with* BERTUCCIO FALIERO
prisoner.

2nd Sig.   We took him in the act
Of issuing from the tower, where, at his order,
As delegated from the Doge, the signal
Had thus began to sound.

1st Sig.   Are all the passes
Which lead up to the palace well secured?

2nd Sig. They are—besides, it matters not; the chiefs
  Are all in chains, and some even now on trial—
  Their followers are dispersed, and many taken.

Ber. F. Uncle!

Doge.   It is in vain to war with Fortune;
  The glory hath departed from our house.

Ber. F. Who would have deem'd it?—Ah! one moment sooner!

Doge. That moment would have changed the face of ages;
  This gives us to eternity—We'll meet it
  As men whose triumph is not in success,
  But who can make their own minds all in all,
  Equal to every fortune. Droop not, 'tis
  But a brief passage—I would go alone,
  Yet if they send us, as 'tis like, together,
  Let us go worthy of our sires and selves.

Ber. F. I shall not shame you, uncle.

1st Sig.   Lords, our orders
  Are to keep guard on both in separate chambers,
  Until the council call ye to your trial.

Doge. Our trial! will they keep their mockery up
  Even to the last? but let them deal upon us,
  As we had dealt on them, but with less pomp.
  'Tis but a game of mutual homicides,
  Who have cast lots for the first death, and they
  Have won with false dice.—Who hath been our Judas?

1st Sig. I am not warranted to answer that.

Ber. F. I'll answer for thee—'tis a certain Bertram,
  Even now deposing to the secret Giunta.

Doge. Bertram, the Bergamask! With what vile tools
  We operate to slay or save! This creature,
  Black with a double treason, now will earn
  Rewards and honours, and be stamp'd in story
  With the geese in the Capitol, which gabbled
  Till Rome awoke, and had an annual triumph,
  While Manlius, who hurl'd down the Gauls, was cast
  From the Tarpeian.

1st Sig.   He aspired to treason,
  And sought to rule the state.

Doge.   He saved the state,
  And sought but to reform what he revived—
  But this is idle——Come, sirs, do your work.

1st Sig. Noble Bertuccio, we must now remove you
  Into an inner chamber.

Ber. F.   Farewell, uncle!
  If we shall meet again in life I know not,
  But they perhaps will let our ashes mingle.

Doge. Yes, and our spirits, which shall yet go forth,
And do what our frail clay, thus clogg'd, hath fail'd in!
They cannot quench the memory of those
Who would have hurl'd them from their guilty thrones,
And such examples will find heirs, though distant.

ACT V

SCENE I

*The Hall of the Council of Ten assembled with the additional Senators,
who, on the Trials of the Conspirators for the Treason of* MARINO
FALIERO, *composed what was called the Giunta.—Guards, Officers,
etc. etc.—*ISRAEL BERTUCCIO *and* PHILIP CALENDARO *as Prisoners.—*BERTRAM, LIONI, *and Witnesses, etc.*

The Chief of the Ten, BENINTENDE.

Ben. There now rests, after such conviction of
Their manifold and manifest offences,
But to pronounce on these obdurate men
The sentence of the law:—a grievous task
To those who hear, and those who speak. Alas!
That it should fall to me! and that my days
Of office should be stigmatized through all
The years of coming time, as bearing record
To this most foul and complicated treason
Against a just and free state, known to all
The earth as being the Christian bulwark 'gainst
The Saracen and the schismatic Greek,
The savage Hun, and not less barbarous Frank;
A city which has open'd India's wealth
To Europe; the last Roman refuge from
O'erwhelming Attila; the ocean's queen;
Proud Genoa's prouder rival! 'Tis to sap
The throne of such a city, these lost men
Have risk'd and forfeited their worthless lives—
So let them die the death.
I. Ber.   We are prepared;
Your racks have done that for us. Let us die.
Ben. If ye have that to say which would obtain
Abatement of your punishment, the Giunta
Will hear you; if you have aught to confess,
Now is your time, perhaps it may avail ye.
I. Ber. We stand to hear, and not to speak.

Ben.   Your crimes
  Are fully proved by your accomplices,
  And all which circumstance can add to aid them;
  Yet we would hear from your own lips complete
  Avowal of your treason: on the verge
  Of that dread gulf which none repass, the truth
  Alone can profit you on earth or heaven—
  Say, then, what was your motive?
I. Ber.   Justice!
Ben.   What
  Your object?
I. Ber.   Freedom!
Ben.   You are brief, sir.
I. Ber. So my life grows: I
  Was bred a soldier, not a senator.
Ben. Perhaps you think by this blunt brevity
  To brave your judges to postpone the sentence?
I. Ber. Do you be brief as I am, and believe me,
  I shall prefer that mercy to your pardon.
Ben. Is this your sole reply to the tribunal?
I. Ber. Go ask your racks what they have wrung from us,
  Or place us there again; we have still some blood left,
  And some slight sense of pain in these wrench'd limbs;
  But this ye dare not do; for if we die there—
  And you have left us little life to spend
  Upon your engines, gorged with pangs already—
  Ye lose the public spectacle, with which
  You would appal your slaves to further slavery!
  Groans are not words, nor agony assent,
  Nor affirmation truth, if nature's sense
  Should overcome the soul into a lie,
  For a short respite—must we bear or die?
Ben. Say, who were your accomplices?
I. Ber.   The Senate!
Ben. What do you mean?
I. Ber.   Ask of the suffering people,
  Whom your patrician crimes have driven to crime.
Ben. You know the Doge?
I. Ber.   I served with him at Zara
  In the field, when *you* were pleading here your way
  To present office; we exposed our lives,
  While you but hazarded the lives of others,
  Alike by accusation or defence;
  And, for the rest, all Venice knows her Doge,
  Through his great actions, and the Senate's insults.
Ben. You have held conference with him?

I. Ber.   I am weary—
    Even wearier of your questions than your tortures:
    I pray you pass to judgment.
Ben.   It is coming.—
    And you, too, Philip Calendaro, what
    Have you to say why you should not be doom'd?
Cal. I never was a man of many words,
    And now have few left worth the utterance.
Ben. A further application of yon engine
    May change your tone.
Cal.   Most true, it *will* do so;
    A former application did so; but
    It will not change my words or, if it did—
Ben. What then?
Cal.   Will my avowal on yon rack
    Stand good in law?
Ben.   Assuredly.
Cal.   Whoe'er
    The culprit be whom I accuse of treason?
Ben. Without doubt, he will be brought up to trial.
Cal. And on this testimony would he perish?
Ben. So your confession be detail'd and full,
    He will stand here in peril of his life.
Cal. Then look well to thy proud self, President!
    For by the eternity which yawns before me,
    I swear that *thou*, and only thou, shalt be
    The traitor I denounce upon that rack,
    If I be stretch'd there for the second time.
One of the Giunta. Lord President, 'twere best proceed to
    judgment;
    There is no more to be drawn from these men.
Ben. Unhappy men! prepare for instant death.
    The nature of your crime, our law, and peril
    The state now stands in, leave not an hour's respite—
    Guards! lead them forth, and upon the balcony
    Of the red columns, where, on festal Thursday,[1]
    The Doge stands to behold the chase of bulls,
    Let them be justified: and leave exposed
    Their wavering relics, in the place of judgment,
    To the full view of the assembled people!—
    And Heaven have mercy on their souls!
The Giunta.   Amen!
I. Ber. Signors, farewell! we shall not all again
    Meet in one place.

---

[1] 'Giovedi grasso'—'fat or greasy Thursday'—which I cannot literally
translate in the text, was the day.

Ben.   And lest they should essay
To stir up the distracted multitude—
Guards! let their mouths be gagg'd[1] even in the act
Of execution.—Lead them hence!

Cal.   What! must we
Not even say farewell to some fond friend,
Nor leave a last word with our confessor?

Ben. A priest is waiting in the antechamber;
But, for your friends, such interviews would be
Painful to them, and useless all to you.

Cal. I knew that we were gagg'd in life; at least
All those who had not heart to risk their lives
Upon their open thoughts; but still I deem'd
That in the last few moments, the same idle
Freedom of speech accorded to the dying,
Would not now be denied to us; but since——

I. Ber. Even let them have their way, brave Calendaro!
What matter a few syllables? let's die
Without the slightest show of favour from them;
So shall our blood more readily arise
To Heaven against them, and more testify
To their atrocities, than could a volume
Spoken or written of our dying words!
They tremble at our voices—nay, they dread
Our very silence—let them live in fear!—
Leave them unto their thoughts, and let us now
Address our own above!—Lead on; we are ready.

Cal. Israel, hadst thou but hearken'd unto me
It had not now been thus; and yon pale villain,
The coward Bertram, would——

I. Ber.   Peace, Calendaro!
What brooks it now to ponder upon this?

Bert. Alas! I fain you died in peace with me:
I did not seek this task: 'twas forced upon me:
Say you forgive me, though I never can
Retrieve my own forgiveness—frown not thus!

I. Ber. I die and pardon thee!

Cal. [*Spitting at him.*]   I die and scorn thee!
        [*Exeunt* ISRAEL BERTUCCIO *and* PHILIP CALENDARO, *Guards,*
                etc.

Ben. Now that these criminals have been disposed of,
'Tis time that we proceed to pass our sentence
Upon the greatest traitor upon record
In any annals, the Doge Faliero!
The proofs and process are complete; the time

---
[1] An historical fact.

And crime require a quick procedure: shall
He now be call'd in to receive the award?
The Giunta. Ay, ay.
Ben.   Avogadori, order that the Doge
Be brought before the council.
One of the Giunta.   And the rest,
When shall they be brought up?
Ben.   When all the chiefs
Have been disposed of.   Some have fled to Chiozza;
But there are thousands in pursuit of them,
And such precaution ta'en on terra firma,
As well as in the islands, that we hope
None will escape to utter in strange lands
His libellous tale of treasons 'gainst the senate.

Enter the DOGE *as Prisoner, with Guards, etc. etc.*

Ben. Doge—for such still you are, and by the law
Must be consider'd, till the hour shall come
When you must doff the ducal bonnet from
That head, which could not wear a crown more noble
Than empires can confer, in quiet honour,
But it must plot to overthrow your peers,
Who made you what you are, and quench in blood
A city's glory—we have laid already
Before you in your chamber at full length,
By the Avogadori, all the proofs
Which have appear'd against you; and more ample
Ne'er rear'd their sanguinary shadows to
Confront a traitor.   What have you to say
In your defence?
Doge.   What shall I say to ye,
Since my defence must be your condemnation?
You are at once offenders and accusers,
Judges and executioners!—Proceed
Upon your power.
Ben.   Your chief accomplices
Having confess'd, there is no hope for you.
Doge. And who be they?
Ben.   In number many; but
The first now stands before you in the court,
Bertram, of Bergamo,—would you question him?
Doge. [*Looking at him contemptuously.*]   No.
Ben.   And two others, Israel Bertuccio,
And Philip Calendaro, have admitted
Their fellowship in treason with the Doge!
Doge. And where are they?

Ben.   Gone to their place, and now
  Answering to Heaven for what they did on earth.
Doge. Ah! the plebeian Brutus, is he gone?
  And the quick Cassius of the arsenal?—
  How did they meet their doom?
Ben.   Think of your own:
  It is approaching.   You decline to plead, then?
Doge. I cannot plead to my inferiors, nor
  Can recognize your legal power to try me.
  Show me the law!
Ben.   On great emergencies,
  The law must be remodell'd or amended:
  Our fathers had not fix'd the punishment
  Of such a crime, as on the old Roman tables
  The sentence against parricide was left
  In pure forgetfulness; they could not render
  That penal, which had neither name nor thought
  In their great bosoms: who would have foreseen
  That nature could be filed to such a crime
  As sons 'gainst sires, and princes 'gainst their realms?
  Your sin hath made us make a law which will
  Become a precedent 'gainst such haughty traitors,
  As would with treason mount with tyranny;
  Not even contented with a sceptre, till
  They can convert it to a two-edged sword!
  Was not the place of Doge sufficient for ye?
  What's nobler than the signory of Venice?
Doge. The signory of Venice!   You betray'd me—
  You—you, who sit there, traitors as ye are!
  From my equality with you in birth,
  And my superiority in action,
  You drew me from my honourable toils
  In distant lands—on flood, in field, in cities—
  You singled me out like a victim to
  Stand crown'd, but bound and helpless, at the altar
  Where you alone could minister.   I knew not,
  I sought not, wish'd not, dream'd not the election,
  Which reach'd me first at Rome, and I obey'd;
  But found on my arrival that, besides
  The jealous vigilance which always led you
  To mock and mar your sovereign's best intents,
  You had, even in the interregnum of
  My journey to the capital, curtail'd
  And mutilated the few privileges
  Yet left the duke: all this I bore, and would
  Have borne, until my very hearth was stain'd

By the pollution of your ribaldry,
And he, the ribald, whom I see amongst you—
Fit judge in such tribunal!——

Ben. [*Interrupting him.*]   Michel Steno
Is here in virtue of his office, as
One of the Forty; 'the Ten' having craved
A Giunta of patricians from the senate
To aid our judgment in a trial arduous
And novel as the present; he was set
Free from the penalty pronounced upon him,
Because the Doge, who should protect the law,
Seeking to abrogate all law, can claim
No punishment of others by the statutes
Which he himself denies and violates!

Doge. His PUNISHMENT! I rather see him *there*,
Where he now sits, and glut him with my death,
That in the mockery of castigation,
Which your foul, outward, juggling show of justice
Decreed as sentence! Base as was his crime,
'Twas purity compared with your protection.

Ben. And can it be, that the great Doge of Venice,
With three parts of a century of years
And honours on his head, could thus allow
His fury, like an angry boy's, to master
All feeling, wisdom, faith, and fear, on such
A provocation as a young man's petulance?

Doge. A spark creates the flame—'tis the last drop
Which makes the cup run o'er, and mine was full
Already: you oppress'd the prince and people;
I would have freed both, and have fail'd in both:
The price of such success would have been glory,
Vengeance, and victory, and such a name
As would have made Venetian history
Rival to that of Greece and Syracuse
When they were freed, and flourish'd ages after,
And mine to Gelon and to Thrasybulus:—
Failing, I know the penalty of failure
Is present infamy and death—the future
Will judge, when Venice is no more, or free;
Till then, the truth is in abeyance. Pause not;
I would have shown no mercy, and I seek none;
My life was staked upon a mighty hazard,
And being lost, take what I would have taken!
I would have stood alone amidst your tombs:
Now you may flock round mine, and trample on it,
As you have done upon my heart while living.

Ben. You do confess then, and admit the justice
   Of our tribunal?
Doge.   I confess to have fail'd;
   Fortune is female: from my youth her favours
   Were not withheld, the fault was mine to hope
   Her former smiles again at this late hour.
Ben. You do not then in aught arraign our equity?
Doge. Noble Venetians! stir me not with questions.
   I am resign'd to the worst; but in me still
   Have something of the blood of brighter days,
   And am not over-patient. Pray you, spare me
   Further interrogation, which boots nothing,
   Except to turn a trial to debate.
   I shall but answer that which will offend you,
   And please your enemies—a host already;
   'Tis true, these sullen walls should yield no echo:
   But walls have ears—nay, more, they have tongues; and if
   There were no other way for truth to o'erleap them,
   You who condemn me, you who fear and slay me,
   Yet could not bear in silence to your graves
   What you would hear from me of good or evil;
   The secret were too mighty for your souls:
   Then let it sleep in mine, unless you court
   A danger which would double that you escape.
   Such my defence would be, had I full scope
   To make it famous; for true *words* are *things*,
   And dying men's are things which long outlive,
   And oftentimes avenge them; bury mine,
   If ye would fain survive me: take this counsel,
   And though too oft ye made me live in wrath,
   Let me die calmly; you may grant me this;—
   I deny nothing, defend nothing, nothing
   I ask of you, but silence for myself,
   And sentence from the court!
Ben.   This full admission
   Spares us the harsh necessity of ordering
   The torture to elicit the whole truth.
Doge. The torture! you have put me there already,
   Daily since I was Doge; but if you will
   Add the corporeal rack, you may: these limbs
   Will yield with age to crushing iron; but
   There's that within my heart shall strain your engines.

Enter an OFFICER.

Officer. Noble Venetians! Duchess Faliero
   Requests admission to the Giunta's presence.

Ben. Say, conscript fathers,[1] shall she be admitted?
One of the Giunta. She may have revelations of importance
    Unto the state, to justify compliance
    With her request.
Ben.   Is this the general will?
All. It is.
Doge.   Oh, admirable laws of Venice!
    Which would admit the wife, in the full hope
    That she might testify against the husband.
    What glory to the chaste Venetian dames!
    But such blasphemers 'gainst all honour, as
    Sit here, do well to act in their vocation.
    Now, villain Steno! if this woman fail,
    I'll pardon thee thy lie, and thy escape,
    And my own violent death, and thy vile life.

The DUCHESS *enters.*

Ben. Lady! this just tribunal has resolved,
    Though the request be strange, to grant it, and
    Whatever be its purport, to accord
    A patient hearing with the due respect
    Which fits your ancestry, your rank, your virtues:
    But you turn pale—ho! there, look to the lady!
    Place a chair instantly.
Ang.   A moment's faintness—
    'Tis past; I pray you pardon me,—I sit not
    In presence of my prince and of my husband,
    While he is on his feet.
Ben.   Your pleasure, lady?
Ang. Strange rumours, but most true, if all I hear
    And see be sooth, have reach'd me, and I come
    To know the worst, even at the worst; forgive
    The abruptness of my entrance and my bearing.
    Is it——I cannot speak—I cannot shape
    The question—but you answer it ere spoken,
    With eyes averted, and with gloomy brows—
    Oh God! this is the silence of the grave!
Ben. [*After a pause.*] Spare us, and spare thyself the repetition
    Of our most awful, but inexorable
    Duty to heaven and man!
Ang.   Yet speak; I cannot—
    I cannot—no—even now believe these things.
    Is *he* condemn'd?
Ben.   Alas!

---

[1] The Venetian senate took the same title as the Roman, of 'conscript fathers.'

Ang.   And was he guilty?
Ben. Lady! the natural distraction of
   Thy thoughts at such a moment makes the question
   Merit forgiveness; else a doubt like this
   Against a just and paramount tribunal
   Were deep offence. But question even the Doge,
   And if he can deny the proofs, believe him
   Guiltless as thy own bosom.
Ang.   Is it so?
   My lord, my sovereign, my poor father's friend,
   The mighty in the field, the sage in council;
   Unsay the words of this man!—Thou art silent!
Ben. He hath already own'd to his own guilt,
   Nor, as thou see'st, doth he deny it now.
Ang. Ay, but he must not die! Spare his few years,
   Which grief and shame will soon cut down to days!
   One day of baffled crime must not efface
   Near sixteen lustres crowded with brave acts.
Ben. His doom must be fulfill'd without remission
   Of time or penalty—'tis a decree.
Ang. He hath been guilty, but there may be mercy.
Ben. Not in this case with justice.
Ang.   Alas! signor,
   He who is only just is cruel; who
   Upon the earth would live were all judg'd justly?
Ben. His punishment is safety to the state.
Ang. He was a subject, and hath served the state;
   He was your general, and hath saved the state;
   He is your sovereign, and hath ruled the state.
One of the Council. He is a traitor, and betray'd the state.
Ang. And, but for him, there now had been no state
   To save or to destroy; and you, who sit
   There to pronounce the death of your deliverer,
   Had now been groaning at a Moslem oar,
   Or digging in the Hunnish mines in fetters!
One of the Council. No, lady, there are others who would die
   Rather than breathe in slavery!
Ang.   If there are so
   Within *these* walls, *thou* art not of the number:
   The truly brave are generous to the fallen!—
   Is there no hope?
Ben.   Lady, it cannot be.
Ang. [*Turning to the Doge.*] Then die, Faliero! since it must be so;
   But with the spirit of my father's friend,
   Thou hast been guilty of a great offence,
   Half-cancell'd by the harshness of these men.

I would have sued to them—have pray'd to them—
Have begg'd as famish'd mendicants for bread—
Have wept as they will cry unto their God
For mercy, and be answer'd as they answer—
Had it been fitting for thy name or mine,
And if the cruelty in their cold eyes
Had not announced the heartless wrath within.
Then, as a prince, address thee to thy doom!

Doge. I have lived too long not to know how to die!
Thy suing to these men were but the bleating
Of the lamb to the butcher, or the cry
Of seamen to the surge: I would not take
A life eternal, granted at the hands
Of wretches, from whose monstrous villainies
I sought to free the groaning nations!

Michel Steno.   Doge,
A word with thee, and with this noble lady,
Whom I have grievously offended. Would
Sorrow, or shame, or penance on my part,
Could cancel the inexorable past!
But since that cannot be, as Christians let us
Say farewell, and in peace: with full contrition
I crave, not pardon, but compassion from you,
And give, however weak, my prayers for both.

Ang. Sage Benintende, now chief judge of Venice,
I speak to thee in answer to yon signor.
Inform the ribald Steno, that his words
Ne'er weigh'd in mind with Loredano's daughter
Further than to create a moment's pity
For such as he is: would that others had
Despised him as I pity! I prefer
My honour to a thousand lives, could such
Be multiplied in mine, but would not have
A single life of others lost for that
Which nothing human can impugn—the sense
Of virtue, looking not to what is call'd
A good name for reward, but to itself.
To me the scorner's words were as the wind
Unto the rock: but as there are—alas!
Spirits more sensitive, on which such things
Light as the whirlwind on the waters; souls
To whom dishonour's shadow is a substance
More terrible than death, here and hereafter;
Men whose vice is to start at vice's scoffing,
And who, though proof against all blandishments
Of pleasure, and all pangs of pain, are feeble

When the proud name on which they pinnacled
Their hopes is breathed on, jealous as the eagle
Of her high aiery; let what we now
Behold, and feel, and suffer, be a lesson
To wretches how they tamper in their spleen
With beings of a higher order.   Insects
Have made the lion mad ere now; a shaft
I' the heel o'erthrew the bravest of the brave;
A wife's dishonour was the bane of Troy;
A wife's dishonour unking'd Rome for ever;
An injured husband brought the Gauls to Clusium,
And thence to Rome, which perish'd for a time;
An obscene gesture cost Caligula
His life, while Earth yet bore his cruelties;
A virgin's wrong made Spain a Moorish province;
And Steno's lie, couch'd in two worthless lines,
Hath decimated Venice, put in peril
A senate which hath stood eight hundred years,
Discrown'd a prince, cut off his crownless head,
And forged new fetters for a groaning people!
Let the poor wretch, like to the courtesan
Who fired Persepolis, be proud of this,
If it so please him—'twere a pride fit for him!
But let him not insult the last hours of
Him, who, whate'er he now is, *was* a hero,
By the intrusion of his very prayers;
Nothing of good can come from such a source,
Nor would we aught with him, nor now, nor ever:
We leave him to himself, that lowest depth
Of human baseness.   Pardon is for men,
And not for reptiles—we have none for Steno,
And no resentment: things like him must sting,
And higher beings suffer, 'tis the charter
Of life.   The man who dies by the adder's fang
May have the crawler crush'd, but feels no anger:
'Twas the worm's nature; and some men are worms
In soul, more than the living things of tombs.

Doge. [*To Ben.*] Signor! complete that which you deem your
    duty.

Ben. Before we can proceed upon that duty,
    We would request the princess to withdraw;
    'Twill move her too much to be witness to it.

Ang. I know it will, and yet I must endure it,
    For 'tis a part of mine—I will not quit,
    Except by force, my husband's side.—Proceed!
    Nay, fear not either shriek, or sigh, or tear;

Though my heart burst, it shall be silent.—Speak!
I have that within that shall o'ermaster all,
Ben. Marino Faliero, Doge of Venice,
   Count of Val di Marino, Senator,
   And some time General of the Fleet and Army,
   Noble Venetian, many times and oft
   Intrusted by the state with high employments,
   Even to the highest, listen to the sentence.
   Convict by many witnesses and proofs,
   And by thine own confession, of the guilt
   Of treachery and treason, yet unheard of
   Until this trial—the decree is death.
   Thy goods are confiscate unto the state,
   Thy name is razed from out her records, save
   Upon a public day of thanksgiving
   For this our most miraculous deliverance,
   When thou art noted in our calendars
   With earthquakes, pestilence, and foreign foes,
   And the great enemy of man, as subject
   Of grateful masses for Heaven's grace in snatching
   Our lives and country from thy wickedness.
   The place wherein as Doge thou shouldst be painted,
   With thine illustrious predecessors, is
   To be left vacant, with a death-black veil
   Flung over these dim words engraved beneath,—
   'This place is of Marino Faliero.
   Decapitated for his crimes.'
Doge.   'His crimes!'
   But let it be so:—it will be in vain.
   The veil which blackens o'er this blighted name,
   And hides, or seems to hide, these lineaments,
   Shall draw more gazers than the thousand portraits
   Which glitter round it in their pictured trappings—
   Your delegated slaves—the people's tyrants!
   'Decapitated for his crimes!'—*What* crimes?
   Were it not better to record the facts,
   So that the contemplator might approve,
   Or at least learn *whence* the crimes arose?
   When the beholder knows a Doge conspired,
   Let him be told the cause—it is your history.
Ben. Time must reply to that; our sons will judge
   Their fathers' judgment, which I now pronounce.
   As Doge, clad in the ducal robes and cap,
   Thou shalt be led hence to the Giants' Staircase,
   Where thou and all our princes are invested;
   And there, the ducal crown being first resumed

Upon the spot where it was first assumed,
Thy head shall be struck off; and Heaven have mercy
Upon thy soul!

Doge.   Is this the Giunta's sentence?

Ben. It is.

Doge.   I can endure it.—And the time?

Ben. Must be immediate.—Make thy peace with God:
Within an hour thou must be in His presence.

Doge. I am already; and my blood will rise
To Heaven before the souls of those who shed it.—
Are all my lands confiscated?

Ben.   They are;
And goods, and jewels, and all kind of treasure,
Except two thousand ducats—these dispose of.

Doge. That's harsh.—I would have fain reserved the lands
Near to Treviso, which I hold by investment
From Laurence the Count-bishop of Ceneda,
In fief perpetual to myself and heirs,
To portion them (leaving my city spoil,
My palace and my treasures, to your forfeit)
Between my consort and my kinsmen.

Ben.   These
Lie under the state's ban; their chief, thy nephew,
In peril of his own life; but the council
Postpones his trial for the present.   If
Thou will'st a state unto thy widow'd princess,
Fear not, for we will do her justice.

Ang.   Signors,
I share not in your spoil! From henceforth, know
I am devoted unto God alone,
And take my refuge in the cloister.

Doge.   Come!
The hour may be a hard one, but 'twill end.
Have I aught else to undergo save death?

Ben. You have nought to do, except confess and die.
The priest is robed, the scimitar is bare,
And both await without.—But, above all,
Think not to speak unto the people; they
Are now by thousands swarming at the gates,
But these are closed: the Ten, the Avogadori,
The Giunta, and the chief men of the Forty,
Alone will be beholders of thy doom,
And they are ready to attend the Doge.

Doge. The Doge!

Ben.   Yes, Doge, thou hast lived and thou shalt die
A sovereign; till the moment which precedes

The separation of that head and trunk,
That ducal crown and head shall be united.
Thou hast forgot thy dignity in deigning
To plot with petty traitors; not so we,
Who in the very punishment acknowledge
The prince.   Thy vile accomplices have died
The dog's death, and the wolf's; but thou shalt fall
As falls the lion by the hunters, girt
By those who feel a proud compassion for thee,
And mourn even the inevitable death
Provoked by thy wild wrath and regal fierceness.
Now we remit thee to thy preparation:
Let it be brief, and we ourselves will be
Thy guides unto the place where first we were
United to thee as thy subjects, and
Thy senate; and must now be parted from thee
As such for ever, on the self-same spot.—
Guards! form the Doge's escort to his chamber.   [*Exeunt.*

SCENE II

The Doge's Apartment

The DOGE *as Prisoner, and the* DUCHESS *attending him.*

Doge. Now, that the priest is gone, 'twere useless all
    To linger out the miserable minutes;
    But one pang more, the pang of parting from thee,
    And I will leave the few last grains of sand,
    Which yet remain of the accorded hour,
    Still falling—I have done with Time.
Ang.   Alas!
    And I have been the cause, the unconscious cause;
    And for this funeral marriage, this black union,
    Which thou, compliant with my father's wish,
    Didst promise at *his* death, thou hast seal'd thine own.
Doge. Not so: there was that in my spirit ever
    Which shaped out for itself some great reverse;
    The marvel is, it came not until now—
    And yet it was foretold me.
Ang.   How foretold you?
Doge. Long years ago—so long, they are a doubt
    In memory, and yet they live in annals:
    When I was in my youth, and served the senate
    And signory as podesta and captain
    Of the town of Treviso, on a day
    Of festival, the sluggish bishop who
    Convey'd the Host aroused my rash young anger,

By strange delay, and arrogant reply
To my reproof; I raised my hand and smote him
Until he reel'd beneath his holy burthen;
And as he rose from earth again, he raised
His tremulous hands in pious wrath towards Heaven.
Thence pointing to the Host, which had fallen from him,
He turn'd to me, and said, 'The hour will come
When he thou hast o'erthrown shall overthrow thee:
The glory shall depart from out thy house,
The wisdom shall be shaken from thy soul,
And in thy best maturity of mind
A madness of the heart shall seize upon thee;
Passion shall tear thee when all passions cease
In other men, or mellow into virtues;
And majesty, which decks all other heads,
Shall crown to leave thee headless; honours shall
But prove to thee the heralds of destruction,
And hoary hairs of shame, and both of death,
But not such death as fits an aged man.'
Thus saying, he pass'd on.—That hour is come.

Ang. And with this warning couldst thou not have striven
To avert the fatal moment, and atone,
By penitence for that which thou hadst done?

Doge. I own the words went to my heart, so much
That I remember'd them amid the maze
Of life, as if they form'd a spectral voice,
Which shook me in a supernatural dream;
And I repented; but 'twas not for me
To pull in resolution: what must be
I could not change, and would not fear.—Nay more,
Thou canst not have forgot, what all remember,
That on my day of landing here as Doge,
On my return from Rome, a mist of such
Unwonted density went on before
The Bucentaur, like the columnar cloud
Which usher'd Israel out of Egypt, till
The pilot was misled, and disembark'd us
Between the pillars of Saint Mark's, where 'tis
The custom of the state to put to death
Its criminals, instead of touching at
The Riva della Paglia, as the wont is,—
So that all Venice shudder'd at the omen.

Ang. Ah! little boots it now to recollect
Such things.

Doge.   And yet I find a comfort in
The thought that these things are the work of Fate;

For I would rather yield to gods than men,
Or cling to any creed of destiny,
Rather than deem these mortals, most of whom
I know to be as worthless as the dust,
And weak as worthless, more than instruments
Of an o'er-ruling power; they in themselves
Were all incapable—they could not be
Victors of him who oft had conquer'd for them!

Ang. Employ the minutes left in aspirations
Of a more healing nature, and in peace
Even with these wretches take thy flight to Heaven.

Doge. I *am* at peace; the peace of certainty
That a sure hour will come, when their sons' sons,
And this proud city, and these azure waters,
And all which makes them eminent and bright,
Shall be a desolation and a curse,
A hissing and a scoff unto the nations,
A Carthage and a Tyre, an Ocean Babel!

Ang. Speak not thus now; the surge of passion still
Sweeps o'er thee to the last; thou dost deceive
Thyself, and canst not injure them—be calmer.

Doge. I stand within eternity, and see
Into eternity, and I behold—
Ay, palpable as I see thy sweet face
For the last time—the days which I denounce
Unto all time against these wave-girt walls,
And they who are indwellers.

Guard [*Coming forward.*]   Doge of Venice,
The Ten are in attendance on your highness.

Doge. Then farewell, Angiolina!—one embrace—
Forgive the old man who hath been to thee
A fond but fatal husband—love my memory—
I would not ask so much for me still living,
But thou canst judge of me more kindly now,
Seeing my evil feelings are at rest.
Besides, of all the fruit of these long years,
Glory, and wealth, and power, and fame, and name,
Which generally leave some flowers to bloom
Even o'er the grave, I have nothing left, not even
A little love, or friendship, or esteem,
No, not enough to extract an epitaph
From ostentatious kinsmen; in one hour
I have uprooted all my former life,
And outlived everything, except thy heart,
The pure, the good, the gentle, which will oft
With unimpair'd but not a clamorous grief

Still keep——Thou turn'st so pale!—Alas! she faints,
She has no breath, no pulse!—Guards! lend your aid—
I cannot leave her thus, and yet 'tis better,
Since every lifeless moment spares a pang.
When she shakes off this temporary death,
I shall be with the Eternal.—Call her women—
One look!—how cold her hand!—as cold as mine
Shall be ere she recovers.—Gently tend her,
And take my last thanks——I am ready now.

[*The Attendants of* ANGIOLINA *enter and surround their mistress,
who has fainted.—Exeunt the* DOGE, *Guards, etc. etc.*

SCENE III

*The Court of the Ducal Palace: The outer gates are shut against the
people.—The* DOGE *enters in his ducal robes, in procession with the
Council of Ten and other Patricians, attended by the Guards, till
they arrive at the top of the 'Giants' Staircase' (where the Doges
took the oaths); the Executioner is stationed there with his sword.—
On arriving, a Chief of the Ten takes off the ducal cap from the
Doge's head.*

Doge. So now the Doge is nothing, and at last
I am again Marino Faliero:
'Tis well to be so, though but for a moment.
Here was I crown'd, and here, bear witness, Heaven!
With how much more contentment I resign
That shining mockery, the ducal bauble,
Than I received the fatal ornament.

One of the Ten. Thou tremblest, Faliero!

Doge.   'Tis with age, then.

Ben. Faliero! hast thou aught further to commend,
Compatible with justice, to the senate?

Doge. I would commend my nephew to their mercy,
My consort to their justice; for methinks
My death, and such a death, might settle all
Between the state and me.

Ben.   They shall be cared for;
Even notwithstanding thine unheard-of crime.

Doge. Unheard of! ay, there's not a history
But shows a thousand crown'd conspirators
Against the people; but to set them free
One sovereign only died, and one is dying.

Ben. And who were they who fell in such a cause?

Doge. The King of Sparta, and the Doge of Venice—
Agis and Faliero!

Ben.   Hast thou more
To utter or to do?

Doge.   May I speak?
Ben.   Thou may'st;
    But recollect the people are without,
    Beyond the compass of the human voice.
Doge. I speak to Time and to Eternity,
    Of which I grow a portion, not to man,
    Ye elements! in which to be resolved
    I hasten, let my voice be as a spirit
    Upon you! Ye blue waves! which bore my banner,
    Ye winds! which flutter'd o'er as if you loved it,
    And fill'd my swelling sails as they were wafted
    To many a triumph! Thou, my native earth,
    Which I have bled for, and thou foreign earth,
    Which drank this willing blood from many a wound!
    Ye stones, in which my gore will not sink, but
    Reek up to Heaven! Ye skies, which will receive it!
    Thou sun! which shinest on these things, and Thou!
    Who kindlest and who quenchest suns!—Attest!
    I am not innocent—but are these guiltless?
    I perish'd, but not unavenged; far ages
    Float up from the abyss of time to be,
    And show these eyes, before they close, the doom
    Of this proud city, and I leave my curse
    On her and hers for ever!——Yes, the hours
    Are silently engendering of the day,
    When she, who built 'gainst Attila a bulwark,
    Shall yield, and bloodlessly and basely yield
    Unto a bastard Attila, without
    Shedding so much blood in her last defence
    As these old veins, oft drain'd in shielding her,
    Shall pour in sacrifice.—She shall be bought
    And sold, and be an appanage to those
    Who shall despise her!—She shall stoop to be
    A province for an empire, petty town
    In lieu of capital, with slaves for senates,
    Beggars for nobles, panders for a people!
    Then when the Hebrew's in thy palaces,[1]
    The Hun in thy high places, and the Greek
    Walks o'er thy mart, and smiles on it for his!
    When thy patricians beg their bitter bread
    In narrow streets, and in their shameful need
    Make their nobility a plea for pity!

[1] The chief palaces on the Brenta now belong to the Jews; who in the earlier times of the republic were only allowed to inhabit Mestri, and not to enter the city of Venice. The whole commerce is in the hands of the Jews and Greeks, and the Huns form the garrison.

Then, when the few who still retain a wreck
Of their great fathers' heritage shall fawn
Round a barbarian Vice of Kings' Vice-gerent,
Even in the palace where they sway'd as sovereigns,
Even in the palace where they slew their sovereign,
Proud of some name they have disgraced, or sprung
From an adulteress boastful of her guilt
With some large gondolier or foreign soldier,
Shall bear about their bastardy in triumph
To the third spurious generation;—when
Thy sons are in the lowest scale of being,
Slaves turn'd o'er to the vanquish'd by the victors,
Despised by cowards for greater cowardice,
And scorn'd even by the vicious for such vices
As in the monstrous grasp of their conception
Defy all codes to image or to name them;
Then when of Cyprus, now thy subject kingdom,
All thine inheritance shall be her shame
Entail'd on thy less virtuous daughters, grown
A wider proverb for worse prostitution;—
When all the ills of conquer'd states shall cling thee,
Vice without splendour, sin without relief
Even from the gloss of love to smooth it o'er,
But in its stead, coarse lusts of habitude,
Prurient yet passionless, cold studied lewdness,
Depraving nature's frailty to an art;—
When these and more are heavy on thee, when
Smiles without mirth, and pastimes without pleasure,
Youth without honour, age without respect,
Meanness and weakness, and a sense of woe
'Gainst which thou wilt not strive, and dar'st not murmur,[1]

[1] If the Doge's prophecy seem remarkable, look to the following, made by Alamanni two hundred and seventy years ago: 'There is one very singular prophecy concerning Venice: "If thou dost not change," it says to that proud republic, "thy liberty, which is already on the wing, will not reckon a century more than the thousandth year." If we carry back the epocha of Venetian freedom to the establishment of the government under which the republic flourished, we shall find that the date of the election of the first Doge is 697; and if we add one century to a thousand, that is, eleven hundred years, we shall find the sense of the prediction to be literally this: "Thy liberty will not last till 1797." Recollect that Venice ceased to be free in the year 1796, the fifth year of the French republic; and you will perceive, that there never was prediction more pointed, or more exactly followed by the event. You will, therefore, note as very remarkable the three lines of Alamanni addressed to Venice; which, however, no one has pointed out:

"Se non cangi pensier, un secol solo
Non conterà sopra 'l millesimo anno
Tua libertà, che va fuggendo a volo."

Many prophecies have passed for such, and many men have been called prophets for much less.'—GINGUENÉ, Hist. Lit. de l'Italie, t. ix., p. 144.

Have made thee last and worst of peopled deserts,
Then, in the last gasp of thine agony,
Amidst thy many murders, think of *mine*!
Thou den of drunkards with the blood of princes![1]
Gehenna of the waters! thou sea Sodom!
Thus I devote thee to the infernal gods!
Thee and thy serpent seed!

> [*Here the* DOGE *turns and addresses the Executioner.*
> Slave, do thine office!

Strike as I struck the foe!   Strike as I would
Have struck those tyrants!   Strike deep as my curse!
Strike—and but once!

> [*The* DOGE *throws himself upon his knees, and as the Executioner
> raises his sword the scene closes.*

SCENE IV

*The Piazza and Piazzetta of Saint Mark's.—The People in crowds
gathered round the grated gates of the Ducal Palace, which are shut*

First Citizen. I have gain'd the gate, and can discern the Ten,
    Robed in their gowns of state, ranged round the Doge.
Second Cit. I cannot reach thee with mine utmost effort.
    How is it? let us hear at least, since sight
    Is thus prohibited unto the people,
    Except the occupiers of those bars.
First Cit. One has approach'd the Doge, and now they strip
    The ducal bonnet from his head—and now
    He raises his keen eyes to Heaven; I see
    Them glitter, and his lips move—Hush! hush!—no,
    'Twas but a murmur—Curse upon the distance!
    His words are inarticulate, but the voice
    Swells up like mutter'd thunder; would we could
    But gather a sole sentence!
Second Cit. Hush! we perhaps may catch the sound.
First Cit.   'Tis vain,
    I cannot hear him.—How his hoary hair

[1] Of the first fifty Doges, *five* abdicated—*five* were banished with their eyes
put out—*five* were MASSACRED—and *nine* deposed; so that *nineteen* out of fifty
lost the throne by violence, besides two who fell in battle: this occurred long
previous to the reign of Marino Faliero. One of his more immediate predecessors, Andrea Dandolo, died of vexation. Marino Faliero himself perished
as related. Amongst his successors, Foscari, after seeing his son repeatedly
tortured and banished, was deposed, and died of breaking a blood-vessel, on
hearing the bell of Saint Mark's toll for the election of his successor. Morosini
was impeached for the loss of Candia; but this was previous to his dukedom,
during which he conquered the Morea, and was styled the Peloponnesian.
Faliero might truly say:
    'Thou den of drunkards with the blood of princes!'

Streams on the wind like foam upon the wave!
Now—now—he kneels—and now they form a circle
Round him, and all is hidden—but I see
The lifted sword in air——Ah! hark! it falls!

[The People murmur.

Third Cit. Then they have murder'd him who would have freed
  us.
Fourth Cit. He was a kind man to the commons ever.
Fifth Cit. Wisely they did to keep their portals barr'd.
  Would we had known the work they were preparing
  Ere we were summon'd here—we would have brought
  Weapons, and forced them!
Sixth Cit.   Are you sure he's dead?
First Cit. I saw the sword fall—Lo! what have we here!

*Enter on the Balcony of the Palace which fronts Saint Mark's Place
  a* CHIEF OF THE TEN,[1] *with a bloody sword. He waves it thrice
  before the people, and exclaims:*
' Justice hath dealt upon the mighty Traitor!'

  *[The gates are opened; the populace rush in towards the 'Giants'
    Staircase,' where the execution has taken place. The fore-
    most of them exclaims to those behind:*
The gory head rolls down the Giants' Steps!

[The curtain falls.

[1] 'Un Capo de' Dieci' are the words of Sanuto's Chronicle

CAIN[1]

A MYSTERY

Now the Serpent was more subtil than any beast of the field which the Lord God had made.—Gen. iii. 1.

[1] [*Cain* was begun at Ravenna, on 16th July 1821, completed on 9th September, and published, in the same volume with *Sardanapalus* and *The Two Foscari*, in December.]

PREFACE

THE following scenes are entitled 'A Mystery,' in conformity with the ancient title annexed to dramas upon similar subjects, which were styled 'Mysteries, or Moralities.' The author has by no means taken the same liberties with his subject which were common formerly, as may be seen by any reader curious enough to refer to those very profane productions, whether in English, French, Italian, or Spanish. The author has endeavoured to preserve the language adapted to his characters; and where it is (and this is but rarely) taken from actual *Scripture*, he has made as little alteration, even of words, as the rhythm would permit. The reader will recollect that the book of Genesis does not state that Eve was tempted by a demon, but by 'the Serpent'; and that only because he was 'the most subtil of all the beasts of the field.' Whatever interpretation the Rabbins and the Fathers may have put upon this, I take the words as I find them, and reply, with Bishop Watson upon similar occasions, when the Fathers were quoted to him, as Moderator in the schools of Cambridge, 'Behold the Book!'—holding up the Scripture. It is to be recollected, that my present subject has nothing to do with the *New Testament*, to which no reference can be here made without anachronism. With the poems upon similar topics I have not been recently familiar. Since I was twenty, I have never read Milton; but I had read him so frequently before, that this may make little difference. Gesner's *Death of Abel* I have never read since I was eight years of age, at Aberdeen. The general impression of my recollection is delight; but of the contents I remember only that Cain's wife was called Mahala, and Abel's Thirza: in the following pages I have called them 'Adah' and 'Zillah,' the earliest female names which occur in Genesis; they were those of Lamech's wives: those of Cain and Abel are not called by their names. Whether, then, a coincidence of subject may have caused the same in expression, I know nothing, and care as little.

The reader will please to bear in mind (what few choose to recollect), that there is no allusion to a future state in any of the books of Moses, nor indeed in the Old Testament. For a reason for this extraordinary omission he may consult Warburton's *Divine Legation*; whether satisfactory or not, no better has yet been assigned. I have therefore supposed it new to Cain, without, I hope, any perversion of Holy Writ.

With regard to the language of Lucifer, it was difficult for me to make him talk like a clergyman upon the same subjects; but I have done what I could to restrain him within the bounds of spiritual politeness. If he disclaims having tempted Eve in the shape of the Serpent, it is only because the book of Genesis has not the most distant allusion to anything of the kind, but merely to the Serpent in his serpentine capacity.

Note.—The reader will perceive that the author has partly adopted in this poem the notion of Cuvier, that the world had been destroyed several times before the creation of man. This speculation, derived from the different strata and the bones of enormous and unknown animals found in them, is not contrary to the Mosaic account, but rather confirms it; as no human bones have yet been discovered in those strata, although those of many known animals are found near the remains of the unknown. The assertion of Lucifer, that the pre-Adamite world was also peopled by rational beings much more intelligent than man, and proportionably powerful to the mammoth, etc. etc., is, of course, a poetical fiction to help him to make out his case.

I ought to add, that there is a 'tramelogedia' of Alfieri, called *Abele.*—I have never read that, nor any other of the posthumous works of the writer, except his Life.

Ravenna,
20th September 1821.

DRAMATIS PERSONÆ

Men.—ADAM
       CAIN
       ABEL

Spirits.—ANGEL OF THE LORD
       LUCIFER

Women.—EVE
       ADAH
       ZILLAH

CAIN

ACT I

The Land without Paradise.—Time, Sunrise

ADAM, EVE, CAIN, ABEL, ADAH, ZILLAH, *offering a Sacrifice.*

Adam. GOD, the Eternal! Infinite! All-wise!—
Who out of darkness on the deep didst make
Light on the waters with a word—all hail!
Jehovah, with returning light, all hail!
Eve. God! who didst name the day, and separate
Morning from night, till then divided never—
Who didst divide the wave from wave, and call
Part of thy work the firmament—all hail!
Abel. God! who didst call the elements into
Earth, ocean, air, and fire, and with the day
And night, and worlds which these illuminate,
Or shadow, madest beings to enjoy them,
And love both them and thee—all hail! all hail!
Adah. God, the Eternal! Parent of all things!
Who didst create these best and beauteous beings,
To be beloved, more than all, save thee—
Let me love thee and them:—All hail! all hail!
Zillah. Oh, God! who loving, making, blessing all,
Yet didst permit the Serpent to creep in,
And drive my father forth from Paradise,
Keep us from further evil:—Hail! all hail!
Adam. Son Cain, my first-born, wherefore art thou silent?
Cain. Why should I speak?
Adam.   To pray.
Cain.   Have ye not pray'd?
Adam. We have, most fervently.
Cain.   And loudly: I
Have heard you.
Adam.   So will God, I trust.
Abel.   Amen!
Adam. But thou, my eldest born, art silent still.
Cain. 'Tis better I should be so.
Adam.   Wherefore so?
Cain. I have nought to ask.

Adam.   Nor aught to thank for?
Cain.   No.
Adam.   Dost thou not live?
Cain.   Must I not die?
Eve.   Alas!
  The fruit of our forbidden tree begins
  To fall.
Adam.   And we must gather it again.
  Oh, God! why didst thou plant the tree of knowledge?
Cain. And wherefore pluck'd ye not the tree of life?
  Ye might have then defied him.
Adam.   Oh! my son,
  Blaspheme not: these are serpent's words.
Cain.   Why not?
  The snake spoke *truth*: it *was* the tree of knowledge;
  It *was* the tree of life: knowledge is good,
  And life is good; and how can both be evil?
Eve. My boy! thou speakest as I spoke, in sin,
  Before thy birth: let me not see renew'd
  My misery in thine. I have repented.
  Let me not see my offspring fall into
  The snares beyond the walls of Paradise,
  Which e'en in Paradise destroy'd his parents.
  Content thee with what *is*. Had we been so,
  Thou now hadst been contented.—Oh, my son!
Adam. Our orisons completed, let us hence,
  Each to his task of toil—not heavy, though
  Needful: the earth is young, and yields us kindly
  Her fruits with little labour.
Eve.   Cain, my son
  Behold thy father cheerful and resign'd,
  And do as he doth.
                  [*Exeunt* ADAM *and* EVE.
Zillah.   Wilt thou not, my brother?
Abel. Why wilt thou wear this gloom upon thy brow,
  Which can avail thee nothing, save to rouse
  The Eternal anger?
Adah.   My beloved Cain,
  Wilt thou frown even on me?
Cain.   No, Adah! no;
  I fain would be alone a little while.
  Abel, I'm sick at heart; but it will pass.
  Precede me, brother—I will follow shortly.
  And you, too, sisters, tarry not behind;
  Your gentleness must not be harshly met:
  I'll follow you anon.

Adah.   If not, I will
  Return to seek you here.
Abel.   The peace of God
  Be on your spirit, brother!
             [*Exeunt* ABEL, ZILLAH, *and* ADAH.
Cain. [*Solus.*]   And this is
  Life!—Toil! and wherefore should I toil?—because
  My father could not keep his place in Eden.
  What had *I* done in this?—I was unborn:
  I sought not to be born; nor love the state
  To which that birth has brought me. Why did he
  Yield to the serpent and the woman? or,
  Yielding, why suffer? What was there in this?
  The tree was planted, and why not for him?
  If not, why place him near it, where it grew,
  The fairest in the centre? They have but
  One answer to all questions, ''Twas *his* will,
  And *he* is good.' How know I that? Because
  He is all-powerful, must all-good, too, follow?
  I judge but by the fruits—and they are bitter—
  Which I must feed on for a fault not mine.
  Whom have we here?—A shape like to the angels,
  Yet of a sterner and a sadder aspect
  Of spiritual essence: why do I quake?
  Why should I fear him more than other spirits,
  Whom I see daily wave their fiery swords
  Before the gates round which I linger oft,
  In twilight's hour, to catch a glimpse of those
  Gardens which are my just inheritance,
  Ere the night closes o'er the inhibited walls
  And the immortal trees which overtop
  The cherubim-defended battlements?
  If I shrink not from these, the fire-arm'd angels,
  Why should I quail from him who now approaches?
  Yet he seems mightier far than them, nor less
  Beauteous, and yet not all as beautiful
  As he hath been, and might be: sorrow seems
  Half of his immortality. And is it
  So? and can aught grieve save humanity?
  He cometh.

              Enter LUCIFER.

Lucifer.   Mortal!
Cain.   Spirit, who art thou?
Lucifer. Master of spirits.

Cain.   And being so, canst thou
  Leave them, and walk with dust?
Lucifer.   I know the thoughts
  Of dust, and feel for it, and with you.
Cain.   How!
  You know my thoughts?
Lucifer.   They are the thoughts of all
  Worthy of thought;—'tis your immortal part
  Which speaks within you.
Cain.   What immortal part?
  This has not been reveal'd: the tree of life
  Was withheld from us by my father's folly,
  While that of knowledge, by my mother's haste,
  Was pluck'd too soon; and all the fruit is death!
Lucifer. They have deceived thee; thou shalt live.
Cain.   I live,
  But live to die: and, living, see nothing
  To make death hateful, save an innate clinging,
  A loathsome, and yet all invincible
  Instinct of life, which I abhor, as I
  Despise myself, yet cannot overcome—
  And so I live. Would I had never lived!
Lucifer. Thou livest, and must live for ever: think not
  The earth, which is thine outward cov'ring, is
  Existence—it will cease, and thou wilt be
  No less than thou art now.
Cain.   No *less!* and why
  No more?
Lucifer.   It may be thou shalt be as we.
Cain. And ye?
Lucifer.   Are everlasting.
Cain.   Are ye happy?
Lucifer. We are mighty.
Cain.   Are ye happy?
Lucifer.   No: art thou?
Cain. How should I be so? Look on me!
Lucifer.   Poor clay!
  And thou pretendest to be wretched! Thou!
Cain. I am:—and thou, with all thy might, what art thou?
Lucifer. One who aspired to be what made thee, and
  Would not have made thee what thou art.
Cain.   Ah!
  Thou look'st almost a god; and——
Lucifer.   I am none:
  And having fail'd to be one, would be nought
  Save what I am. He conquer'd; let him reign!

Cain. Who?
Lucifer.   Thy sire's Maker, and the earth's.
Cain.   And heaven's,
  And all that in them is.   So I have heard
  His seraphs sing; and so my father saith.
Lucifer. They say—what they muſt sing and say, on pain
  Of being that which I am—and thou art—
  Of spirits and of men.
Cain.   And what is that?
Lucifer. Souls who dare use their immortality—
  Souls who dare look the Omnipotent tyrant in
  His everlaſting face, and tell him that
  His evil is not good! If he has made,
  As he saith—which I know not, nor believe—
  But, if he made us—he cannot unmake:
  We are immortal!—nay, he'd *have* us so,
  That he may torture:—let him! He is great—
  But, in his greatness, is no happier than
  We in our conflict! Goodness would not make
  Evil; and what else hath he made?   But let him
  Sit on his vaſt and solitary throne,
  Creating worlds, to make eternity
  Less burthensome to his immense exiſtence
  And unparticipated solitude;
  Let him crowd orb on orb: he is alone
  Indefinite, indissoluble tyrant;
  Could he but crush himself, 'twere the beſt boon
  He ever granted: but let him reign on,
  And multiply himself in misery!
  Spirits and Men, at leaſt we sympathize—
  And, suffering in concert, make our pangs
  Innumerable, more endurable,
  By the unbounded sympathy of all
  With all! But *He!* so wretched in his height,
  So reſtless in his wretchedness, muſt ſtill
  Create, and re-create——
Cain. Thou speak'ſt to me of things which long have swum
  In visions through my thought: I never could
  Reconcile what I saw with what I heard.
  My father and my mother talk to me
  Of serpents, and of fruits and trees: I see
  The gates of what they call their Paradise
  Guarded by fiery-sworded cherubim,
  Which shut them out, and me: I feel the weight
  Of daily toil, and conſtant thought: I look
  Around a world where I seem nothing, with

Thoughts which arise within me, as if they
Could master all things—but I thought alone
This misery was *mine*.—My father is
Tamed down; my mother has forgot the mind
Which made her thirst for knowledge at the risk
Of an eternal curse; my brother is
A watching shepherd boy, who offers up
The firstlings of the flock to him who bids
The earth yield nothing to us without sweat;
My sister Zillah sings an earlier hymn
Than the birds' matins; and my Adah, my
Own and beloved, she, too, understands not
The mind which overwhelms me: never till
Now met I aught to sympathise with me.
'Tis well—I rather would consort with spirits.

Lucifer. And hadst thou not been fit to thine own soul
For such companionship, I would not now
Have stood before thee as I am: a serpent
Had been enough to charm ye, as before.

Cain. Ah! didst *thou* tempt my mother?

Lucifer.   I tempt none,
Save with the truth: was not the tree the tree
Of knowledge? and was not the tree of life
Still fruitful?   Did *I* bid her pluck them not?
Did *I* plant things prohibited within
The reach of beings innocent, and curious
By their own innocence?   I would have made ye
Gods: and even He who thrust ye forth, so thrust ye
Because 'ye should not eat the fruits of life,
And become gods as we.' Were those his words?

Cain. They were, as I have heard from those who heard them.
In thunder.

Lucifer.   Then who was the demon? He
Who would not let ye live, or he who would
Have made ye live for ever in the joy
And power of knowledge?

Cain.   Would they had snatch'd both
The fruits or neither!

Lucifer.   One is yours already,
The other may be still.

Cain.   How so?

Lucifer.   By being
Yourselves, in your resistance.   Nothing can
Quench the mind, if the mind will be itself
And centre of surrounding things—'tis made
To sway.

Cain.   But didst thou tempt my parents?
Lucifer.   I?
  Poor clay! what should I tempt them for, or how?
Cain. They say the serpent was a spirit.
Lucifer.   Who
  Saith that? It is not written so on high:
  The proud One will not so far falsify,
  Though man's vast fears and little vanity
  Would make him cast upon the spiritual nature
  His own low failing. The snake *was* the snake—
  No more; and yet not less than those he tempted
  In nature being earth also—*more* in *wisdom*,
  Since he could overcome them, and foreknew
  The knowledge fatal to their narrow joys.
  Think'st thou I'd take the shape of things that die?
Cain. But the thing had a demon?
Lucifer.   He but woke one
  In those he spake to with his forky tongue.
  I tell thee that the serpent was no more
  Than a mere serpent: ask the cherubim
  Who guard the tempting tree. When thousand ages
  Have roll'd o'er your dead ashes, and your seed's,
  The seed of the then world may thus array
  Their earliest fault in fable, and attribute
  To me a shape I scorn, as I scorn all
  That bows to him, who made things but to bend
  Before his sullen, sole eternity;
  But we, who see the truth, must speak it. Thy
  Fond parents listen'd to a creeping thing,
  And fell. For what should spirits tempt them? What
  Was there to envy in the narrow bounds
  Of Paradise, that spirits who pervade
  Space——but I speak to thee of what thou know'st not,
  With all thy tree of knowledge.
Cain.   But thou canst not
  Speak aught of knowledge which I would not know,
  And do not thirst to know, and bear a mind
  To know.
Lucifer.   And heart to look on?
Cain.   Be it proved.
Lucifer. Darest thou to look on Death?
Cain.   He has not yet
  Been seen.
Lucifer.   But must be undergone.
Cain.   My father
  Says he is something dreadful, and my mother

Weeps when he 's named; and Abel lifts his eyes
To heaven, and Zillah casts hers to the earth,
And sighs a prayer: and Adah looks on me,
And speaks not.

Lucifer.   And thou?

Cain.   Thoughts unspeakable
Crowd in my breast to burning, when I hear
Of this almighty Death, who is, it seems,
Inevitable.   Could I wrestle with him?
I wrestled with the lion, when a boy,
In play, till he ran roaring from my gripe.

Lucifer. It has no shape; but will absorb all things
That bear the form of earth-born being.

Cain.   Ah!
I thought it was a being: who could do
Such evil things to beings save a being?

Lucifer. Ask the Destroyer.

Cain.   Who?

Lucifer.   The Maker—call him
Which name thou wilt: he makes but to destroy.

Cain. I knew not that, yet thought it, since I heard
Of death: although I know not what it is,
Yet it seems horrible.   I have look'd out
In the vast desolate night in search of him;
And when I saw gigantic shadows in
The umbrage of the walls of Eden, chequer'd
By the far-flashing of the cherubs' swords,
I watch'd for what I thought his coming; for
With fear rose longing in my heart to know
What 'twas which shook us all—but nothing came.
And then I turn'd my weary eyes from off
Our native and forbidden Paradise,
Up to the lights above us, in the azure,
Which are so beautiful: shall they, too, die?

Lucifer. Perhaps—but long outlive both thine and thee.

Cain. I'm glad of that: I would not have them die—
They are so lovely.   What is death?   I fear,
I feel, it is a dreadful thing; but what,
I cannot compass: 'tis denounced against us,
Both them who sinn'd and sinn'd not, as an ill—
What ill?

Lucifer.   To be resolved into the earth.

Cain. But shall I know it?

Lucifer.   As I know not death,
I cannot answer.

Cain.   Were I quiet earth
   That were no evil: would I ne'er had been
   Aught else but dust!
Lucifer.   That is a grovelling wish,
   Less than thy father's, for he wish'd to know.
Cain. But not to live, or wherefore pluck'd he not
   The life-tree?
Lucifer.   He was hinder'd.
Cain.   Deadly error!
   Not to snatch first that fruit:—but ere he pluck'd
   The knowledge, he was ignorant of death.
   Alas! I scarcely now know what it is,
   And yet I fear it—fear I know not what!
Lucifer. And I, who know all things, fear nothing; see
   What is true knowledge.
Cain.   Wilt thou teach me all?
Lucifer. Ay, upon one condition.
Cain.   Name it.
Lucifer.   That
   Thou dost fall down and worship me—thy Lord.
Cain. Thou art not the Lord my father worships.
Lucifer.   No.
Cain. His equal?
Lucifer.   No;—I have nought in common with him!
   Nor would: I would be aught above—beneath—
   Aught save a sharer or a servant of
   His power. I dwell apart: but I am great:—
   Many there are who worship me, and more
   Who shall—be thou amongst the first.
Cain.   I never
   As yet have bow'd unto my father's God,
   Although my brother Abel oft implores
   That I would join with him in sacrifice:—
   Why should I bow to thee?
Lucifer.   Hast thou ne'er bow'd
   To him?
Cain.   Have I not said it?—need I say it?
   Could not thy mighty knowledge teach thee that?
Lucifer. He who bows not to him has bow'd to me!
Cain. But I will bend to neither.
Lucifer.   Ne'er the less,
   Thou art my worshipper: not worshipping
   Him makes thee mine the same.
Cain.   And what is that?
Lucifer. Thou'lt know here—and hereafter.

Cain.   Let me but
Be taught the myſtery of my being.
Lucifer.   Follow
Where I will lead thee.
Cain.   But I muſt retire
To till the earth—for I had promised——
Lucifer.   What?
Cain. To cull some firſt-fruits.
Lucifer.   Why?
Cain.   To offer up
With Abel on an altar.
Lucifer.   Saidſt thou not
Thou ne'er hadſt bent to him who made thee?
Cain.   Yes—
But Abel's earneſt prayer has wrought upon me;
The offering is more his than mine—and Adah——
Lucifer. Why doſt thou hesitate?
Cain.   She is my siſter,
Born on the same day, of the same womb; and
She wrung from me, with tears, this promise; and
Rather than see her weep, I would, methinks,
Bear all—and worship aught.
Lucifer.   Then follow me!
Cain. I will.

                        Enter ADAH.

Adah.   My brother, I have come for thee;
It is our hour of reſt and joy—and we
Have less without thee.   Thou haſt labour'd not
This morn; but I have done thy task: the fruits
Are ripe, and glowing as the light which ripens:
Come away.
Cain.   See'ſt thou not?
Adah.   I see an angel;
We have seen many: will he share our hour
Of reſt?—he is welcome.
Cain.   But he is not like
The angels we have seen.
Adah.   Are there, then, others?
But he is welcome, as they were: they deign'd
To be our gueſts—will he?
Cain [*To Lucifer.*]   Wilt thou?
Lucifer.   I ask
Thee to be mine.
Cain.   I muſt away with him.
Adah. And leave us?
Cain.   Ay.

Adah.   And *me?*
Cain.   Beloved Adah!
Adah. Let me go with thee.
Lucifer.   No, she must not.
Adah.   Who
   Art thou that steppest between heart and heart?
Cain. He is a god.
Adah.   How know'st thou?
Cain.   He speaks like
   A god.
Adah.   So did the serpent, and it lied.
Lucifer. Thou errest, Adah!—was not the tree that
   Of knowledge?
Adah.   Ay—to our eternal sorrow.
Lucifer. And yet that grief is knowledge—so he lied not:
   And if he did betray you, 'twas with truth;
   And truth in its own essence cannot be
   But good.
Adah.   But all we know of it has gather'd
   Evil on ill: expulsion from our home,
   And dread, and toil, and sweat, and heaviness;
   Remorse of that which was—and hope of that
   Which cometh not. Cain! walk not with this spirit.
   Bear with what we have borne, and love me—I
   Love thee.
Lucifer.   More than thy mother, and thy sire?
Adah. I do. Is that a sin, too.
Lucifer.   No, not yet;
   It one day will be in your children.
Adah.   What!
   Must not my daughter love her brother Enoch?
Lucifer. Not as thou lovest Cain.
Adah.   Oh, my God!
   Shall they not love and bring forth things that love
   Out of their love? have they not drawn their milk
   Out of this bosom? was not he, their father,
   Born of the same sole womb, in the same hour
   With me? did we not love each other? and
   In multiplying our being multiply
   Things which will love each other as we love
   Them?—And as I love thee, my Cain! go not
   Forth with this spirit; he is not of ours.
Lucifer. The sin I speak of is not of my making
   And cannot be a sin in you—whate'er
   It seem in those who will replace ye in
   Mortality.

Adah. What is the sin which is not
Sin in itself? Can circumstance make sin
Or virtue?—if it doth, we are the slaves
Of——

Lucifer. Higher things than ye are slaves: and higher
Than them or ye would be so, did they not
Prefer an independency of torture
To the smooth agonies of adulation,
In hymns and harpings, and self-seeking prayers,
To that which is omnipotent, because
. It is omnipotent, and not from love,
But terror and self-hope.

Adah. Omnipotence
Must be all goodness.

Lucifer. Was it so in Eden?

Adah. Fiend! tempt me not with beauty; thou art fairer,
Than was the serpent, and as false.

Lucifer. As true.
Ask Eve, your mother: bears she not the knowledge
Of good and evil?

Adah. Oh, my mother! thou
Hast pluck'd a fruit more fatal to thine offspring
Than to thyself; thou at the least hast pass'd
Thy youth in Paradise, in innocent
And happy intercourse with happy spirits:
But we, thy children, ignorant of Eden,
Are girt about by demons, who assume
The words of God, and tempt us with our own
Dissatisfied and curious thoughts—as thou
Wert work'd on by the snake, in thy most flush'd
And heedless, harmless wantonness of bliss.
I cannot answer this immortal thing
Which stands before me; I cannot abhor him;
I look upon him with a pleasing fear,
And yet I fly not from him: in his eye
There is a fastening attraction which
Fixes my fluttering eyes on his; my heart
Beats quick; he awes me, and yet draws me near,
Nearer and nearer:—Cain—Cain—save me from him!

Cain. What dreads my Adah? This is no ill spirit.

Adah. He is not God—nor God's: I have beheld
The cherubs and the seraphs; he looks not
Like them.

Cain. But there are spirits loftier still—
The archangels.

Lucifer. And still loftier than the archangels.

Adah. Ay—but not blessed.

Lucifer.   If the blessedness
  Consists in slavery—no.

Adah.   I have heard it said,
  The seraphs *love most*—cherubim *know most*—
  And this should be a cherub—since he loves not.

Lucifer. And if the higher knowledge quenches love,
  What must *he be* you cannot love when known?
  Since the all-knowing cherubim love least,
  The seraphs' love can be but ignorance:
  That they are not compatible, the doom
  Of thy fond parents, for their daring, proves.
  Choose betwixt love and knowledge—since there is
  No other choice: your sire hath chosen already;
  His worship is but fear.

Adah.   Oh, Cain! choose love.

Cain. For thee, my Adah, I choose not—it was
  Born with me—but I love nought else.

Adah.   Our parents?

Cain. Did they love us when they snatch'd from the tree
  That which hath driven us all from Paradise?

Adah. We were not born then—and if we had been,
  Should we not love them and our children, Cain?

Cain. My little Enoch! and his lisping sister!
  Could I but deem them happy, I would half
  Forget——but it can never be forgotten
  Through thrice a thousand generations! never
  Shall men love the remembrance of the man
  Who sow'd the seed of evil and mankind
  In the same hour! They plucked the tree of science
  And sin—and, not content with their own sorrow,
  Begot *me*—*thee*—and all the few that are,
  And all the unnumber'd and innumerable
  Multitudes, millions, myriads, which may be,
  To inherit agonies accumulated
  By ages!—and *I* must be sire of such things!
  Thy beauty and thy love—my love and joy,
  The rapturous moment and the placid hour,
  All we love in our children and each other,
  But lead them and ourselves through many years
  Of sin and pain—or few, but still of sorrow,
  Intercheck'd with an instant of brief pleasure,
  To Death—the unknown! Methinks the tree of knowledge
  Hath not fulfill'd its promise:—if they sinn'd,
  At least they ought to have known all things that are

Of knowledge—and the mystery of death.
What do they know?—that they are miserable.
What need of snakes and fruits to teach us that?
Adah. I am not wretched, Cain, and if thou
Wert happy——
Cain.   Be thou happy, then, alone—
I will have nought to do with happiness,
Which humbles me and mine.
Adah.   Alone I could not,
Nor *would* be happy: but with those around us
I think I could be so, despite of death,
Which, as I know it not, I dread not, though
It seems an awful shadow—if I may
Judge from what I have heard.
Lucifer.   And thou couldst not
Alone, thou say'st, be happy?
Adah.   Alone! Oh, my God!
Who could be happy and alone, or good?
To me my solitude seems sin; unless
When I think how soon I shall see my brother,
His brother, and our children, and our parents.
Lucifer. Yet thy God is alone; and is he happy,
Lonely, and good?
Adah.   He is not so; he hath
The angels and the mortals to make happy,
And thus becomes so in diffusing joy?
What else can joy be, but the spreading joy?
Lucifer. Ask of your sire, the exile fresh from Eden;
Or of his first-born son: ask your own heart;
It is not tranquil.
Adah.   Alas! no! and you—
Are you of heaven?
Lucifer.   If I am not, inquire
The cause of this all-spreading happiness
(Which you proclaim) of the all-great and good
Maker of life and living things: it is
His secret, and he keeps it. *We* must bear,
And some of us resist, and both in vain,
His seraphs say: but it is worth the trial,
Since better may not be without: there is
A wisdom in the spirit, which directs
To right, as in the dim blue air the eye
Of you, young mortals, lights at once upon
The star which watches, welcoming the morn.
Adah. It is a beautiful star; I love it for
Its beauty.

Lucifer.   And why not adore?
Adah.   Our father
  Adores the Invisible only.
Lucifer.   But the symbols
  Of the Invisible are the loveliest
  Of what is visible; and yon bright star
  Is leader of the host of heaven.
Adah.   Our father
  Saith that he has beheld the God himself
  Who made him and our mother.
Lucifer.   Hast *thou* seen him?
Adah. Yes—in his works.
Lucifer.   But in his being?
Adah.   No—
  Save in my father, who is God's own image;
  Or in his angels, who are like to thee—
  And brighter, yet less beautiful and powerful
  In seeming: as the silent sunny noon,
  All light, they look upon us; but thou seem'st
  Like an ethereal night, where long white clouds
  Streak the deep purple, and unnumber'd stars
  Spangle the wonderful mysterious vault
  With things that look as if they would be suns;
  So beautiful, unnumber'd, and endearing,
  Not dazzling, and yet drawing us to them,
  They fill my eyes with tears, and so dost thou.
  Thou seem'st unhappy: do not make us so,
  And I will weep for thee.
Lucifer.   Alas! those tears!
  Couldst thou but know what oceans will be shed——
Adah. By me?
Lucifer.   By all.
Adah.   What all?
Lucifer.   The million millions—
  The myriad myriads—the all-peopled earth—
  The unpeopled earth—and the o'er-peopled Hell,
  Of which thy bosom is the germ.
Adah.   O Cain!
  This spirit curseth us.
Cain.   Let him say on;
  Him will I follow.
Adah.   Whither?
Lucifer.   To a place
  Whence he shall come back to thee in an hour;
  But in that hour see things of many days.
Adah. How can that be?

Lucifer.   Did not your Maker make
  Out of old worlds this new one in few days?
  And cannot I, who aided in this work,
  Show in an hour what he hath made in many,
  Or hath destroy'd in few?
Cain.   Lead on.
Adah.   Will he,
  In sooth, return within an hour?
Lucifer.   He shall.
  With us acts are exempt from time, and we
  Can crowd eternity into an hour,
  Or stretch an hour into eternity:
  We breathe not by a mortal measurement—
  But that's a mystery.   Cain, come on with me.
Adah. Will he return?
Lucifer.   Ay, woman! he alone
  Of mortals from that place (the first and last
  Who shall return, save ONE), shall come back to thee,
  To make that silent and expectant world
  As populous as this: at present there
  Are few inhabitants.
Adah.   Where dwellest thou?
Lucifer. Throughout all space.   Where should I dwell? Where are
  Thy God or Gods—there am I: all things are
  Divided with me; life and death—and time—
  Eternity—and heaven and earth—and that
  Which is not heaven nor earth, but peopled with
  Those who once peopled or shall people both—
  These are my realms!   So that I do divide
  His, and possess a kingdom which is not
  His.   If I were not that which I have said,
  Could I stand here?   His angels are within
  Your vision.
Adah.   So they were when the fair serpent
  Spoke with our mother first.
Lucifer.   Cain! thou hast heard.
  If thou dost long for knowledge, I can satiate
  That thirst; nor ask thee to partake of fruits
  Which shall deprive thee of a single good
  The conqueror has left thee.   Follow me.
Cain. Spirit, I have said it.

                            [*Exeunt* LUCIFER *and* CAIN.
Adah. [*Follows, exclaiming.*]   Cain! my brother! Cain!

ACT II

SCENE I

The Abyss of Space

Cain. I tread on air, and sink not; yet I fear
  To sink.
Lucifer.   Have faith in me, and thou shalt be
  Borne on the air, of which I am the prince.
Cain. Can I do so without impiety?
Lucifer. Believe—and sink not! doubt—and perish! thus
  Would run the edict of the other God,
  Who names me demon to his angels; they
  Echo the sound to miserable things,
  Which, knowing nought beyond their shallow senses,
  Worship the word which strikes their ear, and deem
  Evil or good what is proclaim'd to them
  In their abasement.   I will have none such:
  Worship or worship not, thou shalt behold
  The worlds beyond thy little world, nor be
  Amerced for doubts beyond thy little life,
  With torture of *my* dooming.   There will come
  An hour, when, toss'd upon some water-drops,
  A man shall say to a man, 'Believe in me,
  And walk the waters'; and the man shall walk
  The billows and be safe.   *I* will not say,
  Believe in *me*, as a conditional creed
  To save thee; but fly with me o'er the gulf
  Of space an equal flight, and I will show
  What thou dar'st not deny,—the history
  Of past, and present, and of future worlds.
Cain. Oh, God, or demon, or whate'er thou art,
  Is yon our earth?
Lucifer.   Dost thou not recognize
  The dust which form'd your father?
Cain.   Can it be?
  Yon small blue circle, swinging in far ether,
  With an inferior circlet near it still,
  Which looks like that which lit our earthly night?
  Is this our Paradise?   Where are its walls,
  And they who guard them?
Lucifer.   Point me out the site
  Of Paradise.
Cain.   How should I?   As we move
  Like sunbeams onward, it grows small and smaller,

And as it waxes little, and then less,
Gathers a halo round it, like the light
Which shone the roundest of the stars, when I
Beheld them from the skirts of Paradise:
Methinks they both, as we recede from them,
Appear to join the innumerable stars
Which are around us; and, as we move on,
Increase their myriads.

Lucifer.   And if there should be
Worlds greater than thine own, inhabited
By greater things, and they themselves far more
In number than the dust of thy dull earth,
Though multiplied to animated atoms,
All living, and all doom'd to death, and wretched,
What wouldst thou think?

Cain.   I should be proud of thought
Which knew such things.

Lucifer.   But if that high thought were
Link'd to a servile mass of matter, and,
Knowing such things, aspiring to such things,
And science still beyond them, were chain'd down
To the most gross and petty paltry wants,
All foul and fulsome, and the very best
Of thine enjoyments a sweet degradation,
A most enervating and filthy cheat
To lure thee on to the renewal of
Fresh souls and bodies, all foredoom'd to be
As frail, and few so happy——

Cain.   Spirit! I
Know nought of death, save as a dreadful thing
Of which I have heard my parents speak, as of
A hideous heritage I owe to them
No less than life; a heritage not happy,
If I may judge, till now.   But, spirit! if
It be as thou hast said (and I within
Feel the prophetic torture of its truth),
Here let me die; for to give birth to those
Who can but suffer many years, and die,
Methinks is merely propagating death,
And multiplying murder.

Lucifer.   Thou canst not
All die—there is what must survive.

Cain.   The Other
Spake not of this unto my father, when
He shut him forth from Paradise, with death
Written upon his forehead.   But at least

Let what is mortal of me perish, that
I may be in the rest as angels are.
Lucifer. *I* am angelic: wouldst thou be as I am?
Cain. I know not what thou art: I see thy power
And see thou show'st me things beyond *my* power,
Beyond all power of my born faculties,
Although inferior still to my desires
And my conceptions.
Lucifer.   What are they which dwell
So humbly in their pride, as to sojourn
With worms in clay?
Cain.   And what art thou who dwellest
So haughtily in spirit, and canst range
Nature and immortality—and yet
Seem'st sorrowful?
Lucifer.   I seem that which I am;
And therefore do I ask of thee, if thou
Wouldst be immortal?
Cain.   Thou hast said, I must be
Immortal in despite of me. I knew not
This until lately—but since it must be,
Let me, or happy or unhappy, learn
To anticipate my immortality.
Lucifer. Thou didst before I came upon thee.
Cain.   How?
Lucifer. By suffering.
Cain.   And must torture be immortal?
Lucifer. We and thy sons will try. But now, behold!
Is it not glorious?
Cain.   Oh, thou beautiful
And unimaginable ether! and
Ye multiplying masses of increased
And still increasing lights! what are ye? what
Is this blue wilderness of interminable
Air, where ye roll along, as I have seen
The leaves along the limpid streams of Eden?
Is your course measured for ye? Or do ye
Sweep on in your unbounded revelry
Through an aërial universe of endless
Expansion—at which my soul aches to think—
Intoxicated with eternity?
Oh God! Oh Gods! or whatsoe'er ye are!
How beautiful ye are! how beautiful
Your works, or accidents, or whatsoe'er
They may be! Let me die, as atoms die,
(If that they die) or know ye in your might

And knowledge! My thoughts are not in this hour
Unworthy what I see, though my dust is;
Spirit! let me expire, or see them nearer.
Lucifer. Art thou not nearer? look back to thine earth!
Cain. Where is it? I see nothing save a mass
Of most innumerable lights.
Lucifer.   Look there!
Cain. I cannot see it.
Lucifer.   Yet it sparkles still.
Cain. That!—yonder!
Lucifer.   Yea.
Cain.   And wilt thou tell me so?
Why, I have seen the fire-flies and fire-worms
Sprinkle the dusky groves and the green banks
In the dim twilight, brighter than yon world
Which bears them.
Lucifer.   Thou hast seen both worms and worlds,
Each bright and sparkling—what dost think of them?
Cain. That they are beautiful in their own sphere,
And that the night, which makes both beautiful,
The little shining fire-fly in its flight,
And the immortal star in its great course,
Must both be guided.
Lucifer.   But by whom or what?
Cain. Show me.
Lucifer.   Dar'st thou behold?
Cain.   How know I what
I *dare* behold? As yet, thou hast shown nought
I dare not gaze on further.
Lucifer.   On, then, with me.
Wouldst thou behold things mortal or immortal?
Cain. Why, what are things?
Lucifer.   *Both* partly: but what doth
Sit next thy heart?
Cain.   The things I see.
Lucifer.   But what
Sate nearest it?
Cain.   The things I have not seen,
Nor ever shall—the mysteries of death.
Lucifer. What, if I show to thee things which have died,
As I have shown thee much which cannot die?
Cain. Do so.
Lucifer.   Away, then! on our mighty wings.
Cain. Oh! how we cleave the blue! The stars fade from us!
The earth! where is my earth? Let me look on it,
For I was made of it.

Lucifer.   'Tis now beyond thee,
  Less, in the universe, than thou in it;
  Yet deem not that thou canst escape it; thou
  Shalt soon return to earth, and all its dust;
  'Tis part of thy eternity, and mine.
Cain. Where dost thou lead me?
Lucifer.   To what was before thee!
  The phantasm of the world; of which thy world
  Is but the wreck.
Cain.   What! is it not then new?
Lucifer. No more than life is; and that was ere thou
  Or *I* were, or the things which seem to us
  Greater than either: many things will have
  No end; and some, which would pretend to have
  Had no beginning, have had one as mean
  As thou; and mightier things have been extinct
  To make way for much meaner than we can
  Surmise; for *moments* only and the *space*
  Have been and must be all *unchangeable*.
  But changes make not death, except to clay;
  But thou art clay—and canst but comprehend
  That which was clay, and such thou shalt behold.
Cain. Clay, spirit! what thou wilt, I can survey.
Lucifer. Away, then!
Cain.   But the lights fade from me fast,
  And some till now grew larger as we approach'd,
  And wore the look of worlds.
Lucifer.   And such they are.
Cain. And Edens in them?
Lucifer.   It may be.
Cain.   And men?
Lucifer. Yea, or things higher.
Cain.   Ay? and serpents too?
Lucifer. Wouldst thou have men without them? must no reptiles
  Breathe, save the erect ones?
Cain.   How the lights recede!
  Where fly we?
Lucifer.   To the world of phantoms, which
  Are beings past, and shadows still to come.
Cain. But it grows dark, and dark—the stars are gone!
Lucifer. And yet thou seest.
Cain.   'Tis a fearful light!
  No sun, no moon, no lights innumerable.
  The very blue of the empurpled night
  Fades to a dreary twilight, yet I see
  Huge dusky masses: but unlike the worlds

We were approaching, which, begirt with light,
Seem'd full of life even when their atmosphere
Of light gave way, and show'd them taking shapes
Unequal, of deep valleys and vast mountains;
And some emitting sparks, and some displaying
Enormous liquid plains, and some begirt
With luminous belts, and floating moons, which took,
Like them, the features of fair earth:—instead,
All here seems dark and dreadful.

Lucifer.   But distinct.
Thou seekest to behold death, and dead things?

Cain. I seek it not; but as I know there are
Such, and that my sire's sin makes him and me,
And all that we inherit, liable
To such, I would behold at once, what I
Must one day see perforce.

Lucifer.   Behold!

Cain.   'Tis darkness.

Lucifer. And so it shall be ever; but we will
Unfold its gates!

Cain.   Enormous vapours roll
Apart—what's this?

Lucifer.   Enter!

Cain.   Can I return?

Lucifer. Return! be sure: how else should death be peopled?
Its present realm is thin to what it will be,
Through thee and thine.

Cain.   The clouds still open wide
And wider, and make widening circles round us.

Lucifer. Advance!

Cain.   And thou!

Lucifer.   Fear not—without me thou
Couldst not have gone beyond thy world. On! on!

[*They disappear through the clouds.*

SCENE II

Hades

Enter LUCIFER *and* CAIN.

Cain. How silent and how vast are these dim worlds!
For they seem more than one, and yet more peopled
Than the huge brilliant luminous orbs which swung
So thickly in the upper air, that I
Had deem'd them rather the bright populace
Of some all unimaginable Heaven,
Than things to be inhabited themselves,

But that on drawing near them I beheld
Their swelling into palpable immensity
Of matter, which seem'd made for life to dwell on,
Rather than life itself. But here, all is
So shadowy and so full of twilight, that
It speaks of a day past.

Lucifer.   It is the realm
Of death:—Wouldst have it present?

Cain.   Till I know
That which it really is, I cannot answer.
But if it be as I have heard my father
Deal out in his long homilies, 'tis a thing—
Oh God! I dare not think on't! Cursed be
He who invented life that leads to death!
Or the dull mass of life, that, being life,
Could not retain, but needs must forfeit it—
Even for the innocent!

Lucifer.   Dost thou curse thy father?

Cain. Cursed he not me in giving me my birth?
Cursed he not me before my birth, in daring
To pluck the fruit forbidden?

Lucifer.   Thou say'st well:
The curse is mutual 'twixt thy sire and thee—
But for thy sons and brother?

Cain.   Let them share it
With me, their sire and brother! What else is
Bequeath'd to me? I leave them my inheritance.
Oh, ye interminable gloomy realms
Of swimming shadows and enormous shapes,
Some fully shown, some indistinct, and all
Mighty and melancholy—what are ye?
Live ye, or have ye lived?

Lucifer.   Somewhat of both.

Cain. Then what is death?

Lucifer.   What? Hath not he who made ye
Said 'tis another life?

Cain.   Till now he hath
Said nothing, save that all shall die.

Lucifer.   Perhaps
He one day will unfold that further secret.

Cain. Happy the day!

Lucifer.   Yes; happy! when unfolded,
Through agonies unspeakable, and clogg'd
With agonies eternal, to innumerable
Yet unborn myriads of unconscious atoms,
All to be animated for this only!

Cain. What are these mighty phantoms which I see
    Floating around me?—They wear not the form
    Of the intelligences I have seen
    Round our regretted and unenter'd Eden,
    Nor wear the form of man as I have view'd it
    In Adam's and in Abel's, and in mine,
    Nor in my sister-bride's, nor in my children's:
    And yet they have an aspect, which, though not
    Of men nor angels, looks like something, which
    If not the last, rose higher than the first,
    Haughty, and high, and beautiful, and full
    Of seeming strength, but of inexplicable
    Shape; for I never saw such. They bear not
    The wing of seraph, nor the face of man,
    Nor form of mightiest brute, nor aught that is
    Now breathing; mighty yet and beautiful
    As the most beautiful and mighty which
    Live, and yet so unlike them, that I scarce
    Can call them living.
Lucifer.   Yet they lived.
Cain.   Where?
Lucifer.   Where
    Thou livest.
Cain.   When?
Lucifer.   On what thou callest earth
    They did inhabit.
Cain.   Adam is the first.
Lucifer. Of thine, I grant thee—but too mean to be
    The last of these.
Cain.   And what are they?
Lucifer.   That which
    Thou shalt be.
Cain.   But what *were* they?
Lucifer.   Living, high,
    Intelligent, good, great, and glorious things,
    As much superior unto all thy sire,
    Adam, could e'er have been in Eden, as
    The sixty-thousandth generation shall be,
    In its dull damp degeneracy, to
    Thee and thy son;—and how weak they are, judge
    By thy own flesh.
Cain.   Ah me! and did *they* perish?
Lucifer. Yes, from their earth, as thou wilt fade from thine.
Cain. But was *mine* theirs?
Lucifer.   It was.

Cain.   But not as now.
  It is too little and too lowly to
  Sustain such creatures.
Lucifer.   True, it was more glorious.
Cain. And wherefore did it fall?
Lucifer.   Ask him who fells.
Cain. But how?
Lucifer.   By a most crushing and inexorable
  Destruction and disorder of the elements,
  Which struck a world to chaos, as a chaos
  Subsiding has struck out a world: such things,
  Though rare in time, are frequent in eternity.—
  Pass on, and gaze upon the past.
Cain.   'Tis awful!
Lucifer. And true.   Behold these phantoms! they were once
  Material as thou art.
Cain.   And must I be
  Like them?
Lucifer.   Let He who made thee answer that.
  I show thee what thy predecessors are,
  And what they *were* thou feelest, in degree
  Inferior as thy petty feelings and
  Thy pettier portion of the immortal part
  Of high intelligence and earthly strength.
  What ye in common have with what they had
  Is life, and what ye *shall* have—death: the rest
  Of your poor attributes is such as suits
  Reptiles engender'd out of the subsiding
  Slime of a mighty universe, crushed into
  A scarcely-yet shaped planet, peopled with
  Things whose enjoyment was to be in blindness—
  A Paradise of Ignorance, from which
  Knowledge was barr'd as poison.   But behold
  What these superior beings are or were;
  Or, if it irk thee, turn thee back and till
  The earth, thy task—I'll waft thee there in safety.
Cain. No: I'll stay here.
Lucifer.   How long?
Cain.   For ever!   Since
  I must one day return here from the earth,
  I rather would remain; I am sick of all
  That dust has shown me—let me dwell in shadows.
Lucifer. It cannot be: thou now beholdest as
  A vision that which is reality.
  To make thyself fit for this dwelling, thou

Must pass through what the things thou see'st have pass'd—
The gates of death.

Cain.   By what gate have we enter'd
Even now?

Lucifer.   By mine! But, plighted to return,
My spirit buoys thee up to breathe in regions
Where all is breathless save thyself. Gaze on;
But do not think to dwell here till thine hour
Is come.

Cain.   And these, too; can they ne'er repass
To earth again?

Lucifer.   *Their* earth is gone for ever—
So changed by its convulsion, they would not
Be conscious to a single present spot
Of its new scarcely harden'd surface—'twas—
Oh, what a beautiful world it *was!*

Cain.   And is.
It is not with the earth, though I must till it,
I feel at war, but that I may not profit
By what it bears of beautiful, untoiling,
Nor gratify my thousand swelling thoughts
With knowledge, nor allay my thousand fears
Of death and life.

Lucifer.   What thy world is, thou see'st,
But canst not comprehend the shadow of
That which it was.

Cain.   And those enormous creatures,
Phantoms inferior in intelligence
(At least so seeming) to the things we have pass'd,
Resembling somewhat the wild habitants
Of the deep woods of earth, the hugest which
Roar nightly in the forest, but ten-fold
In magnitude and terror; taller than
The cherub-guarded walls of Eden, with
Eyes flashing like the fiery swords which fence them,
And tusks projecting like the trees stripp'd of
Their bark and branches—what were they?

Lucifer.   That which
The Mammoth is in thy world;—but these lie
By myriads underneath its surface.

Cain.   But
None on it?

Lucifer.   No: for thy frail race to war
With them would render the curse on it useless—
'Twould be destroy'd so early.

Cain.   But why *war?*

Lucifer. You have forgotten the denunciation
   Which drove your race from Eden—war with all things,
   And death to all things, and disease to most things,
   And pangs, and bitterness; these were the fruits
   Of the forbidden tree.
Cain.   But animals—
   Did they, too, eat of it, that they must die?
Lucifer. Your Maker told ye, *they* were made for you,
   As you for him.—You would not have their doom
   Superior to your own? Had Adam not
   Fallen, all had stood.
Cain.   Alas! the hopeless wretches!
   They too must share my sire's fate, like his sons;
   Like them too, without having shared the apple;
   Like them, too, without the so dear-bought *knowledge*!
   It was a lying tree—for we *know* nothing.
   At least it *promised knowledge* at the *price*
   Of death—but *knowledge* still: but what *knows* man?
Lucifer. It may be death leads to the *highest* knowledge;
   And being of all things the sole thing certain,
   At least leads to the *surest* science: therefore
   The tree was true, though deadly.
Cain.   These dim realms!
   I see them, but I know them not.
Lucifer.   Because
   Thy hour is yet afar, and matter cannot
   Comprehend spirit wholly—but 'tis something
   To know there are such realms.
Cain.   We knew already
   That there was death.
Lucifer.   But not what was beyond it.
Cain. Nor know I now.
Lucifer.   Thou knowest that there is
   A state, and many states beyond thine own—
   And this thou knewest not this morn.
Cain.   But all
   Seems dim and shadowy.
Lucifer.   Be content; it will
   Seem clearer to thine immortality.
Cain. And yon immeasurable liquid space
   Of glorious azure which floats on beyond us,
   Which looks like water, and which I should deem
   The river which flows out of Paradise
   Past my own dwelling, but that it is bankless
   And boundless, and of an ethereal hue—
   What is it?

Lucifer.   There is still some such on earth,
   Although inferior, and thy children shall
   Dwell near it—'tis the phantasm of an ocean.
Cain. 'Tis like another world, a liquid sun—
   And those inordinate creatures sporting o'er
   Its shining surface?
Lucifer.   Are its habitants,
   The past leviathans.
Cain.   And yon immense
   Serpent, which rears his dripping mane and vasty
   Head ten times higher than the haughtiest cedar
   Forth from the abyss, looking as he could coil
   Himself around the orbs we lately look'd on—
   Is he not of the kind which bask'd beneath
   The tree in Eden?
Lucifer.   Eve, thy mother, best
   Can tell what shape of serpent tempted her.
Cain. This seems too terrible.   No doubt the other
   Had more of beauty.
Lucifer.   Hast thou ne'er beheld him?
Cain. Many of the same kind (at least so call'd),
   But never that precisely which persuaded
   The fatal fruit, nor even of the same aspect.
Lucifer. Your father saw him not?
Cain.   No: 'twas my mother
   Who tempted him—she tempted by the serpent.
Lucifer. Good man! whene'er thy wife, or thy sons' wives,
   Tempt thee or them to aught that's new or strange,
   Be sure thou see'st first who hath tempted *them*.
Cain. Thy precept comes too late: there is no more
   For serpents to tempt woman to.
Lucifer.   But there
   Are some things still which woman may tempt man to,
   And man tempt woman:—let thy sons look to it!
   My counsel is a kind one; for 'tis even
   Given chiefly at my own expense; 'tis true,
   'Twill not be follow'd, so there's little lost.
Cain. I understand not this.
Lucifer.   The happier thou!—
   Thy world and thou are still too young!   Thou thinkest
   Thyself most wicked and unhappy: is it
   Not so?
Cain.   For crime, I know not; but for pain,
   I have felt much.
Lucifer.   First-born of the first man!
   Thy present state of sin, and thou art evil—

Of sorrow, and thou sufferest—are both Eden
In all its innocence compared to what
Thou shortly may'st be; and that state again,
In its redoubled wretchedness, a Paradise
To what thy sons' sons' sons, accumulating
In generations like to dust (which they
In fact but add to), shall endure and do,—
Now let us back to earth!

Cain.   And wherefore didst thou
   Lead me here only to inform me this?

Lucifer. Was not thy quest for knowledge?

Cain.   Yes: as being
   The road to happiness.

Lucifer.   If truth be so,
   Thou hast it.

Cain.   Then my father's God did well
   When he prohibited the fatal tree.

Lucifer. But had done better in not planting it.
   But ignorance of evil doth not save
   From evil; it must still roll on the same,
   A part of all things.

Cain.   Not of all things.   No:
   I'll not believe it—for I thirst for good.

Lucifer. And who and what doth not?   *Who* covets evil
   For its own bitter sake?—*None*—nothing! 'tis
   The leaven of all life, and lifelessness.

Cain. Within those glorious orbs which we behold,
   Distant and dazzling, and innumerable,
   Ere we came down into this phantom realm,
   Ill cannot come: they are too beautiful.

Lucifer. Thou hast seen them from afar.

Cain.   And what of that?
   Distance can but diminish glory—they,
   When nearer, must be more ineffable.

Lucifer. Approach the things of earth most beautiful,
   And judge their beauty near.

Cain.   I have done this—
   The loveliest thing I know is loveliest nearest.

Lucifer. Then there must be delusion.—What is that,
   Which being nearest to thine eyes is still
   More beautiful than beauteous things remote?

Cain. My sister Adah.—All the stars of heaven,
   The deep blue noon of night, lit by an orb
   Which looks a spirit, or a spirit's world—
   The hues of twilight—the sun's gorgeous coming—
   His setting indescribable, which fills

My eyes with pleasant tears as I behold
Him sink, and feel my heart float softly with him
Along that western paradise of clouds—
The forest shade, the green bough, the bird's voice—
The vesper bird's, which seems to sing of love,
And mingles with the song of cherubim,
As the day closes over Eden's walls;—
All these are nothing, to my eyes and heart,
Like Adah's face: I turn from earth and heaven
To gaze on it.

Lucifer.   'Tis fair as frail mortality,
In the first dawn and bloom of young creation
And earliest embraces of earth's parents,
Can make its offspring; still it is delusion.

Cain. You think so, being not her brother.

Lucifer.   Mortal!
My brotherhood's with those who have no children.

Cain. Then thou canst have no fellowship with us.

Lucifer. It may be that thine own shall be for me.
But if thou dost possess a beautiful
Being beyond all beauty in thine eyes,
Why art thou wretched?

Cain.   Why do I exist?
Why art *thou* wretched? why are all things so?
Ev'n he who made us must be, as the maker
Of things unhappy! To produce destruction
Can surely never be the task of joy,
And yet my sire says he's omnipotent:
Then why is evil—he being good? I ask'd
This question of my father; and he said,
Because this evil only was the path
To good. Strange good, that must arise from out
Its deadly opposite. I lately saw
A lamb stung by a reptile; the poor suckling
Lay foaming on the earth, beneath the vain
And piteous bleating of its restless dam;
My father pluck'd some herbs, and laid them to
The wound; and by degrees the helpless wretch
Resumed its careless life, and rose to drain
The mother's milk, who o'er it tremulous
Stood licking its reviving limbs with joy.
Behold, my son! said Adam, how from evil
Springs good!

Lucifer.   What didst thou answer?

Cain.   Nothing; for
He is my father: but I thought, that 'twere

A better portion for the animal
Never to have been *stung at all*, than to
Purchase renewal of its little life
With agonies unutterable, though
Dispell'd by antidotes.
Lucifer.   But as thou saidst
Of all beloved things thou lovest her
Who shared thy mother's milk, and giveth hers
Unto thy children——
Cain.   Most assuredly:
What should I be without her?
Lucifer.   What am I?
Cain. Dost thou love nothing?
Lucifer.   What does thy God love?
Cain. All things, my father says; but I confess
I see it not in their allotment here.
Lucifer. And, therefore, thou canst not see if *I* love
Or no, except some vast and general purpose,
To which particular things must melt like snows.
Cain. Snows! what are they?
Lucifer.   Be happier in not knowing
What thy remoter offspring must encounter;
But bask beneath the clime which knows no winter.
Cain. But dost thou not love something like thyself?
Lucifer. And dost thou love *thyself*?
Cain.   Yes, but love more
What makes my feelings more endurable,
And is more than myself, because I love it.
Lucifer. Thou lovest it, because 'tis beautiful,
As was the apple in thy mother's eye;
And when it ceases to be so, thy love
Will cease, like any other appetite.
Cain. Cease to be beautiful! how can that be?
Lucifer. With time.
Cain.   But time has pass'd, and hitherto
Even Adam and my mother both are fair:
Not fair like Adah and the seraphim—
But very fair.
Lucifer.   All that must pass away
In them and her.
Cain.   I'm sorry for it; but
Cannot conceive my love for her the less.
And when her beauty disappears, methinks
He who creates all beauty will lose more
Than me in seeing perish such a work.
Lucifer. I pity thee who lovest what must perish.

Cain. And I thee who lov'st nothing.
Lucifer.   And thy brother—
  Sits he not near thy heart?
Cain.   Why should he not?
Lucifer. Thy father loves him well—so does thy God.
Cain. And so do I.
Lucifer.   'Tis well and meekly done.
Cain. Meekly!
Lucifer.   He is the second born of flesh,
  And is his mother's favourite.
Cain.   Let him keep
  Her favour, since the serpent was the first
  To win it.
Lucifer.   And his father's?
Cain.   What is that
  To me? should I not love that which all love?
Lucifer. And the Jehovah—the indulgent Lord,
  And bounteous planter of barr'd Paradise—
  He, too, looks smilingly on Abel.
Cain.   I
  Ne'er saw him, and I know not if he smiles.
Lucifer. But you have seen his angels.
Cain.   Rarely.
Lucifer.   But
  Sufficiently to see they love your brother:
  His sacrifices are acceptable.
Cain. So be they! wherefore speak to me of this?
Lucifer. Because thou hast thought of this ere now.
Cain.   And if
  I *have* thought, why recall a thought that——[*He pauses, as
      agitated.*]—Spirit!
  Here we are in *thy* world; speak not of *mine.*
  Thou hast shown me wonders; thou hast shown me those
  Mighty pre-Adamites who walk'd the earth
  Of which ours is the wreck; thou hast pointed out
  Myriads of starry worlds, of which our own
  Is the dim and remote companion, in
  Infinity of life: thou hast shown me shadows
  Of that existence with the dreaded name
  Which my sire brought us—Death; thou hast shown me
      much—
  But not all: show me where Jehovah dwells,
  In his especial Paradise—or *thine*:
  Where is it?
Lucifer.   *Here*, and o'er all space.

Cain.   But ye
  Have some allotted dwelling—as all things;
  Clay has its earth, and other worlds their tenants;
  All temporary breathing creatures their
  Peculiar element; and things which have
  Long ceased to breathe *our* breath, have theirs, thou say'ſt;
  And the Jehovah and thyself have thine—
  Ye do not dwell together?
Lucifer.   No, we reign
  Together; but our dwellings are asunder.
Cain. Would there were only one of ye! perchance
  An unity of purpose might make union
  In elements which seem now jarr'd in ſtorms.
  How came ye, being spirits, wise and infinite,
  To separate? Are ye not as brethren in
  Your essence, and your nature, and your glory?
Lucifer. Art thou not Abel's brother?
Cain.   We are brethren,
  And so we shall remain; but were it not so,
  Is spirit like to flesh? can it fall out?
  Infinity with Immortality?
  Jarring and turning space to misery—
  For what?
Lucifer.   To reign.
Cain.   Did ye not tell me that
  Ye are both eternal?
Lucifer.   Yea!
Cain.   And what I have seen.
  Yon blue immensity, is boundless?
Lucifer.   Ay.
Cain. And cannot ye both *reign* then?—is there not
  Enough?—why should ye differ?
Lucifer.   We *both* reign.
Cain. But one of you makes evil.
Lucifer.   Which?
Cain.   Thou! for
  If thou canſt do man good, why doſt thou not?
Lucifer. And why not he who made? *I* made ye not;
  Ye are *his* creatures, and not mine.
Cain.   Then leave us
  His creatures, as thou say'ſt we are, or show me
  Thy dwelling, or *his* dwelling.
Lucifer.   I could show thee
  Both; but the time will come thou shalt see one
  Of them for evermore.
Cain.   And why not now?

Lucifer. Thy human mind hath scarcely grasp to gather
　　The little I have shown thee into calm
　　And clear thought; and *thou* wouldst go on aspiring
　　To the great double Mysteries! the *two Principles!*
　　And gaze upon them on their secret thrones!
　　Dust! limit thy ambition; for to see
　　Either of these, would be for thee to perish!
Cain. And let me perish, so I see them!
Lucifer.　　　　　　　　　　　　　　There
　　The son of her who snatch'd the apple spake!
　　But thou wouldst only perish, and not see them;
　　That sight is for the other state.
Cain.　　　　　　　　　　　Of death?
Lucifer. That is the prelude.
Cain.　　　　　　　　　Then I dread it less,
　　Now that I know it leads to something definite.
Lucifer. And now I will convey thee to thy world,
　　Where thou shalt multiply the race of Adam,
　　Eat, drink, toil, tremble, laugh, weep, sleep, and **die.**
Cain. And to what end have I beheld these things
　　Which thou hast shown me?
Lucifer.　　　　　　　　　Didst thou not require
　　Knowledge? And have I not, in what I show'd,
　　Taught thee to know thyself?
Cain.　　　　　　　　　Alas! I seem
　　Nothing.
Lucifer.　　　And this should be the human sum
　　Of knowledge, to know mortal nature's nothingness;
　　Bequeath that science to thy children, and
　　'Twill spare them many tortures.
Cain.　　　　　　　　　　Haughty spirit!
　　Thou speak'st it proudly; but thyself, though proud,
　　Hast a superior.
Lucifer.　　　　　No! By heaven, which he
　　Holds, and the abyss, and the immensity
　　Of worlds and life, which I hold with him—No!
　　I have a victor—true; but no superior.
　　Homage he has from all—but none from me:
　　I battle it against him, as I battled
　　In highest heaven. Through all eternity,
　　And the unfathomable gulfs of Hades,
　　And the interminable realms of space,
　　And the infinity of endless ages,
　　All, all, will I dispute! And world by world,
　　And star by star, and universe by universe,
　　Shall tremble in the balance, till the great

Conflict shall cease, if ever it shall cease,
Which it ne'er shall, till he or I be quench'd!
And what can quench our immortality,
Or mutual or irrevocable hate?
He as a conqueror will call the conquer'd
Evil; but what will be the *good* he gives?
Were I the victor, *his* works would be deem'd
The only evil ones.   And you, ye new
And scarce-born mortals, what have been his gifts
To you already, in your little world?
Cain. But few; and some of those but bitter.
Lucifer.   Back
With me, then, to thine earth, and try the rest
Of his celestial boons to you and yours.
Evil and good are things in their own essence,
And not made good or evil by the giver;
But if he gives you good—so call him; if
Evil springs from *him*, do not name it *mine*,
Till ye know better its true fount; and judge
Not by words, though of spirits, but the fruits
Of your existence, such as it must be.
One good gift has the fatal apple given—
Your *reason*:—let it not be oversway'd
By tyrannous threats to force you into faith
'Gainst all external sense and inward feeling:
Think and endure,—and form an inner world
In your own bosom—where the outward fails;
So shall you nearer be the spiritual
Nature, and war triumphant with your own.   [*They disappear.*

ACT III

The Earth, near Eden, as in Act I

Enter CAIN *and* ADAH.

Adah. Hush! tread softly, Cain.
Cain.   I will; but wherefore?
Adah. Our little Enoch sleeps upon yon bed
Of leaves, beneath the cypress.
Cain.   Cypress! 'tis
A gloomy tree, which looks as if it mourn'd
O'er what it shadows; wherefore didst thou choose it
For our child's canopy?

Adah.   Because its branches
   Shut out the sun like night, and therefore seem'd
   Fitting to shadow slumber.

Cain.   Ay, the laſt—
   And longeſt; but no matter—lead me to him.
                        [*They go up to the child.*
   How lovely he appears! his little cheeks,
   In their pure incarnation, vying with
   The rose leaves ſtrewn beneath them.

Adah.   And his lips, too,
   How beautifully parted!   No; you shall not
   Kiss him, at leaſt not now; he will awake soon—
   His hour of mid-day reſt is nearly over;
   But it were pity to diſturb him till
   'Tis closed.

Cain.   You have said well; I will contain
   My heart till then.   He smiles, and sleeps!—Sleep on
   And smile, thou little, young inheritor
   Of a world scarce less young: sleep on, and smile!
   Thine are the hours and days when both are cheering
   And innocent! *thou* haſt not pluck'd the fruit—
   Thou know'ſt not thou art naked!   Muſt the time
   Come thou shalt be amerced for sins unknown,
   Which were not thine nor mine?   But now sleep on!
   His cheeks are reddening into deeper smiles,
   And shining lids are trembling o'er his long
   Lashes, dark as the cypress which waves o'er them;
   Half open, from beneath them the clear blue
   Laughs out, although in slumber.   He muſt dream—
   Of what?   Of Paradise!—Ay! dream of it,
   My disinherited boy!   'Tis but a dream;
   For never more thyself, thy sons, nor fathers,
   Shall walk in that forbidden place of joy!

Adah.   Dear Cain!   Nay, do not whisper o'er our son
   Such melancholy yearnings o'er the paſt:
   Why wilt thou always mourn for Paradise?
   Can we not make another?

Cain.   Where?

Adah.   Here, or
   Where'er thou wilt: where'er thou art, I feel not
   The want of this so much regretted Eden.
   Have I not thee, our boy, our sire, and brother,
   And Zillah—our sweet siſter, and our Eve,
   To whom we owe so much besides our birth?

Cain.   Yes—death, too, is amongſt the debts we owe her.

Adah. Cain! that proud spirit, who withdrew thee hence,
    Hath sadden'd thine still deeper. I had hoped
    The promised wonders which thou hast beheld,
    Visions, thou say'st, of past and present worlds,
    Would have composed thy mind into the calm
    Of a contented knowledge; but I see
    Thy guide hath done thee evil: still I thank him,
    And can forgive him all, that he so soon
    Hath given thee back to us.

Cain.   So soon?

Adah.   'Tis scarcely
    Two hours since ye departed: two *long* hours
    To *me*, but only *hours* upon the sun.

Cain. And yet I have approach'd that sun, and seen
    Worlds which he once shone on, and never more
    Shall light; and worlds he never lit: methought
    Years had roll'd o'er my absence.

Adah.   Hardly hours.

Cain. The mind then hath capacity of time,
    And measures it by that which it beholds,
    Pleasing or painful; little or almighty.
    I had beheld the immemorial works
    Of endless beings; skirr'd extinguish'd worlds;
    And, gazing on eternity, methought
    I had borrow'd more by a few drops of ages
    From its immensity: but now I feel
    My littleness again. Well said the spirit,
    That I was nothing!

Adah.   Wherefore said he so?
    Jehovah said not that.

Cain.   No: *he* contents him
    With making us the *nothing* which we are;
    And after flattering dust with glimpses of
    Eden and Immortality, resolves
    It back to dust again—for what?

Adah.   Thou know'st—
    Even for our parents' error.

Cain.   What is that
    To us? they sinn'd, then *let them* die!

Adah. Thou hast not spoken well, nor is that thought
    Thy own, but of the spirit who was with thee.
    Would *I* could die for them, so *they* might live!

Cain. Why, so say I—provided that one victim
    Might satiate the insatiable of life,
    And that our little rosy sleeper there

Might never taste of death nor human sorrow,
Nor hand it down to those who spring from him.

Adah. How know we that some such atonement one day
    May not redeem our race?

Cain.   By sacrificing
    The harmless for the guilty? what atonement
    Were there? why, *we* are innocent: what have we
    Done, that we must be victims for a deed
    Before our birth, or need have victims to
    Atone for this mysterious, nameless sin—
    If it be such a sin to seek for knowledge?

Adah. Alas! thou sinnest now, my Cain: thy words
    Sound impious in mine ears.

Cain.   Then leave me!

Adah.   Never,
    Though thy God left thee.

Cain.   Say, what have we here?

Adah. Two altars, which our brother Abel made
    During thine absence, whereupon to offer
    A sacrifice to God on thy return.

Cain. And how knew *he*, that *I* would be so ready
    With the burnt offerings, which he daily brings
    With a meek brow, whose base humility
    Shows more of fear than worship, as a bribe
    To the Creator?

Adah.   Surely, 'tis well done.

Cain. One altar may suffice; *I* have no offering.

Adah. The fruits of the earth, the early, beautiful
    Blossom and bud, and bloom of flowers, and fruits,
    These are a goodly offering to the Lord,
    Given with a gentle and a contrite spirit.

Cain. I have toil'd, and till'd, and sweaten in the sun
    According to the curse:—must I do more?
    For what should I be gentle? for a war
    With all the elements ere they will yield
    The bread we eat? For what must I be grateful?
    For being dust, and grovelling in the dust,
    Till I return to dust? If I am nothing—
    For nothing shall I be an hypocrite,
    And seem well-pleased with pain? For what should I
    Be contrite? for my father's sin, already
    Expiate with what we all have undergone,
    And to be more than expiated by
    The ages prophesied, upon our seed.
    Little deems our young blooming sleeper, there,
    The germs of an eternal misery

To myriads is within him! better 'twere
I snatch'd him in his sleep, and dash'd him 'gainst
The rocks, than let him live to——
Adah.   Oh, my God!
  Touch not the child—my child! *thy* child! Oh Cain!
Cain. Fear not! for all the stars, and all the power
  Which sways them, I would not accost yon infant
  With ruder greeting than a father's kiss.
Adah. Then, why so awful in thy speech?
Cain.   I said,
  'T were better that he ceased to live, than give
  Life to so much of sorrow as he must
  Endure, and, harder still, bequeath; but since
  That saying jars you, let us only say—
  'Twere better that he never had been born.
Adah. Oh, do not say so! Where were then the joys,
  The mother's joys of watching, nourishing,
  And loving him? Soft! he awakes. Sweet Enoch!
                                    [*She goes to the child.*
  Oh Cain! look on him; see how full of life,
  Of strength, of bloom, of beauty, and of joy,
  How like to me—how like to thee, when gentle,
  For *then* we are *all* alike; is't not so, Cain?
  Mother, and sire, and son, our features are
  Reflected in each other; as they are
  In the clear waters, when *they* are *gentle*, and
  When *thou* art *gentle*. Love us, then, my Cain!
  And love thyself for our sakes, for we love thee.
  Look! how he laughs and stretches out his arms,
  And opens wide his blue eyes upon thine,
  To hail his father; while his little form
  Flutters as wing'd with joy. Talk not of pain!
  The childless cherubs well might envy thee
  The pleasures of a parent! Bless him, Cain!
  As yet he hath no words to thank thee, but
  His heart will, and thine own too.
Cain.   Bless thee, boy!
  If that a mortal blessing may avail thee,
  To save thee from the serpent's curse!
Adah.   It shall.
  Surely a father's blessing may avert
  A reptile's subtlety.
Cain.   Of that I doubt;
  But bless him ne'er the less.
Adah.   Our brother comes.
Cain. Thy brother Abel.

Enter ABEL.

Abel.   Welcome, Cain! My brother,
  The peace of God be on thee!
Cain.   Abel, hail!
Abel. Our sister tells me that thou hast been wandering,
  In high communion with a spirit, far
  Beyond our wonted range. Was he of those
  We have seen and spoken with, like to our father?
Cain. No.
Abel.   Why then commune with him? he may be
  A foe to the Most High.
Cain.   And friend to man.
  Has the Most High been so—if so you term him?
Abel. Term him! your words are strange to-day, my brother.
  My sister Adah, leave us for awhile—
  We mean to sacrifice.
Adah.   Farewell, my Cain:
  But first embrace thy son. May his soft spirit,
  And Abel's pious ministry, recall thee
  To peace and holiness!

                              [*Exit* ADAH, *with her child.*

Abel.   Where hast thou been?
Cain. I know not.
Abel.   Nor what thou hast seen?
Cain.   The dead,
  The immortal, the unbounded, the omnipotent,
  The overpowering mysteries of space—
  The innumerable worlds that were and are—
  A whirlwind of such overwhelming things,
  Suns, moons, and earths, upon their loud-voiced spheres
  Singing in thunder round me, as have made me
  Unfit for mortal converse: leave me, Abel.
Abel. Thine eyes are flashing with unnatural light—
  Thy cheek is flush'd with an unnatural hue—
  Thy words are fraught with an unnatural sound—
  What may this mean?
Cain.   It means——I pray thee, leave me.
Abel. Not till we have pray'd and sacrific'd together.
Cain. Abel, I pray thee, sacrifice alone—
  Jehovah loves thee well.
Abel.   *Both* well, I hope.
Cain. But thee the better: I care not for that;
  Thou art fitter for his worship than I am;
  Revere him, then—but let it be alone—
  At least, without me.

Abel.   Brother, I should ill
Deserve the name of our great father's son,
If, as my elder, I revered thee not,
And in the worship of our God call'd not
On thee to join me, and precede me in
Our priesthood—'tis thy place.

Cain.   But I have ne'er
Asserted it.

Abel.   The more my grief; I pray thee
To do so now: thy soul seems labouring in
Some strong delusion; it will calm thee.

Cain.   No;
Nothing can calm me more. *Calm!* say I? Never
Knew I what calm was in the soul, although
I have seen the elements still'd. My Abel, leave me!
Or let me leave thee to thy pious purpose.

Abel. Neither; we must perform our task together.
Spurn me not.

Cain.   If it must be so——well, then,
What shall I do?

Abel.   Choose one of those two altars.

Cain. Choose for me: they to me are so much turf
And stone.

Abel.   Choose thou!

Cain.   I have chosen.

Abel.   'Tis the highest,
And suits thee, as the elder. Now prepare
Thine offerings.

Cain.   Where are thine?

Abel.   Behold them here—
The firstlings of the flock, and fat thereof—
A shepherd's humble offering.

Cain.   I have no flocks;
I am a tiller of the ground, and must
Yield what it yieldeth to my toil—its fruit:

                         [*He gathers fruits.*
Behold them in their various bloom and ripeness.

         [*They dress their altars and kindle a flame upon them.*

Abel. My brother, as the elder, offer first
Thy prayer and thanksgiving with sacrifice.

Cain. No—I am new to this; lead thou the way,
And I will follow—as I may.

Abel. [*Kneeling.*]   Oh God!
Who made us, and who breathed the breath of life
Within our nostrils, who hath blessed us,
And spared, despite our father's sin, to make

His children all lost, as they might have been,
Had not thy justice been so temper'd with
The mercy which is thy delight, as to
Accord a pardon like a Paradise,
Compared with our great crimes:—Sole Lord of light!
Of good, and glory, and eternity;
Without whom all were evil, and with whom
Nothing can err, except to some good end
Of thine omnipotent benevolence—
Inscrutable, but still to be fulfill'd—
Accept from out thy humble first of shepherd's
First of the first-born flocks—an offering,
In itself nothing—as what offering can be
Aught unto thee?—but yet accept it for
The thanksgiving of him who spreads it in
The face of thy high heaven, bowing his own
Even to the dust, of which he is, in honour
Of thee, and of thy name, for evermore!

Cain [*Standing erect during this speech.*] Spirit! whate'er or whoso-
        e'er thou art,
Omnipotent, it may be—and, if good,
Shown in the exemption of thy deeds from evil;
Jehovah upon earth! and God in heaven!
And it may be with other names, because
Thine attributes seem many, as thy works:—
If thou must be propitiated with prayers,
Take them! If thou must be induced with altars,
And soften'd with a sacrifice, receive them!
Two beings here erect them unto thee.
If thou lov'st blood, the shepherd's shrine, which smokes
On my right hand, hath shed it for thy service
In the first of his flock, whose limbs now reek
In sanguinary incense to thy skies;
Or if the sweet and blooming fruits of earth,
And milder seasons, which the unstain'd turf
I spread them on now offers in the face
Of the broad sun which ripen'd them, may seem
Good to thee, inasmuch as they have not
Suffer'd in limb or life, and rather form
A sample of thy works, than supplication
To look on ours! If a shrine without victim,
And altar without gore, may win thy favour,
Look on it! and for him who dresseth it,
He is—such as thou mad'st him; and seeks nothing
Which must be won by kneeling: if he's evil,
Strike him! thou art omnipotent, and may'st—

For what can he oppose?   If he be good,
Strike him, or spare him, as thou wilt! since all
Rests upon thee; and good and evil seem
To have no power themselves, save in thy will;
And whether that be good or ill I know not,
Not being omnipotent, nor fit to judge
Omnipotence, but merely to endure
Its mandate; which thus far I have endured.

[*The fire upon the altar of* ABEL *kindles into a column of the
brightest flame, and ascends to heaven; while a whirlwind
throws down the altar of* CAIN, *and scatters the fruits abroad
upon the earth.*

Abel. [*Kneeling.*] Oh, brother, pray! Jehovah's wroth with
thee.

Cain. Why so?

Abel.   Thy fruits are scatter'd on the earth.

Cain. From earth they came, to earth let them return;
Their seed will bear fresh fruit there ere the summer:
Thy burnt flesh-off'ring prospers better: see
How heav'n licks up the flames, when thick with blood!

Abel. Think not upon my offering's acceptance,
But make another of thine own before
It is too late.

Cain.   I will build no more altars,
Nor suffer any.—

Abel. [*Rising.*]   Cain! what meanest thou?

Cain. To cast down yon vile flatt'rer of the clouds,
The smoky harbinger of thy dull pray'rs—
Thine altar, with its blood of lambs and kids,
Which fed on milk, to be destroy'd in blood.

Abel. [*Opposing him.*] Thou shalt not:—add not impious works
to impious
Words! let that altar stand—'tis hallow'd now
By the immortal pleasure of Jehovah,
In his acceptance of the victims.

Cain.   His!
His pleasure! what was his high pleasure in
The fumes of scorching flesh and smoking blood,
To the pain of the bleating mothers, which
Still yearn for their dead offspring? or the pangs
Of the sad ignorant victims underneath
Thy pious knife? Give way! this bloody record
Shall not stand in the sun, to shame creation!

Abel. Brother, give back! thou shalt not touch my altar
With violence: if that thou wilt adopt it,
To try another sacrifice, 'tis thine.

Cain. Another sacrifice!   Give way, or else
  That sacrifice may be——
Abel.   What mean'st thou?
Cain.   Give—
  Give way!—thy God loves blood!—then look to it:—
  Give way, ere he hath *more*!
Abel.   In *his* great name,
  I stand between thee and the shrine which hath
  Had his acceptance.
Cain.   If thou lov'st thyself,
  Stand back till I have strew'd this turf along
  Its native soil:—else——
Abel. [*Opposing him.*]   I love God far more
  Than life.
Cain. [*Striking him with a brand, on the temples, which he snatches from
    the altar.*] Then take thy life unto thy God,
  Since he loves lives.
Abel. [*Falls.*]   What hast thou done, my brother?
Cain. Brother!
Abel.   Oh, God! receive thy servant, and
  Forgive his slayer, for he knew not what
  He did.—Cain, give me—give me thy hand; and tell
  Poor Zillah——
Cain. [*After a moment's stupefaction.*] *My* hand! 'tis all red, and
    with—
  What?

                        [*A long pause.—Looking slowly round.*
            Where am I? alone!   Where's Abel? where
  Cain?   Can it be that I am he?   My brother,
  Awake!—why liest thou so on the green earth?
  'Tis not the hour of slumber:—why so pale?
  What, hast thou!——thou wert full of life this morn!
  Abel! I pray thee, mock me not!   I smote
  Too fiercely, but not fatally.   Ah, why
  Wouldst thou oppose me?   This is mockery;
  And only done to daunt me:—'twas a blow—
  And but a blow.   Stir—stir—nay, only stir!
  Why, so—that's well!—thou breath'st! breathe upon me!
  Oh, God!   Oh, God!
Abel. [*Very faintly.*]   What's he who speaks of God?
Cain. Thy murderer.
Abel.   Then may God forgive him!   Cain,
  Comfort poor Zillah:—she has but one brother
  Now.   [ABEL *dies.*
Cain.   And I none!—Who makes me brotherless?
  His eyes are open! then he is not dead!

Death is like sleep; and sleep shuts down our lids.
His lips, too, are apart; why then he breathes;
And yet I feel it not.—His heart!—his heart!—
Let me see, doth it beat? methinks——No!—no!
This is a vision, else I am become
The native of another and worse world.
The earth swims round me:—what is this?—'tis wet;

[*Puts his hand to his brow, and then looks at it.*

And yet there are no dews! 'Tis blood—my blood—
My brother's and my own; and shed by me!
Then what have I further to do with life,
Since I have taken life from my own flesh?
But he cannot be dead!—Is silence death?
No; he will wake; then let me watch by him.
Life cannot be so slight, as to be quench'd
Thus quickly!—he hath spoken to me since—
What shall I say to him?—My brother!—No:
He will not answer to that name; for brethren
Smite not each other. Yet—yet—speak to me.
Oh! for a word more of that gentle voice,
That I may bear to hear my own again!

Enter ZILLAH.

Zillah. I heard a heavy sound; what can it be?
'Tis Cain; and watching by my husband. What
Doſt thou there, brother? Doth he sleep? Oh, heav'n!
What means this paleness, and yon ſtream?—No, no!
It is not blood; for who would shed his blood?
Abel! what's this?—who hath done this? He moves not;
He breathes not: and his hands drop down from mine
With ſtony lifelessness! Ah! cruel Cain!
Why cam'ſt thou not in time to save him from
This violence? Whatever hath assail'd him,
Thou wert the ſtronger, and shouldſt have ſtepp'd in
Between him and aggression! Father!—Eve!—
Adah!—come hither! Death is in the world!

[*Exit* ZILLAH, *calling on her Parents, etc.*

Cain. [*Solus.*] And who hath brought him there?—I—who abhor
The name of Death so deeply, that the thought
Empoison'd all my life, before I knew
His aspeƈt—I have led him here, and giv'n
My brother to his cold and ſtill embrace,
As if he would not have asserted his
Inexorable claim without my aid.
I am awake at laſt—a dreary dream
Had madden'd me;—but *he* shall ne'er awake!

Enter ADAM, EVE, ADAH, *and* ZILLAH.

Adam. A voice of woe from Zillah brings me here.—
    What do I see?—'Tis true!—My son!—my son!
    Woman, behold the serpent's work, and thine!   [*To* EVE.
Eve. Oh! speak not of it now: the serpent's fangs
    Are in my heart. My best beloved, Abel!
    Jehovah! this is punishment beyond
    A mother's sin, to take *him* from me!
Adam.   Who,
    Or what hath done this deed?—speak, Cain, since thou
    Wert present; was it some more hostile angel,
    Who walks not with Jehovah? or some wild
    Brute of the forest?
Eve.   Ah! a livid light
    Breaks through, as from a thunder-cloud! yon brand,
    Massy and bloody! snatch'd from off the altar,
    And black with smoke, and red with——
Adam.   Speak, my son!
    Speak, and assure us, wretched as we are,
    That we are not more miserable still.
Adah. Speak, Cain! and say it was not *thou*!
Eve.   It was.
    I see it now—he hangs his guilty head,
    And covers his ferocious eye with hands
    Incarnadine.
Adah.   Mother, thou dost him wrong—
    Cain! clear thee from this horrible accusal,
    Which grief wrings from our parent.
Eve.   Hear, Jehovah!
    May the eternal serpent's curse be on him!
    For he was fitter for his seed than ours.
    May all his days be desolate! May——
Adah.   Hold!
    Curse him not, mother, for he is thy son—
    Curse him not, mother, for he is my brother,
    And my betroth'd.
Eve.   He hath left thee no brother—
    Zillah no husband—me *no son*!—for thus
    I curse him from my sight for evermore!
    All bonds I break between us, as he broke
    That of his nature, in yon——Oh death! death!
    Why didst thou not take *me*, who first incurr'd thee?
    Why dost thou not so now?
Adam.   Eve! let not this,
    Thy natural grief, lead to impiety!

A heavy doom was long forespoken to us;
And now that it begins, let it be borne
In such sort as may show our God, that we
Are faithful servants to his holy will.

Eve. [*pointing to Cain.*] *His will!* the will of yon incarnate spirit
Of death, whom I have brought upon the earth
To strew it with the dead.   May all the curses
Of life be on him! and his agonies
Drive him forth o'er the wilderness, like us
From Eden, till his children do by him
As he did by his brother!   May the swords
And wings of fiery cherubim pursue him
By day and night—snakes spring up in his path—
Earth's fruits be ashes in his mouth—the leaves
On which he lays his head to sleep be strew'd
With scorpions!   May his dreams be of his victim!
His waking a continual dread of death!
May the clear rivers turn to blood as he
Stoops down to stain them with his raging lip!
May every element shun or change to him!
May he live in the pangs which others die with!
And death itself wax something worse than death
To him who first acquainted him with man!
Hence, fratricide! henceforth that word is *Cain*,
Through all the coming myriads of mankind,
Who shall abhor thee, though thou wert their sire!
May the grass wither from thy feet! the woods
Deny thee shelter! earth a home! the dust
A grave! the sun his light! and heaven her God!

[*Exit* EVE.

Adam. Cain! get thee forth: we dwell no more together.
Depart! and leave the dead to me—I am
Henceforth alone—we never must meet more.

Adah. Oh, part not with him thus, my father: do not
Add thy deep curse to Eve's upon his head!

Adam. I curse him not: his spirit be his curse.
Come, Zillah!

Zillah.   I must watch my husband's corse.

Adam. We will return again, when he is gone
Who hath provided for us this dread office.
Come, Zillah!

Zillah.   Yet one kiss on yon pale clay,
And those lips once so warm—my heart! my heart!

[*Exeunt* ADAM *and* ZILLAH, *weeping.*

Adah. Cain! thou hast heard, we must go forth.   I am ready,
So shall our children be.   I will bear Enoch,

And you his sister.   Ere the sun declines
Let us depart, nor walk the wilderness
Under the cloud of night.—Nay, speak to me.
To *me—thine own.*
Cain.   Leave me!
Adah.   Why, all have left thee.
Cain. And wherefore lingerest thou?   Dost thou not fear
To dwell with one who hath done this?
Adah.   I fear
Nothing except to leave thee, much as I
Shrink from the deed which leaves thee brotherless.
I must not speak of this—it is between thee
And the great God.
A Voice from within exclaims, Cain! Cain!
Adah.   Hear'st thou that voice?
The Voice within. Cain! Cain!
Adah.   It soundeth like an angel's tone.

Enter the ANGEL *of the Lord.*

Angel. Where is thy brother Abel?
Cain.   Am I then
My brother's keeper?
Angel.   Cain, what hast thou done?
The voice of thy slain brother's blood cries out,
Even from the ground, unto the Lord!—Now art thou
Cursed from the earth, which opened late her mouth
To drink thy brother's blood from thy rash hand.
Henceforth, when thou shalt till the ground, it shall not
Yield thee her strength; a fugitive shalt thou
Be from this day, and vagabond on earth!
Adah. This punishment is more than he can bear.
Behold, thou drivest him from the face of earth,
And from the face of God shall he be hid.
A fugitive and vagabond on earth,
'Twill come to pass, that whoso findeth him
Shall slay him.
Cain.   Would they could! but who are they
Shall slay me?   Where are these on the lone earth
As yet unpeopled?
Angel.   Thou hast slain thy brother,
And who shall warrant thee against thy son?
Adah. Angel of Light! be merciful, nor say
That this poor aching breast now nourishes
A murderer in my boy, and of his father.
Angel. Then he would but be what his father is.
Did not the milk of Eve give nutriment

To him thou now see'st so besmear'd with blood?
The fratricide might well engender parricides.—
But it shall not be so—the Lord thy God
And mine commandeth me to set his seal
On Cain, so that he may go forth in safety.
Who slayeth Cain, a sevenfold vengeance shall
Be taken on his head.   Come hither!

Cain. What
Wouldst thou with me?

Angel. To mark upon thy brow
Exemption from such deeds as thou hast done.

Cain. No, let me die!

Angel. It must not be.

[*The* ANGEL *sets the mark on* CAIN's *brow.*

Cain. It burns
My brow, but nought to that which is within it.
Is there more? let me meet it as I may.

Angel. Stern hast thou been and stubborn from the womb,
As the ground thou must henceforth till; but he
Thou slew'st was gentle as the flocks he tended.

Cain. After the fall too soon was I begotten!
Ere yet my mother's mind subsided from
The serpent, and my sire still mourn'd for Eden.
That which I am, I am; I did not seek
For life, nor did I make myself; but could I
With my own death redeem him from the dust—
And why not so? let him return to day,
And I lie ghastly! so shall be restored
By God the life to him he loved; and taken
From me a being I ne'er loved to bear.

Angel. Who shall heal murder? what is done is done;
Go forth! fulfil thy days! and be thy deeds
Unlike the last! [*The* ANGEL *disappears.*

Adah. He's gone, let us go forth;
I hear our little Enoch cry within
Our bower.

Cain. Ah! little knows he what he weeps for!
And I who have shed blood cannot shed tears!
But the four rivers would not cleanse my soul.[1]
Think'st thou my boy will bear to look on me?

Adah. If I thought that he would not, I would—

Cain. [*Interrupting her.*] No,
No more of threats: we have had too many of them:
Go to our children; I will follow thee.

---

[1] The 'four rivers' which flowed round Eden, and consequently the only waters with which Cain was acquainted upon the earth.

Adah. I will not leave thee lonely with the dead;
    Let us depart together.
Cain.   Oh! thou dead
    And everlasting witness! whose unsinking
    Blood darkens earth and heaven! what thou *now* art
    I know not! but if *thou* see'st what *I* am,
    I think thou wilt forgive him, whom his God
    Can ne'er forgive, nor his own soul.—Farewell!
    I must not, dare not touch what I have made thee.
    I, who sprung from the same womb with thee, drain'd
    The same breast, clasp'd thee often to my own,
    In fondness brotherly and boyish, I
    Can never meet thee more, nor even dare
    To do that for thee, which thou shouldst have done
    For me—compose thy limbs into their grave—
    The first grave yet dug for mortality.
    But who hath dug that grave? Oh, earth! Oh, earth!
    For all the fruits thou hast render'd to me, I
    Give thee back this.—Now for the wilderness.
                [ADAH *stoops down and kisses the body of* ABEL.
Adah. A dreary, and an early doom, my brother,
    Has been thy lot! Of all who mourn for thee,
    I alone must not weep. My office is
    Henceforth to dry up tears, and not to shed them;
    But yet of all who mourn, none mourn like me,
    Not only for thyself, but him who slew thee.
    Now, Cain! I will divide thy burden with thee.
Cain. Eastward from Eden will we take our way;
    'Tis the most desolate, and suits my steps.
Adah. Lead! thou shalt be my guide, and may our God
    Be thine! Now let us carry forth our children.
Cain. And *he* who lieth there was childless. I
    Have dried the fountain of a gentle race,
    Which might have graced his recent marriage couch,
    And might have temper'd this stern blood of mine,
    Uniting with our children Abel's offspring!
    O Abel!
Adah.   Peace be with him.
Cain.   But with *me!*—   [*Exeunt.*

APPENDIX

THE WANDERINGS OF CAIN

A FRAGMENT

By S. T. COLERIDGE, Esq.

'A LITTLE further, O my father, yet a little further, and we shall come into the open moonlight!' Their road was through a forest of fir-trees; at its entrance the trees stood at distances from each other, and the path was broad, and the moonlight and the moonlight shadows reposed upon it, and appeared quietly to inhabit that solitude. But soon the path winded and became narrow; the sun at high noon sometimes speckled, but never illumined it, and now it was dark as a cavern.

'It is dark, O my father!' said Enos, 'but the path under our feet is smooth and soft, and we shall soon come out into the open moonlight. Ah! why dost thou groan so deeply?'

'Lead on, my child,' said Cain; 'guide me, little child.' And the innocent little child clasped a finger of the hand which had murdered the righteous Abel; and he guided his father. 'The fir branches drip upon thee, my son.'—'Yea, pleasantly, father, for I ran fast and eagerly to bring thee the pitcher and the cake, and my body is not yet cool. How happy the squirrels are that feed on these fir-trees! they leap from bough to bough, and the old squirrels play round their young ones in the nest. I clomb a tree yesterday at noon, O my father, that I might play with them; but they leapt away from the branches, even to the slender twigs did they leap, and in a moment I beheld them on another tree. Why, O my father, would they not play with me? Is it because we are not so happy as they? Is it because I groan sometimes even as thou groanest?' Then Cain stopped, and stifling his groans, he sank to the earth, and the child Enos stood in the darkness beside him, and Cain lifted up his voice, and cried bitterly, and said, 'The Mighty One that persecuteth me is on this side and on that; he pursueth my soul like the wind, like the sand-blast he passeth through me; he is around me even as the air; O that I might be utterly no more! I desire to die— yea, the things that never had life, neither move they upon the earth—behold they seem precious to mine eyes. O that a man might live without the breath of his nostrils, so I might abide in darkness and blackness, and an empty space! Yea, I would

lie down, I would not rise, neither would I stir my limbs till I
became as the rock in the den of the lion, on which the young
lion resteth his head whilst he sleepeth. For the torrent that
roareth far off hath a voice; and the clouds in heaven look
terribly on me; the Mighty One who is against me speaketh in
the wind of the cedar-tree; and in silence am I dried up.' Then
Enos spake to his father,—'Arise, my father, arise; we are but
a little way from the place where I found the cake and the pitcher.'
And Cain said, 'How knowest thou?' and the child answered—
'Behold, the bare rocks are a few of thy strides distant from the
forest; and while even now thou wert lifting up thy voice, I
heard the echo.' Then the child took hold of his father, as if
he would raise him; and Cain, being faint and feeble, rose slowly
on his knees and pressed himself against the trunk of a fir, and
stood upright and followed the child. The path was dark till
within three strides' length of its termination, when it turned
suddenly: the thick black trees formed a low arch, and the
moonlight appeared for a moment like a dazzling portal.
Enos ran before and stood in the open air; and when Cain, his
father, emerged from the darkness, the child was affrighted, for
the mighty limbs of Cain were wasted as by fire; his hair was
black, and matted into loathly curls, and his countenance was
dark and wild, and told, in a strange and terrible language, of
agonies that had been, and were, and were still to continue to be.

The scene around was desolate; as far as the eye could reach,
it was desolate; the bare rocks faced each other, and left a long
and wide interval of thin white sand. You might wander on
and look round and round, and peep into the crevices of the
rocks, and discover nothing that acknowledged the influence of
the seasons. There was no spring, no summer, no autumn;
and the winter's snow, that would have been lovely, fell not on
these hot rocks and scorching sands. Never morning lark had
poised himself over this desert; but the huge serpent often
hissed there beneath the talons of the vulture, and the vulture
screamed, his wings imprisoned within the coils of the serpent.
The pointed and shattered summits of the ridges of the rocks
made a rude mimicry of human concerns, and seemed to
prophesy mutely of things that then were not; steeples, and
battlements, and ships with naked masts. As far from the wood
as a boy might sling a pebble of the brook, there was one rock
by itself at a small distance from the main ridge. It had been
precipitated there, perhaps, by the terrible groan the earth gave
when our first father fell. Before you approached, it appeared
to lie flat on the ground, but its base slanted from its point, and
between its points and the sands a tall man might stand upright.
It was here that Enos had found the pitcher and cake, and to this

place he led his father; but, ere they arrived there, they beheld a human shape; his back was towards them, and they were coming up unperceived when they heard him smite his breast, and cry aloud, 'Woe is me! woe is me! I must never die again, and yet I am perishing with thirst and hunger.'

The face of Cain turned pale; but Enos said, 'Ere yet I could speak, I am sure, O my father, that I heard that voice. Have not I often said that I remembered a sweet voice? O my father! this is it'; and Cain trembled exceedingly. The voice was sweet indeed, but it was thin and querulous, like that of a feeble slave in misery, who despairs altogether, yet cannot refrain himself from weeping and lamentation. Enos crept softly round the base of the rock, and stood before the stranger, and looked up into his face. And the Shape shrieked, and turned round, and Cain beheld him, that his limbs and his face were those of his brother Abel whom he had killed; and Cain stood like one who struggles in his sleep, because of the exceeding terribleness of a dream; and ere he had recovered himself from the tumult of his agitation, the Shape fell at his feet, and embraced his knees, and cried out with a bitter outcry, 'Thou eldest born of Adam, whom Eve, my mother, brought forth, cease to torment me! I was feeding my flocks in green pastures by the side of quiet rivers, and thou killedst me; and now I am in misery.' Then Cain closed his eyes, and hid them with his hands—and again he opened his eyes, and looked around him, and said to Enos, 'What beholdest thou? Didst thou hear a voice, my son?'— 'Yes, my father, I beheld a man in unclean garments, and he uttered a sweet voice, full of lamentation.' Then Cain raised up the Shape that was like Abel, and said, 'The Creator of our father, who had respect unto thee, and unto thy offering, wherefore hath he forsaken thee?' Then the Shape shrieked a second time, and rent his garment, and his naked skin was like the white sands beneath their feet; and he shrieked yet a third time, and threw himself on his face upon the sand that was black with the shadow of the rock, and Cain and Enos sate beside him; the child by his right hand, and Cain by his left. They were all three under the rock, and within the shadow. The Shape that was like Abel raised himself up, and spake to the child. 'I know where the cold waters are, but I may not drink; wherefore didst thou then take away my pitcher?' But Cain said, 'Didst thou not find favour in the sight of the Lord thy God?' The Shape answered, 'The Lord is God of the living only, the dead have another God.' Then the child Enos lifted up his eyes and prayed; but Cain rejoiced secretly in his heart. 'Wretched shall they be all the days of their mortal life,' exclaimed the Shape, 'who sacrifice worthy and acceptable sacrifices to the God of the

dead; but after death their toil ceaseth. Woe is me, for I was
well beloved by the God of the living, and cruel wert thou, O
my brother, who didst snatch thee away from his power and his
dominion.' Having uttered these words, he rose suddenly, and
fled over the sands; and Cain said in his heart, 'The curse of the
Lord is on me—but who is the God of the dead?' and he ran
after the Shape, and the Shape fled shrieking over the sands, and
the sands rose like white mists behind the steps of Cain, but the
feet of him that was like Abel disturbed not the sands. He
greatly outrun Cain; and, turning short, he wheeled round, and
came again to the rock where they had been sitting, and where
Enos still stood; and the child caught hold of his garment as he
passed by, and he fell upon the ground; and Cain stopped, and
beholding him not, said, 'he has passed into the dark woods,'
and walked slowly back to the rocks, and when he reached it,
the child told him that he had caught hold of his garment as he
passed by, and that the man had fallen upon the ground; and
Cain once more sate beside him, and said—'Abel, my brother, I
would lament for thee, but that the spirit within me is withered,
and burnt up with extreme agony. Now, I pray thee, by thy
flocks and by thy pastures, and by the quiet rivers which thou
lovedst, that thou tell me all that thou knowest. Who is the God
of the dead? where doth he make his dwelling? what sacrifices
are acceptable unto him? for I have offered, but have not been
received; I have prayed, and have not been heard; and how can I
be afflicted more than I already am?' The Shape arose and
answered—'O that thou hadst had pity on me as I will have pity
on thee. Follow me, son of Adam! and bring thy child with
thee': and they three passed over the white sands between the
rocks, silent as their shadows.

END OF VOLUME II

Canto III IX

He had quaff'd too quickly she found
The dregs were wormwood.